THE MEANINGS OF AGE

THE MEANINGS OF AGE

Selected Papers of
BERNICE L. NEUGARTEN

Edited and with a Foreword by
Dail A. Neugarten

THE UNIVERSITY OF CHICAGO PRESS
Chicago & London

BERNICE L. NEUGARTEN is Professor Emerita in the Department of Behavioral Science and the College, and Rothschild Distinguished Scholar in the Center for Aging, Health, and Society, at the University of Chicago.

THE UNIVERSITY OF CHICAGO PRESS, Chicago 60637
THE UNIVERSITY OF CHICAGO PRESS, LTD., London

© 1996 by The University of Chicago
All rights reserved. Published 1996

Printed in the United States of America
05 04 03 02 01 00 99 98 97 96   1 2 3 4 5

ISBN: 0-226-57383-4 (cloth)
      0-226-57384-2 (paper)

Library of Congress Cataloging-in-Publication Data

Neugarten, Bernice Levin, 1916–
    The meanings of age : selected papers of Bernice L. Neugarten /
edited and with a foreword by Dail A. Neugarten.
        p.   cm.
    Includes bibliographical references and index.
    ISBN 0-226-57383-4 (cloth : alk. paper). — ISBN 0-226-57384-2
(paper : alk. paper)
    1. Aged—United States.   2. Aging—United States.   3. Gerontology—
United States.   I. Neugarten, Dail Ann.   II. Title.
HQ1064.U5N296   1996
305.26—dc20   96-14865
                                                                 CIP

CONTENTS

ACKNOWLEDGMENTS

This book represents a collaborative effort—not only between members of the Neugarten family but also between Neugartens and many of our colleagues and friends. Special appreciation is due to the following individuals:

- Robert H. Binstock, Professor of Aging, Health and Society, Case Western Reserve University, who, throughout the years, sharpened Bernice's thinking about the social policy issues facing our aging society
- David L. Gutmann, Professor of Psychiatry and Education, Northwestern University, who began as one of Bernice's most prized students and became one of her most creative and respected colleagues
- Gunhild O. Hagestad, Professor of Sociology, University of Oslo, and Associate Professor of Human Development and Social Policy, Northwestern University, with whom Bernice shared many a late night exploring and crafting the study of lives
- Margie E. Lachman, Professor of Psychology, Brandeis University, who was a most conscientious and thoughtful reviewer of an early manuscript draft
- George L. Maddox, Professor of Sociology and of Medical Sociology, Duke University, who, with Bernice and other colleagues, pioneered the field of aging and became one of Bernice's long-term friends, and
- Jerrold L. Neugarten, Bernice's son and my brother, who, after completing an *Oral History of Bernice L. Neugarten* (1994, available in the Oral History Research Office, Butler Library, Columbia University), served as a commentator and constructive critic of this manuscript.

D.A.N.
1996

Bernice L. Neugarten and the Meanings of Age

Dail A. Neugarten

We (Bernice, Dail, and Jerrold Neugarten) began this book some time ago. It grew from a conviction that academics, students, and practitioners in disciplines as diverse as psychology, sociology, education, law, medicine, and social policy—to say nothing of the discipline of gerontology—would welcome a compilation of Bernice L. Neugarten's most significant works.

Choosing 34 from over 160 journal articles, book chapters, research reports, speeches, and testimonies in the field of adult development and aging was not an easy task. For Neugarten's productivity and the breadth of her interests and ideas have been extensive.

The first of these papers was written in 1958 and the last in 1994—a period of over thirty-five years. In truth, Neugarten's professional career spanned some fifty years; her first manuscript was written in 1946 and her most recent in 1995. What a long time to raise important questions about the nature and patterns of lives and about the social as well as personal consequences of increased longevity. What a long time to pioneer new lines of inquiry that helped frame and clarify concerns of persons as they age and of policy makers and practitioners as they allocated resources and served those in need.

What a long time to conduct research that drew attention to previously unrecognized topics—topics such as menopause, grandparenthood, and parentcaring—and that relied upon quantitative as well as qualitative methods of data analysis. What a long time to coin terms that have become everyday parlance—terms such as "on-time and off-time," "the social clock," "the fluid life cycle," "the young-old and the old-old," "the age-integrated society," and "age-irrelevance." And what a long time to refine her thinking—thinking which began by suggesting that the field of gerontology should grow and develop and ended by raising the question of whether there should be a field named gerontology at all. Given her innate curiosity Neugarten constantly reinvented the field of adult development and aging and, in so doing, consistently revitalized her students, her colleagues, and herself.

Neugarten began her career with research that focused on aging persons—on changes in personality over the adult life span, changes in age-sex roles as individuals matured, adjustments to life events (such as retirement and widowhood), and social and psychological patterns of aging. She went on to examine the sociology of age—the changing age-status system, age norms as systems of social control, and age distinctions as they are embodied in the law—and social policies that affect the old as well as the young. Most recently, Neugarten concentrated on the subject of age versus need in an aging society. While creatively exploring concepts and constructs, she followed her interests as she moved from discipline to discipline and from disciplinary to interdisciplinary modes of study.

As she worked, Neugarten raised fundamental questions about the nature of lives (especially the second half of lives), their social contexts, and the social policy concerns affecting an aging society—questions such as:

- How do people change as they grow up and grow old?
- What, if anything, is unique about the second half of life?
- What are the continuities and discontinuities in personality and behavior over time?
- How do people adapt to significant life events and to life changes, and are there consistent differences between men and women? Is it the anticipated or the unanticipated events that produce more stress?
- How does one maintain a concept of "self" in the face of changing life circumstances?
- What constitutes "successful aging"?
- How do age norms operate and do they create serious constraints on behavior?
- What, if any, are age-appropriate behaviors, and how do those change over time?
- What are the ethical and public policy implications of an increasing proportion of older persons?
- Can there truly be an "age irrelevant" society?

As she continued to work, Neugarten concluded that:

- It is the study of lives—their continuities and discontinuities—that is the proper domain for research and theory building in the field of human development.
- Adulthood, middle age, and old age have their unique developmental tasks, and development does not end when a man or woman enters any of these life periods.
- Middle and old age are significant periods in the life cycle although they are not separate or disjunctive times.
- Aging itself need not be considered a problem. Aging is normal, not pathological.

- Throughout the life course there are expected and unexpected life events, but when and how they occur makes their impacts different. Men and women differ in their coping strategies.
- Personality develops only through interactions between individuals and their social environments. There are strong relationships between biological, psychological, and social factors, and persons are never separate from their social contexts.
- People need to create coherence in their lives, and therefore they construct and reconstruct their autobiographies. In addition, they rehearse their futures in order to prepare for significant life events.
- There is no single pattern of successful aging. The patterns are many, and a person's satisfaction with his or her life is contingent upon many interrelated variables.
- Age norms exist, and they serve to socialize people with respect to "age-appropriate behavior." These norms change over time.
- Chronological age in adulthood is not a measure of functional capacity, economic status, intellectual ability, or social values. Stereotypes of "the elderly" should be abolished.
- Tremendous diversity exists among middle- and old-aged people. Lives "fan out"; the older one becomes, the more different one is from others.
- Although there may never be a totally "age-irrelevant" society, constructive social policies will reflect a more thoughtful balance of age with need.
- The "aging society" brings with it many challenges and opportunities for both aging persons and for the society at large.

These queries and discoveries are addressed in this book.

A few comments about the book itself: The papers we included were originally written for many audiences. Some were prepared in response to specific requests—from lawyers, doctors, educators, psychologists, sociologists, and older people themselves who wished to know more about age and the aging society. Others grew from Neugarten's own interests and her desire to share what she and her numerous colleagues had learned. The papers (many of which were coauthored and thus illustrate Neugarten's collaborative nature) are reprinted, with occasional minor deletions, as they initially appeared. There is therefore some redundancy in ideas. Too, there is some overlap with a book previously edited by Bernice L. Neugarten: *Middle Age and Aging: A Reader in Social Psychology* (Chicago: University of Chicago Press, 1968). There are also data that are outmoded and some archaic use of language. Neugarten used the generic "he," for example, to refer to both males and females, and "Negro" would now be replaced with "African American." We presume that readers will regard these outdated usages as historical artifacts and not as oversights.

The papers are arranged chronologically (where appropriate) within each of the four major parts. Although not written in the sequence in which they appear here, they have been arranged to assure an internal coherence to this book. Readers interested in a chronological account of Neugarten's scholarly works may refer to the Bibliography of Bernice L. Neugarten at the end of this volume.

Many readers of *The Meanings of Age* will be acquainted personally with Bernice Neugarten, for her intelligence and warmth have drawn them into her classes, her symposia, her conferences, and her proverbial "Hyde Park kitchen table." Others will know her through her ideas. She has made lasting contributions to existing academic disciplines and has defined a discipline that has come to be called "the study of lives." Still others will not know her at all, but will be curious about a book titled *The Meanings of Age*. These readers will be impressed not only by Neugarten's clarity of thought but by her common sense. For at all times she exhibited enormous respect for individuals as makers and shapers of their own lives, and at all times she focused on normal reactions by real people facing genuine events. Her writings and her own life illustrate that old age connotes not only frailty and loss but also wisdom, health, and an appreciation and acceptance of the complexities of life.

Bernice Neugarten has lived a long life and has been a lifelong learner. She has had continuity of place, of institution, and of colleagues. She has also had discontinuities and unexpected events that have interrupted her plans. Her four colleagues, who graciously wrote introductory essays to sections of this book, provide testimonies to the ways in which Bernice Neugarten has lived and the ways in which her scholarship has stood the test of time.

INTRODUCTION
The Aging Society and My Academic Life

In pondering how best to address the theme, social structures and human lives, I have elected to comment primarily on a set of changes in academic perspectives and structures that reflect the dramatic change in the age structure of the population—for, historically speaking, it is the attention to aging and the aging society that is the context for viewing my own academic career.

My graduate education took form in what was then a newly created program in the Division of the Social Sciences at the University of Chicago called Human Development. That program was and is a multidisciplinary one, whose faculty are drawn primarily from anthropology, psychology, and sociology; and whose faculty and students draw upon those disciplines in studying the course of lives and issues of continuity and change from infancy to old age.

This is not the occasion for a conceptual analysis, but it should be said that Human Development is a broader program than those that, in many other universities, are called Developmental or Life-Span Psychology, for while attention is given to changes that occur within the individual, the focus is on the individual-in-society; on the social structures and on the culture as much as on the mind and the psyche. The program centers on processes of socialization, on personal change and social change as they interact throughout life time. The social structures of the society are regarded as fundamental in shaping the individual's experience, but at the same time persons are perceived as proactive, not merely reactive. From this perspective, people can be said to invent their future lives, just as, in the telling and retelling, they reinvent their past lives.

The Committee on Human Development is the oldest of many interdisciplinary committees at the University of Chicago. It began as the Committee on Child Development, created in 1930 by a group of social scientists and biologists who undertook studies of children and adolescents within the contexts of the family, the school, and the community. By 1940 those interests had widened and studies of older people were also under way. The name was therefore changed from Child Develop-

Reprinted by permission from *Sociological Lives,* edited by M. W. Riley (Newbury Park, CA: Sage Publications, 1988), 91–106.

ment to Human Development. The first Chairman was Ralph Tyler, later Dean of the Division of Social Sciences at Chicago, and later still, Director of the Center for Advanced Study in the Behavioral Sciences in Palo Alto. Its second Chairman was Robert J. Havighurst, who played the major role in building the curriculum and in planning many of the major research programs for which the Committee became known.

In the late 1940s a course was created called Maturity and Old Age, the first of its kind so far as I can determine. That course was joined with those in childhood and adolescence to form the core sequence for the Ph.D., and together with courses from the supporting disciplines, there was for the first time an interdisciplinary Ph.D. program in place organized around continuity and change across lives from birth to death.

The Committee has flourished over the years, with an active research faculty, a succession of communitywide studies and other large-scale research, and more than 400 Ph.D. graduates. Programs called Human Development have appeared in many other universities, many of them patterned after the one at Chicago. The term "life-span development" was coined later (by others) and has become widely used among developmental psychologists; and the "life-span perspective" is now appearing in many other of the social sciences (Featherman, 1983). Historically speaking, it was first the cultural anthropologists who adopted this perspective, with their studies of age grading and their interests in life histories. It was next the personality psychologists with what they called the studies of lives, and next, as already mentioned, the developmental psychologists. Sociologists, although concerned with individual social mobility and status attainment since Sorokin's work appeared, have only recently come forward with their work on age stratification and the sociology of age—represented in particular by the work of Matilda Riley and her colleagues (Riley, Johnson, and Foner, 1972). A new bridge between sociologists and historians is presently leading to a proliferation of studies of "the life course"—studies of the timing and sequencing of life events and role transitions, focused usually on intercohort comparisons (Neugarten and Hagestad, 1976; Hagestad and Neugarten, 1985). A number of economists have adopted the life-course perspective in their studies of economic and consumer behavior, as have a few political scientists, in studies of political socialization and participation. It is apparent that investigators of many persuasions are now organizing their data and reexamining their theories to reckon with change over the lifetime.

AGING AS AN ACADEMIC FIELD

It was the attention to aging that led historically to the definition of the academic field called Human Development. But the study of aging has also had a vigorous independent development.

At Chicago, social science research in aging began in the early 1940s with relatively large-scale studies undertaken by Ernest Burgess, Robert Havighurst, Ethel Shanas, and others—studies, for example, of work and retirement and of psychosocial adaptations to old age. (It is probably a little-known fact that, as early as 1943, the Social Science Research Council created a subcommittee called Social Adjustment in Old Age, headed by Burgess and Havighurst, to survey what was known about aging and to suggest directions for research. That group issued its report and bibliography in 1946.)

By the end of the 1940s dissertations in aging had begun to appear in Human Development, and a few in Sociology. In subsequent years, the Committee on Human Development became a major center for social science research in aging and a center for training Ph.D.s in this area. For over 20 years I directed a special training program in adult development and aging, first funded in the late 1950s by the National Institute of Mental Health, then through the Program on Adult Development and Aging of the National Institute on Child Health and Human Development when that institute was formed in the early 1960s, then by the National Institute on Aging when that institute was formed in the mid-1970s. During that 20-year period, some 80 Ph.D.s graduated from our special program, almost all of whom are now on university faculties around the country, teaching and carrying out research, with some who are administering multidisciplinary gerontology centers. Insofar as these former students represent a strategic population of teachers and researchers, it can be said fairly that the Chicago program played the leading role in creating the academic field of adult development and aging. The fact that I was the formal director of that training program for those 20 years does not mean that it was all a single-handed effort. There were as many as a dozen faculty in Human Development in some of those years who were committed to research in aging and another dozen in other parts of the university who helped guide dissertations that crosscut their own fields.

In subsequent years, academic programs in aging have appeared in many other universities, some of them doctoral programs in the biological or social sciences, but many more at the master's level in professional areas such as nursing, social work, or public administration. In most instances, aging represents an area of specialization within a degree program in an established department or School, but in a few places a degree called Gerontology is offered at the bachelor's or master's level.

It is understandable that the dramatic increase in life expectancy and the increased proportion of older people in the society should have created the so-called demographic imperative that is having its effects on academia. In the 40 years since the first course was given at Chicago, some 1100 colleges and universities in the country have begun offering courses or special certificates or degree programs in aging. Gerontological societies, scientific and professional, are flourishing in this country and have appeared in more than 50 other countries over the world, all with the express purpose of furthering research and education. There are now some 70 journals in the field, research oriented or practice oriented. It is against this background of aging as a growth industry in academia that my own academic life has taken shape.

MY FORMAL CAREER

The formal outline of my career can be set forth in brief terms. I came from a small town in Nebraska to the University of Chicago; I took an undergraduate degree in English and French literatures, a master's degree in educational psychology, and a Ph.D. in Human Development. (It happens that I was the first person to complete the Ph.D. after the Committee changed its name from Child to Human Development. Presumably this makes me the first fully credentialed Human Developer—an obvious anomaly of labeling, given all the poets and philosophers who through the ages have reflected upon the course of human lives, often in more insightful ways than the social scientists.)

I then spent an eight-year period "out," as it is often ironically referred to, raising two children, doing part-time writing and research jobs, becoming involved in local independent politics, and, with my husband, in organizational efforts aimed at building a racially-integrated community.

In 1951 I returned to the university to join the faculty in Human Development. At my request, I remained on part-time appointment for five years, then moved onto the tenure track, and was tenured four years later. (It happens that I was the first person to be given tenure in Human Development alone—that is, without a joint appointment in another department. Thus, so to speak, Human Development itself was also tenured in this same move—a certain milestone in the changing structure of the Social Sciences at Chicago.)

After another four years I was promoted to professor; and five years later I began a stint as Chairman of the Committee. Altogether I spent 30 years on the faculty at Chicago, then took an early retirement in 1980 and moved to Northwestern University to begin a new academic program called Human Development and Social Policy. (The 30 years at the same institution, plus all my student years there, probably makes me one of the least geographically mobile academics in this country.)

To flesh out this outline a bit: For one thing, although I was paying it little attention for most of the time, this progression of events was unusual for a woman of my birth cohort or my academic cohort. For another thing, it is likely that my research interests in the sociology of age and age-norms that I pursued later in my career stemmed in part from the fact that I was so "off time" in my youth. I was carrying courses in high school when I was 11 years old; and, after high school, I marked time for two years before coming as a teenager into the intellectual excitement and the sometimes buzzing confusion that marked the undergraduate "Hutchins's College" at Chicago in the 1930s. There it was not altogether rare to have a 14- or 15-year-old fellow student among us; and because we met degree requirements by placement tests and comprehensive examinations, not by number of courses or length of residence, academic acceleration was a common pattern. Although I tried to stretch things out, I had a master's degree by the time I was 21 and I looked much too young to find a job as a high school teacher. I was rescued when one of my professors called to offer me an assistantship if I would enter the doctoral program under the Committee on Child Development. Thus I was already one of its students when that committee later changed its name to Human Development.

Things slowed down thereafter, for, after several graduate assistantships, I was approximately on schedule in terms of academic age norms when I finished the Ph.D. at age 27; "late" when I joined the faculty at 35; and in a different sense, "on time" again when, at age 40, I published my first paper on middle age.

RESEARCH AND TEACHING

The substantive or intellectual side of my career is more difficult to summarize. My interest in sociological issues was evident from the first: My dissertation dealt with social class as a determining factor in the friendship patterns of children and adolescents; I taught courses in educational sociology for a brief time; and then collaborated with Robert Havighurst in producing a text in that field titled *Society and Education* (Havighurst and Neugarten, 1957). Some years later, in connection with the Kansas City Studies of Adult Life, I coauthored with Richard P. Coleman a book on the social class structure of Kansas City in the 1950s (Coleman and Neugarten, 1971).

At the same time, I also pursued psychological topics: personality changes in adolescence, a cross-cultural study of moral and emotional development in children of six American Indian tribes, and so on.

It was an accident that led me to concentrate on the study of adult development and aging. A year or two after I returned to the university, the course that I have already mentioned, Maturity and Old Age, needed a teacher. I was invited to give that course and, at the same time, to join the research team that was beginning a communitywide study of middle-aged and aging persons in the metropolitan area of Kansas City. Had it been the course in child development that needed an instructor, I might well have wound up today as a child psychologist. Thus, despite the fact that I was aware that the changing age structure of the population had enormous implications for the society at large, and despite the fact that I might have chosen to enter the field of aging because of it, it was not foresight or planning, but chance that was the major

foresight

factor. (This unpredicted turn of events in my own career may be one of the reasons for my belief that, in the study of human lives, insufficient attention has been given to the unanticipated and the off-time events, to the discontinuities as well as the continuities [Neugarten, 1969].)

The following six months were spent reading all I could find about personality change in adulthood (there was very little except for Erik Erikson's work) and all the theoretical and empirical work I could find in the social sciences on age, aging, and age structures. In the early 1950s this task could be accomplished in six months. Now one cannot keep up even with the titles, let alone the content of publications, in aging, and the problem has become how to separate the new from the redundant.

I reorganized the course, renamed it Adult Development and Aging, and have given ever-changing versions of the course every year since.

In the next three years, I published my first paper on the psychology of aging, a paper that appeared in a volume titled *Potentialities of Women in the Middle Years* (Gross, 1956). The editor of that volume was ahead of her time, for the book appeared well before any attention was given, in the women's movement of the 1960s and 1970s, to middle-aged and older women. A year afterward I published my first paper written from the societal perspective, a paper on social change and the aging population. My studies have been of these two general categories ever since, a point I will return to in a later section of this essay.

In my forties, most of my publications were reports of empirical studies, often carried out in collaboration with colleagues and graduate students. In my fifties, although I undertook new empirical researches, more of my publications were "think pieces"—essays and review chapters. My fifties were also a period in which more of my time went to administrative roles, and much more to teaching, especially to the one-to-one teaching involved in dissertation supervision. Various kinds of rewards accumulate over the course of a long career, but two were of special significance to me in this period: the first, when in a single year four of my former students authored textbooks in middle age and aging, something I myself have never done; and, second, when I received a national award for graduate teaching.

By my early sixties, I was involved in the policy field. Earlier, much in the pattern typical of academics, I had served on study sections and advisory panels in the National Institutes of Health and in other parts of the Department of Health and Human Services and the Department of Education. But these groups had all been research related. Now I was appointed to the Federal Council on Aging, a 15-person group appointed by the president, with the mandate to report each year to the president and to Congress on the situation of older people, and to make recommendations regarding legislative and executive initiatives. In my three years there, I began *insufficient*

to learn about policymaking and politics. Not that the Federal Council on Aging was an important or even visible body, as such things go, but it was a place where an array of major policy issues were studied and debated.

A year later I was appointed a Deputy Chairman of the 1981 White House Conference on Aging—where, amusingly enough, because of a slipup by a staff member, my first inkling of this appointment was when I was asked to appear at the White House to be sworn in—this, without ever having been told that such a post existed, much less ever being asked if I wanted it. Although I was then of the opinion, as I am today, that there was no national need for a White House Conference on Aging, I decided that if that conference were to take place, I would welcome the opportunity to help shape its agenda. I spent a good deal of time in Washington for the next 15 months, planning the organization of the conference and the range of issues to be dealt with; I was then summarily removed when the administration changed in 1981; then a few months later, I was reappointed by that new administration to a different but still visible role in the conference. I have never had any political visibility, so mine is an instance of an academic maintaining the role of an academic. But by now I had learned a good bit more about policymaking and politics. More important, I learned that an academic has something to learn from, but also something to offer to, the policymaking endeavor.

By now, too, I had become convinced that for students in the social sciences— whether in aging or any other related field—it is important that they understand the significance of policy decisions in influencing the course of lives. So, by my early sixties, it seemed natural enough that, building on my own experiences, I should want to organize a new type of doctoral program that would bridge the social sciences and policymaking in the study of lives. Thus I moved from Chicago to Northwestern in 1980, at the persuasion of a new dean there who had been my colleague at Chicago, and who has facilitated the creation of the new graduate program called Human Development and Social Policy—a program in which, not surprisingly, I have been concentrating on policies related to the aging society.

If, then, I entered the field of aging by accident, I have stayed in it by design. And I suppose it can be said that the changing age structure of the society has not only influenced, but has indirectly created the context and the content of my academic life.

THE ISSUE OF GENDER

Because I am a woman—and because we have not yet created a climate in which that fact is insignificant in considering the career of an academic—I should comment here on how changes in societal structures that relate to gender have affected my academic life. It may appear strange to the reader to be told first that my experience in this regard has been singularly atypical for a woman of my cohort—for I do not re-call a single instance in which the fact that I was a woman worked to my disadvan-tage, or to my advantage, in my education or in my research career.

I had encouragement all the way: first from my parents, particularly my father, then from teachers. When I was in high school, the superintendent of schools called me into his office several times to explain that there was a man at the University of Chicago named Robert Maynard Hutchins who had exciting ideas about education and that it was therefore the place I must go. He made no mention of possible diffi-culties because I was female, nor did I hear any such mention made throughout my student years at Chicago.

In Human Development there were approximately equal numbers of men and women students each year; fellowships were awarded without attention to the sex of the applicant; and there were always women as well as men faculty. (In the program with which I am now associated at Northwestern, we have equal numbers of men and women faculty, but of thirty Ph.D. students, only four are men, a historical change in the sex ratio of graduate students that is appearing in many social science departments throughout the country.) It happens also that among the many stu-dents whose dissertation committees I have chaired over the years, there have been—without planning it that way—about equal numbers of men and women.

In another respect, also, Human Development at Chicago was unusual, for be-ginning in the late 1950s we saw fit, at my suggestion, to admit for the Ph.D. a num-ber of middle-aged women who had been housewives for most of their lives—this at a time when such admissions were rare in top-rated universities. These women proved to be as successful as younger men or women in completing their degrees. In fact, they had one major advantage, for while some had trouble at first in making the transition into the student role, none of them suffered, as did young women stu-dents, over sex role conflict—they did not worry that to take a Ph.D. might dimin-ish their femininity, either in their own or other people's minds.

I recall that when I was chairman of Human Development at Chicago in the early 1970s a form letter arrived from the women's caucus of the American Psychological Association, asking me to describe my efforts to hire a woman faculty member, and if those efforts had met with any success. I sent back information about the sex dis-tribution of our faculty, and said that although the wording of their letter seemed to be an instance of the approach to data-gathering that can be characterized as "When did you stop beating your wife?" I was nevertheless strongly supportive of their goals, as I hoped our record in Human Development would show.

Although I was never aware of any obstacles put in my way because I was a woman, still I did not go untouched by the women's movement of the late 1960s and 1970s. The major instance of student protest on the Chicago campus in

1968–1969—and the sit-in that paralyzed much of the university for a few weeks—was triggered by the fact that a young woman faculty member who held a joint appointment in the Committee on Human Development and the Department of Sociology was not reappointed. The student leaders held that it was because she was a woman and because she held radical political views; and they did not waver when it was pointed out that both these facts, particularly the first, had been well known to all those involved in her original appointment.

The student protest was taken very seriously in all parts of the university. I spent much of my time for several months working with a small group of other faculty and students in altering the governance procedures in Human Development to give students a greater role. Probably because I happened to be the only woman in the Council of the University Senate at the time, I was appointed chairman of the first Committee on Women of the University of Chicago. That committee was created as an arm of the Council and was given access to all confidential data regarding faculty appointments for both women and men over the years—data regarding recruitment efforts, salaries, promotions—a fact that made our group something of an exception during that period when women faculty groups were organizing on other campuses to protest inequitable treatment and were often dealt with by administrators as outsiders rather than insiders.

Our Committee on Women gathered a great deal of local and national data, and issued a long report that was widely circulated over the country (Committee on University Women, 1970). (This is not the occasion to discuss the findings of that report, but it may be of interest to mention here that the Department of Sociology was one of the departments at Chicago that had never had a tenured woman—a situation that changed, happily enough, as one of the outcomes of our Committee's efforts.)

I was also elected Chairman of the Committee on Human Development in that year—a role that senior faculty members were expected to take turns in filling, but that I had hoped to defer for several more years.

All this affected my scholarly productivity, for I was at the time completing work on three book-length manuscripts, one on the sociology of age, one on middle age, and one on patterns of aging. All this work was laid aside for what I regarded as compelling reasons; but the manuscripts grew cold; and they were never published (some of the research findings appeared later as journal articles). I took comfort some years afterward when a publisher told me that the student movement of the late 1960s had evidently had a similar effect on many other social scientists, for the number of manuscripts he and other publishers received for several years thereafter had been noticeably fewer than before.

It is fair to say, then, that in those years, as the university dealt with the issue of gender and the closely related issue of student empowerment, the changes—whether or not they were far-reaching enough to satisfy many of us—had their effects on my own academic career.

INTELLECTUAL DEVELOPMENT

My pattern of research has been to open up new topic areas rather than to follow a single line of inquiry; to use sometimes qualitative, sometimes quantitative methods; to prefer exploration to replication—in short, to map out some of the landscape of what had earlier been the neglected territory of the second half of life.

As already mentioned, my studies have been of two general types: the first relates to aging persons—to such topics as changes in personality and in age-sex roles, the diversity of patterns of aging, middle-aged parenting and grandparenting, adjustment to retirement, the changing meanings of age to the individual, and the internalized social clock that tells people if they are "on time" in following the social timetables.

The second category relates to the sociology of age from the societal perspective—to such topics as the changing age-status system, age norms as systems of social control, societal implications of the lengthened life span, the relations among age groups and the rise of the young-old, age distinctions as they are embodied in the law, and policy issues related to the aging society.

I have chosen illustrations from that work that I hope will serve to indicate how my thinking about these particular topics has developed over time.

Early on, I began to study the life events that in the 1950s were touted, as they still are today, as the significant transitions of middle age. I found that the menopause was a psychological nonevent to most women; that the so-called emptying of the nest—that is, when children grow up and leave home—was not a loss event to mothers or fathers (unless it occurred later than anticipated and therefore signified delayed maturity in the child). We found also that most middle-aged and older people had never experienced—nor had they perceived in others—a mid-life crisis (Neugarten and Datan, 1974). (This, despite the journalists who seized on the term as a revealed truth and treated it as high drama.)

Drawing from my own studies but also from the work of others, I learned that retirement is welcomed by most men if they have adequate income (we knew little about formal retirement in women, for it was then a relatively rare occurrence); that health improves rather than deteriorates after retirement; that most older people have high levels of life satisfaction, and, of equal significance, that in the second half of life, the level of life satisfaction is not related to age. And so on. It became clear that the myths and the negative stereotypes about middle age and old age did not fit the realities. The large majority of older persons, although retired, are vigorous and competent people, active in their families and communities. I called them the "young-old," described them as a new historical phenomenon in postindustrial societies, and suggested that the young-old represent a major resource to the aging societies in which we live, but a resource thus far underutilized (Neugarten, 1974, 1975). The term "old-old" I reserved for that minority of frail older people who need special care and support. I pointed out that the distinction between young-old and old-old was of central importance in policymaking, for the desires and needs of the two groups are very different.

It became clear also, from the work my colleagues and I were doing, that there was no single pattern of social-psychological aging, nor a single pattern of optimal or so-called "successful" aging (Neugarten, Havighurst, and Tobin, 1968). The widely held view that the person who remains active and maintains the social role pattern of middle age is the successful ager—the so-called "activity theory"—and the contrasting view that aging is an inherent and universal process of mutual withdrawal between the individual and the society, and that the successful ager is the person who has disengaged—the so-called "disengagement theory" set forth by Cumming and Henry (1961), and so hotly debated by gerontologists in 1960s and early 1970s—these are both reductionist theories that do not account for the diversity of patterns.

Not only do people grow old in very different ways, but the range of individual differences becomes greater with the passage of life time. Age therefore becomes a poor predictor of the adult's physical or social or intellectual competence, of the person's needs or capacities. In this sense, as compared to earlier periods in history, age has declined in significance in distinguishing among middle-aged and older people. (In different terms, age turns out to be a very weak variable in multivariable analyses.)

The corollary is that change over adulthood is not "ordered" change, as stage theorists would have it (Neugarten, 1979b), and further, that patterns of adulthood and aging are affected by, but not determined by, early experience. These ideas are not yet altogether popular among developmental psychologists, so some of the papers I have written on these topics have not always been happily received.

As another step in my thinking, I noted that, despite the fact that age is becoming less useful or less relevant in assessing adult competencies and needs, we have witnessed a proliferation of policy decisions and benefit programs in which target groups are defined on the basis of age, a trend particularly evident with regard to older people. At federal, state, and local levels of government, programs are created that provide persons with income, health services, social services, transportation, housing, and special tax benefits on the basis of their age. Much the same is true in the private sector, where civic, educational, and religious bodies create special programs for older people in health care, education, recreation, and other community services. (Thus, what social scientists know is one thing; what policymakers do is quite another—not, in itself, a new discovery.)

I pondered this anomaly, and in the past few years I have written several policy papers that have made me something of a controversial figure to the special interest groups in aging—in particular, to the so-called "age-advocacy organizations" that, in their efforts to influence government and governmental programs, claim to speak for older people as a group. I have suggested, for instance, that age-entitlement programs be reexamined from the perspective of need entitlement (Neugarten, 1979a, 1982)—a suggestion that is anathema to many persons who have labored long to improve the economic and social status of older people in this country, and who fear that those gains would be reversed if anything so radical were even to be contemplated. I persist, nevertheless, in believing that all of us, young and old, would be well ahead if policymakers would focus not on age, but on more relevant dimensions of human competencies and human needs.

To return to the theme of social science research: On the societal level, it is clear enough that age status and age-stratification systems are themselves dynamic; that age-group definitions, age distinctions, and age norms are constantly altered in concert with other types of social change (Neugarten, 1968; Neugarten & Peterson, 1957; Neugarten, Moore, & Lowe, 1965; Neugarten & Neugarten, 1986; Passuth, Maines, & Neugarten, 1984). Both the study of lives and the study of social change must therefore be seen as the constant interweaving of life time, socially defined time, and historical time. It has long been understood that the course of human lives—and, therefore, patterns of aging—are different in different societies, in different subgroups, and at different points in history. Aging, then, is not an immutable process, either in the social or the biological patterning of lives, as the increase in average life expectancy itself has made so clear.

This common knowledge has not always been taken seriously by social science investigators. Some gerontologists searched at first for a common social pattern of aging or for "laws" of change that would be neither culture-bound nor history-bound. Today most would agree that all that can be said for certain on this topic is that people are born, grow up, and die, and that in postindustrial societies most people now grow old before they die. Although we do not yet know the limits of mutability—that is, how much change can be achieved—the new view is that a vast range of positive interventions can be made in patterns of aging. To have laid the basis for changing the climate of opinion in this way has surely been a major contribution of both the social and the biological scientists over the past 40 years.

Looking back, I sometimes wonder why it was that many researchers were preoccupied with questions about social and psychological aging that now seem so naive. Perhaps it is only an instance of that for which we social scientists are often criticized—that we elaborate what is common sense. Yet, it often turns out that common sense is not so common; and that to document one version of common sense over another may itself be an important achievement.

A colleague once asked what my personal goal was in studying aging. I laughed and said "To return old people to the human race—to make it clear that they are not a special species, nor creatures from another planet." I think we social science researchers, as a group, have now accomplished that task. We have come to realize that the same general theories regarding the nature of human nature will serve us as well—or as poorly—for older people as for younger.

THE FUTURE

It is unlikely that, in the future, social scientists will make dramatic theoretical advances in the study of aging. Conceptual ones, yes, as in the conceptualizations of the age-stratification and age-norm systems, and in the perspective that the course of lives and the course of social change are mutually interactive, as the essays in this volume are illustrating. Some of us will develop new conceptual approaches, and others of us will carry out the descriptive and analytic studies that will continue to be important.

Still others of us I hope will take a new direction: To turn matters around, as it were, and to ask not only "How do societal changes influence the lives of older people?" but also "How does the presence of increasing numbers of older people affect the society at large?"

To elaborate on this point: In all parts of the world, societies are undergoing change that is perhaps as fundamental as any in human history, change that comes with the increase in life expectancy and the increasing proportions of older persons in the population. These demographic trends have been dramatic in industrialized countries in the last 80 years; and it is being projected—barring catastrophic famines or wars—that the numbers of older people will increase at as rapid a rate in the developing countries over the next 20 years as in developed countries over the past 80 years.

We have created an aging population, but we do not know much about its effects on our social institutions and social structures. We know, for instance, that the family has become a multigenerational structure, but we know little about patterns of social interaction or economic transfers in the four- or five-generation unit. What is the influence of the changing age distribution on our educational institutions? On systems of medical and social services? On the social structures of communities and the relations among age groups? On our political structures, laws, and legal institutions? On the responsibilities of government for the support of the young and the old? On the meanings of age as a dimension of social organization?

It is not altogether a secret that we students of society have sometimes missed out on some of the big social issues of our times. If, for example, more of us had studied race relations in the 1950s and 1960s, we might not have been so surprised by the form of the civil rights movement in the early 1960s and by the riots that occurred in some of our cities. Some readers may recall Everett Hughes's Presidential address to the American Sociological Associations when he asked, "How did it happen that we missed the boat on race relations?" and when he suggested that perhaps it was our own professionalism that had blocked our view.

Another example is our failure, as psychologists and sociologists and anthropologists alike, to give sufficient attention to family patterns and motivations for parenthood, with the result that so many of us were caught by surprise by the baby boom, soon to become the senior boom. Are we now missing the boat on the aging society?

This is not, of course, the first time it has been suggested that we should attend to the social implications of the aging population. A decade ago a colleague and I coedited two publications that dealt with social policy, social ethics, and the aging society (Neugarten & Havighurst, 1976, 1977), but, as long ago as the 1950s, sociologists like Ernest Burgess were pointing to the need to study the impact of older people on the society. Thus far, few of us have heeded that advice.

Things may change. As a straw in the wind, the National Academy of Sciences recently created a short-lived, but nevertheless active Committee on the Aging Society, whose purpose was to stimulate research on this topic in the various parts of the Academy. And the book called *Our Aging Society: Paradox and Promise* (Pifer and Bronte, 1986), a collection of essays written by a varied group of academics, may help create an agenda for empirical research.

It is my hope, then, that social scientists will pursue the questions of how societies, not only populations, grow old, a set of issues that is highly significant for the society in which we live. Pursuing these questions might lead to new conceptualizations of the nature of social change and to new conceptualizations of the interplay between changing social structures and the course of human lives.

References

Committee on University Women. 1970. *Women in the University of Chicago.* Chicago: University of Chicago.

Coleman, R. P., and Neugarten, B. L. 1971. *Social Status in the City.* San Francisco: Jossey-Bass.

Cumming, E., and W. E. Henry, 1961. *Growing Old.* New York: Basic Books.

Featherman, D. L. 1983. "The Life Span Perspective in Social Science Research." In *Life-Span Development and Behavior,* Vol. 5, edited by P. B. Baltes and O. G. Brim, Jr. New York: Academic Press.

Gross, I. W., ed. 1956. *Potentialities of Women in the Middle Years.* East Lansing: Michigan State University Press.

Hagestad, G. O., and B. L. Neugarten. 1985. "Age and the Life Course." Pp. 35–61 in *Handbook of Aging and the Social Sciences,* edited by B. Binstock and E. Shanas. New York: Van Nostrand Reinhold.

Havighurst, R. J., and Neugarten, B. L. 1957. *Society and Education.* Boston: Allyn & Bacon (2nd ed., 1962; 3rd ed., 1967; 4th ed., 1975).

Neugarten, B. L. 1968. "The Changing Age Status System." Pp. 5–21 in *Middle Age and Aging: A Reader in Social Psychology,* edited by B. L. Neugarten. Chicago: University of Chicago Press.

———. 1969. "Continuities and Discontinuities of Psychological Issues into Adult Life." *Human Development* 12:121–130.

———. 1974. "Age Groups in American Society and the Rise of the Young-Old." *The Annals of the American Academy of Political and Social Sciences,* pp. 187–198.

———. 1975. "The Future and the Young-Old." *Gerontologist* 15(1, Pt. 2):4–9.

———. 1979a. "Policy for the 1980s: Age-Entitlement or Need-Entitlement?" Pp. 48–52 in *National Journal Issues Book, Aging: Agenda for the Eighties.* Washington, DC: Government Research Corporation.

———. 1979b. "Time, Age, and the Life Cycle." *American Journal of Psychiatry* 136(7):887–894.

———, ed. 1982. *Age or Need? Public Policies for Older People.* Beverly Hills, CA: Sage.

———, and N. Datan. 1974. "The Middle Years." Pp. 592–608 in *American Handbook of Psychiatry,* Vol. 1. *The Foundations of Psychiatry,* edited by S. Arieti. New York: Basic Books.

Neugarten, B. L., and G. O. Hagestad. 1976. "Age and the Life Course." Pp. 626–649 in *Handbook of Aging and the Social Sciences,* edited by B. B. Binstock and E. Shanas. New York: Van Nostrand Reinhold.

Neugarten, B. L., and R. J. Havighurst. 1976. *Social Policy, Social Ethics, and the Aging Society* (Report prepared for the National Science Foundation). Washington, DC: Government Printing Office (Stock #038-000-00299-6; 121 pages).

———. 1977. *Extending the Human Life Span: Social Policy and Social Ethics* (Report prepared for the National Science Foundation). Washington, DC: Government Printing Office (Stock #038-000-00337-2; 70 pages).

———, and S. S. Tobin. 1968. "Personality and Patterns of Aging." Pp. 173–177 in *Middle Age and Aging: A Reader in Social Psychology,* edited by B. L. Neugarten. Chicago: University of Chicago Press.

Neugarten, B. L., J. W. Moore, and J. C. Lowe. 1965. "Age Norms, Age Constraints, and Adult Socialization." *American Journal of Sociology* 70:710–717 (Reprinted in Neugarten, *Middle Age and Aging,* 1968).

Neugarten, B. L., and D. A. Neugarten. 1986. "The Changing Meanings of Age in the Aging Society." Pp. 33–51 in *Our Aging Society: Paradox and Promise,* edited by A. Pifer and L. Bronte. New York: Norton.

Neugarten, B. L., and W. A. Peterson. 1957. "A Study of the American Age-Grade

System." Pp. 497–502 in *Proceedings of the Fourth Congress of the International Association of Gerontology,* Merano, Bolzano, Italy, July 14–19. Vol. 3. *Sociological Division.* Firenze: Mattioli.

Passuth, P. M., D. R. Maines, and B. L. Neugarten. 1984. "Age Norms and Age Constraints Twenty Years Later." Paper presented at the Midwest Sociological Society Meeting, Chicago.

Pifer, A., and L. Bronte, eds. 1986. *Our Aging Society: Paradox and Promise.* New York: Norton.

Riley, M. W., M. E. Johnson, and A. Foner, eds. 1972. *Aging and Society,* Vol. 3. *A Sociology of Age Stratification.* New York: Russell Sage.

PART ONE

Age as a Dimension of Social Organization

Definitions and Descriptions of Age

George L. Maddox

unters with Bernice Neugarten, whether in conversation or in print, tend to be
orable. An immense vitality pervades her observations about people and
ts, and her incisive analyses quickly get to the heart of any issue. She has persis-
y highlighted issues in late adulthood with profoundly significant but simple
ses that demanded and received attention. Phrases like "an age-irrelevant soci-
' "the end of gerontology," "returning older people to the human race," and "the
ig society" proved to be productively provocative over a long career in which
nice Neugarten helped set the intellectual agenda in gerontology. The changing
ial meaning of age is a case in point.

The Irrelevance of Age

Chronological age has had and continues to have an obvious practical significance in
everyday life. People know their age. Bureaucratic organizations and social programs
record and attach significance to age as a criterion of certain social rights and responsibilities. Age 65 is a prime correlate of retirement, Social Security, Medicare, and the
beginning of old age. Schooling is organized by age. Social scientists analyze their
evidence "controlling for age," as though age is a predictor of important social
outcomes. Isn't it nonsense to declare the irrelevance of age?

With a provocative generalization about "the age-irrelevant society," Bernice
Neugarten gets your attention and invites a response. While all societies pay attention to some form of age grading, the meanings and significance of chronological age
vary in important ways through time and over space. The meanings of age at any
time in our society typically are convenient constructs that we use to serve our social
purposes. The prevailing consensus in a society about how to use age—to signal normative expectations about being on track and on time in development—can and
does serve to conveniently organize behavior, beginning with the age-graded organization of our schools and workplaces. And we use age to signal qualification for
political office, a driver's license, or Social Security.

George L. Maddox is Professor of Sociology and Medical Sociology, Duke University.

The *age-relevant* society, however, becomes problematic when social change makes the prevailing age norms increasingly impractical in dealing with the observed complexity of how adult lives actually develop. When is one too young to drink or vote, or too old to drive or hold high public office? We are less certain today than yesterday. Neugarten observed that, particularly in late adulthood, existing age norms are increasingly irrelevant as precise guides for behavior. For even the casual observer in the United States recognizes that the Social Security and Medicare declaration that 65 is *old* is a bureaucratic convenience which does not square well with reality, a conclusion that research investigators in aging have drawn for at least three decades. Recent national legislation has forbidden mandatory retirement based on age alone for most occupations and, by the turn of the century, age 67 will become the normal age for drawing full Social Security benefits. Actuaries will continue to calculate active life expectancy and remaining years of life by chronological age. But Neugarten's declaration of diversity in the later adult years, illustrated by differentiating older adults broadly into *young-old, old, and old-old,* has seemed eminently sensible to most observers and has been widely accepted in both popular and professional writing. British geriatricians, who never accepted our American specification of oldness, declared years ago that the domain of geriatric medicine properly begins at 75. In the United States today, age 65, while still popular as a marker in public bureaucracy, is being rethought. The *age-irrelevant* society has not arrived. But age certainly has more varied, flexible, and changing meanings today than two decades ago when Bernice Neugarten forecast the age-irrelevant society.

DIVERSITY AND THE END OF GERONTOLOGY

Calling our attention to the dynamic social processes that have been reconstructing the meaning of age in the United States, Neugarten highlighted how the older associations between age, social roles, and rules for organizing adult development have been blurred. Her observations about diversity in later life and about how poorly chronological age captured this diversity, struck a responsive chord among scholars. She correctly sensed changes in age-related norms, a concern that was reflected in her quick response when asked about her most satisfying contribution to gerontology. With only a moment's reflection she said, "Helping return older people to the human race." Older adults are never free from time-dependent physiological changes, but they can be freed from the arbitrary constraints of socially constructed meanings of being older.

Neugarten made the same point, but with a more dramatic flare, in a presentation to a seminar for young geronologists at an annual meeting of the Gerontological Society of America. As one of the recognized pioneers of gerontology, Neugarten received the attention she intended when she announced the "end of gerontology." No one really believes that the Gerontological Society of America, which celebrated its fiftieth anniversary in 1995, is likely to disappear soon. Systematic study of later life is here to stay, as is some governmental apparatus which finds chronological age to be convenient for planning, financing, and managing services for older adults. Neugarten's point, however, is both subtle and correct. Late life is currently being viewed both popularly and professionally as more differential and complex than we ever imagined. And our understanding of late adulthood is improved by seeing the human life course whole, by seeing the substantial continuities which generally bind old age to the adult years. She might have said, "Expect the end of gerontology as we know it." She would have been more correct in her forecast but would have generated much less interest and less productive conversation.

The Societal Context of Aging

Neugarten understood that serving older adults could and did produce both a service and a research industry of adult professionals, an outcome which Carroll Estes (1981) popularized and criticized as "the aging enterprise." This aging enterprise had and has a stake in constructing and controlling its territory which is organized by age. Such behavior is common and easily recognized in a society familiar with interest group politics. What was troublesome about this, Neugarten felt, was that the aging enterprise focused too narrowly on individuals and, worse, assumed that all adults at the same chronological age were potential clients or patients eligible for age-defined benefits, such as pensions or special services, without regard to established need. Such a distinction asks whether *need* or *age* is the better criterion for allocating societal resources. There was no question of Neugarten's personal preference. Age per se, she knew, was not a strong predictor of need for publicly provided compensatory services. Her conclusion rattled the bureaucratic strongholds of age-based entitlements and services associated with Social Security and Medicare. The Americans with Disabilities Act of 1990, however, expressed in legislation one implication of Neugarten's forecast: disability as the dominant criterion for compensatory social assistance is a reasonable alternative to chronological age for developing social policy. Such a conclusion poses a substantial challenge for age-based services, particularly in housing. Historically, advocates for housing for older adults wanted just that in Housing and Urban Development regulations. But today housing initially intended for older adults turns out to include a large segment of disabled adults, not necessarily old. And Supplemental Social Insurance, an add-on to Social Security, now serves a majority of disabled poor younger adults and children. The trend is increasingly in this direction.

AGING SOCIETY

Although Bernice Neugarten is most often claimed by psychologists as their own, she was very much a product of the interdisciplinary Committee on Human Development at the University of Chicago. She was deeply interested in individuals as they change over their lifetimes, a perspective which tended to dominate the early history of gerontology, sometimes to the neglect of the context in which individuals age. Interested as she was in individuals, she nevertheless also reasserted an interdisciplinary interest in social environments as the contexts in which individuals age.

An early opportunity for her to declare the importance of context was her challenge to the individualistic, biologically reductionistic theory of disengagement proposed in the Kansas City Study of Adulthood in which she was an investigator. The outcomes of aging which might be called successful, she affirmed, are substantially defined and facilitated socially. In proof she offered comparative research documenting cross-national differences in adaptation to retirement.

Social context also figured prominently in her early discussion of age as a determinant of normative expectations about behavior. It is not news that age-related norms are socially constructed. What is news is that such norms are, under conditions of social change, continually reconstructed. Societies, not just individuals, age and develop as populations age. In her writing she noted the work of historians such as Philippe Ariès (1962) who documented, notably in his *Centuries of Childhood*, that societies over time and across space can and do divide up the life course differently. In Western societies, childhood as we know it is a rather recent social invention. The invention of adolescence is even more recent. And the expansion of old age into subcategories of *young-old, old*, and *old-old* is on today's agenda. Contemporary adults have a good deal of social space within which to maneuver in the construction of their social personae, and the meaning of age continues to be modifiable.

Society, however, is more than its culturally defined age-relevant roles and rules. Social and public policies structure the allocation of resources differentially over the life course. The equity of the prevailing rules for allocating resources between age categories appears currently in discussions of intergenerational fairness. Neugarten's interest did not lie primarily in establishing what is intergenerationally fair. Rather she was interested in the potential mismatching of institutional structures, particularly in the family and the workplace, that had a high probability of thwarting the intentions of older individuals able and willing to explore new roles for themselves. She was, expectedly, interested in how to make workplaces and families more age irrelevant.

She and I jointly authored the Social and Behavioral Sciences section of the new National Institute on Aging's first report to the Congress. It was titled *Our Future Selves: Behavioral and Social Research* and written in 1977. She insisted that we stress the implications of an aging society as well as of aging individuals. Society—its demographics, its resource allocations, and its institutional provisions for politics, education, family, and work—is appropriately an object for study as an independent set of external variables that is fundamental to understanding aging processes and the experience of aging. Matilda Riley (1994) has made this type of research a major emphasis of her work over the past two decades at the National Institute of Aging. In this research the differentiation and modifiability of behavior in later life figure prominently.

Neugarten's emphasis on the interaction of people and their social environment was intended to focus on the dynamics of and potential for purposive change. What are the meanings of age? We observe changing meanings. Testing the limits of desirable change in inventing the future of aging is the continuing challenge which lies ahead.

References

Aries, P. 1962. *Centuries of Childhood.* New York: Knopf.

Estes, C. 1981. *The Aging Enterprise.* San Francisco: Jossey-Bass.

Neugarten, B., and Maddox, G. 1977. *Our Future Selves: Behavioral and Social Research.* Bethesda, MD: National Institute of Aging, National Institutes of Health.

Riley, M. W., Kahn, R. L., and Foner, A. (eds). 1994. *Age and Structural lag.* New York: John Wiley.

ONE

Age Norms, Age Constraints, and Adult Socialization

Bernice L. Neugarten, Joan W. Moore, and John C. Lowe

In all societies, age is one of the bases for the ascription of status and one of the underlying dimensions by which social interaction is regulated. Anthropologists have studied age-grading in simple societies, and sociologists in the tradition of Mannheim have been interested in the relations between generations; but little systematic attention has been given to the ways in which age groups relate to each other in complex societies or to systems of norms which refer to age-appropriate behavior. A promising group of theoretical papers which appeared twenty or more years ago have now become classics (Benedict, 1938; Davis, 1940; Linton, 1936; Lowie, 1920; Mannheim, 1952; Parsons, 1942; Prins, 1953; Van Gennep, 1908), but with the exceptions of a major contribution by Eisenstadt (1956) and a provocative paper by Berger (1960), little theoretical or empirical work has been done in this area in the two decades that have intervened, and there has been little development of what might be called a sociology of age.

The present paper deals with two related issues: first, with the degree of constraint perceived with regard to age norms that operate in American society; second, with adult socialization to those norms.[1] Preliminary to presenting the data that bear upon these issues, however, a few comments regarding the age-norm system and certain illustrative observations gathered earlier may help to provide context for this study.

BACKGROUND CONCEPTS AND OBSERVATIONS

Expectations regarding age-appropriate behavior form an elaborated and pervasive system of norms governing behavior and interaction, a network of expectations that is embedded throughout the cultural fabric of adult life. There exists what might be called a prescriptive timetable for the ordering of major life events: a time in the life span when men and women are expected to marry, a time to raise children, a time to retire. This normative pattern is adhered to, more or less consistently, by most per-

Reprinted by permission from *American Journal of Sociology* 70, no. 6 (May 1965): 710–17; © 1965 by The University of Chicago; all rights reserved.

sons in the society. Although the actual occurrences of major life events for both men and women are influenced by a variety of life contingencies, and although the norms themselves vary somewhat from one group of persons to another, it can easily be demonstrated that norms and actual occurrences are closely related. Age norms and age expectations operate as prods and brakes upon behavior, in some instances hastening an event, in others delaying it. Men and women are aware not only of the social clocks that operate in various areas of their lives, but they are aware also of their own timing and readily describe themselves as "early," "late," or "on time" with regard to family and occupational events.

Age norms operate also in many less clear-cut ways and in more peripheral areas of adult life as illustrated in such phrases as "He's too old to be working so hard" or "She's too young to wear that style of clothing" or "That's a strange thing for a man of his age to say." The concern over age-appropriate behavior is further illustrated by colloquialisms such as "Act your age!"—an exhortation made to the adult as well as to the child in this society.

Such norms, implicit or explicit, are supported by a wide variety of sanctions ranging from those, on the one hand, that relate directly to the physical health of the transgressor to those, on the other hand, that stress the deleterious effects of the transgression on other persons. For example, the fifty-year-old man who insists on a strenuous athletic life is chastised for inviting an impairment of his own health; a middle-aged woman who dresses like an adolescent brings into question her husband's good judgment as well as her own; a middle-aged couple who decide to have another child are criticized because of the presumed embarrassment to their adolescent or married children. Whether affecting the self or others, age norms and accompanying sanctions are relevant to a great variety of adult behaviors; they are both systematic and pervasive in American society.

Despite the diversity of value patterns, life styles, and reference groups that influence attitudes, a high degree of consensus can be demonstrated with regard to age-appropriate and age-linked behaviors as illustrated by data shown in Table 1.1. The table shows how responses were distributed when a representative sample of middle-class men and women aged forty to seventy[2] were asked such questions as: "What do you think is the best age for a man to marry? . . . to finish school?" "What age comes to your mind when you think of a 'young' man? . . . an 'old' man?" "At what age do you think a man has the most responsibilities . . . accomplishes the most?"[3]

The consensus indicated in the table is not limited to persons residing in a particular region of the United States or to middle-aged persons. Responses to the same set of questions were obtained from other middle-class groups: one group of fifty men and women aged twenty to thirty residing in a second midwestern city, a group of sixty Negro men and women aged forty to sixty in a third midwestern city, and a

Table 1.1. Consensus in a Middle-Class, Middle-Aged Sample Regarding Various Age-Related Characteristics

	Age Range Designated as Appropriate or Expected	Percent Who Concur	
		Men (N = 50)	Women (N = 43)
Best age for a man to marry	20–25	80	90
Best age for a woman to marry	19–24	85	90
When most people should become grandparents	45–50	84	79
Best age for most people to finish school and go to work	20–22	86	82
When most men should be settled on a career	24–26	74	64
When most men hold their top jobs	45–50	71	58
When most people should be ready to retire	60–65	83	86
A young man	18–22	84	83
A middle-aged man	40–50	86	75
An old man	65–75	75	57
A young woman	18–24	89	88
A middle-aged woman	40–50	87	77
An old woman	60–75	83	87
When a man has the most responsibilities	35–50	79	75
When a man accomplishes most	40–50	82	71
The prime of life for a man	35–50	86	80
When a woman has the most responsibilities	25–40	93	91
When a woman accomplishes most	30–45	94	92
A good-looking woman	20–35	92	82

group of forty persons aged seventy to eighty in a New England community. Essentially the same patterns emerged in each set of data.

THE PROBLEM AND THE METHOD

Based upon various sets of data such as those illustrated in Table 1.1, the present investigation proceeded on the assumption that age norms and age expectations operate in this society as a system of social control. For a great variety of behaviors, there is a span of years within which the occurrence of a given behavior is regarded as appropriate. When the behavior occurs outside that span of years, it is regarded as inappropriate and is negatively sanctioned.

The specific questions of this study were these: How do members of the society vary in their perception of the strictures involved in age norms, or in the degree of constraint they perceive with regard to age-appropriate behaviors? To what extent are personal attitudes congruent with the attitudes ascribed to the generalized other?

Finally, using this congruence as an index of socialization, can adult socialization to age norms be shown to occur as respondents themselves increase in age?

The instrument.—A questionnaire was constructed in which the respondent was asked on each of a series of items which of three ages he would regard as appropriate or inappropriate, or which he would approve or disapprove. As seen in the illustrations below the age spans being proposed were intended to be psychologically rather than chronologically equal in the sense that for some events a broad age span is appropriate, for others, a narrow one.

> A woman who feels it's all right at her age to wear a two-piece bathing suit to the beach:
> > When she's 45 (approve or disapprove)
> > When she's 30 (approve or disapprove)
> > When she's 18 (approve or disapprove).

Other illustrative items were:

> A woman who decides to have another child (when she's 45, 37, 30).
>
> A man who's willing to move his family from one town to another to get ahead in his company (when he's 45, 35, 25).
>
> A couple who like to do the "Twist" (when they're 55, 30, 20).
>
> A man who still prefers living with his parents rather than getting his own apartment (when he's 30, 25, 21).
>
> A couple who move across country so they can live near their married children (when they're 40, 55, 70).

The thirty-nine items finally selected after careful pretesting are divided equally into three types: those that relate to occupational career; those that relate to the family cycle; and a broader grouping that refer to recreation, appearance, and consumption behaviors. In addition, the items were varied systematically with regard to their applicability to three periods: young adulthood, middle age, and old age.

In general, then, the questionnaire presents the respondent with a relatively balanced selection of adult behaviors which were known from pretesting to be successful in evoking age discriminations. A means of scoring was devised whereby the score reflects the degree of refinement with which the respondent makes age discriminations. For instance, the respondent who approves of a couple dancing the "Twist" if they are twenty, but who disapproves if they are thirty, is placing relative age constraint upon this item of behavior as compared to another respondent who approves the "Twist" both at age twenty and at age thirty, but not at age fifty-five. The higher the score, the more the respondent regards age as a salient dimension across a wide variety of behaviors and the more constraint he accepts in the operation of age norms.[4]

The sample.—A quota sample of middle-class respondents was obtained in which level of education, occupation, and area of residence were used to determine social class. The sample is divided into six age-sex cells: fifty men and fifty women aged twenty to thirty, one hundred men and one hundred women aged thirty to fifty-five, and fifty men and fifty women aged sixty-five and over. Of the four hundred respondents, all but a few in the older group were or had been married. The great majority were parents of one or more children.

The only known bias in the sample occurs in the older group (median age for men is sixty-nine; for women seventy-two) where most individuals were members of Senior Citizens clubs and where, as a result, the subsample is biased in the direction of better health and greater community involvement than can be expected for the universe of persons in this age range. While Senior Citizens is a highly age-conscious and highly age-graded association from the perspective of the wider society, there is no evidence that the seventy-year-old who joins is any more or any less aware of age discriminations than is the seventy-year-old who does not join.[5] The older group was no more or less homogeneous with regard to religious affiliation, ethnic background, or indexes of social class than were the other two age groups in this sample.

Administration.—To investigate the similarity between personal attitudes and attitudes ascribed to the generalized other, the questionnaire was first administered with instructions to give "your personal opinions" about each of the items; then the respondent was given a second copy of the questionnaire and asked to respond in the way he believed "most people" would respond.[6]

In about half the cases, both forms of the instrument were administered consecutively in personal interviews. In the remainder of the cases, responses on the first form were gathered in group sessions (in one instance, a parents' meeting in a school), and the second form was completed later and returned by mail to the investigator.

The two types of administration were utilized about evenly within each age-sex group. No significant differences in responses were found to be due to this difference in procedure of data-gathering.

FINDINGS

The findings of this study can be read from Figure 1.1. The figure shows a striking convergence with age between the two sets of attitudes.

1. Age trends within each set of data are opposite in direction. With regard to personal opinions, there is a highly significant increase in scores with age—that is, an increase in the extent to which respondents ascribe importance to age norms and place constraints upon adult behavior in terms of age appropriateness.

2. With regard to "most people's opinions" there is a significant decrease in scores

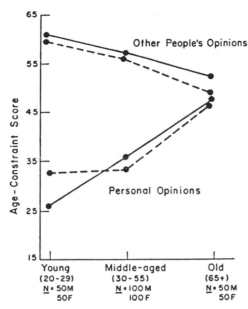

FIG. 1.1. Perception of age constraints in adulthood, by age and sex. An analysis of variance for the data on "personal opinions" showed that age was a highly significant variable (F is statistically reliable beyond the .001 level); and the interaction between age and sex was significant (F is reliable at the .05 level). For the data on "other people's opinions," age alone is a significant variable (F is reliable beyond the .001 level). Dotted line, women; solid line, men.

with age—that is, a decrease in the extent to which age constraints are perceived in the society and attributed to a generalized other.

3. Sex differences are minimal with the exception that young women stand somewhat outside the general trend on "personal opinions," with scores that differentiate them from young men but not from middle-aged women.

Discussion

The difference shown in these data between personal attitudes and attitudes attributed to the generalized order (a finding that holds true for all but the oldest respondents) implies that age norms operate like other types of norms insofar as there is some lack of congruence between that which is acknowledged to be operating in the society and that which is personally accepted as valid. It is noteworthy, on the one hand, that age norms are uniformly acknowledged to exist in the minds of "most people." While the data are not shown here, on each one of the thirty-nine behavioral items some 80 percent or more of all respondents made age discriminations when asked for "most people's opinions." In other words, general consensus exists that behaviors described in the test instrument are age-related. On the other hand, respondents uniformly attributed greater stricture to age norms in the minds of other people than in their own minds. This difference was reflected in the scores for every respondent as well as in the mean scores.

These findings indicate that there is an overriding norm of "liberal-mindedness" regarding age, whereby men and women consistently maintain that they hold more liberal views than do others. In many ways this situation is reminiscent of the phenomenon of pluralistic ignorance, in which no respondent's personal view of the attitudes of others is altogether correct (Allport, 1924). In other ways, however, this may be a situation in which respondents tend to exaggerate, rather than to misconstrue, the opinions of others. A young person who says, in effect, "I am not strict about age norms, but other people are," is indeed correct that other people are stricter than he is (as shown in these data on "personal opinions"); but he exaggerates, for other people are not so strict as he thinks. Similarly, when an old person says, in effect, "I think this is the norm, and other people think so, too," he is also partly correct that other old people agree with him, but he ignores what *young* people think.

These partial misconceptions have at least two implications: first, when a person's own opinions differ from the norms he encounters, he may exaggerate the differences and place the norms even further away from his own opinions than is warranted. Second, it may be that in considering age norms the individual gives undue weight to the opinion of persons who are older or stricter than himself and ignores the opinions of others who are younger or less strict. In both instances, the norm image is not the average of all opinions encountered but the image of the "ideal" norm. In the case of age norms, the "ideal" norms may well be those held by older persons.

The findings of this study are also of interest when viewed within the context of adult socialization. Cross-sectional data of this type must be interpreted with caution since the differences between age groups may reflect historical changes in values and attitudes as much as changes that accompany increased age itself. Still, the findings seem congruent with a theory of adult socialization: that personal belief in the relevance and validity of social norms increases through the adult life span and that, in this instance, as the individual ages he becomes increasingly aware of age discriminations in adult behavior and of the system of social sanctions that operate with regard to age appropriateness. The middle-aged and the old seem to have learned that age is a reasonable criterion by which to evaluate behavior, that to be "off-time" with regard to life events or to show other age-deviant behavior brings with it social and psychological sequelae that cannot be disregarded. In the young, especially the young male, this view is only partially accepted; and there seems to be a certain denial of age as a valid dimension by which to judge behavior.

This age-related difference in point of view is perhaps well illustrated by the response of a twenty-year-old who, when asked what he thought of marriage between seventeen-year-olds, said, "I suppose it would be all right if the boy got a good job, and if they loved each other. Why not? It isn't age that's the important thing." A forty-five-year-old, by contrast, said, "At that age, they'd be foolish. Neither one of them is settled enough. A boy on his own, at seventeen, couldn't support a wife, and he certainly couldn't support children. Kids who marry that young will suffer for it later."

Along with increased personal conviction regarding the validity of age norms goes a decreased tendency to perceive the generalized other as restrictive. The overall convergence in the data, a convergence which we have interpreted in terms of adult socialization, may reflect status and deference relationships between age groups in American society, where high status is afforded the middle-aged and where social enforcement of norms may generally be said to be vested in the mature rather than the young. The young person, having only recently graduated from the age-segregated world of adolescents, and incompletely socialized to adult values, seems to perceive a psychological distance between himself and "most people" and to feel only partially identified with the adult world. This is evidenced by the fact that when asked, "Whom do you have in mind when you think of 'most people'?" young adults tended to answer, "Older people."

Only for old people is there a high degree of congruence between personal opinions and the opinions ascribed to others. This may reflect not only the accumulated effects of adult socialization and the internalization of age norms, but also a certain crystallization of attitudes in the aged. Older respondents volunteered the most vehement and the most opinionated comments as they moved from item to item, as if to underscore the fact that their attitudes with regard to age and age-related behaviors are highly charged emotionally. Under these circumstances, there is likely to be a blurring of distinctions between what the respondent himself regards as right and what he thinks other people would "naturally" regard as right.

With regard to sex differences, the fact that young women perceive greater constraints regarding age-appropriate behavior than do young men is generally congruent with other evidence of differences in socialization for women and men in our society. Young women are probably more highly sensitized to the imperatives of age norms than are young men, given the relatively more stringent expectations regarding age at marriage for women.

It should be recalled that the present study is based upon quota samples of middle-class respondents and that accordingly the findings cannot be readily generalized to other samples. Nevertheless, the findings support the interpretation that age norms are salient over a wide variety of adult behaviors and support the view that adult socialization produces increasingly clear perception of these norms as well as an increasing awareness that the norms provide constraints upon adult behavior.

Notes

1. With some exceptions, sociologists have as yet given little attention to the broader problem of adult socialization.

2. The sample was drawn by area-probability methods (a 2 percent listing of households in randomly selected census tracts) with the resulting pool of cases then stratified by age, sex, and socioeconomic status. Using the indexes of occupation, level of education, house type, and area of residence, these respondents were all middle class. The data were gathered in connection with the Kansas City Studies of Adult Life, a research program carried out over a period of years under the direction of Robert J. Havighurst, William E. Henry, Bernice L. Neugarten, and other members of the Committee on Human Development, University of Chicago.

3. For each item in the table, the percentages that appear in the third and fourth columns obviously vary directly with the breadth of the age span shown for that item. The age span shown was, in turn, the one selected by the investigators to produce the most accurate reflection of the consensus that existed in the data.

The way in which degree of consensus was calculated can be illustrated on "Best age for a man to marry." Individuals usually responded to this item in terms of specific years, such as "20" or "22" or in terms of narrow ranges, such as "from 20 to 23." These responses were counted as consensus within the five-year age range shown in Table 1.1, on the grounds that the respondents were concurring that the best age was somewhere between twenty and twenty-five. A response such as "18 to 20" or "any time in the 20's" was outside the range regarded as consensus and was therefore excluded.

4. For each item of behavior, one of the ages being proposed is scored as the "appropriate" age; another, the "marginal"; and the third, the "inappropriate" (the age at which the behavior is usually proscribed on the basis of its transgression of an age norm). A response which expresses disapproval of only the "inappropriate" age is scored 1, while a response which expresses disapproval of not only the "inappropriate" but also the "marginal" age receives a score of 3. The total possible score is 117, a score that could result only if the respondent were perceiving maximum age constraint with regard to every one of the thirty-nine items. A response which expresses approval or disapproval of all three ages for a given behavior is scored zero, since for that respondent the item is not age-related, at least not within the age range being proposed.

The "appropriate" age for each item had previously been designated by the investigators on the basis of previous findings such as those illustrated on Table 1.1 of this report. That the designations were generally accurate was corroborated by the fact that when the present instrument was administered to the four hundred respondents described here, more than 90 percent of respondents on successive test items checked "approve" for the "appropriate" one of the three proposed ages.

5. On the other hand, members of Senior Citizens are more likely to be activists and to re-

gard themselves as younger in outlook than persons who do not join such groups. If this is true, the age differences to be described in the following sections of this paper might be expected to be even more marked in future studies in which samples are more representative.

6. The problem being studied here relates to problems of conformity, deviation, and personal versus public attitudes. As is true of other empirical research in these areas, the terms used here are not altogether satisfactory, in part because of the lack of uniform terminology in this field. For example, while age norms are in some respects related to "attitudinal" and "doctrinal" conformity as posed by Merton (1959), these data do not fit that analytical framework because age norms are less clear-cut than the norms Merton discusses, and the realms of attitudinal and doctrinal conformity are less prescribed.

Similarly, the projection of personal attitudes upon the generalized other has been studied by Getzels and Walsh (1958) but their theoretical model is not altogether applicable because in the present research the phenomenon of projection cannot be demonstrated. The same lack of fit exists with the concepts used by Rokeach (1960); and with the concepts of social norms, norms of common consent, and personal norms as used by Bott (1957). The *self, generalized other* terminology is therefore regarded as the most appropriate for describing the present data.

References

Allport, Floyd H. 1924. *Social Psychology.* Boston: Houghton Mifflin Co.

Benedict, Ruth. 1938. Continuities and Discontinuities in Culture Conditioning. *Psychiatry* I:161–67.

Berger, Bennett M. 1960. How Long is a Generation? *British Journal of Sociology* 11:10–23.

Davis, Kingsley. 1940. The Sociology of Parent-Youth Conflict. *American Sociological Review* 5:523–35.

Eisenstadt, S. N. 1956. *From Generation to Generation: Age Groups and the Social Structure.* New York: Free Press of Glencoe.

Linton, Ralph. 1936. *The Study of Man.* New York: Appleton-Century-Crofts, Inc.

Lowie, Robert H. 1920. *Primitive Society.* New York: Harper and Row Publishers, Inc.

Mannheim, Karl. 1952. The Problem of Generations. In *Essays on the Sociology of Knowledge.* New York: Oxford University Press, Inc.

Parsons, Talcott, 1942. Age and Sex in the Social Structure of the United States. *American Sociological Review* 7:604–16.

Prins, A. H. J. 1953. *East African Age-Class Systems.* Groningen: J. B. Wolters.

Van Gennep, Arnold. 1908. *The Rites of Passage.* Chicago: The University of Chicago Press, 1960.

TWO

Age Groups in American Society and the Rise
of the Young-Old

Ours is a society characterized by longevity. While the natural limits of the human life span have probably not changed since ancient times, an ever increasing number of persons now live to age 80 or 90, thus approaching what appears to be the natural, probably genetically fixed limit. Put in different words, advances in biomedical science and other social, political and economic changes have resulted in a redistribution of deaths so that deaths now occur much less frequently at the beginning of the life span—in infancy and childhood—and more frequently at the end—in old age. Continued medical advances are expected to add only a few more years to average life expectancy, and most biologists—a few to the contrary notwithstanding—believe that no major scientific breakthrough or anti-aging treatment is likely to appear within the next two decades to produce a dramatic extension of the life span. Nevertheless, because more people live to old age, the numbers of older persons in the United States will continue to rise sharply. Future numbers cannot be translated directly into future proportions, because future birth rates—and, therefore, the future total population—are uncertain; however, the numbers of older people can be accurately predicted because these persons are already born. At present, 20 million persons are aged 65 and over; the number will grow to 28 million by 1990 and to 40 million by 2020; the pulse, or swell, in numbers will be due to the aging of large cohorts of people who are presently young.

The age distribution of a population is both the result and the cause of pervasive changes in economic, political and other aspects of social organization. Some of the implications become obvious enough when a developing nation in Asia, Latin America or Africa is compared with an economically developed society such as our own. In the former, during the period 1965 to 1970, roughly 41 percent of a national population was under age 15 and only 3 percent was over age 65. By contrast, in the developed nation the parallel figures were 27 percent under 15 and 10 percent over 65.[1]

Reprinted by permission from *Annals of the American Academy of Political and Social Science* 415 (September 1974): 187–98.

Relations among Age Groups

The relative numbers of young, middle-aged and old affect every aspect of life, particularly the relations among age groups. In most societies in most periods of history an equilibrium becomes established whereby all age groups receive an appropriate share of goods and services and an appropriate place for their different world views. Unusual circumstances sometimes arise, however, in which relations among age groups become strained and customary modes of accommodation are no longer regarded as equitable.

For instance, in some countries the appearance of large numbers of older persons has been relatively sudden—as in the United States within the past fifty years—and dislocations have occurred because these societies have been unprepared—that is, unprepared by prevailing value systems which determine human priorities—to meet the newly emerging needs. In the United States a sizable proportion of older people have suffered from inadequate income, poor housing, and a host of other social and economic ills; thus, they have constituted a disproportionately disadvantaged group. A large minority of needy aged grew up who created acute problems in the fields of social and medical welfare. Although our Social Security program was established in the late 1930s it is only within the last decade that a wide range of remedial and palliative public and private programs have been initiated.

It is perhaps equally cogent that fluctuations in birth rates in the United States have also led to an enormous population pulse of young persons who are presently 15 to 25. With the growth of technology and an economy which provides insufficient work opportunities, and with a system of secondary and higher education which fails to provide meaningful experience for a growing minority of young people—particularly those from low occupational levels—the problems with regard to the young may be as serious as those with regard to the old.

Is Ageism Increasing or Decreasing?

Some observers believe that not only inequities, but conflicts, between age groups are increasing in the direction of both young and old; that a new age divisiveness is appearing; and that new antagonisms, which can be called ageism, are growing. Some have said that the Western world is entering a period of social change not unlike earlier eras marked by struggles for political and economic rights; however, the present struggle is for age rights, and it is being joined not only by the young, but also by the old who might otherwise become its victims. Some decry the trend toward age segregation, pointing to the high school and college as age ghettos for the young and to age-segregated residential areas—whether new retirement communities or deteriorated neighborhoods in the inner city where the old are left behind—as age ghettos for the old. Just as anger toward the young was on the rise in the 1960s, with the attention drawn to the youthful law offender, the student activist and the hippie, so these observers believe that anger toward the old may rise as a growing proportion of power positions in the judiciary, legislative, business and professional arenas are occupied by older people; as the number of retirees increases and Social Security taxes rise; and as the economic burden is perceived—rightly or wrongly—as falling more and more upon the middle-aged taxpayer.

Other observers take a more optimistic view. They point to new attempts to integrate the young into the adult society—as witnessed by the lowering of the voting age from 21 to 18; to the greater permissiveness toward the new life styles of the young; to the deference given to their technical expertise. In the other direction, they point to the fact that while a substantial minority of older persons has been economically disadvantaged, there has been a regular rise in overall purchasing power in the hands of older people; that in the past five years Social Security payments have increased nearly 70 percent—although inflation has offset much of this gain; and that the proportion of older persons who are poor has dropped dramatically. In this view age-segregated communities, at least for that large majority of older persons who are not poor, are a sign of the greater permissiveness toward the new life styles of the old, for older persons move into these communities by choice and are therefore responding to the new options being offered them. In some segments of American society older people are becoming a visible and contented leisure class, helped along by a change in national values from instrumentality to expressivity and from a work ethic to a leisure ethic.

Regardless of the special problems of the young and the question of whether ageism is waxing or waning, it is true that in the United States—as in other industrialized societies—both young and old must adapt to new phenomena resulting from added longevity. Moreover, all members of society must adapt to multigenerational families, retirement and trends toward gerontocracy. From this perspective, increased numbers of older persons—whether they are needy or affluent—pose the problem of major social readjustments, and their presence leads to the need for new alignments among all age groups.

CHANGING PERCEPTIONS OF THE LIFE CYCLE

The relations among age groups are also influenced by changing perceptions of the life cycle and the periods of life. Age groups have become increasingly differentiated over time. For instance, it was not until the seventeenth and eighteenth centuries, with industrialization, the appearance of a middle class, and formal educational institutions, that childhood became a discernible period of life with its special needs and characteristics.[2] The concept of adolescence can be viewed as an invention of the twentieth century. Now, a case is being made for a new stage called youth; this stage has appeared only in the last few decades as the transition from childhood to adulthood has been increasingly prolonged, resulting in a free-choice period between high school and first job or marriage for a growing number of young persons.[3]

Also, in the past few decades middle age has become a newly delineated stage in the life cycle, due not only to increased longevity and improved health, but also to the historically changing rhythm of events in the family cycle. Since the turn of the century marriage and parenthood occur earlier; children—whose births are spaced closer together—grow up and leave home earlier. Thus, before retirement there is now a period, which begins around 40, when most parents consider themselves to be middle aged. The perception is widely shared that persons no longer move abruptly from adulthood—the period of full commitment to work and family responsibilities—into old age, but that they go, instead, through a relatively long interval during which family responsibilities are diminished, work continues, even though specific work roles may change—for example, women reentering the labor market in their 40s and 50s—and physical vigor remains high.

The Young-Old

We are presently undergoing still another changing perception of the life cycle and still another meaningful division is appearing: namely, a division between the young-old and the old-old. Although chronological age is not a satisfactory marker, it is nevertheless an indispensable one. At the risk of oversimplification, the young-old come from the group composed of those who are approximately 55 to 75—as distinguished from the old-old, who are 75 and over.

There is undoubtedly overlap between the middled aged and the young-old. Indeed, in terms of self-perceptions, many persons call themselves middle aged until their 70s, thereby expressing a sense of continued youthfulness and/or a denial of aging. However, putting aside self-perceptions—which tend, at best, to be inconsistent from one group to another—the young-old are distinguishable primarily by the fact of retirement. Granted that the use of a single life event as the criterion is arbitrary, retirement is nevertheless a meaningful marker with regard to the young-old, just as the departure of children from the home is a useful marker with regard to middle age.

This 55 to 75 grouping is not one to which we have been accustomed. Ever since the beginning of our Social Security system, we have used age 65, not age 55, as the economic—then, as the social and psychological—marker of old age. For various other historical reasons a set of stereotypes have grown up about old age which are based primarily upon the old-old. Moreover, although the stereotypes of older persons as sick, poor, enfeebled, isolated and desolated have been greatly overdrawn even for the old-old, they have become uncritically attached to the whole group over 65. These stereotypes are only now beginning to yield to reality.

For one thing, 65 as a marker of economic old age is becoming less consistent. For example, by 1973 the number of retirees drawing Social Security benefits who were 62 to 64 and who were not disabled had already grown to over 1.5 million. In some occupational groups eligibility for pensions was and is determined not by chronological age, but by the number of years of service. It is not unimportant also that the wide array of federally supported services provided through the Older Americans Act go to persons aged 60 and over rather than 65 and over.

Age 55 is beginning to be a meaningful lower age limit for the young-old because of the lowering age of retirement. Many workers are now voluntarily retiring just as soon as they think they can live comfortably on their retirement incomes—for example, auto workers who exercise their option to retire at 55. In other industries where overall employment is declining, the downward trend in age of retirement is dramatic—whether most retirements are voluntary or involuntary. The 1970 census showed that a significant drop in the proportion of all men in the labor force occurs by age 55, when 81 percent of 55- to 64-year-olds are in the labor force, as compared to 92 percent of the next younger age group.

Whether this trend toward earlier retirement will continue in the future depends upon a large number of other factors: rates of economic and technological growth, the number of young workers, the number of women workers, increases in part-time work opportunities and a possible share-the-work movement. Most observers predict, however, that the downward trend will continue over the next two or three decades.[4] By and large, then, the young-old will increasingly become a retired group.

It is already a relatively healthy group. Table 2.1 shows that about 15 percent of 45- to 64-year-olds need to limit their major activities because of health, while just under 40 percent of all those 65 and over must do so. If the young-old group were differentiated in these data, the proportion with health limitations would probably be between 20 and 25 percent.

OTHER CHARACTERISTICS OF THE YOUNG-OLD

Because of the enormous diversity of life styles among the young-old, meaningful differences are obscured in aggregated data of the type shown in Table 2.1. Nevertheless, the gross characteristics of this age group are worth noting.

At present the young-old group numbers roughly 31 million and constitutes more than 15 percent of the total population—as compared with the old-old, who constitute less than 4 percent. Their proportion is expected to remain about the same over the next three decades—depending, of course, upon birth rates and total size of population.

Table 2.1. Characteristics of the Young-Old and the Old-Old, 1970

| Characteristics | Young-Old | | Old-Old |
	55 to 64	65 to 74	75 and Over
Numbers: Total (millions)	19	12	8
men	9	5	3
women	10	7	5
percent total population	9	6	4
percent increase 1960–1970	19	15	43
Projections, 2000: Total	22.5	16	12.5
men	10.5	7	4.5
women	12	9	8
percent total population*	9	7	5
percent increase 1970–2000	21	31	64
Marital status (%)			
men: married, wife present	82	75	56
widowed	4	11	28
women: married, husband present	64	44	19
widowed	20	42	68
Living arrangements (%)			
men: heads of household†	95	93	86
in institutions	1	2	7
women: heads of household§	27	42	51
in institutions	1	2	11
same house as in 1965	72	73	71
moved, same county	16	15	16
In labor force (%)			
men	81	32	12
women	42	14	5
Median income			
all white families (age of head)	$10,680‡	$5,260§	
only husband worked	9,150	5,740	
husband and wife worked	13,400	9,730	
Percent who were poor			
1967	—	29.6§	
1971	11.6	21.6	
1972	10.8	18.6¶	
Median years schooling completed			
men	10.2	8.7	8.3
women	10.8	9.0	8.6
projected, 1990 (M + F)	12.3	11.9§	

continued

Table 2.1. *Continued*

Characteristics	Young-Old		Old-Old
	55 to 64	65 to 74	75 and Over
Health status (%)			
limitation or inability to			
carry on major activity:			
men	17[‖]		43[§]
women	14[‖]		35
Political behavior			
highest of all age groups			
on overall participation	X[#]		
highest of all age groups			
on voting			X^{§**}

* Based on Series E census projections; birth-rate, 2.1. This is higher than the actual birthrates of the past two years.

† Head of family or primary individual.

‡ The comparable figure for 45 to 54-year-olds is $12,580.

§ Data refer to total group 65 and over.

¶ The percent poor has dropped further since 1972, due to the 20 percent increase in Social Security benefits in 1973, the 11 percent cost-of-living increase in Social Security in 1974, and the Supplemental Security Income system in 1974 which provides minimum incomes for those aged 65 and over.

‖ Data refer to the total group 45 to 64.

\# For the age group 51 to 65; data are corrected for income and education. See S. Verba and N. H. Nie, *Participation in America* (New York: Harper and Row, 1972).

** Data are corrected for income; see Verba and Nie, *Participation*.

Because mortality rates for women are lower, women outnumber men by a sizable proportion; this imbalance is expected to grow even larger. Nevertheless, because most men marry women somewhat younger than themselves, the young-old as a total group are more like their younger, than their older, counterparts with regard to marital status and family relations. About 80 percent of the young-old men and well over half the women were married in 1970 and living with their spouses. The rates of widowhood are, of course, very different for the two sexes; about 7 percent of the men, but over 30 percent of the women, are widowed. By far the common pattern is husband-wife families living in their own households—some 70 percent owning their own homes—and only a very small number moving from one house to another within a five-year interval. Of married men living with their wives, 95 percent are heads of their households. In other words, very few such couples live in households where a child or a relative is the head of the household.

The young-old see their children frequently, often living near to at least one child. They expect that when they grow to advanced old age and can no longer manage for themselves, their children will come to their aid—not financially, for the government is looked to as the expected source of financial and medical assistance, but emotionally. As a number of studies have shown, assistance and services are being exchanged across generational lines, and affectional ties are strong. Thus, the family continues to be an important part of daily life.

It is noteworthy that a large proportion of young-old have a living parent. The estimate is that one of every three 60-year-olds had a living parent in 1972; furthermore, this proportion will increase, because the numbers of old-old are growing faster than the numbers of young-old. Although the care of an aged parent poses problems, the fact that a parent is still living usually contributes to a sense of youthfulness in the young-old child.

The economic status of the young-old is less easily summarized. Income from work is a major factor in economic status, and for most persons income drops precipitously upon retirement. In 1970 the average income for white families was about 15 percent lower for the 55 to 64 age group than for the 45 to 54 group; it dropped to half the latter amount for those over 65. These are data for different groups of persons rather than for the same persons at different ages; therefore, the statistics may be deceptive with regard to change over the life span. Nevertheless, if present trends continue, the adjustment to lower incomes for most persons may be timed closer to age 55 than to age 65. The anticipation of a longer period of life at a reduced income may affect monetary savings plans in young adulthood, just as it affects pension plans; however, such consequences are presently unpredictable.

Neither can the economic position of this age group relative to other age groups be easily determined. While income drops sharply for most persons upon retirement, current money income is only part of total economic resources—for instance, government in-kind transfers, such as Medicare, value of rent to homeowner, net worth holdings, tax adjustments, intrafamily transfers and other components need to be included in assessing economic status.

The relative economic status of the young-old compared to other age groups is similarly unpredictable for future decades, for the distribution of goods and services among age groups and the degree to which direct income payments to retirees will outweigh the provisions of services—indirect income—remain to be seen. Whether or not affluence will be increasingly equalized by age is an open question, even though the trend has now been toward improved economic status for older people.

It is likely that economic hazards for both the young-old and the old-old will be reduced in the near future, even if economic status is not equalized with that of younger groups. The rise in Social Security payments, the new cost-of-living increases which protect against inflation, and the new federalization of the welfare system—the Supplemental Security Income system which makes the income of the poorest old people somewhat more adequate than before—together constitute one major step forward. Second, it is almost certain that a form of national health insurance will soon be instituted to meet an increasing proportion of health costs for persons of all ages; for older persons it will be a marked improvement over Medicare. Third, private and public pensions and profit-sharing plans have spread. Currently, the need for improving their operation is recognized in Congress and elsewhere. To the extent that these and other changes occur, the major threats to economic well-being of older persons will be effectively diminished—with the outcome that the future young-old will be much more financially secure than their predecessors.

The young-old are already much better educated than the old-old, but the more important fact is that in the near future they will be in a less disadvantaged position in comparison to the young. So marked are the gains in educational level in successive cohorts of the population that by 1980 the average 55-year-old will be a high school graduate; by 1990 this will be true of all the young-old as a group. Furthermore, with the anticipated growth in higher education for adults, whether degree-oriented or not, and the even greater growth in what the Carnegie Commission calls "further education"—that is, education, both part-time and full-time, which occurs in settings other than college campuses and which is not aimed at academic degrees—it can also be anticipated that the educational differences which presently exist between young, middle-aged and young-old will be much reduced.[5]

With regard to political participation there is no evidence that age blocks are forming or that a politics of age is developing in the United States.[6] A quite different picture emerges, however, when general political participation and voting patterns are examined. Verba and Nie show that, when their national data are corrected for income and education, overall political participation—for example, voting, persuading others to vote a certain way, actively working for party or candidate, working with others on local problems—is highest for the age group 51 to 65. It falls off only a little for persons over 65.[7] For voting alone—and, again, when the data are corrected for income levels—the peak is the period after age 65. Thus, the young-old group are a highly active political group as compared to other age groups, and within the electorate as a whole they are disproportionately influential.

WHAT WILL THE YOUNG-OLD WANT?

These, then, are some of the characteristics of that 15 percent of the total population who are the young-old. As a group they are markedly different from the outmoded stereotypes of old age. Although they are relatively free from traditional social responsibilities of work and family, they are relatively healthy, relatively affluent, and they are politically active.

A vigorous and educated young-old group can be expected to develop a variety of new needs with regard to the meaningful use of time. They are likely to want a wide range of options and opportunities, both for self-enhancement and for community participation.

They will probably want a wider range of options with regard to work. Some will opt for early retirement; some will want to continue working beyond age 65; some will want to undertake new work careers at one or more times after age 40. They are likely to encourage those economic policies which hasten the separation between income and work and which move toward the goal of providing retirees with sufficient income to approximate their preretirement living standards.

We are already seeing a trend which will probably accelerate: a wider range of life patterns with regard to the three related areas of work, education and leisure. More middle-aged and older people are returning to education, some because of obsolescence of work skills and others for recreation or self-fulfillment. Plans are now going forward in various parts of the country to create inter-generational campuses with housing for older people, and in this and other ways to help bring into reality the so-called learning society.

The needs of the young-old in housing, location and transportation will be increasingly affected by the decisions they make with regard to the use of leisure time. The large majority will be living independently, apart from children and other relatives. This fact, combined with the desire to find interesting things to do, will lead them to seek environments which maximize options for meaningful pursuits. The extent to which age-segregated communities will increase depends, presumably, upon the extent to which the young-old will be provided opportunities for meaningful community participation in their present locations.

The vast majority will be living as married couples, but the large number of widows and single and divorced will probably lead to the formation of more group households composed of nonfamily members. At the same time, many will want housing arrangements which make it possible to maintain an aged parent at home. Perhaps an incentive system will be undertaken whereby family care of an old-old relative will not only be possible, but even remunerative. Family interactions of other types may also increase rather than decrease. Some observers predict that as the more instrumental aspects of life—education, income maintenance, health services—are increasingly shifted to other social institutions, the family may become more, rather than less, important within the expressive aspects of life—that is, in providing lasting emotional ties, and a sense of identity and self-worth.

The young-old are also likely to want greater options with regard to cultural enrichment, community participation and local political involvement—in general, for what might be called an age-irrelevant society in which arbitrary constraints based on chronological age are removed and in which all individuals, whether they are young or old, have opportunities consonant with their needs, desires and abilities. Over all, as the young-old articulate their needs and desires, the emphasis is likely to be upon improving the quality of life and upon increasing the choices of life styles.

THE YOUNG-OLD IN 1990

If the young-old in the 1970s have moved far from the stereotypes of old age, what can be said of those who will constitute the young-old in the 1990s? The group will include those who are presently 30 to 40 years old, those who are actively participating in the major political and cultural movements which are presently altering our traditional social institutions. This age group includes those who challenged government leaders over the issue of a land war in Southeast Asia in the 1960s; those who were involved in the civil rights movement, the Women's Liberation movement and the antipollution movement; those who are now activists in an era during which corporate enterprise has come under attack as the result of the consumer movement and the office of the presidency has come under attack as the result of Watergate.

These are parents of school-age children at the time when the public schools are being challenged to provide better outcomes for disadvantaged groups and when the issues of desegregation and busing have become personal issues. These are persons who have grown up in an age of organ transplants, legalization of abortion, the problems of cities, crime, the energy crisis. Furthermore, they have come into political maturity in an age when persons look increasingly to government—whether federal or local—not only to provide essential services and to protect citizens from harm, but also to improve the quality of their lives.

These experiences and these attitudes, combined with their higher educational and occupational levels, will probably lead the future young-old to exert a potent influence upon government. Compared to the young-old of the 1970s, the young-old of the 1990s are likely to wield their influence through direct political action and to make demands of both the public and private sectors to bring the benefit structure in line with their raised expectations.

THE OLD-OLD

This focus upon the young-old is not meant to denigrate the old-old, nor to neglect their needs. For one thing, the number of those over 75 is growing at an increasing rate. Their legitimate claims upon the society are at least as compelling as those of other age groups.

Their needs for meaningful ways of spending time, for special housing and for transportation will depend in large measure upon health status. Probably an increasing minority will remain active and productive and, because this is true, increased options in all areas of life will be important. The majority will probably live independently, but they will need both supportive social services and special features in the physical environment to enable them to function as fully as possible. Not only will the old-old require health services geared toward slowing physical and mental deterioration, but social services designed to prevent unnecessary decline in the individual's feelings of self-worth and dignity. In this respect opportunities for social interaction and social contributions will continue to be important.

For the old-old, as the probability of illness increases, some will require nursing home care; others who wish to remain at home will require new forms of home health services. There is no denying the fact that at the very end of life there will be a shorter or longer period of dependency and that increased numbers of the old-old will need special care, either in their own homes or in institutional settings. Thus, a larger share of the service budget of the nation will go to the old-old.

With regard to persons who are terminally ill or incapacitated, society will continue to face the problems of providing the maximum social supports, the highest possible levels of care and comfort, the assurance of dignified death and an increasing element of choice for the individual himself or for members of his family in deciding how and when his life shall end. The future will probably see the spread of educational programs aimed at the public at large, as well as at various professional groups, for achieving a "best death" for each individual.

THE FUTURE ROLES OF THE YOUNG-OLD

To return now to the broader question of the relationship among age groups in a modern society and to the broader historical perspective: the role of the older person vis-à-vis other age groups has undergone a major transition. Although the point has often been exaggerated, it is true that as a result of a slow historical process the older person is no longer the repository of wisdom which he may have been in simpler and more stable societies. More recently, he is also moving away from the role of economic producer—or the role of worker, as we have usually used that term. He has now become the user of leisure time. In that new role the young-old may be regarded as the first age group to reach the society of the future. Will they experiment with what some observers would call their truly human condition—the condition of freedom from work and freedom from want?

If our portrait of the young-old is correct, then, with their relative good health, education, purchasing power, free time and political involvement, they are not likely to become the neglected, the isolated or the expendables of the society. Will they, instead, become the social contributors, as well as the self-fulfilled? Will they be the first to create, on a large scale, new service roles and to offer their services to the community without regard to direct financial remuneration?

If, as seems presently true, the young-old will not form a strong age-group identification of their own, they might become the major agents of social change in building the age-irrelevant society. If they create an attractive image of aging, thus allay the fears of the young about growing old, and if they help to eradicate those age norms which are currently meaningless and those age attitudes which are currently divisive, they will do the society an untold service. Theirs is an enormous potential.

Notes

1. P. M. Hauser, "Extension of Life: Demographic Considerations" (Paper presented at the Twenty-Fifth Annual Conference on Aging, Institute of Gerontology, University of Michigan, Ann Arbor, Michigan, 12 September 1972).

2. P. Aries, *Centuries of Childhood* (New York: Vintage Books, 1962).

3. *Youth: Transition to Adulthood,* Report of a panel of the President's Social Science Advisory Committee, J. S. Coleman, Chairman (Washington, D.C.: U.S. Government Printing Office, 1974).

4. A. J. Jaffe, "Has the Retreat from the Labor Force Halted? A Note on Retirement of Men, 1930–1970," *Industrial Gerontology* (Spring 1971), pp. 1–12.

5. Carnegie Commission on Higher Education, *Toward a Learning Society* (New York: McGraw-Hill, 1973).

6. A. Campbell, "Politics through the Life Cycle," *Gerontologist* 11, no. 2 (Summer 1971), pp. 112–117.

7. S. Verba and N. H. Nie, *Participation in America* (New York: Harper and Row, 1972).

THREE

The Young-Old and the Age-Irrelevant Society

In the past century medical and social advances have produced the most dramatic of changes in the human life cycle—its increased duration. The facts need no elaboration here, nor the fact that average life expectancy is expected to continue to increase, although very slowly, over the next few decades in industrialized countries. (In the so-called developing countries, it is expected to jump dramatically and to approach that of the developed countries.)

The social implications of life extension have been both good and bad. The long period of the life cycle in which people remain physically and intellectually vigorous has been lengthening, and, in this sense, man may be said to be slowly creating his Fountain of Youth. At the same time life extension is producing a larger proportion of ill and frail persons of advanced old age. The problem for biological and biomedical gerontologists is how to increase the active and vigorous part of life without increasing the period of disability, a problem whose solution may continue to escape us for the foreseeable future.

The lengthening life cycle has led to the appearance of what can be called the young-old, as differentiated from the old-old. Because these terms have now taken on a certain currency, we need only be reminded briefly that the young-old are persons in the second half of their lives who are the healthy and vigorous retirees and their spouses. This large group of people is relatively comfortable financially; they are integrated members of their families and their communities; they are increasingly well-educated, with half who have more than a high school education; and they are politically active. The young-old seek meaningful ways to use their time. Some want to work, either in remunerated or non-remunerated jobs, some seek self-fulfillment through education or through various types of leisure, some seek new ways of serving their communities.

The old-old, by contrast, are persons who, because of physical or mental deterioration or losses in their ordinary social support systems, have come to require a range

Reprinted from the proceedings of a conference entitled "The Young-Old: A New North American Phenomenon," Couchinching Institute, Toronto, Canada, February 1979, pp. 1–12.

of supportive and restorative health and social services. Essentially these are persons who are in need of special care.

While most of the young-old are in their late fifties, sixties and seventies, and while most of the old-old are in their late seventies, eighties and nineties, it is not age which is the relevant factor. (Indeed the terms young-old and old-old were originally suggested as a gross way of acknowledging some of the enormous diversity among older persons, and of suggesting that there are at least two very different sets of social policy issues involved in meeting the needs of older persons.) Some 80-year-olds are obviously more vigorous and youthful than some 60-year-olds. And it does not help us much in predicting a person's health, or his marital status, or economic status, or pattern of interests or general life style to know that he is 60 rather than 50, or that she is 70 rather than 60. This is what gerontologists mean when they say that in the second half of life—just as is true throughout the whole long period of adulthood—age is a poor predictor of psychological, intellectual or social performance.

We should also be reminded that the longer people live, the more different they become, at least until a final biological change levels out the differences. Lives fan out with time as people develop their own patterns of interests and commitments, their own sequences of life choice, their own psychological turning points and their own patterns of relationships with the few significant other people whose development impinges most directly on their own. One has only to attend a twenty-fifth reunion of one's high school or college class to recognize how much more different people have become at age 45, say, than they were at age 20. And by age 60 they will have become more different still.

This is but another way of making the same point: that age itself is not a good index for predicting how a person is living out his life. (This is especially true for a person living out *her* life.)

There are still other ways of making this same point. There are, for instance, changes in the traditional rhythm of the life cycle: increasing numbers of men and women who marry, divorce, then remarry; increasing numbers who rear children in two-parent, then one-parent, then two-parent households; some men who, in May–December marriages, create second families when they are middle-aged or young-old. There are increasing numbers of women, but also of men, who enter, exit, and re-enter school; who enter and re-enter the labor force; who change jobs at various points and who undertake second and third careers. All this adds up to what some observers are calling the "fluid life cycle," one marked by an increasing number of role transitions, by the proliferation of timetables, and by the lack of synchrony among age-related roles.

Society is becoming accustomed to the 70-year-old student, the 30-year-old college president, the 22-year-old-mayor, the 35-year-old grandmother, the 50-year-old retiree, the 65-year-old father of a preschooler, and even the 85-year-old mother caring for her 65-year-old son. Age norms and age expectations, thus, are diminishing in importance as regulators of behavior, and in this sense, too, we are moving toward an age-irrelevant society.

From this broad perspective, the appearance of the young-old is itself a good example of how age is losing its relevance. It is not age, but the event of retirement, that differentiates the young-old from the middle-aged. And because retirement occurs to different people at different ages, the young-old are not to be identified as those who reach, say, 55 or 65. Age of retirement has been dropping dramatically in the United States, where a greater number of persons begin to draw Social Security benefits at age 62 than at 65; where increasing numbers choose to retire after a given number of years of service; and where increasing numbers are taking at least their first retirement at 55. Now that the Congress has passed a law forbidding private employers to retire persons on the basis of age, there will be even greater variability in the age of retirement.

Age at retirement is becoming more blurred also by the extent to which persons retire from one job, take another, then retire again; or who phase out their work lives gradually, moving from full-time to part-time work. Retirement is not such a clear-cut transition as we often make it out to be.

It is also attended now by a new set of positive images. In a recent book, *In Search of the New Old,* Calhoun sets forth the proposition that it was the 25 years from 1945 to 1970 that saw a major transformation in the image of old age—and in particular, the image of retirement—from negative to positive. The change, he argues, was engineered by gerontologists, social workers, educators, big business, labor, the advertising industry and the mass media, each group for its own self-interest as well as for the presumed advantage to older people. For instance, business has a stake in promoting a positive image of retirement if it is to keep control over the size of the labor force, for it is easier to retire older workers when retirement is made attractive. Another major influence on the image of the elderly has been the recognition by advertisers that older people are a significant consumer group.

In my own view the transformation in images is not so clear nor so unidirectional as Calhoun suggests. It is true that the stereotype of the aged as poor, sick, needy, isolated and desolated has given way to the more complex realities, and like any other period of life, growing old is acknowledged to have its victories as well as its losses. And the stereotype that retirement brings with it loss of self-worth, illness and even premature death has also given way to the more complex realities that, like any other major life event, retirement brings its losses and its gains, its stresses and its challenges. Also, like any other major life event, the vast majority of men and women make the transition with relative success and work out a new and satisfying pattern of activities and a new life style.

Whether it comes early or late, and whether it is first anticipated by the individual in primarily positive or negative terms, retirement brings with it a wide range of options with regard to the use of time. Just as at other periods of life, the most important thing in life for the young-old is health; second, enough money to live on comfortably; the third, interesting things to do. But the young-old have one great advantage over others—for them, it is socially acceptable not to work. Indeed, as the leisure ethic has come to temper, if not to replace, the work ethic in America, and as the term "workaholic" has entered the language, in some quarters it is bad to be a young workaholic, but even worse to be an old workaholic. Some of us become so uncomfortable in the presence of a 65- or 75-year-old who is engrossed in his work that we set about redefining his activity, saying, "Well, of course, for him it's not work—it's play."

Whether work is work, or work is play, and whether some people have to work hard at getting any fun out of their play, all these patterns are socially approved options for the young-old. Their freedoms are greatly increased. They can choose the "I'll-stay-in-harness-till-I-die" style, or the rocking chair style, or the Sun City style, any one of them with society's approval.

It is not only with regard to work and leisure that the young-old want a wide range of options: they want (and they are getting) a wide range of educational opportunities in formal and informal settings. Within the formal educational institution they want (and get) adaptations in curricula, scheduling, and other administrative procedures to accommodate their interests. And they have easy access to informal learning situations in churches, museums and the mass media.

The young-old want a wide range of options, also, with regard to housing and living arrangements. Some choose age-segregated communities. For instance, because there are large numbers of widowed and single and divorced, they want opportunities to form group households, with appropriate financing arrangements. And because a large proportion have an old-old parent, and because "parent-caring" is becoming the significant problem of family life (that is, the concern over how to arrange appropriate care for a parent), many want housing arrangements that make it possible to maintain the aged parent in the parent's own home or in the home of the child.

How well our society is meeting the needs of the young-old, and how well the young-old are creating for themselves the life patterns they want, cannot be measured easily. But here are a few illustrations of programs that are now spreading over the U.S.:

Programs to help expand employment opportunities: for instance, in Chicago a program called ABLE (Ability Based on Life Experience) is sponsored by the organization of community trusts and foundations. A network of public and voluntary agencies has been created whose goals are to strengthen existing employment agencies and services, to promote public awareness of the needs for employment for older persons, and to bring about equality of employment for persons over 55.

At the federal level there is the Fair Employment Practices Act which prohibits discrimination against older workers; and most recently, new regulations in the Comprehensive Employment and Training Act (CETA) which provides large funds for training and employment opportunities for the unemployed and underemployed. Henceforth an equitable proportion of CETA funds must go to older persons.

An example of a different type lies in the field of education where the trend is toward the concept of lifelong education. Colleges and universities are seeking to serve the new adult clientele as the number of younger students decline, and a small but growing proportion of that new clientele are the young-old. In 1976, about 5 percent of all persons 55 to 64 reported that they were taking courses in an educational institution. This figure does not include the much larger numbers engaged in educational activities in museums, libraries, churches, neighborhood clubs, nor that very large number who pursue self-taught projects which run the gamut from homemaking skills to various esoteric forms of knowledge.

Many young-old are engaged as teachers as well as students. A report published a few months ago by the Academy for Educational Development estimated that there are at least one million young-old now educating others. They teach in schools and other settings, they counsel, they lead groups in self-awareness, and they tutor everyone in everything. Most of these people are serving as volunteers, with only a small fraction getting wages, stipends or honoraria. The same report described the eleven federally administered programs in the U.S. in which older people serve in volunteer roles. These include the Retired Senior Volunteer Program, Foster Grandparents, Green Thumb, the Peace Corps of Retired Executives, and so on. Of the total of the quarter-million persons engaged in these programs, nearly 2 of 5 are serving in educational roles.

So education is an important arena for the young-old, both as teachers and as learners.

With regard to the broader array of volunteer roles, in a national survey in 1975 over 20 percent of all people over 65 reported that they were doing some kind of volunteer work. The percentage is considerably higher among those who are better off financially and those with the most education but it includes many persons from minority groups and many from poverty levels. A great variety of jobs are being carried out—in health, civic affairs, social services, family services, and so on. Many of these jobs involve counseling, working with drug abuse cases, mentally ill and the physically impaired.

Let us turn now to some of the implications for social policy. To what extent are we developing policies that are in line with the new realities regarding age and age groups?

A case can be made that at the same time that age is becoming irrelevant in the society, our legislatures are proliferating laws and regulations that are age-based. In the legitimate concern over the welfare of older people, we have seized upon age as the convenient dimension for creating programs of income maintenance, housing, transportation, health services, social services and tax benefits. Thus not only is the major part of the Social Security system pegged to age, as is reasonable enough, but Medicare is pegged to age, and we also have a special nationwide government network created through the Administration on Aging for providing social services to persons over 60.

There has been a certain justification for this approach, of course. In the 1950s and 1960s a large proportion of older people in the U.S. were poor and were without health insurance or easy access to health services or social services. To create programs based on age eligibility did, in fact, catch a large proportion of persons who were in need. But today the situation is changing. In the U.S. the numbers of old persons under the poverty line is not much different from the number of younger persons under the poverty line. In fact, if one counts in all the income support programs for both young and old that are government supported—the transfer programs and the in-kind programs like Social Security, Supplementary Security Income, Medicare, Medicaid, Aid to Dependent Children, food stamps, rent subsidies, tax benefits—then it turns out that the proportion of the old who are poor is substantially lower than the proportion of young who are poor. And just to remind ourselves that there are many ways of looking at economic well-being, if we look at what people report about themselves, then in a national survey in 1975 about 15 percent of people over 65, but 18 percent of people under 65, said they did not have enough money to live on.

This is not to say that, as a "caring" society, we have done enough about the problem of poverty in the aged, or poverty in the wider population. Neither can it be said that the old are not getting a fair share of these efforts. Indeed, some observers are saying we have done enough for the old—even that the old are now an advantaged rather than a disadvantaged group.

To argue that we have done enough for the old is, of course, the same kind of oversimplification that arises whenever we talk about "the old" as if it were a single group. So long as we do not draw distinctions between the young-old and the old-old, or between the needy and the non-needy, then we are vulnerable to this kind of uncritical argument.

Age-based legislation may have the eventual effect of denying services to those older persons who are most in need. By most estimates it is about 10 to 15 percent of people over 65 who require some form of special health or social services. The worry is that this 15 percent may not be served adequately because it is being obscured by the other 85 percent in the age category.

Thus we must be wary lest we define our target populations in ways that are not meaningful, but only expedient for the legislator and the administrator. There is still another danger—if age-based rather than need-based legislation continues, those of us who consider ourselves advocates for older people may inadvertently be creating age discrimination at the very same time we decry it. We may be creating new forms of ageism, some of them at the cost of the young, some that may boomerang upon us, and some that create divisiveness in the society at large.

But the policy questions are complex and do not take, in the actual instance, the simple either/or forms I have thus far suggested. It is usually some combination of age and need that policy makers are struggling with. Let me draw some examples.

There is now a major concern in the U.S. focussed on the so-called "greying of the budget," an issue which is causing great concern among policy makers. Our Secretary of Health, Education and Welfare has made a number of speeches in the last few months calling attention to the fact that in 1978 some 24 percent of the total federal budget went to older people, and that it may rise over the next several decades to some 40 percent. The alarm is that there will be fewer workers to support the greater numbers of retirees, so that the total economy will be out of joint and the Social Security system may even collapse altogether.

Such fears seem to me to be ill-founded, for Congress is continually altering the financial base of the Social Security system. That activity is unlikely to come to a sudden halt. Nor are we likely to abandon programs of income maintenance for older people. For one thing, the young-old will be an important political force in this regard. And for another thing, younger workers are not likely to overlook the fact that it is preferable to support their aged family members through a Social Security system than to place the responsibility back on individual families.

Some policy analysts are suggesting that one thing to do about the future is to raise the age of eligibility for Social Security benefits—a suggestion that sets of immediate opposition from others who argue that more incentives should be created to keep people at work—such as extra benefits for every additional year beyond 65 spent in the labor market, a procedure which would weigh years-in-service more heavily than age. New kinds of work arrangements such as improved conditions in the workplace, more part-time jobs, flextime and phased retirement could also be increased—in short, to create, not a longer work life for everybody, but greater options for everybody.

Shall we deal with the problem, then, by manipulating age as the variable, or by building upon economic and other motivational factors that underlie the diversities among people?

Another example: the age-based advocacy groups in the U.S. such as the National Association of Retired Federal Employees, the National Council of Senior Citizens, and particularly the American Association of Retired Persons (the Grey Panthers are thus far following a somewhat different direction) are not only growing in size but are becoming more sophisticated as legislative advocates. It has been accepted wisdom that there is no real politics of age in the U.S.; that age has not been a sufficiently potent factor to cause persons of diverse economic and political persuasions to form cohesive political groups, that the age-based organizations are therefore paper tigers. In short, political behavior has been considered an area in which age is not the relevant factor.

All this is probably true, but there is some reason for uneasiness that the age-advocacy groups may become a divisive force in American life, especially if economic and demographic changes lead to a drop in pension levels or in service programs for older people.

From my own perspective, the growth of age-based advocacy groups is another example of how the irrelevant factor, age, may create an artificial social grouping—artificial, that is, with regard to policy initiatives. These age-based organizations may become the advocates for the problem elderly—those who are still below the poverty line, those who need long-term health care and so on. Or they might put their efforts toward increasing the quality of life for the population at large. But if, instead, they advocate for older people as an age group, they may create a backlash in which the needs of the needy aged will be lost out.

An example of a very different kind is the Age Discrimination Act passed by the U.S. Congress in 1975 which prohibits discrimination on the basis of age in any and all programs receiving federal support. The act itself is a step in the right direction, for it is making the point—although in a proscriptive rather than a prescriptive way—that age should not be permitted to be relevant in distributing goods and services. The problems are enormous, however, in implementing the Act and in deciding what is age discrimination. Is it discriminatory, for instance, to give special benefits to the elderly? Or to require a 65-year-old, but not a 64-year-old, to pass a test of vision before obtaining a driver's license? Or to allow a 16-year-old, but not a 15-year-old, to drive an automobile? What kinds of age distinctions are justified? Which ones are based on scientific evidence, and which ones on stereotypes?

There are many other examples that could be offered. And common to them all are very difficult ethical and philosophical as well as political issues. There is, for instance, the value position that because a person is old he deserves more support than a person who is young—a value position that is rejected by others. If we move toward restructuring government policies to support the disabled or the poor, rather than to support persons who happen to be old, then what new definitions of need shall be constructed? And if need-entitlement is to be substituted for age-entitlement, it raises the specter that so-called "means" tests are demeaning, and that people, especially old people, should not be asked to establish their poverty status before becoming eligible for services. To what extent does this last-mentioned value come into conflict with other values of equity and justice for the population at large? And to what extent are attitudes against the means test likely to be present in successive generations? As people grow accustomed to the role of government in equalizing opportunity, will there be more or less opposition to means testing and needs testing? All these are very troublesome questions.

Because they are so difficult, and because they require much more searching examination, I do not presume to offer any resolutions. I do suggest, however, that for the present we should begin to rethink our policies which are based on age.

There are different ways of being a friend of the aged: one way has been to establish special programs, but another might be to "return" older people to the human race by ignoring age differences wherever possible and by focussing on more relevant dimensions of human differences. In the caring society of the future, what will be the best way to care about older people?

Reference

Calhoun, Richard B. 1978. *In Search of the New Old.* New York: Elsevier Press.

FOUR

Age Distinctions and Their Social Functions

Among social scientists and legal scholars an interest in the relationship between age and the law has been spurred by two recent legislative actions of Congress. The first was the enactment of the Age Discrimination Act of 1975.[1] The ADA bars discrimination on the basis of age in any program receiving federal support if that program was not explicitly aimed at a particular age group. The ADA applies across the age spectrum, to both the young and the old.

The second action was the 1978 amendment to the Age Discrimination in Employment Act of 1967.[2] The original Act barred discrimination in the workplace for persons age 40 to 65.[3] The 1978 amendment raised the protections to age 70,[4] prohibited mandatory retirement in the private sector before age 70,[5] and prohibited mandatory retirement altogether for most federal employees.[6]

These two new laws come at a time when public concern over the legal rights of children and adolescents, the so-called children's movement, has been growing. With reference, then, to both the young and the old, age rights constitute a new focus in the arena of civil rights, and age, like race or gender or physical handicap, is coming into public awareness as a dimension of human difference that calls for legal regulation.

A few examples will delineate some of the issues. Under the regulations promulgated by the United States Department of Health and Human Services pursuant to the ADA, each federal agency which extends federal financial assistance to any program or activity is required to conduct a review of the age distinctions it imposes on its recipients by regulations, policies, and administrative practices in order to eliminate those distinctions that are impermissible under the ADA.[7] Similar steps are to be followed by all public and private agencies at the state and local level that are recipients of federal funds.[8] In the interpretation of the ADA made by the Department of Health and Human Services in formulating its regulations, major exceptions were permitted which seem to water down the effects of the ADA.[9] The ADA is nevertheless an important step in setting forth the view that the age of the beneficiary should not itself be a relevant characteristic in the distribution of public funds.

Reprinted by permission from *Chicago Kent Law Review* 57, no. 4 (fall 1981): 809–25.

The problems are enormous in implementing the ADA and in deciding what constitutes age discrimination.[10] Is it discriminatory toward younger people when special benefit programs like Medicare are created for older people? And at the state level, is it discriminatory to require a 65-year-old, but not a 64-year-old, to pass a vision test before obtaining a driver's license or to allow a 16-year-old, but not a 15-year-old, to drive an automobile? Such distinctions are presently legal, but they may come to be regarded as unjust or inequitable as the ADA adds to a rising public consciousness about age distinctions and age rights.

Another example is one that deals with the young and with changes in legal definitions of maturity. A California law passed in 1979, known as the Emancipation of Minors Act,[11] is designed to help teen-agers who have fled intolerable family situations. Children who are at least 14 can be declared independent of their parents and, if they are living away from home and supporting themselves, can receive the right to be treated for most legal purposes as adults.[12] A similar law was passed in Connecticut in 1979 whereby minors 16 and older who are seeking emancipation can petition the Superior Court for Juvenile Matters.[13] If the court finds that they are capable of supporting themselves and are willingly living apart from their parents, they may be declared legally emancipated.[14] These two laws are significant examples of changing attitudes towards age distinctions and concepts of maturity.

Implicitly or explicitly, these illustrations involve many of the issues that intrigue social scientists who turn their attention to age and the law. Attempts to analyze the interactions of law and society rest on two fundamental premises: that legal systems exist within an encompassing sociocultural system and that much of the social fabric is woven together with the threads of legal license and mandate.[15] These tenets reflect the further understanding that the legal system and other social systems interact in mutually determining ways. Embedded in that interaction are a number of common issues such as legitimation, authority, social change, the nature of consensus, and conflict resolution. These general points need no elaboration here. But it happens that, with a few notable exceptions, social scientists have given little attention to such issues as they bear upon questions of age and the law.[16]

The first set of questions that arises for social scientists relates to changing social values and attitudes with regard to age distinctions, how age distinctions become formalized in the legal system, and how legal decisions, whether statutory, regulatory, or judicial, shape these attitudes.

Another set of questions relates to the use of age as a proxy for some other attribute which is deemed significant in making distinctions between members of society. In the case of the emancipation of minors, that attribute might be called social maturity. In the case of mandatory retirement, it might be called incompetence in the workplace. When is it reasonable to use age as a proxy? What is the scientific evidence that age is reliably related to the attribute under discussion? When age is used as a proxy, at what particular ages are the distinctions to be drawn? In the emancipation of minors, why is 14 the age of eligibility in California, but 16 in Connecticut? And in the example of mandatory retirement, why is it permissible to retire persons above but not those below age 70?

A special set of questions arises in determining discrimination under the ADA. Here, discrimination does not relate to an age distinction per se, but to the age distribution of persons served by a given government program when compared to the age distribution of the population eligible for the service. How much discrepancy between the two age distributions constitutes discrimination?

An additional set of questions relates to the individual versus the group. When it is reasonable to treat the individual as a member of the age group to which he belongs, and when must individual differences be respected? For example, in the emancipation of minors, it is only certain 16-year-olds, those who can demonstrate to the satisfaction of the court that they are economically independent, who are given freedom from parents. Yet, in the situation of mandatory retirement, it has been held equitable to retire a person who is performing satisfactorily merely because it can be shown that in the population at large certain types of intellectual decline appear in persons over 70.[17] In the first instance, the law is saying that not every 16-year-old is the same. But in the second instance, the law is saying, in effect, that every 70-year-old is the same.

The lawyer will recognize that such questions relate directly to various legal issues such as whether or not issues of constitutional rights are involved, what are the bases for redress, what is the definition of suspect classes, when is the strict scrutiny or the minimum rationality standard to be used in judicial review, what are the questions of due process and equal protection under the law, when are categories of persons over- or under-inclusive, when are conclusive presumptions operating, and what is prima facie evidence of discrimination. And obviously enough, issues of social equity and justice under the law underlie all the questions raised here. But analyses of the legal, philosophical, and ethical doctrines lie beyond the scope of this paper. The comments which follow are addressed to only a few of the social science questions. The intent is first to describe, in broad strokes, the social processes which give rise to age distinctions and age discriminations, then to illustrate briefly a few of the problems in determining discrimination, and in doing so, to indicate some of the ways in which social scientists and legal scholars come together in pursuing issues of age and the law.

AGE-STATUS SYSTEMS

To the anthropologist and the sociologist, age is a major dimension of social organization. To the psychologist, it is a major dimension by which the individual organizes his life course and interprets his life experience. The age structure of society is a socially and psychologically meaningful system. It is within this system that age distinctions are created and age discrimination arises.

All societies rationalize the passage of life time, divide life time into socially relevant units, and thus transform biological time into social time. Certain biological or social events come to be regarded as significant punctuation marks in the life course and to signify the transition points from one age status to the next. Thus, to take a familiar example, puberty is regarded in some societies as the event which marks the entry into adulthood, and elaborate *rites de passage* mark its importance. In other societies like our own, puberty carries little significance with regard to age status, and entry into adulthood is marked instead by marriage and parenthood or by the achievement of economic independence.

In all societies, age-status systems emerge in which rights, rewards and responsibilities are differentially distributed to socially defined age groups. Life periods in the lives of individuals become parallel with age grades in the society; and age grades in turn constitute an age-stratification structure.[18]

In societies where the division of labor is simple and the rate of social change is slow, a single over-arching age-status system may emerge in which family, work, political, and religious roles are synchronized, allocated, and regulated according to the individual's position in the age structure.

To call attention to such societies is not to equate a simple society with a modern industrial society, but to help clarify the functions of age distinctions. Thus, in some East African societies, males born over a given period of time are assigned membership in a given age-set and then proceed as a group from one age-grade to the next. In one such society there are six overlapping age-grades after childhood: the junior warrior or "youth," occupied by males aged 14 to 23; the senior warrior, occupied from about 20 to 30; the learning elder status, from 14 until the oldest child is to be circumcised; the junior elder status; the senior elder status; and the priestly status. Men move from warrior to elder status when they marry; they reach priestly status only when all their children are circumcised and when they no longer have wives of childbearing age.[19]

Age-status systems are built upon functional age. That is, as the individual's physical, mental, and social competencies change over time, he is able to carry out different social functions. Those competencies are utilized and systematized in the interests of the society at large. Social age distinctions appear, therefore, because they are inherently functional to the society.

In modern, complex societies, plural systems of age-status arise, also based on perception of functional age, but are differentiated in relation to particular social institutions. These multiple systems make use of the common index of chronological age, but age distinctions vary in the extent to which they become explicit and formal.

Age-grading in a typical American school, for instance, is much more formal than in the typical American family. Social age definitions may be inconsistent from one institutional setting to the next, as in the case when persons marry and become parents and are therefore considered adult in the family system, but at the same time continue in school and are not yet adult in the economic system. In modern societies, then, age-role transitions are often asynchronous.

Any age system, whether in a simple or a complex society, thus performs two functions. For the individual, it establishes a series of social positions that provides clarity and predictability, regular movement from lower to higher rungs of the age-status ladder, and a certain coherence as new role patterns are automatically assigned with increasing age. For the society, it provides for an effective division of labor, in the broadest sense of that term, thereby establishing a social mechanism for maintaining the economy, the educational system, the family system, and the military, political, and religious systems.

Age Distinctions and Age Norms

Age status systems, by definition, create age distinctions, and along with them, a pattern of norms and expectations regarding age-appropriate behavior. Age norms vary in the degree to which they are formalized and in the strength of the sanctions attached to them. Some operate on the basis of informal consensus; others are stipulated in the laws. In both instances they are mechanisms of social control.

It might be noted, parenthetically, that age norms form a network of expectations that pervade the whole cultural fabric. Men and women are aware of the social clocks that operate in various areas of their lives and they are aware of their own timing. In our society, people readily describe themselves as being early, late, or on time with regard to family and occupational events. In different words, age norms act as prods and brakes upon behavior, in some instances hastening a life event, in other instances delaying it. But age norms also operate in more peripheral areas of life, as when a woman is told, "You're too old to be working so hard," or a man is told, "You're too young to dress like that." Adults as well as children are constantly exhorted to act their age.

Although social scientists have given relatively little attention to age norms, there are at least a few studies that demonstrate a high degree of consensus with regard to age-appropriate behaviors, with common patterns of approval and disapproval expressed by representative groups of adults. It also appears that young persons perceive more age constraints operating in the society than do middle-aged or older people, a finding that parallels the fact that a great number of laws exist that regulate the rights and responsibilities of young people.[20] Finally, in this connection, there are sets of data indicating that age norms and age constraints may, at least in some ways, be losing their saliency as regulators of the life course[21] at the same time that age distinctions are increasing in the law.

Historical Change

Age status systems become altered over time as they reflect other kinds of social changes. For example, with increased longevity, the timing of the life course has changed. Historians say that in Western societies it was not until the 17th and 18th centuries, with the growth of industrialization, the appearance of a middle class, and the emergence of formal educational institutions, that childhood became a discernible period of life, one with special needs and characteristics.[22] The concept of adolescence took on its present meaning in the last part of the 19th century, but became a widespread concept only in the 20th century.[23] A new stage called youth has emerged in the last few decades as the transition from adolescence to adulthood has been prolonged.[24] And in the second half of the life course, there is now a delineated period called middle age;[25] and more recently still, the recognition that the young-old should be differentiated from the old-old.[26]

As the United States has moved from the agrarian to the industrialized, from small town to metropolis, there have been other alterations in our age-status systems. The family cycle may be said to have quickened as marriage, parenthood, and grandparenthood occur earlier now than in 1900, but as widowhood occurs later. In our economic institutions, points of entry and exit from the labor market are differently timed as the growth of technology and the lengthened period of education have led to a delay, particularly for men, in reaching maturity, and as the trend toward earlier retirement has led to an earlier old age as socially defined. In our political institutions, maturity now comes earlier, with the eligibility to vote at 18 rather than 21. And there has been a proliferation of laws relating to pensions, housing, and medical and social services for older persons that, as some have described it, are creating a separate status for the old.[27]

Social lags and social strains are often reflected in age-status systems, and social and legal age definitions that have been functional in one period of history may become dysfunctional in another. To take another example from an African society: There may be times when, to create a group large enough to be functional in the society, the limits of an age-set are widened. When such an age-set reaches the point of becoming junior elders, it may include, as anticipated, men of marriageable age, but it may also include other men who, if the rules of the system were to be followed, would have been held back from marriage and parenthood. This would create intolerable strains both for the individuals involved and for the whole community.[28] Or, when such a society comes into contact with a western culture and many young men move to the city in search of jobs, there are too few males left in the village to carry out the essential social tasks. As a result, the rules of the age-status system are changed to accommodate such situations.

The same general principle operates in more complex societies. In the United States, the presence of large numbers of vigorous older persons, together with the changes in the economy that motivate them to continue in the labor market, produce pressures for change in the systems that regulate retirement. Modifications in the law, as in the ADEA amendment mentioned earlier, constitute change in the age-status system. Another example, also mentioned earlier, is the lowered age of voting. The appearance of large numbers of politically active young people in the late 1960s, their presumed greater maturity as compared to preceding generations, and the fact that 18-year-olds were in the armed forces but were being denied the franchise until age 21—itself an excellent example of the asynchronous nature of our age systems— led to the 26th amendment. Lowering the voting age to 18 was a change in the rules regarding age status. Still another example arises in the present public debate over legalized abortion, where some of the arguments on the issue of the age at which a fetus becomes a "person" with rights to legal protection.

In all three examples—the first related to the economy, the second to the political system, and the third to the family—the questions are the same: How and where should an age distinction be created? When does an age distinction become age discrimination?

These points can be summarized as follows: Functional age becomes transformed into social age, and social ages into age distinctions. A pervasive network of age norms and age expectations becomes a system of social control. Some age distinctions become formalized in the laws. In a bureaucratic society like our own, chronological age becomes the index of social age and is used as the proxy for functional age. As the age-status system adapts to other forms of social change, various chronological ages embedded in the laws lose their original value. Some become outmoded; others become discriminatory in the views of legislators, administrators, and the courts.

New Images of Old Age

Perceptions of age groups are reflected in the social policies of a modern society, and therefore in the laws. These perceptions, as already implied, relate to the size of an age-status group and to the characteristics perceived to be common to members of that group. These issues are taking on new importance with regard to old age. Who is to be regarded as old? What should be the lower age boundary? And because of what characteristics? These are very real questions in political decision-making and in the formulation of government policies and programs.[29]

In the past several decades there has been an image of older people as persons in need. Thus, there are the programs of Supplementary Security Income, Medicare, senior centers, and publicly subsidized housing. All these are legal expressions of the view that older persons are economically disadvantaged, physically ill or vulnerable, diminished in intellectual and social competence, and therefore deserving of special concern and protection.

At the same time, there is the view, based on equally compelling sets of data, that most older people are healthy and active and relatively comfortable financially; that they constitute a major resource in the nation's economic and community life; and that the policy goal is, therefore, to remove constraints which affect their employment and create various other forms of social segregation.

This disparity of images is well illustrated in the rising debate over changes in the Social Security system. The Social Security program began with the premise that it is appropriate and socially desirable for persons to retire at age 65. But the present trend toward abolishing mandatory retirement, and the view that the right to continue to work is a civil right, are based on a contrary premise—that it is appropriate and desirable to prolong the work life of older people.

To take another example: The establishment of senior centers, nutrition sites and elderly housing projects are based on the premise that at least a certain degree of age segregation is reasonable and even desirable. At the same time, such programs as Foster Grandparents are promoted as a means of combating age segregation. An even more telling example is the paradox that exists within a single law. The 1978 amendments to the Older Americans Act confirmed the age-categorical programs established under that Act, but at the same time added a general prohibition against age discrimination.

If cohesive and rational policies are to be created regarding government responsibility for older people, these disparate images will need to be reconciled. One astute observer has delineated three alternatives.[30] The first stems from the view that age itself is a poor predictor of the adult's capacity, circumstance, or need. Like gender or race, age does not determine health, marital status, economic status, or intellectual or social competence. If the role of government is to provide opportunities commensurate with the individual's abilities and services commensurate with the individual's needs, then programs should be age-neutral rather than age-categorical. Efforts should be targeted at various needy groups rather than at the old as a group.[31]

This view, sometimes called the "age-irrelevant" view, would lead to laws that eliminate age discrimination not only in employment practices, but in credit practices, professional licensing and other public regulatory activities; to age desegregation of publicly subsidized housing; to the conversion of age-based tax exemptions and income transfer programs into income-based eligibility; and to the conversion of Medicare into an income-based program like Medicaid or a national health insurance program that would cover persons of all ages. Under this view, the goal is to mainstream older people into the larger society; to move away, wherever possible, from the use of age as a proxy; and to move to direct measures of competence or need.

The second alternative is to redefine old age by moving it up to age 75, and to work toward synchronization of the laws in this respect. Thus, instead of the multiple definitions that now exist in the statutes, a single definition would be the basis for special benefits and protections. Such a policy would reaffirm the notion that there is an increased frequency of economic, social, and health needs, as well as an increased prevalence of frailty and impairment, in persons over 75, and that programs should be tailored accordingly. This position would lead to laws prohibiting mandatory retirement until age 75, and laws based on 75 as the age of eligibility for Medicare, subsidized housing, and subsidized social services. Under this alternative, chronological age would still be used as the proxy for need, and the problem of how to avoid an over- or under-inclusive age group would remain.

The third alternative is called veteranship and is based on the view that old age is an earned status that should provide special rewards and benefits. This alternative recognizes the value of long life experience. Because older persons have contributed throughout their lives to the good of society as parents, workers and community supporters, old age should become the occasion for the community's repayment. Older people are a group who deserve special respect, enhanced authority and prestige. They should be given the status of elders, in the best sense of that term.

In providing a full range of life options for older people, and an end to age segregation and age discrimination, the goal is much the same as in the "age-irrelevant" position. The difference is that the veteranship view would lead to a wide array of laws creating special benefit programs for older people. Chronological age would still be the basis for eligibility, and the problem would remain of determining what particular chronological age should denote admission to the status of veteran or elder.

These alternative views of old age provide a timely example of how perceptions of age groups are changing, and how such changes affect the laws. It remains to be seen if one or another of these views will become the prevailing one in the decade ahead.

DISTINCTIONS AND DISCRIMINATIONS UNDER THE LAW

As is true in other areas, the laws that establish age distinctions are sometimes proscriptive, sometimes prescriptive, and sometimes permissive. They pervade most areas of life, including the allocation of public resources, the extension and denial of benefits, the imposition of legal burdens, and the relaxation of legal responsibilities. There are other familiar examples. The age of the perpetrator, or even that of the victim, is sometimes an element of a criminal offense; state laws bar the hiring of police officers or firemen over age 35; public schools may bar 3-year-olds; and zoning laws may exclude children, thus creating communities that are only for the elderly. Special legal protections exist for the young and the old, as in guardianship cases where the principle of *parens patriae*[32] is invoked.

The Pervasiveness of the Law

That age distinctions are embodied in the laws is not surprising; however, the extent to which such laws create a system of social control has seldom been documented. A study conducted twenty-seven years ago illustrates one type of research that would be enlightening, research that today, given the advent of the computer, might be more easily undertaken. In 1954, an analysis of the Illinois laws containing references to age disclosed 178 such statutes.[33] Nearly 75 percent of those laws referred to the years of life from birth through age 21. Most of them aimed at the protection of children, and, as might be expected, most of them dealt with the provision of physical care and education, the prohibition of child labor, and responsibility for criminal offenses. Those statues that referred to ages 16 to 21 were usually enabling in nature, providing for adult participation in the society. There were very few laws dealing with the years between 22 and 50. Of the 20 percent of the statutes that referred to ages above 50, most dealt with pensions or age of retirement in various occupations, or with protections for frail older persons. While this 1954 study of Illinois law may be dated, it is still noteworthy, for it indicates the pervasive role of the law in creating and maintaining the age-status system.

Changes in the Legal Culture

It has been noted above that alterations in age-status accompany other types of social change. As is true of the family or the economy, changes in the legal system itself and in the culture that surrounds it affect the extent to which age distinctions become formalized in the law. The scope of due process under the law has been broadened in this country over the past few decades. More people now have a voice about more things that come before the courts, and the courts have confirmed some rights that formerly did not exist. New branches of the law have emerged, such as consumer law and environmental law, and civil rights law has been applied to new situations. New forums have emerged for the community's intervention in governmental and court decisions.

There has been an increase in the use of the law as a means of social control. Not only have levels of legal activity risen, but perceptions and attitudes about the law have shifted. We have been witnessing the appearance of the so-called litigious society, in which individuals increasingly turn to the courts for the resolution of conflicts that would earlier have been resolved privately.

Again, research is lacking with regard to the effects of these changes on the age-status system, but two statutes, the Age Discrimination in Employment Act and the Age Discrimination Act, are good examples of how the legal system now governs new areas of life and how it operates to sharpen age distinctions and discriminations.

Age as a Proxy

In discussing the pervasiveness of the laws regarding age, a parallel point which should be noted is that age is used as a proxy for a wide range of characteristics such as intellectual and emotional maturity (e.g., minimum ages for entering school), readiness to assume adult responsibilities (e.g., minimum ages for voting, drinking, driving, and marrying), physical strength or speed of response (e.g., maximum ages for policemen, bus drivers, or airline pilots), economic productivity (e.g., age of retirement), and various types of debility (e.g., ages for eligibility for medical services and social services).

The use of age as a proxy has a major advantage and a major disadvantage. The advantage is that age is a classic example of a "formally realizable rule."[43] That is, there is little or no discretion needed in determining how to apply it. Either a person is 18 years old or he is not. Thus, the use of age takes on new social functions in a bureaucratic society. It makes decision-making easier for law-makers and government officials, as well as for judges. It is less costly than using more individualized assessments of functional age. Expediency and cost-effectiveness are important social values.

The major disadvantage is that the validity of using age as a proxy depends upon the correspondence between age and the characteristic for which it stands, and the presumed correspondence often is not based on good evidence, but on age stereotypes (e.g., it is often presumed that most older people are poor, but in fact, the proportion of older people who are poor is not much different from the proportion of younger people who are poor). Furthermore, to use age as a proxy means to use particular ages as cut-off points. The age classifications that result are then under-inclusive (some 14-year-olds are as mature as the 16-year-olds who are permitted to drive) or over-inclusive (not all 65-year-olds are in need of tax relief).

Thus, the use of age as a proxy involves a trade-off between different social values—expediency versus accuracy. The extent to which a category is over- or under-inclusive is an important determinant of the constitutionality of legal classifications. But an imperfect classification may be allowed to stand if, in the eyes of the law, it is based on some degree or rationality or "reasonableness." Thus, it is a legitimate interest of the state to ensure a vigorous judiciary; and it is regarded as reasonable that because persons over 70 are usually less vigorous than younger persons, judges should be retired at age 70. There are sometimes dramatic differences between the legal definition of reasonableness, the social scientist's definition (as based on evidence of individual differences), and the social ethicist's definition (as based on the rights of individuals).

Discrepant Age Distributions

Age discrimination is an elusive enough concept when it relates to an age distinction. But it is also elusive when, as under the ADA, discrimination relates to age distributions: that is, when the age distribution of beneficiaries in a given program is compared to the age distribution of the eligible population in determining whether the two distributions are congruent.

When the ADA was first passed in 1975, Congress recognized that the extent of age discrimination in federal programs was unknown. It instructed the Commission on Civil Rights to undertake a study of the matter, saying that, in the light of the findings, the ADA would be amended as necessary and then implemented. The Commission on Civil Rights studied ten major programs and concluded that age discrimination was present in all of them, sometimes with regard to younger groups, and sometimes with regard to older persons.[35] This method of comparing distribution is, however, only a first step in determining discrimination. For if differences occur, it still must be decided if the discrimination is real or only apparent. Thus, the second step is to determine if the observed disparity is justifiable or not. This requires a value judgment. For instance, it is well known that older people constitute 11 percent of the population of the United States, but that they utilize more than 30 percent of all health expenditures. This fact is not usually regarded as discriminatory toward younger people because it can be demonstrated that older people more often suffer from ill health and therefore have greater need of health services.

This is the problem that arises at the operational level under the ADA. It is the same kind of problem that often arises in cases of alleged race or sex discrimination, where, for example, a whole array of data dealing with the hiring practices of a company is a whole is often scrutinized for evidence of discrimination rather than just the specific data regarding a particular plaintiff.

In relation to the ADA, a study by the Urban Institute focused on the Vocational Rehabilitation Program, one of the programs cited by the Commission on Civil Rights.[36] In this instance, older persons were underrepresented among program beneficiaries. But in analyzing the data further, there are many factors which can be construed as reasonable bases for differential treatment. One factor is the source of referral. Younger clients are more often referred by educational institutions while older clients are referred by physicians. Many physicians believe older disabled persons should not work, and therefore do not refer them to the program. Another factor is that interactions between federal programs themselves affect the number of persons who apply. Many older persons, if successfully rehabilitated so that they become able to work, would lose other federal benefits. Other older persons are reluctant to be rehabilitated for lower-paying jobs than those they had earlier. Still another factor relates to outcomes, whereby there may be greater difficulty in placing an older worker after rehabilitation than a younger disabled worker. If equal numbers of older persons were to be served under the program, the cost-benefit ratio for the program would be unfavorable.

Thus, the determination of discrimination becomes as complex here as in the first category. Whether the question relates to a particular age distinction or to a distribution of beneficiaries, there is a wide area of discretion left to the administrators who write the regulations and the judges who make the decisions. Over the long term, the decisions will reflect the value patterns of the society and the perceptions of age groups that prevail at a given time in history.

Age distinctions of more subtle types can also arise from the tendency of those in the legal system to perceive age groups in stereotyped ways. These age-based stereotypes may influence legal decisions in a variety of covert ways.[37] These issues, like some of the others mentioned above, have seldom been studied. They are worthy of the research efforts of both social scientists and legal scholars.

CONCLUSION

This paper has dealt with only a small number of the issues and the complexities that face us in considering age distinctions, age discriminations, and the law. A case may be made that age is becoming an increasingly significant dimension of social organization. The changing demography is one contributing factor, but there are other factors. Some believe that age segregation is growing, although this itself is not a simple question. Bureaucracy brings with it the increasing use of age in sorting and sifting people. There are increasing numbers of government programs aimed at the young and at the old, and age criteria are increasingly being codified into law. Age is becoming accentuated in the formation of political interest groups. Age and the law will become an increasingly important area for scholarship as well as legal practice.

Notes

1. Pub. L. No. 94-135, tit. III, §§ 301-308, 89 Stat. 728 (codified at 42 U.S.C. §§ 6101-6107 (1976 & Suppl. III 1979)) [hereinafter referred to as the ADA]. The ADA provides:

Pursuant to regulations prescribed under section 6103 of this title . . . no person in the United States shall, on the basis of age, be excluded from participation in, be denied the benefits of, or be subjected to discrimination under, any program or activity receiving Federal financial assistance.

Id. § 6102.

As originally enacted, the ADA provided that no regulations promulgated for its enforcement would be effective before January 1, 1979. 42 U.S.C. § 6103(a)(5) (1976) (amended 1978). The 1978 amendments to the ADA extended that date to July 1, 1979. 42 U.S.C. § 6103(a)(5) (Supp. III 1979). The United States Department of Health and Human Services subsequently promulgated regulations for the enforcement of the ADA. 45 C.F.R. §§ 90.1-90.62 (1980).

2. Age Discrimination in Employment Act Amendments of 1978, Pub. L. No. 95-256, 92 Stat. 189 (amending 29 U.S.C. §§ 621-634 (1976)).

3. 29 U.S.C. § 631 (1976) (amended 1978).

4. 29 U.S.C. § 631(a) (Supp. III 1979).

5. *Id.* § 623(f)(2). This section provides that no seniority system or employee benefit plan shall require or permit the involuntary retirement on the basis of age of any individual to whom the Act applies.

6. *Id.* § 631(b). This section sets a lower limit of 40 years of age for the protected federal employees listed in § 633(a) of the Act but sets no upper age limit.

7. 45 C.F.R. §§ 90.32-90.34 (1980).

8. *Id.* §§ 90.41-90.50. Indeed, the regulations expressly state that the recipient agencies have primary responsibility to ensure that their programs and activities are in compliance with the ADA. *Id.* § 90.42(a).

9. For example, 45 C.F.R. § 90.14 (1980) provides:
A recipient is permitted to take an action, otherwise prohibited by section 90.12, if the action reasonably takes into account age as a factor necessary to the normal operation or the achievement of any statutory objective of a program or activity. An action reasonably takes into account age as a factor necessary to the normal operation or the achievement of any statutory objective of a program or activity, if:
  (a) Age is used as a measure or approximation of one or more other characteristics; and
  (b) The other characteristic(s) must be measured or approximated in order for the normal operation of the program or activity to continue, or to achieve any statutory objective of the program or activity; and
  (c) The other characteristic(s) can be reasonably measured or approximated by the use of age; and
  (d) The other characteristic(s) are impractical to measure directly on an individual basis.
Similarly, 45 C.F.R. § 90.15 (1980) provides:
A recipient is permitted to take an action otherwise prohibited by section 90.12 which is based on a factor other than age, even though that action may have a disproportionate effect on persons of different ages. An action may be based on a factor other than age only if the factor bears a direct and substantial relationship to the normal operation of the program or activity or to the achievement of a statutory objective.

10. *See* Schuck, *The Graying of Civil Rights Law: The Age Discrimination Act of 1975*, 89 YALE L.J. 27 (1979).

11. CAL. CIV. CODE §§ 60-70 (West 1980).

12. *Id.* § 64.

13. CONN. GEN. STAT. ANN. §§ 46b-150 to 46b-150e (West Supp. 1981).

14. *Id.* § 46b-150b.

15. *See* L. FRIEDMAN, THE LEGAL SYSTEM (1975); H. HART, THE CONCEPT OF LAW (1961).

16. *See* H. PRATT, THE GRAY LOBBY (1976): Cain, *Aging and the Law,* in HANDBOOK OF AGING AND THE SOCIAL SCIENCES 342 (1976); Cottrell, *Governmental Functions and the Politics of Age,* in HANDBOOK OF SOCIAL GERONTOLOGY 624 (C. Tibbitts ed. 1960); Hudson & Binstock, *Political systems and Aging,* in HANDBOOK OF AGING AND THE SOCIAL SCIENCES 369 (1976); Schmidhauser, *Age and Judicial Behavior: American Higher Appellate Judges,* in POLITICS OF AGE 101 (1962) [hereinafter referred to as *Age and Judicial Behavior*]; Cain, *The Growing Importance of Legal Age in Determining the Status of the Elderly,* 14 GERONTOLOGIST 167 (1974) [hereinafter referred to as *Growing Importance*]; Marks, *Detours on the Road to Maturity: A View of the Legal Conception of Growing Up and Letting Go,* 39 L. & CONTEMP. PROB. 78 (1975); L. Cain, Counting Backward From Projected Death: An Alternative to Chronological Age in Assigning Status to the Elderly (March 22, 1978) (paper presented at a conference of the Policy Center on Aging, Syracuse University); J. Schmidhauser, Changing Age Structure of American Political Leadership (1977) (paper presented at the 30th Annual Meeting of the Gerontological Society, San Francisco, Cal.).

17. *See* Trafelet v. Thompson, 594 F.2d 623 (7th Cir.), *cert. denied,* 444 U.S. 906 (1979).

18. *See* 3 M. RILEY, M. JOHNSON & A. FONER, AGING AND SOCIETY—A SOCIOLOGY OF AGE STRATIFICATION (1972).

19. *See* A. PRINS, EAST AFRICAN AGE-CLASS SYSTEMS (1953); Gulliver, *Age Differentiation,* in 1 INTERNATIONAL ENCYCLOPEDIA OF THE SOCIAL Sciences 157 (D. Sills ed. 1968).

20. *See* Neugarten, Moore & Lowe, *Age Norms, Age Constraints, and Adult Socialization,* 70 AM. J. Soc. 710 (1965).

21. *See* P. Passuth, Continuity and Change in Age Norms and Age Constraints (April 15, 1981) (unpublished paper in Northwestern University Department of Sociology Library); R. Sills, H. Zepelin & M. Brill, Age Norms: 1960s and 1980s Compared (Nov. 14, 1980) (paper presented at the 33d Annual Meeting of the Gerontological Society, San Diego, Cal.).

22. *See* P. ARIES, CENTURIES OF CHILDHOOD: A SOCIAL HISTORY OF FAMILY LIFE (1962).

23. *See* J. GILLIS, YOUTH AND HISTORY (1974); Demos & Demos, *Adolescence in Historical Perspective,* 31 J. MARR & FAM. 632 (1969).

24. *See* PRESIDENT'S SCIENCE ADVISORY COMM., PANEL ON YOUTH, YOUTH: TRANSITION TO ADULTHOOD (1973); Keniston, *Youth: A New Stage of Life,* 39 AM. SCHOLAR 631 (1970).

25. *See* Neugarten, *The Awareness of Middle Age,* in MIDDLE AGE AND AGING: A READER IN SOCIAL PSYCHOLOGY 93 (B. Neugarten ed. 1968).

26. *See* Neugarten, *Age Groups in American Society and the Rise of the Young-Old,* 415 ANNALS OF THE AMERICAN ACADEMY OF POLITICAL AND SOCIAL SCIENCES 187 (1974).

27. *See Growing Importance, supra* note 16.

28. *See* Foner & Kertzer, *Intrinsic and Extrinsic Sources of Change in Life-Course Transitions,* in AGING FROM BIRTH TO DEATH 121 (M. Riley ed. 1979).

29. *See generally How Old Is "Old"? The Effects Of Aging On Learning And Working: Hearing Before the Sen. Special Comm. on Aging,* 96th Cong., 2d Sess. (1980).

30. D. Nelson, Observations on Current and Future Bases for Effective National Policy Advocacy on Behalf of Older People (Sept. 15, 1980) (paper prepared for the Federal Council on Aging, Washington, D.C.).

31. *See* Neugarten, *Policy for the 1980s: Age or Need Entitlement?*, in AGING: AGENDA FOR THE EIGHTIES 48 (1979).

32. *Parens patriae* refers to the role of the state as the sovereign and guardian of persons under a legal disability. BLACK'S LAW DICTIONARY 1003 (5th ed. 1979).

33. L. Evans, Legal Definition of Age as Contained in Illinois Statute Law (Aug. 1954) (unpublished master's degree thesis in University of Chicago Library).

34. *See* Kennedy, *Form and Substance in Private Law Adjudication*, 89 HARV. L. REV. 1685 (1976).

35. U.S. COMM'N ON CIVIL RIGHTS, THE AGE DISCRIMINATION STUDY (PART I) (1977).

36. *See* M. GUTOWSKI & J. KOSHEL, METHODS FOR ASSESSING AGE DISCRIMINATION IN FEDERAL PROGRAMS (1977).

37. *See Age and Judicial Behavior, supra* note 16.

FIVE

The Changing Meanings of Age

Bernice L. Neugarten and Dail A. Neugarten

In our society, as in most others, age is a major dimension of social organization. Our school system, to name one example, is carefully arranged around the students' ages, and the behavior of all students is clearly differentiated from the behavior of adult teachers. Similarly, to a greater or lesser extent, families, corporations, even whole communities are organized by age.

Age also plays an important part in how people relate to one another across the whole range of everyday experience. When a young man sits down in an airplane and glances at the person in the next seat, the first thing to cross his mind is likely to be "That's an old man," or "That's a young man like me," and he automatically adjusts his behavior accordingly—his language, manners and conversation.

Age is also a major touchstone by which individuals organize and interpret their own lives. Both children and adults continually ask of themselves, "How well am I doing for my age?"

From all three perspectives, our changing society has brought with it changes in the social meanings of age: blurred boundaries between the periods of life, new definitions of age groups, new patterns in the timing of major life events and new inconsistencies in what is considered age-appropriate behavior.

In all societies, lifetime is divided into socially relevant periods, age distinctions become systematized and rights and responsibilities are distributed according to social age. Even the simplest societies define at least three periods: childhood, adulthood and old age. In more complex societies, a greater number of life periods are differentiated, and transition points are differently timed in different areas of life. In modern America people are considered adults in the political system when they reach 18 and are given the right to vote; but they are not adults in the family system until they marry and take on the responsibilities of parenthood. Or people may be adult in the family system, but if they are still in school they are not yet adult in the economic system.

Reprinted by permission from *Psychology Today,* May 1987: 29–30, 32-33; © 1987 Sussex Publishers, Inc. This essay was adapted from an article entitled "Age in the Aging Society" that originally appeared in *Daedalus,* winter 1986: 31–49.

Historians have described how life periods became demarcated in Western societies over the past few centuries. Only with industrialization and the appearance of a middle class and formally organized schools did childhood become a clearly definable period of life. Adolescence took on its present meaning in the late 19th century and became widespread in the 20th, as the period of formal education lengthened and the transition to adulthood was increasingly delayed. A stage called youth took on its modern meaning only a few decades ago, as growing numbers of young people, after leaving high school and before marrying or making occupational choices, opted for a period of time to explore various life roles.

It was only a few decades ago, too, that middle age became identified, largely a reflection of the historically changing rhythm of events in the family cycle. With fewer children per family, and with births spaced closer together, middle age became defined as the time when children grow up and leave the parents' home. In turn, as the concept of retirement took hold, old age came to be regarded as the time following retirement from the labor force. It was usually perceived as a distinct period marked by the right to lead a life of leisure, declining physical and intellectual vigor, social disengagement and, often, isolation and desolation.

Life periods were closely associated with chronological age, even though age lines were seldom sharply drawn.

But the distinctions between life periods are blurring in today's society. The most dramatic evidence, perhaps, is the appearance of the so-called "young-old." It is a recent historical phenomenon that a very large group of retirees and their spouses are healthy and vigorous, relatively well-off financially, well-integrated into the lives of their families and communities and politically active. The term "young-old" is becoming part of everyday parlance, and it refers not to a particular age but to health and social characteristics. A young-old person may be 55 or 85. The term represents the social reality that the line between middle age and old age is no longer clear. What was once considered old age now characterizes only that minority of older persons who have been called the "old-old," that particularly vulnerable group who often are in need of special support and special care.

When, then, does old age now begin? The usual view has been that it starts at 65, when most people retire. But in the United States today the majority begin to take their Social Security retirement benefits at 62 or 63; and at ages 55 to 64 fewer than three of every four men are in the labor force. At the same time, with continued good health, some people are staying at work, full-time or part-time, into their 80s. So age 65 and retirement are no longer clear dividers between middle age and old age.

Alternatively, old age is often said to begin when poor health creates a major limitation on the activities of everyday life. Yet in a 1981 survey, half of all people 75 to 84 reported no such health limitations. Even in the very oldest group, those older than 85, more than a third reported no limitations due to health, and another one-third reported minor limitations; only one in three said they were unable to carry out any of their everyday activities. So health status is also becoming a poor age marker.

It is not only in the second half of life that the blurring of life periods can be seen. Adults of all ages are experiencing changes in the traditional rhythm and timing of events of the life cycle. More men and women marry, divorce, remarry and divorce again up through their 70s. More stay single. More women have their first child before they are 15, and more do so after 35. The result is that people are becoming grandparents for the first time at ages ranging from 35 to 75. More women, but also increasing numbers of men, raise children in two-parent, then one-parent, then two-parent households. More women, but also increasing numbers of men, exit and reenter school, enter and reenter the work force and undertake second and third careers up through their 70s. It therefore becomes difficult to distinguish the young, the middle-aged, and the young-old—either in terms of major life events or the ages at which those events occur.

The line between adolescence and adulthood is also being obscured. The traditional transitions into adulthood and the social competencies they implied—full-time jobs, marriage and parenthood—are disappearing as markers of social age. For some men and women, the entry into a job or profession is being delayed to age 30 as education is prolonged. For others, entry into the work force occurs at 16 or 17. Not only are there more teenage pregnancies but also more teenage women who are mothering their children. All this adds up to what has been aptly called "the fluid life cycle."

This is not to deny that our society still recognizes differences between adolescents, young people and old people, and that people still relate to each other accordingly. Yet we are less sure today where to place the punctuation marks in the life line and just what those punctuation marks should be. All across adulthood, age has become a poor predictor of the timing of life events, just as it is a poor predictor of health, work status, family status, interests, preoccupations and needs. We have conflicting images rather than stereotypes of age: the 70-year-old in a wheelchair, but also the 70-year-old on the tennis court; the 18-year-old who is married and supporting a family, but also the 18-year-old college student who brings his laundry home to his mother each week.

Difference among individuals, multiple images of age groups and inconsistencies in age norms were surely present in earlier periods of our history, but as our society has become more complex, the irregularities have become increasingly a part of the social reality.

These trends are reflected in public perceptions, too. Although systematic research is sparse, there are a few studies that show a diminishing public consensus about the periods of life and their markers. In the early 1960s, for instance, a group of middle-class, middle-aged people were asked about the "best" ages for life transitions (such as completing school, marrying, retiring) and the ages they associated with such phrases as "a young man," "an old woman" and "when a man (or woman) has the most responsibilities." When the same questions were asked of a similar group of people two decades later, the earlier consensus on every item of the questionnaire had disappeared. In the first study, nearly 90 percent had replied that the best age for a woman to marry was between 19 and 24; in the repeat study, only 40 percent gave this answer. In the first study, "a young man" was said to be a man between 18 and 22; in the repeat study, "a young man" was anywhere from 18 to 40. These findings are based on a very small study, but they illustrate how public views are changing.

In some respects, the line between childhood and adulthood is also fading. It is a frequent comment that childhood as we once knew it is disappearing. Increasingly children and adults have the same preferences in styles of dress, forms of language, games and television shows. Children know more about once-taboo topics such as sex, drugs, alcoholism, suicide and nuclear war. There is more adult-like sexual behavior among children, and more adult-like crime. At the same time, with the pressures for achievement rising, we have witnessed the advent of "the hurried child" and "the harried child."

We have also become accustomed to the descriptions of today's adults as narcissistic, self-interested and self-indulgent. Yuppies are described in the mass media as the pace-setters. While they work hard to get ahead, they are portrayed as more materialistic even than the "me" generation that preceded them, interested primarily in making money and in buying the "right" cars, the "best" housing and the most expensive gourmet foods. Overall, today's adults have fewer lasting marriages, fewer lasting commitments to work or community roles, more uncontrolled expressions of emotion, a greater sense of powerlessness—in short, more childlike behavior.

This picture may be somewhat overdrawn. Both children and adults are continually exhorted to "act your age," and they seldom misunderstand what that means. Yet the expectations of appropriate behavior for children and adults are certainly less differentiated than they once were. We are less sure of what intellectual and social competencies to expect of children—not only because some children are teaching their teachers how to use computers, but also because so many children are streetwise by age 8 and so many others, in the wake of divorce, are the confidantes of their parents by age 12.

Some observers attribute the blurring of childhood and adulthood primarily to the effects of television, which illuminates the total culture and reveals the secrets that adults have traditionally withheld from children. But it is not only television. A report in *The New York Times* underlines the fact that children are being socialized in new ways today by parents, schools, churches, and peer groups as well. The Girl Scouts of the U.S.A., according to the *Times* article, had decided finally to admit 5-year-olds. The national executive director was quoted as saying, "The decision to admit five-year-olds reflects the change in the American labor market. Women are working for part or all of their adult lives now. The possibilities are limitless but you need to prepare. So we think six is not too early to learn about career opportunities, and we also think that girls need to learn about making decisions. When you're five, you're not too young."

The blurring of traditional life periods does not mean that age norms are disappearing altogether. We still have our regulations about the ages at which children enter and exit from school, when people can marry without the consent of parents, when they are eligible for Social Security benefits. And less formal norms are still operating. Someone who moves to the Sun Belt to lead a life of leisure is socially approved if he is 70, but not if he is 30. An unmarried mother meets with greater disapproval if she is 15 than if she is 35. A couple in their 40s who decide to have another child are criticized for embarrassing their adolescent children. At the door of a discotheque a young person who cannot give proof of being "old enough" may be refused admission, while inside a gray-haired man who dances like those he calls youngsters meets the raised eyebrows and mocking remarks of the other dancers. As in these examples, expectations regarding age-appropriate behavior still form an elaborate and pervasive system of norms, expectations that are woven into the cultural fabric.

Both legal and cultural age norms are mirrored in the ways people behave and the ways they think about their own lives. Today, as in the past, most people by the time they are adolescents develop a set of anticipations of the normal, expectable life cycle: expectations of what the major life events and turning points will be and when they should occur. People internalize a social clock that tells them if they are on time or not.

Although the actual timing of life events for both women and men has always been influenced by various life contingencies, the norms and the actual occurrences have been closely connected. It may be less true today, but most people still try to marry or have a child or make a job change when they think they have reached the "right" age. They can still easily report whether they were early, late or on time with regard to one life event after another. "I married early," we hear, or "I had a late start because I served in Vietnam."

The life events that occur on time do not usually precipitate life crises, for they have been anticipated and rehearsed. The so-called "empty nest," for instance, is not itself stressful for most middle-aged parents. Instead, it is when children do not leave home at the appropriate time that stress occurs in both the parent and the child. For most older men, if it does not occur earlier than planned, retirement is taken in stride as a normal, expectable event. Widowhood is less often a crisis if it occurs at 65 rather than at 40.

It is the events that upset the expected sequence and rhythm of the life cycle that cause problems—as when the death of a parent comes during one's adolescence rather than in middle age; when marriage is delayed too long; when the birth of a child comes too early; when occupational achievement is slowed; when the empty nest, grandparenthood, retirement, major illness or widowhood occurs "out of sync." Traditional timetables still operate.

For the many reasons suggested earlier, the traditional time schedules do not in today's society produce the regularities anticipated by adolescents or young adults. For many men and women, to be out of sync may have lost some of its importance, but for others, the social clocks have not stopped ticking. The incongruities between the traditional norms and the fluid life cycle represent new freedoms for many people; for other people, new uncertainties and strains.

There is still another reality to be reckoned with. Some timetables are losing their significance, but others are more compelling than ever. A young man may feel he is a failure if he has not "made it" in his corporation by the time he is 35. A young woman may delay marriage because of her career, but then hurry to catch up with parenthood. The same young woman may feel under pressure to marry, bear a child and establish herself in a career all within a five-year-period—even though she knows she is likely to live to 85.

Sometimes both traditional and nontraditional views are in conflict in the mind of the same person. The young woman who deliberately delays marriage may be the same woman who worries that she has lost status because she is not married by 25. A middle-aged man starts a second family, but feels compelled to justify himself by explaining that he expects to live to see his new children reach adulthood. Or an old person reports that because he did not expect to live so long, he is now unprepared to take on the "new ways" of some of his peers. Some people live in new ways, but continue to think in old ways.

Given such complications, shall we say that individuals are paying less or more attention to age as a prod or a brake upon their behavior? That age consciousness is decreasing or increasing? Whether or not historical change is occurring, it is fair to say that one's own age remains crucial to every individual, all the way from early childhood through advanced old age. A person uses age as a guide in accommodating to others, in giving meaning to the life course, and in contemplating the time that is past and the time that remains.

In sum, there are multiple levels of social and psychological reality based on social age, and in modern societies, on calendar age as the marker of social age. The complexities are no fewer for the individual than for society at large.

PART TWO
The Life Course

Thoughts about the Life Course

Gunhild O. Hagestad

Part 2 of this book clearly illustrates two key characteristics of Bernice Neugarten as a scholar: her ability to capture complex phenomena in clear and simple language and her wide disciplinary horizon. Many times she has given us words for realities we have known but lacked the terms to describe. The papers in this section include many such terms. Neugarten may not have always been the person to coin them, but she introduced them in a way which made them part of our vocabulary, our reflections, and our research. Examples are "timetables," "social clocks," "on- and off-time events," "young-old and old-old," "kinkeeping" and "parentcaring."

Bernice Neugarten could be described as a sociologist's psychologist and a psychologist's sociologist. For most of her professional life, she has been a card-carrying member of both professional associations. Because of the dual disciplinary involvement, her writing has had a wide audience. Her focus on developing individuals in a changing social context has inspired a variety of work done under the rubrics of life span developmental psychology and life course analysis. Over the last two decades, the life course perspective has steadily gained ground as a meeting place between disciplines: anthropology, demography, history, psychology, and sociology. At the time when most of the papers in this section were written, the life course was yet to become a commonly used concept. The term used by Neugarten was the *life cycle*, but these papers are remarkable as vanguard examples of a life course approach. She anticipated concepts, substantive questions, and analytical challenges which remain central to scholars who apply the life course perspective today. Let me list a few such enduring issues and briefly trace them to current work.

CONTINUITIES AND DISCONTINUITIES

When colleagues and former students recently created a volume honoring Neugarten's scholarly contribution by giving illustrations of work it inspired, it was natural to choose a title focused on continuities and discontinuities (Bengtson, 1996). More than any other issue, this has been a recurrent theme in her writing. Her 1969

Gunhild O. Hagestad is Professor of Sociology at the University of Oslo and Associate Professor of Human Development and Social Policy at Northwestern University.

paper, the first in this section of this book, is a classic. The central question addressed is how psychological issues in childhood are related to those in adulthood. In this and many subsequent papers, Neugarten warned researchers that adulthood has its own unique set of challenges and preoccupations for the developing person. She also raised a question which she repeatedly posed: How and to what extent does the individual maintain an inner sense of continuity in the face of external discontinuity? Both in life span developmental psychology and life course analysis, authors have pondered the relationship between transitions and self. How is a core persona—what Kaufman (1987) calls the ageless self—maintained in the face of life changes which may represent discontinuities (Brim and Kagan, 1980; Brim and Ryff, 1980)?

The issue of discontinuities also appears in discussions of life course patterns on a societal level. A number of European authors have recently argued that after a period of institutionalization of the life course and a socially created "normal biography," we may now be witnessing a "deinstitutionalization, characterized by disorder and discontinuity" (Buchmann, 1989; Held, 1986; Kohli, 1986). During the last decade, German scholars have provided extensive discussions of how societal conditions may create life course discontinuities, for example, in the transition to adulthood (Heinz, 1991, 1992). In these works, one often finds echoes of Benedict's (1938) classic analysis of cultural discontinuity in the transition from adolescence to adulthood in Western society. In the field of gerontology, sociologists have described how culture and socialization patterns (Rosow, 1974) or "structural lag" (Riley, Kahn and Foner, 1994) confront aging individuals with biographical discontinuities.

Closely related to issues of stability and change in the life course are questions about inter-individual differences across life. Both in life span developmental psychology (Baltes, 1987) and in sociological discussions of the life course, it has been argued that, as members of a birth cohort age, life patterns become more heterogeneous. Neugarten may have been the first to discuss this as a fanning out of lives across time. Dannefer (1988) suggests that the increased variability with age reflects "Matthew effects": social inequalities which widen over time.

Discussions of continuities and discontinuities inevitably led us to another key Neugarten theme.

LIVES EXPERIENCED VERSUS LIVES OBSERVED

Throughout her work, Neugarten has pointed to possible tensions between the perspective of an observer and that of the person whose life is being studied. Many recent publications leave the connection between societally created life trajectories and individual awareness a moot point. If societies, through structural arrangements and social policies, create standard pathways, are individuals aware of such life structuring? Kohli (1986) suggests that the same processes which give rise to standardization of the life course also create new "mentalities," such as increased cultural awareness of chronological age. Similar arguments are found in Chudacoff's (1989) analysis of age consciousness in American culture and Meyer's (1986) discussion of how life course programs are tied to metaphors, motives, and reasons. In her groundbreaking work on social timetables for key life transitions, Neugarten's focus was subjective awareness of social clocks and the extent to which they serve as a basis for planning and self-evaluation. Some authors have recently attempted to link subjective perceptions of age structures and career timetables to actual career ladders in given social organizations. Results indicate that there are often discrepancies between the two (Lawrence, 1988).

Neugarten took the issue of subjective awareness versus observable life patterns one step further, outlining two layers of subjectivity. She warned that possible changes in the inner life may not appear in awareness. An example of work which links outwardly observable role changes with internal reorganization which can only be captured in projective measures is her much-cited work on age-sex roles (see part 3), later elaborated by her coauthor Gutmann (1987).

In spite of the complexities of capturing subjective awareness and relating it to observable phenomena, Neugarten has repeatedly warned scholars that in designing research, they must not lose sight of what is considered important by the people they study. The individual's own construction of life's journey from the vantage point of an ever-changing present has recently been given much attention in work on autobiography, life history, and personal narratives (e.g., Bertaux and Kohli, 1984; Denzin, 1989; McAdams, 1993).

THE IMPORTANCE OF TIME DIMENSIONS

Neugarten was among the first to talk about the complex interrelationships of chronological age or biographical time, social age systems, and historical time. Her outlook reflected the influence of two important mentors. Very early in her career, she worked with sociologist Lloyd Warner, the man who gave us the first systematic discussion of age grading in North America (see Cain, 1964). Later, Robert Havighurst sensitized her to how developmental tasks in different phases of life represent a combination of maturation and aging on the one hand and societal demands and resources on the other. In much of her work, Neugarten discussed how the personal experience of time and age is shaped by social age systems, which, in turn, are affected by the forces of history. With the movement of history, new life phases and age groups emerge.

In the 1960s, Neugarten was among the first to describe the markers of middle age. She pointed to such phenomena as changing time orientation, stocktaking and a new sense of competency and freedom—themes which are central in a current popular book on passages in adulthood (Sheehy, 1995). A decade later, she urged us to take a more nuanced view of old age, separating the old-old and the young-old. In arguing for this distinction, she used cohort comparisons to show the emergence of a "new old age." Although she always reminded us not to lose sight of the person, she used an analytical approach which has been quite common in life course analysis: describing "the statistical histories of birth cohorts," to use Winsborough's (1980) term. Cohort composites are used to illustrate historical change in the contours of lives, including what Cain (1967) calls "watersheds."

Rich illustrations of the complex interplay of individual life time and historical time have emerged in the research programs of sociologist Glen Elder (Elder, 1974; Elder and Caspi, 1988; Elder and O'Rand, 1995) and family historian Tamara Hareven (1977, 1986). Both of these scholars emphasize the importance of an intermediate level of time structuring: family time. They stress the interdependence of life careers in the family and the significance of altered family rhythms. Again, we find early discussion of such themes in Neugarten's work.

CHANGING FAMILY CONTEXTS

Neugarten used aggregate cohort comparisons to show how social and demographic changes had created new life patterns among midlife women. She pointed to what she called "a quickening of the family cycle," the closer spacing of early family transitions within a context of increasing life expectancy. Such early family starts, combined with longer lives, she argued, create new generational constellations. Among such emerging family structures are four-generational families with two middle generations, a new context for sorting out needs and resources in the family. In the late 1970s, she discussed topics which received fairly massive attention in the following decade: parentcaring and the stress of being "women in the middle" (Brody, 1981). Earlier, she suggested that to vigorous young-old individuals, grandparenthood takes on new role meanings. Thirty years after it was written, her paper on grandparenthood is still widely cited, because in the 1990s, grandparenthood and its significance in the lives of the old as well as children has for the first time become a high priority research topic.

In her discussions of grandparenthood, kinkeeping and parentcaring, she emphasized that men and women often have strikingly different role patterns and perceptions.

GENDERED LIVES

Although Neugarten's classic discussion of how aging holds different meanings for men and women appears in part 3 of this book, it also deserves mention here. She made it quite clear that there is a "his" and a "her" middle age, and that this difference goes beyond biological changes. In much of her work, she emphasized age and sex as twin statuses which are subject to joint cultural constructions. Although sociology has two classic papers by Linton (1942) and Parsons (1942) on this issue, it continues to be in need of systematic exploration. To a considerable degree, gender and age are discussed in separate literatures. There are by now numerous publications on women and aging (e.g., Turner and Troll, 1994) but few systematic analyses of the social meanings of age for men and women (Arber and Ginn, 1955; Hagestad, 1994).

In summary, Bernice Neugarten's papers on the many meanings of time and age in the life course raised challenges and provided conceptual tools which will inspire reflection and observation for years to come.

References

Arber, S. and Ginn, J. (eds.). 1995. *Connecting gender and aging.* Buckingham, U.K.: Open University Press.

Baltes, P. B. 1987. Theoretical propositions of life-span developmental psychology: On the dynamics between growth and decline. *Developmental Psychology,* 5, 611–626.

Benedict, R. 1938. Continuities and discontinuities in cultural conditioning. *Psychiatry,* 1, 161–167.

Bengtson, V. L. (ed.). 1996. *Adulthood and Aging: Research on continuities and discontinuities.* New York: Springer Publishers.

Bertaux, D. and Kohli, M. 1984. The life story approach: A continental view. *Annual Review of Sociology,* 215–262.

Brim, O. G. and Kagan, J. 1980. *Constancy and change in human development.* Cambridge, Mass.: Harvard University Press.

Brim, O. G. and Ryff, C. D. 1980. On the properties of life events. In Baltes, P. B. and Brim, O. G. (eds.). *Life-span development and behavior.* Vol. 3. New York: Academic Press, 367–388.

Brody, E. M. 1981. "women in the middle" and family help to older people. *The Gerontologist,* 21, 471–80.

Buchmann, M. 1989. *The script of life in modern society.* Chicago: The University of Chicago Press.

Cain, L. 1964. Life course and social structure. In Faris, R. (ed.) *Handbook of modern sociology,* ch. 8. Chicago: Rand McNally.

Cain, L. 1967. Age status and generational phenomena: The new old people in contemporary America. *The Gerontologist,* 7, 83–92.

Chudacoff, H. P. 1989. *How old are you? Age consciousness in American culture.* Princeton, NJ: Princeton University Press.

Dannefer, D. 1988. Differential gerontology and the stratified life course. *Annual Review of Gerontology.* 3–36.

Denzin, N. K. 1989. *Interpretive biography.* Newbury Park, CA: Sage.

Elder, G. H. 1974. *Children of the great depression.* Chicago: University of Chicago Press.

Elder, G. H. and Caspi, A. 1988. Human development and social change: An emerging perspective on the life course. In Bolger, N., Caspi, A. Downey, G. and Moorehouse, M. (eds.). *Persons in context: Developmental processes,* 77–113. Cambridge, England: Cambridge University Press.

Elder, G. H. and O'Rand, A. M. 1995. Adult lives in a changing society. In Cook, K. S., Fine, G. A. and House, J. S. (eds.). *Sociological perspectives on social psychology,* New York: Allyn and Bacon, 452–475.

Gutmann, D. 1987. *Reclaimed Powers: Toward a new psychology of men and women in later life.* New York: Basic Books.

Hagestad, G. O. 1994. The social meanings of age for men and women. In Stevenson, M. R. (ed.). *Gender roles through the life span.* Muncie, IN: Ball State University Press.

Hareven, T. K. 1977. Family time and historical time. *Daedalus,* 106, 57–70.

Hareven, T. K. 1986. *Family time and industrial time.* New York: Cambridge University Press.

Heinz, W. R. 1991. Theoretical advances in life course research. Vol. I: Status passages and the life course. Weinheim: Deutscher Studien Verlag.

Heinz, W. R. 1992. Theoretical advances in life course research. Vol. III: Status passages, institutions and gatekeeping. Weinheim: Deutscher Studien Verlag.

Held, T. 1986. Institutionalization and deinstitutionalization of the life course. *Human Development,* 29, 157–162.

Kaufman, S. R. 1987. *The ageless self.* Madison, WI: University of Wisconsin Press.

Kohli, M. 1986. Social organization and subjective construction of life course. In Sorensen, A. B., Weinert, F. E. and Sherrod, L. R. (eds.). *Human development and the life course: Multidisciplinary perspectives,* 271–292. Hillsdale, NJ: Lawrence Erlbaum Associates.

Lawrence, B. S. 1988. New wrinkles in the theory of age: Demography, norms, and performance ratings. *Academy of Management Journal,* 31, 309–337.

Linton, R. A. 1942. Age and sex categories. *American Sociological Review,* 7, 589–603.

McAdams, D. P. 1993. *The stories we live by: Personal myths and the making of the self.* New York: W. Morrow.

Meyer, J. W. 1986. The institutionalization of the life course and its effects on the self. In Sorensen, A. B. et al. (eds.). *Human development and the life course: Multidisciplinary perspectives,* 199–216. Hillsdale, NJ: Lawrence Erlbaum Associates.

Parsons, T. 1942. Age and sex in the social structure of the United States. *American Sociological Review,* 7, 604–616.

Riley, M. W., Kahn, R. L. and Foner, A. (eds.). 1994. *Age and structural lag: Changes in work, family, retirement, and other structures.* New York: Wiley and Sons.

Rosow, I. 1974. *Socialization to old age.* Berkeley: University of California Press.

Sheehy, G. 1995. *New passages: Mapping your life across time.* New York: Random House.

Turner, B. and Troll, L. H. 1994. Women growing older: *Psychological Perspectives.* Thousand Oaks, CA: Sage.

Winsborough, H. H. 1980. A demographic approach to the life cycle. In Back, K. W. (ed.). *Life course: Integrative theories and exemplary populations.* 65–75. Boulder, CO: Westview Press.

Continuities and Discontinuities of Psychological Issues into Adult Life

I am impressed more by the discontinuities than by the continuities of psychological issues into adult life. For we shall not understand the psychological realities of adulthood by projecting forward the issues that are salient in childhood—neither those issues that concern children themselves, nor those that concern child psychologists as they study cognitive development and language development and the resolution of the Oedipal.

Many investigators who have been focussing upon infancy, childhood and adolescence are dealing with issues that are not the significant issues to adults. To illustrate very briefly, and not to dwell upon the obvious:

In the adolescent we are accustomed to thinking that the major psychological task is the formation of identity. For the period that immediately follows, Kenneth Keniston has recently suggested the title "youth," distinguishing it from young adulthood, as the time when the major task for the ego is the confrontation of the society, the sorting out of values, and making a "fit" between the self and society.

In young adulthood, the issues are related to intimacy, to parenthood, and to meeting the expectations of the world of work, with the attendant demands for restructuring of roles, values, and sense of self—in particular, the investment of self into the lives of a few significant others to whom one will be bound for years to come.

In middle age, some of the issues are related to new family roles—the responsibilities of being the child of aging parents, and the reversal of authority which occurs as the child becomes the decision-maker for the parent . . . the awareness of the self as the bridge between the generations . . . the confrontation of a son-in-law or daughter-in-law with the need to establish an intimate relation with a stranger under very short notice . . . the role of grandparenthood.

Some of the issues are related to the increased stock-taking, the heightened introspection and reflection that become characteristic of the mental life . . . the changing time-perspective, as time is restructured in terms of time-left-to-live rather than time-since-birth . . . the personalization of death, bringing with it, for women, the

Reprinted by permission from *Human Development* 12 (1969): 121–30.

rehearsal for widowhood, and for men, the rehearsal of illness; and for both, the new attention to body-monitoring.

Some of the issues relate to the creation of social heirs (in contrast to biological heirs) . . . the concomitant attention to relations with the young—the need to nurture, the care not to overstep the delicate boundaries of authority relationships, the complicated issues over the use of one's power—in short, the awareness of being the socializer rather than the socialized.

And in old age, the issues are different again. Some are issues that relate to renunciation—adaptation to losses of work, friends, spouse, the yielding up of a sense of competency and authority . . . reconciliation with members of one's family, one's achievements, and one's failures . . . the resolution of grief over the death of others, but also over the approaching death of self . . . the need to maintain a sense of integrity in terms of what one has been, rather than what one is . . . the concern with "legacy" . . . how to leave traces of oneself . . . the psychology of survivorship . . .

All these are psychological issues which are "new" at successive stages in the life cycle; and as developmental psychologists we come to their investigation ill-equipped, no matter how sophisticated our approaches to child development.

The issues of life, and the content and preoccupation of the mental life, are different for adults than for children. Furthermore, as psychologists, we deal in a sense with different organisms. Let me illustrate again, only briefly, that which we all know:

As the result of accumulative adaptations to both biological and social events, there is a continuously changing basis within the individual for perceiving and responding to new events in the outer world. People change, whether for good or for bad, as the result of the accumulation of experience. As events are registered in the organism, individuals inevitably abstract from the traces of those experiences and they create more encompassing as well as more refined categories for the interpretation of new events. The mental filing system not only grows larger, but it is reorganized over time, with infinitely more cross-references. This is merely one way of saying that not only do the middle-aged differ from the young because they were subject to different formative experiences, but because of the unavoidable effects of having lived longer and of having therefore a greater apperceptive mass or store of past experience.

Because of longer life-histories, with their complicated patterns of personal and social commitments, adults are not only much more complex than children, but they are more different one from another, and increasingly different as they move from youth to extreme old age.

More important, the adult is a self-propelling individual who manipulates the environment to attain his goals. He creates his environment, more or less (and varying in degree, of course, by the color of his skin and the size of his own or his father's bank account). He *invents* his future self, just as he recreates or *reinvents* his past self. We cannot go far in understanding adult psychology, then, without giving a central position to purposive behavior, to what Charlotte Buhler calls intentionality, or to what Brewster Smith has called the self-required values, or to what Marjorie Lowenthal refers to as the reassessment of goals as itself the measure of adaptation.

These are not new ideas, but because they are such striking features of the adult as compared to the child, they create special problems for the student of the life cycle when he turns to problems of prediction, for we do not yet know how to capture the phenomena of decision-making.

Another factor is the adult's sense of time and timing. The adult, surely by middle age, with his highly refined powers of introspection and reflection, is continually busying himself in making a coherent story out of his life history. He reinterprets the past, selects and shapes his memories, and reassesses the significance of past events in his search for coherence. An event which, at the time of its occurrence, was "unexpected" or arbitrary or traumatic becomes rationalized and interwoven into a context of explanation in its retelling 20 years later.

The remembrance of things past is continually colored by the encounter with the present, of course; just as the present is interpreted in terms of the past. To deal with both the past and the present simultaneously is a unique characteristic of human personality. It is a set of mental processes which vary according to the sensitivity of the individual, probably with his educational level and his ability to verbalize, but a set of mental processes which probably also follow a distinguishable course with increasing age. In a study presently under way in Chicago, for instance, the data seem to show that middle-aged people utilize their memories in a somewhat different fashion than do old people. The middle-aged draw consciously upon past experience in the solution of present problems; the old seem to be busy putting their store of memories in order, as it were, dramatizing some, striving for consistency in others, perhaps as a way of preparing an ending for that life-story.

There is another way in which issues of time and timing are of central importance in the psychology adulthood: namely, the ways in which the individual evaluates himself in relation to socially-defined time. Every society is age-graded, and every society has a system of social expectations regarding age-appropriate behavior. The individual passes through a socially-regulated cycle from birth to death as inexorably as he passes through the biological cycle; and there exists a socially-prescribed timetable for the ordering of major life events: a time when he is expected to marry, a time to raise children, a time to retire. Although the norms vary somewhat from one socioeconomic, ethnic, or religious group to another, for any social group it can easily be demonstrated that norms and actual occurrences are closely related.

Age norms and age expectations operate as a system of social controls, as prods and brakes upon behavior, in some instances hastening an event, in others, delaying it. Men and women are aware not only of the social clocks that operate in various areas of their lives; but they are aware also of being "early," "late," or "on time" with regard to major life events.

Being on time or off time is not only a compelling basis for self-assessment with regard to family events, but also with regard to occupational careers, with both men and women comparing themselves with their friends or classmates or siblings in deciding whether or not they have made good.

Persons can describe ways in which being on-time or off-time has other psychological and social accompaniments. Thus, in a study of Army officers (the Army is a clearly age-graded occupation, where expectations with regard to age and grade are formally set forth in the official Handbook) the men who recognized themselves as being too long in grade—or late in career achievement—were also distinguishable on an array of social and psychological attitudes toward work, family, community participation, and personal adjustment.

When factors such as these are added to the inexorable biological changes, the individual develops a concept of the "normal, expectable life-cycle"—a phrase which I have borrowed from Dr. Robert Butler and which owes much, of course, to Hartmann's "normal, expectable environment." Adults carry around in their heads, whether or not they can easily verbalize it, a set of anticipations of the normal, expectable life-cycle. They internalize expectations of the consensually-validated sequences of major life events—not only what those events should be, but when they should occur. They make plans and set goals along a time-line shaped by these expectations.

The individual is said to create a sense of self very early in life. Freud, for example, in describing the development of the ego; and George Mead, in describing the differentiation between the "I" and the "me," placed the development of self very early in childhood. But it is perhaps not until adulthood that the individual creates a sense of the life-cycle; that is, an anticipation and acceptance of the inevitable sequence of events that will occur as men grow up, grow old and die—in adulthood, that he understands that the course of his own life will be similar to the lives of others, and that the turning points are inescapable. This ability to interpret the past and foresee the future, and to create for oneself a sense of the predictable life-cycle differentiates the healthy adult personality from the unhealthy, and it underlies the adult's self-assessment.

The self-concept of the adult has the elements of the past contained within it. The adult thinks of himself in the present in terms of where he has come from; what he has become; how content he is at 50 compared to the time when he was 40.

All this differentiates the adult as subject from the psychologist as observer. The adult has a built-in dimension of thought that is the present-relative-to-the-past—but the psychologist has not yet created dimensions of this type in capturing the psychological realities of the life-cycle and in studying antecedent-consequent relations. In fact, it is the specific aim of most investigators to keep separate Time 1 from Time 2 observations and evaluations, on the premise that to do otherwise is to contaminate the data.

To put this differently, to the subject, the blending of past and present is psychological reality. To the investigator, validity (and therefore, reality) lies in keeping time segments independent of each other.

Thus, to repeat, some of the problems that face us in attempting to build a psychology of the life-cycle stem from the facts that the salient issues of the mental life are different for adults than for children; the underlying relations of the individual to his social environment are different; the relations of the investigator to his subject are different; and the salient dimensions psychologists use to describe and measure mental and emotional life *should* be different.

I am suggesting, then, that our foremost problem in studying the life span is to create a frame of reference and sets of dimensions that are appropriate to the subject-matter, and that are valid in the sense that they are fitting ways of capturing reality. To do this, it might be added, we need first a great wealth of descriptive studies, based on various methods that stem from naturalistic observational approaches.

Let me turn now more specifically to the studies which are emerging in which the attempt is made to relate findings on childhood and adulthood in the lives of the same individual—in short, to longitudinal studies which form the foundation of a psychology of the life cycle.

The longitudinal studies may be seen, in overly simplified and overly-dichotomized terms, as being of two major types: first are those I shall refer to as "trait" or "dimension" oriented, studies addressed to questions of stability and change along given dimensions of ability and personality; second are those I shall call "life-outcomes" oriented, those which pose such questions as these: What kind of child becomes the achieving adult? The middle-aged failure? The successful ager? The psychiatric casualty? What constellation of events are predictive of outcomes?

In the first type of research, the investigators have been preoccupied with such problems as whether or not the individual who is aggressive at age 3 is aggressive at age 30, or whether the high IQ child turns out to be the high IQ adult. There are also studies in which the ipsative approach is taken, and in which the stability of personality types is the question being pursued—the difference being, that is, that attention is focussed upon the patterns of traits rather than individual traits, and the degree to which these patterns show stability or change.

In such studies, the investigator is plagued with questions of validity of his measures over time—is the concept of aggression or intelligence the same concept for 3- and 30-year-olds? Are we measuring the same phenomenon? These studies have proceeded without regard to the events of the life-cycle, and the passage of calendar time is itself taken to be the sufficient variable. As in Kagan and Moss's studies from birth to maturity or Nancy Bayley's studies of cognitive development, or Oden's latest follow-up of the Terman gifted group, the presumption seems to be that the same changes can be expected between age 3 and 30 whether or not marriage has intervened, or parenthood, or job failure or widowhood. "Time" is treated as independent from the biological and social events that give substance to "time," and independent from the events that might be regarded as the probable psychological markers of time.

In studies of life-outcomes, we need, of course, studies of traits and dimensions; but we are in particular need of studies aimed at determining which life events produce change and which do not—which ones leave measurable traces in the personality structure, and which ones call forth new patterns of adaptation.

Let me illustrate: parenthood might be presumed to be an event that has a transforming effect upon the personality, whether one reasons from psychoanalytic theory, or role theory, or learning theory; and whether one conceptualizes the event in terms of elaboration and differentiation of the ego, or in terms of adjustment to a major new set of social roles, or in terms of the development of new sets of responses to the demands of a new significant other. Yet we have no systemic studies of the effects of parenthood upon personality development; and no good evidence that parenthood is more significant, say, than college attendance or marriage or widowhood.

To take another example: some of my own work on middle-aged women has led me to conclude that the menopause is not the transforming event in personality development that puberty is; nor is the departure of children from the home of the same importance as parenthood.

We need to establish which life events are the important ones, but we need to study also when the event occurs, in terms of its social "appropriateness." (To marry at age 30 is a different psychological event than to marry at age 16; and to be widowed at age 40 may be more significant than to be widowed at age 65, for in either case, the event comes off-time and does not fit the anticipations of the normal, expectable life-cycle.)

Among the longitudinal and long term follow-up studies presently available, investigators have taken both prospective and retrospective approaches. They begin with a group of infants or young children and follow them forward in time; or they begin with a group of adults and look backward in their life-histories to identify the predictors or antecedents of present adult status. In both instances, what is most striking is the relative lack of predictability from childhood to adulthood with regard to life-outcomes. To mention only a few very recent studies: Hoyt's review of the literature indicates that we cannot predict from school success to vocational success. . . . Robins' study of deviant children grown up shows that while anti-social behavior in childhood is predictive of sociopathic behavior in adults, the withdrawn personality characteristics of childhood are not associated with later adult pathology of any kind. . . . Rogler and Hollingshead's study in Puerto Rico indicates that experiences in childhood and adolescence of schizophrenic adults do not differ noticeably from those of persons who are not afflicted with the illness. . . . Baller's follow-up of mid-life attainment of the mentally retarded shows low predictability from childhood, with persons of below-70 IQ faring vastly better than anyone anticipated.

I recognize that, in some ultimate sense, we may never be able to make satisfactory predictions regarding life-outcomes, no matter how well we choose our variables or how well we manage to identify the important and unimportant life events, for we shall probably never be able to predict the changes that will occur in an individual's social environment, nor the particular contingencies and accidents that will arise in an individual life, nor—equally important—the ways his life cycle is affected by those of the significant others with whom his life is intertwined. Furthermore, the psychologist, no matter how sophisticated his methods, will need the sociologist, the anthropologist, and the historian, to say nothing of the developmental biologist, to help him. Thus the study of lives will flourish only to the extent that a truly interdisciplinary behavioral science is created. Perhaps we shall have to leave the field to the creative writer, the philosopher, or the archivist for a long time still to come, and decide that the life-cycle as a unit of study in the behavioral sciences is one with which we are not yet prepared to deal.

Yet we developmental psychologists are not likely to abandon the subject matter that intrigues us; and in the immediate future, as we work in our own areas, we can probably gain enormously in our ability to predict outcomes if we focus more of our attention upon the things that are of concern to the individuals we are studying— what the subject selects as important in his past and in his present; what he plans to do with his life; what he predicts will happen; and what strategies he elects—in short, if we make greater use of the subject himself as the reporting and predicting agent.

I am reminded in this connection that Jean McFarlane recently told me that after her intensive and intimate study of her subjects over a 30-year period, she was continuously surprised to see how her people turned out. In going back over the data that she and Marjorie Honzik had painstakingly amassed, she found that much of what her subjects told her had been important to them when they were children or adolescents was not even to be found in her records—in other words, that which the investigators had regarded as important and had bothered to record was not the same as that which the subjects themselves had regarded as important at the time.

I suggest therefore that in future studies we pay more attention to gathering systematic and repeated self-reports and self-evaluations, and in doing so, to utilize what I shall call the "clinical" as well as the "observer's" approach. In the one case, the clinical psychologist tries to put himself into the frame of reference of his patient or client and to see the world through that person's eyes. In the other case, the "observer" psychologist brings his own frame of reference to the data and interprets according to his own theories.

We need to gather longitudinal data of both types (as by collecting autobiographies from our subjects at repeated intervals, and by creating a set of dimensions and measures that are appropriate to that data). We need, in other words, to use a double perspective: that of the observer and that of the person whose life it is.

In conclusion, I have been drawing attention to the discontinuities between a psychology of childhood and a psychology of adulthood, between the perspectives of the investigator and that of the subject himself, between the stances of the clinician and the psychometrician. If, at the present time, we have only a few elements of a life-span developmental psychology, I am suggesting a few of the elements that are conspicuously missing.

SEVEN

Sociological Perspectives on the Life Cycle

Bernice L. Neugarten and Nancy Datan

I. INTRODUCTION

Students of the life cycle have given much attention to the biological timetable of human development, using such concepts as maturation, age, and stage as major dimensions in mapping significant changes. Much less attention has been given to the socio-historical context and to the development of concepts for mapping changes in the social environment as they affect the way in which an individual's life is lived. Although there have been scattered but significant attempts by psychologists to understand the lives of noted individuals in relation to historical change (such as Freud's [1939] study of Moses and monotheism, and Erikson's [1958, 1969] studies of Luther and Gandhi), for the most part, psychologists have left it to biographers, novelists, and historians to study the personalities of the eminent and to elucidate both the forces that shape the individual and the effect of the individual upon his time.

Developmentally oriented studies have appeared which deal with the impact of single historical events upon the life course of groups of individuals. For example, the effects of World War II have been studied in a variety of ways, as in studies of the long-term effects on British children evacuated from London during the Blitz (Maas, 1963), or the effects of the Depression upon the subsequent social development of children (Elder, 1973), or in a study of middle-aged women 25 years after they had experienced concentration camps (Antonovsky, Maoz, Datan, and Wijsenbeek, 1971).

While there are many such studies of the significance of given historical events, the socio-historical perspective on the life cycle has not as yet received widespread, systematic treatment. On the contrary, studies of development are more often characterized by a search for a universal sequence of personality change comparable to, if not paced by, the maturational timetable, rather than a search for the sequences of personality changes that can be shown to reflect sequences of historical and social events. A major problem lies in the fact that we lack a set of conceptual tools by which

Reprinted by permission from *Life-Span Developmental Psychology: Personality and Socialization,* edited by P. B. Baltes and K. W. Schaie (New York and London: Academic Press, 1973), 53–79.

to integrate maturatinal, psychological, sociological, and historical perspectives on the life cycle.

The purpose of this paper is to remind the reader of a few sociological concepts that have been of significance in understanding human personality, and then to turn to the life cycle seen in three dimensions of time: life time, or the individual's chronological age; social time, or the system of age grading and age expectations that shapes the life cycle; and historical time, or the succession of political, economic, and social events that shape the setting into which the individual is born and make up the dynamic, constantly changing background against which his life is lived.

II. Sociological Concepts

From the sociological perspective, personality is generally seen as an emergent of the interaction between the biological organism and the social context, and the task of the sociologist has been to explore this interaction from the standpoint of social organization. Thus, speaking very generally, sociologists often move from a study of the social organization to the consideration of its consequences for personality, viewing personality as the outcome of social learning.

In relating the individual to his social surrounding, the concepts of social system, social role, and socialization have repeatedly been set forth in the sociological and social–psychological literature. (Recent expositions are given, for example, in Brim and Wheeler, 1966; Clausen, 1968; Goslin, 1969; and Riley, Johnson, and Foner, 1972.) Although not each of these concepts was originally intended for this purpose, each can be related to a time dimension in looking at the life course.

A. The Social System and Social Role

Parsons and Shils (1951b) have expressed the distinction between the psychological and sociological levels of analysis in their description of the social system as made up of the actions of individuals. The actions constituting the *social system* are the same actions that make up the personality systems of the individual actors, but these two systems are analytically discrete entities despite the identity of their basic components. The difference lies in the different foci of organization and each system involves different functional problems in operation. The individual actor is not the unit of study in the social system; rather, for most purposes, it is the *role* that is being examined. A role is a sector of an individual actor's range of action, but it is also a specific set of behaviors having a particular function for a social institution—e.g., fatherhood is a role with specific functions for the family (and thus for the larger society) and at the same time, it is a role with specific functions for the individual. Any role or role constellation has different significance according to whether it is viewed from the individual or the societal perspective; but from both perspectives, the individual learns to think and to behave in ways that are consonant with the roles he plays, so that performance in a succession of roles leads to predictable personality configurations. Indeed, for some sociologists, personality itself is perceived as the sum of the individual's social roles. For purposes of the present discussion, the life cycle can be seen as a succession of roles and changing role constellations, and a certain order and predictability of behavior occurs over time as individuals move through a given succession of roles.

B. Socialization and Social Learning

The process by which the human infant is transformed into a member of a particular society and learns the roles appropriate to his or her sex, social class, and ethnic group, is called socialization. (Social classes have been shown by sociologists to be subcultures with differentiated norms and institutions.) LeVine (1969) has distinguished three different views of the process of socialization which correspond approximately to the disciplinary orientations of cultural anthropology, personality psychology, and sociology. For the anthropologist, socialization involves the transmission of cultural values and traditions from generation to generation. To some psychologists, the major task in socialization is the channeling of instinctual drives into socially useful forms. For the sociologist, socialization is a process of training the child for participation in society, with the emphasis upon positive social prescriptions growing out of the needs of the social structure.

In all three views, however, socialization can be seen as a process of social learning or of training through which individuals acquire the knowledge, skills, attitudes and values, the needs and motivations, and the cognitive, affective and conative patterns that relate them to their socio-cultural setting. The success of the socialization process is measured by the ability of the individual to perform well in the roles he takes on (Inkeles, 1969).

While socialization was once conceived as a process by which the infant was transformed into an adult of his culture, and thus the process was essentially complete at adulthood, more recently, sociologists have come to describe socialization as a lifelong process (Brim and Wheeler, 1966), one that involves new learning in adulthood in response to rapid social change and in response to the succession of life tasks. Although anthropologists such as Benedict (1938) have long pointed to discontinuities in cultural conditioning at various points in the life cycle, the recognition of the need for resocialization in adulthood is relatively new.

In summary then, from the sociological perspective, the life cycle can be described as a succession of social roles, and personality can be described as the product of changing patterns of socialization.

III. THREE DIMENSIONS OF TIME
A. Life Time

From the ancient poets through Shakespeare to Erikson (1950, 1959), people have viewed the life cycle as a series of orderly changes, from infancy through childhood, adolescence, maturity, and old age with the biological timetable governing the sequence of changes in the process of growing up and growing old. Although for the developmental psychologist there are a host of conceptual and methodological issues involved in the use of chronological age or *life time* as an index of change (see, e.g., Baer, 1970; Baltes and Goulet, 1971; Looft, 1973; Wohlwill, 1970a), chronological age is nevertheless the most frequently used index. It is a truism that chronological age is at best only a rough indicator of an individual's position on any one of numerous physical or psychological dimensions, for from earliest infancy on, individual differences emerge in development. Nor is age a meaningful predictor of many forms of social and psychological behavior, unless there is accompanying knowledge of the particular society as a frame of reference. An obvious example is the fact that in the United States the typical 14-year-old girl is a schoolgirl, while in a rural village in the Near East she may be the mother of two children. The significance of a given chronological age, or a given marker of life time, when viewed from a sociological or anthropological perspective, is a direct function of the social definition of age, or of *social time*.

B. Social Time

Social time refers to the dimension that underlies the age-grade system of a society. Anthropologists were the first to introduce the concept of age grading (see, e.g., Eisenstadt, 1956; Warner, 1958). It is characteristic in a preliterate society to have *rites-de-passage* marking the transition from one age status to the next, such as the passage from youth to maturity and to marriageability (Van Gennep, 1960). Only a rough parallel exists between social time and life time, for although in simple societies a girl may be considered marriageable when she reaches puberty, in a modern society she is not considered marriageable until long thereafter. In short, social timing is not synchronous with biological timing. There are also different sets of age expectations and age statuses in different societies, further demonstrating that neither chronological age (nor maturational stage) is itself the determinant of age status, but that it merely signifies the biological potentiality upon which a system of age norms and age grading can operate to shape the life cycle.

C. Historical Time

Historical time shapes the social system, and the social system, in turn, creates a changing set of age norms and a changing age-grade system which shapes the individual life cycle. Ariès (1962) has traced the social history of family life in Western society, suggesting that not until the seventeenth and eighteenth centuries, with the growth of industrialization, the formation of a middle class, and the appearance of formal educational institutions, did the concept emerge that childhood is a distinct phase of life, a period that has its specific characteristics and needs. The concept of adolescence as a distinctive period in the life cycle appeared in the twentieth century (Demos and Demos, 1969). Keniston (1970) has suggested that in the past few decades, when the speed of social change has been so great, a stage called youth, in which a new form of reconciliation of the self with the changing social order follows upon the earlier task of identity formation, can now be noted. Similarly, the period of middle age is a recently delineated stage in the life cycle resulting from the enormous increase in longevity that has occurred since the beginning of this century, together with the changing rhythm of the work cycle and the family cycle.

Historical time refers not only to long-term processes, such as industrialization and urbanization which create the social-cultural context and changing definitions of the phases of the life cycle. History is also a series of economic, political, and social events that directly influence the life course of the individuals who experience those events. The life cycle of an individual is shaped, then, by the long term historical processes of change that gradually alter social institutions; but the life cycle is also affected by discrete historical events. Some sense of the interplay between historical time and life time emerges if, for example, one considers World War II as it impinged on a young man, a child, or a young mother.

In the first case, a young man who becomes a soldier may achieve some resolution of masculine identity by taking on a highly stereotyped male role. In the second case, the child may go fatherless for the first few years of his life, with the attendant consequences for parental identification and oedipal resolution. In the third case, a mother whose husband has gone to war faces child rearing with reduced economic, physical, and psychological resources as she takes on both father's and mother's roles. This example merely illustrates the obvious point that the same historical event takes on very different psychological meanings depending on the point in the life cycle at which the event occurs.

Behavioral scientists have recognized the importance of the timing of major historical events in the life line of the individual, and *cohort analysis* (cf. Cain, 1967; Schaie, 1968) is a tool originally developed by demographers in an attempt to relate life time to historical time. A *cohort* is a group defined by calendar year of birth (a given year or some prescribed number of years). The characteristics of cohorts are analyzed in an attempt to explore *cohort effects,* that is, the effect of membership in a particular cohort with its unique background and demographic composition (cf. Riley, 1971; Riley *et al.,* 1972). For instance, Cain (1967) has presented sets of data to show that a historical "hinge" or "watershed" developed in America at the end of World War I with regard to levels of education, fertility patterns, sexual mores, reduction of hours in the work week, labor force participation patterns, and so on. This watershed produced a sharp contrast in life styles between the cohort of persons born before the turn of the century (persons who are presently over 70) and the cohort born after 1900 (persons who are now entering old age), with the results indicating that the needs of the new cohort of the aged will be very different from the needs of cohorts that preceded it. Another watershed probably occurred with the Great Depression of the 1930s.

It might be pointed out that cohort, like the dimension age, is in itself without psychological meaning, and that psychologists must eventually be able to specify the events that give meaning to cohort differences. For the present it is not known, except in the most general way, which historical events are more significant than other events in influencing the course of personality development over the life cycle—a problem which must somehow be resolved if cohort analysis is to become a powerful tool in analyzing life histories.

IV. Social Time and the Age Status Structure

The concepts of historical time and life time are well understood, even though they have not often been used in juxtaposition in studies undertaken by developmental psychologists. The concept of social time, on the other hand, probably needs fuller exposition.

Age grade systems are expressions of the fact that all societies rationalize the passage of life time, divide life time into socially relevant units, and thus can be said to transform calendar time (or biological time) into social time. As already noted, the concept of age grading comes from anthropological studies of simple societies where the life cycle may consist of a succession of formally age-graded, ascriptive roles: A male, for example, may pass from infancy to childhood to warrior-apprentice to warrior (and simultaneously to husband and father), and finally to elder, a status terminated by death. Age-strata and age-status systems emerge in all societies; and duties, rights, and rewards are differentially distributed to age groups which themselves have been socially defined. In societies where the division of labor is simple and the rate of social change is slow, a single age-grade system becomes formalized; and family, work, religious, and political roles are allocated and regulated accordingly. A modern complex society, by contrast, is characterized by plural systems of age status that become differentiated in relation to particular social institutions.

American society is characterized by a comparatively fluid and differentiated age-status system; yet despite its fluidity, and despite overlapping systems of age grading, there are some ascriptive age statuses that are systematically tied to chronological age, such as entry into school, age at eligibility to vote, age of legal responsibility, and so on.

The age-grade system institutionalizes cultural values and constitutes a social system that shapes the life cycle. Every society has a system of social expectations regarding age-appropriate behavior, and these expectations are internalized as the individual grows up and grows old, and as he moves from one age stratum to the next. There is a time when he is expected to go to work, to marry, a time to raise children, a time to retire, even a time to grow sick and to die.

As an example of the way in which age expectations are institutionalized, most children in American society must attend school between the ages of 6 and 16; at 18, they acquire the right to vote. This is to say that American society views a lengthy education as a prerequisite for adult responsibility; there are social institutions to provide this education; there is an age-grade and age-norm system that prevents the assumption of adult responsibilities—work, marriage, voting, legal liability—until compulsory education is ended. The total network of age-associated institutions is far more complex than this example can indicate, and the system of age grading is primarily consensual rather than formal, but the example serves to illustrate the close correspondence between age norms and age expectations on the one hand, and social and cultural values on the other.

That these concepts of social time, age grading, age status, and age norms refer to present-day social realities is demonstrated in a series of empirical studies by the first-named author begun over 15 years ago. Many of these studies remain unpublished, but it will be useful to draw upon them here in elaborating upon the concept of social time.

One of the first in this series of studies explored regularities in age expectations among adults. It was found that middle-aged people perceive adulthood as composed of four different life periods, each with its characteristic pattern of personal and social behavior: young adulthood, maturity, middle age, and old age (Neugarten and Paterson, 1957). Progression from one period to the next was described along one or more of five underlying dimensions of life: career line (e.g., major promotion, retirement), health and physical vigor, the family cycle (e.g., children entering school, children departing the family home), psychological attributes (e.g., "Middle age is when you become mellow"), or social responsibilities ("Old age is when you can take things easy and let others do the worrying").

From these data it was possible to delineate the first gross outline of an age structure and a system of age expectations that cross-cut various areas of adult life. There appears to be a set of social age definitions that provide a frame of reference by which the experiences of adult life are perceived as orderly and rhythmical. Although perceptions vary somewhat by age and sex, and especially by social class (for example, middle age and old age are seen as beginning earlier by working-class men and women than by middle-class), it was the high degree of consensus that was striking in these data.

Expectations regarding the timing of major life events can also be charted. Interviewees respond easily to questions such as: "What is the best age for a man to marry?"; or "the best age to become a grandmother?" and they readily give chronological ages for phrases such as: "a mature woman"; or "when a man should hold his top job." Moreover, there is widespread consensus on items such as these that deal with the timing of work and family events, attitudes, and psychological characteristics. There also appears to be a prescriptive timetable by which major events are ordered along the individual's life line, and consensual definition of the chronological ages that correspond to phases in the life span. For example, most middle-class men and women agreed that a man is young between 18 and 22, middle-aged between 40 and 50, and old between 65 and 75; and that men have the most responsibilities between 35 and 50. Youth, middle age, and old age were similarly defined for women, but women are seen as moving through major phases of the life line earlier than men (Neugarten, Moore, and Lowe, 1965). There is greater consensus regarding age-appropriate behavior for women than for men; and greater consensus regarding age expectations for the period of young adulthood, as if the normative system bears more heavily on individuals as they enter adulthood than when they move on to successive phases of maturity and old age.

V. Age Norms as a System of Social Control

If the system of age expectations is a normative one, as hypothesized, then it should be more or less compelling for everybody; that is, individuals should feel some degree of social pressure to conform to expectations. One of the ways this issue was pursued was to ask to what extent an individual is consistent in meeting various age norms. The data were examined to identify persons who fell at the extremes of the age distribution on an early life event—for instance, men who had married comparatively early or late—and to see to what extent these persons maintained an early or late position relative to their own social class group on successive life events. Although these data are spotty thus far, the size of the sample precludes statistical testing, in examining individual cases it was observed that early or late individuals move toward the norm on the next major event in the life line. The implication is, then, that there is a "pull" in the age system, just as there is in other normative systems, so that individuals who are age-deviant on one event tend to move back toward the norm on the next event.

Individuals themselves are aware of age norms and age expectations in relation to their own patterns of timing. In adults of varying ages, it has been found that every

person can report immediately whether he was "late," "early," or "on time," on one
life event after another (e.g., "I married early," or "I was late getting started, because
of the Depression"). This high degree of awareness of timing has been interpreted as
further evidence that age expectations form a normative system, that social definitions of age are commonly accepted and meaningful, and that patterns of timing
play an important role with respect to self-concept and self-esteem.

Another question relates to the process of socialization by which age norms are
learned. Respondents have been asked how their ideas about age norms originated,
but people seem to take age-norms so much for granted that they are unable to describe their learning experiences. One conclusion has been that the norms are probably learned in such a wide range of contexts and are so imbedded in experience that
it is not feasible to attempt to disentangle the socialization experiences by direct
questioning.

It may be reasoned, however, that if a normative system is operating, people are
probably aware of the sanctions in the system and are sensitive to social approval and
disapproval. Attempts to explore this question through a study of individuals who
were "off-time" in major life events convinced the investigators that age deviancy is
always of psychological significance to the individual, even though a systematic elu-
cidation has not yet been achieved of the mechanisms involved in the social sanctioning of age deviancy.

Another research approach has permitted some inferences about age norms as a
system of social constraints. Such questions as these were asked:

> Would you approve of a woman who decides to have another child at 40? at 35?
> at 30?
> What about a couple who moved across the country to live near their married
> children when they are 40? 55? 75?

In analyzing responses to such items, a significant increase with age has been found
in the extent to which respondents attach importance to age norms and view age appropriateness as a constraint upon behavior. It can be inferred then, that the middle-
aged and the old, who see greater constraints in the age-norm system than do the
young, have learned that to be off-time with regard to major life events entails negative consequences, and that, therefore, age and age appropriateness are reasonable
criteria by which to evaluate behavior. The young, by contrast, tend to deny that age
is a valid criterion by which to judge behavior (Neugarten *et al.*, 1965).

These studies illustrate the point that the age-status structure of a society, age-
group identifications, the internalization of age norms, and age norms as a network
of social controls are important dimensions of the social and cultural context in
which the life course must be viewed. Many of the major punctuation marks of the

life cycle are not only orderly and sequential, but many are social rather than biological in nature, and their timing is socially regulated. These concepts point to one way of structuring the passage of time in the life span of the individual; and in delineating a social time clock that can be superimposed upon the biological clock, these concepts are helpful in comprehending the life cycle.

VI. AGE STRATIFICATION

A complementary perspective on the dimension of age emerges from the literature on age stratification in society. Mannheim (1952b) and more recently, Riley and her associates (Riley, 1971; Riley *et al.*, 1972) have viewed the study of the age structure of society along two dimensions: the life course dimension; and the historical dimension, seen as coordinates for locating the individual in the age structure of society.

The life course dimension is roughly indexed by chronological age which serves as an indicator of the individual's experience, including age-related organic changes affecting physical and mental functioning, and including the probability of certain psychological and social experiences. The historical dimension includes the political, social, and cultural changes in society. In Riley's view, integration of these two dimensions provides a perspective on the life course, and the concept of cohort is a link between the two dimensions.

In Mannheim's concept of a generation, he bridges historical time and life time. Mannheim suggested that the sociological significance of generations is predicated upon, but not defined by, the rhythm of the biological succession of generations. Individuals sharing the same year of birth are endowed with a potentially common location in "the historical dimension of the social process." A common year of birth does not in itself constitute a similarity of location: rather, a generation by its date of birth is limited to a particular range of possible experiences. Similarity of location results from the fact that a particular generation, or what we now call age cohort, experiences the same events at the same points in the life cycle, and thus "these experiences impinge upon a similarly stratified consciousness" (Mannheim, 1952b, p. 310). The sense of belonging to a generation is only a *potentiality* based upon the biological succession of generations. Furthermore, "whether a new *generation style* emerges every year, every thirty, every hundred years, or whether it emerges rhythmically at all, depends entirely on the trigger action of the social and cultural process" (Mannheim, 1952b, p. 310). Mannheim thus moves from the historical context to the level of individual consciousness by the intervening concepts of "generations" and "generational consciousness."

Riley (1971), using Mannheim's dimensions of historical time and life time, deals with the effect of the process of aging on the social structure of society. After describing a society as a structure composed of age strata, her concern is the sociology of age stratification as the expression of the rhythm of generations. Following Mannheim's conceptualization, each cohort by the fact of its year of birth is limited to a certain range of experience; and the consequence is that when, at a given point in time, individuals of varying age levels are studied, they differ in ways that cannot be accounted for solely on the basis of aging. Instead, each age stratum has its distinctive subculture which is the product of the historical events the individuals experience at a particular period in their lives.

At any point in time, then, society consists of a set of age strata each of which is characterized by its own pattern of labor force participation, consumer behavior, leisure-time activities, marital status, religious behavior, education, nativity, fertility, and childbearing practices. Differences (or similarities) between age strata are to be understood on the two dimensions of life course and historical change.

Both Mannheim and Riley, then, are concerned with only two of the three time dimensions under discussion here, and both of them link historical time to life time by the use of such intermediary concepts as generation and age cohort. The relations between historical time and life time can be better understood, however, if social time is added as a third interrelated dimension and if age statuses and age norms can be seen as forming a social-psychological system that stands parallel to the age-stratification structure.

The conceptual framework put forward here, then, might be restated as follows: The age-stratification structure described by Riley and the age-status structure as described in the present paper can be seen as descriptions of two types of sociological reality. Age norms as a system of social control can be seen as a description of social-psychological reality. All three are based upon age as a dimension of social organization; and all three imply that an individual can be located within an age structure and that his behavior is controlled by the age system of which he is part. Similarly, in turning from concepts of social structure to dimensions of time, historical time and life time need to be complemented by the dimension of social time. In moving from the socio-historical context to the form and content of the life cycle, and in considering the psychological significance of historical events, social time and social age become particularly useful as intermediary concepts. The effects of historical events upon the individual can be said to be "filtered" through the age-status system. For example, the effect of World War II upon an 18-year-old man is different from its effect upon a 25-year-old man not only because the second, having lived longer, is different biologically from the first, but because he is different sociologically from the first. The two individuals have been socially "placed" in different age strata; they have different age statuses, and the age-related expectations of behavior that are binding upon them are different.

Some of these points will emerge again in the following illustration of how historical time, social time, and life time are intertwined in the currently changing rhythm of the life cycle.

VII. The Changing Rhythm of the Life Cycle

As American society has changed from agrarian to industrialized, from small town to metropolis, there have been corresponding changes in the social definitions of age groups, in age norms, and in relations between age groups. Only a few aspects of the changing rhythm of the life cycle will be described here to show how major life events are now differently timed and to indicate that the difference in timing is an accompaniment of underlying biological, social, and economic changes in the society. (Much of this section is taken from Neugarten and Moore, 1968.)

Medical advances are among the many factors that have led to growth and redistribution of the population, with presently high proportions of the young and the old, due in turn to reductions in infant mortality and to a striking increase in longevity. Technological change and urbanization have created alterations in the economic system and the family system which are superimposed upon this changing biological base. One result is a new rhythm of life timing and aging.

Concepts of social age and age status are readily illustrated within the institution of the family. The points along the life line at which the individual moves from "child" to "adolescent" to "adult" are socially defined, although they are timed in relation to biological development. After physical maturity is reached, social age continues to be marked off by relatively clear-cut biological or social events in the family cycle. Thus, marriage marks the beginning of one social age period, as does the appearance of the first child, the departure of children from the home, and the birth of the first grandchild. At each stage, the individual takes on new roles and his prestige is altered in relation to other family members.

As shown by the data for women in Table 7.1, changes in timing in the family cycle have been dramatic over the past several decades as age at marriage has dropped, as children are born earlier in the marriage and are spaced closer together, and as longevity of both sexes, and consequently the duration of marriage has increased. (The data for men show parallel trends. In 1890, the median age at marriage for men was 26; at birth of first child, 36; at marriage of last child, 59; at widowhood, 57. In 1959, the respective median ages were 22, 28, 49, and 66.)

Changes in work patterns have been even more dramatic (see Fig. 7.1). In 1890 less than 30% of all women at age 20 were in the labor force, and this was the highest percentage for any age group. The proportions dropped by age, so that at age 50 only about 12% were workers. But by 1966, womens' participation in the labor force had increased so dramatically that over 50% of all 20-year-old women were working.

Table 7.1. Changes in the Timing of Life Events[a]

Median age at:	1890	1966
Leaving school	14	18
Marriage	22	20
Birth of first child	24–25	21
Birth of last child	32	26
Death of husband	53	64
Marriage of last child	55	48
Death	68	78

[a] Data are taken from Glick, Heer, and Beresford, 1963. The entries in the table do not, of course, represent the same women, but various groups of women at each of the two calendar years. The timing of future events for, say, women who in 1966 were marrying at average age 20 cannot be directly extrapolated from the table. At the same time, the interpretation of these data may be seen as a quickening family cycle over calendar time. This is but another instance in which developmental psychologists draw longitudinal inferences from cross-sectional data.

The percentage dropped off only a little among 30-year-olds, and then rose again so that over 50% of all 50-year-old women were in the labor force.

Historically, then, the family cycle has quickened as marriage, parenthood, empty nest (and grandparenthood) all occur earlier. The trend is toward a more rapid rhythm of events through most of the family cycle, then an extended interval (now some 16 years) when husband and wife are the remaining members of the household. Widowhood occurs much later, and the life span for women has lengthened enormously.

These general trends are not expected to be reversed, even though today a slight upturn in age of marriage (in 1972, it was 20.8 rather than 20.2 for women), more unmarried families, more communal and other experimental forms of family life may be noted. While the family cycle runs its course a few years later for women at higher-than-average levels of education, the general pattern of historical change just described is the same for both highly-educated and poorly-educated women.

Over the past 80 years, an interesting and important difference has been developing between men and women with respect to the timing of family and work cycles. Marriage no longer signifies that the man is ready to be the breadwinner. With the needs of the American economy for technical and professional workers, the length of time devoted to education has increased for more and more young persons, but there has not been an accompanying delay of marriage. In 1966 of all men attending college or graduate school, nearly one in four was married (for those men aged 25–29, it was nearly three out of four) as was one of every seven women.

The accompanying phenomenon is the young wife who works to support her husband through school. The changing sex-role patterns are reflected in the rising

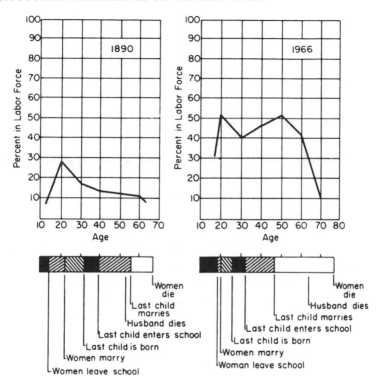

FIG. 7.1. Work in relation to significant stages in the lives of women. [From Neugarten (Ed.), *Middle age and aging: A reader in social psychology.* Chicago: The University of Chicago Press, 1968. © 1968 by The University of Chicago. *Sources:* National Manpower Council, *Womanpower* (New York: Columbia University Press, 1957), p. 307. Right-hand portion of figure has been revised based on labor-force data taken from *1967 Manpower Report,* U.S. Department of Labor, Table A-2, p. 202, and on family cycle data taken from Glick, Heer, and Beresford, 1963, p. 12.]

proportion of young married women in the labor force: In 1890, it was only 6% of those aged 14–24; in 19690, it was 31%. While these percentages reflect marriages in which husbands are working as well as those in which husbands are still in school, they show in both instances not only that young wives are increasingly sharing the economic burdens of new households, but also that women are doing so at younger and younger ages. Thus, the age of economic maturity has been deferred for men, but not for women. It has become socially acceptable for men to reverse the traditional sequence of events, and for family maturity to precede rather than to follow economic maturity.

Furthermore, men's work life has been shortened over the past decades as young

men are increasingly delayed from entering the labor force (at technical and professional levels, because of increased length of education; at lower occupational levels,
because of the diminishing need for unskilled workers) and as older men are increasingly retiring at younger ages (for men over 65, only one of four is now in the labor
force). In short, the trend for men is to be older when they start to work, and younger
when they retire. Women still spend much less time in the labor force than men, on
the average, but the historical trend for women is the opposite—women are younger
when they start to work; they work much longer than before, whether or not they are
married and whether or not they have children; and they are older when they retire.

The new rhythms of social maturity impinge also upon other aspects of family
life. Parent-child relationships are influenced in many subtle ways by the fact that
half of all new fathers in the 1960s were under 23 and half of all new mothers under
21. Changes in parental behavior, with fathers reportedly becoming less authoritarian and with both parents sharing more equally in tasks of homemaking and childrearing, may reflect, in part, this increased youthfulness. It is the relative youth of
both parents and grandparents, furthermore, that may be contributing to the complex patterns of help between generations in the family that are now becoming evident, including the widespread financial help that flows from parents downward to
their adult children. Similarly, with more grandparents surviving per child, and with
an extended family system that encompasses several generations, new patterns of
child-rearing are emerging in which child–grandparent relations may be taking on
changing significance.

VIII. Toward a Social Psychology of the Life Cycle

Changes in the life cycle, such as those just described, have their effects upon personality, and it is likely that the personalities of successive age cohorts will, therefore,
be different in measurable ways, especially if the sociologist's view of personality is
adopted. (This is not the occasion to discuss varying conceptions of personality, except to acknowledge their great diversity, and to suggest that from most points of
view, including those of psychoanalysis and ego psychology, social change can be expected to have at least some systematic effects upon personality development.) It
nevertheless remains for future personality psychologists to turn attention to the interplay between history and personality, as indicated at the outset of this chapter, and
to undertake empirical studies that will elucidate, for example, the changes in self-
concepts, the sense of efficacy, and even the balance between the rational and the impulsive components of personality as these are affected by the changing social
context.

Developmental theorists are lacking, as yet, an overarching theory of development over the life cycle. In part, this is so because we have not fully recognized the complex interplay between maturational sequences and social-cultural forces, and have often tended to view the latter as complications that "obscure" the invariant sequence of developmental change. What is needed is to view maturational change as only one of the major components of development, and to forego the constraining analogy that compels us to search only for corresponding invariant timetables of psychological change. The present authors are not, of course, the first to argue that the specific historical context is as valid a frame of reference for the study of the development of personality as is the maturational timetable, and that both are required. The point can be stated more accurately: namely, the task is to study sequences of change for the purpose of determining *which ones* are primarily developmental (in the sense of being tied to maturational change), and *which ones* are primarily situational—if, indeed, this distinction can be made at all.

For example, how will life-cycle change and social change be related in the life course of present-day youth, a problem that is as current as this morning's headlines and as relevant as any to which the developmental psychologist can address himself? As this chapter is being written, the morning newspaper carries a story about high school radicals and the fact that by the time they reach college they seem to have exhausted their political energies—that is, the "little brother" about whom the campus radical used to warn us only a year or two ago seems already to have burned out and to be leading a more conventional life as a college student than his big brother. What is the relation of *timing* and commitment to social causes, and the relation of both to personality development? What does it mean to become an activist at 15, as compared to 20, or 45?

Shall we re-examine our earlier views that extremism and idealism among the young are an accompaniment of underlying biological change? Why was it the 20-year-old who was the activist in 1968, the 15-year-old in 1970, but neither in 1972? And what difference will it make to the particular individuals by the time they reach middle age?

To make another example, what are the changes in the personalities of women that may be anticipated as the accompaniment of the women's liberation movement? Specifically, what are the effects if the woman is young and is choosing to postpone marriage and childbearing, perhaps to forego them altogether, as compared to the effects if the woman is 40 and engaged in that period of self-evaluation whose outcome will determine the course of her old age?

Obviously the relations of life time, social time, and historical time pose enormously complicated questions, but it is precisely this complexity to which students of the life cycle should be willing to address themselves.

References

Antonovsky, A., Maoz, B., Datan, N., and Wijsenbeek, H. Twenty-five years later: A limited study of sequelae of the concentration camp experience. *Social Psychiatry,* 1971, **6**, 186–193.

Aries, P. *Centuries of childhood.* New York: Random House, 1962.

Baer, D. M. An age-irrelevant concept of development. *Merrill-Palmer Quarterly,* 1970, **16**, 230–245.

Baltes, P. B., and Goulet, L. R. Exploration of developmental variables by manipulation and simulation of age differences in behavior. *Human Development,* 1971, **14**, 149–170.

Benedict, R. Continuities and discontinuities on cultural conditioning. *Psychiatry,* 1938, **1**, 161–167.

Brim, O. G., and Wheeler, S. *Socialization after childhood: Two essays.* New York: Wiley, 1966.

Cain, L. D., Jr. Age status and generational phenomena: The new old people in contemporary America. *Gerontologist,* 1967, 7, 83–92.

Clausen, J. A. (Ed.) *Socialization and society.* Boston: Little, Brown and Company, 1968.

Demos, J., and Demos, V. Adolescence in historical perspective. *Journal of Marriage and the Family,* 1969, **31**, 632–638.

Eisenstadt, S. N. *From generation to generation: Age groups and social structure.* Glencoe, Illinois: Free Press, 1956.

Elder, G. H., Jr. *Children of the great depression.* New York: Markham Press, 1973, in press.

Erikson, E. H. *Childhood and society.* New York: Norton, 1950, 1963.

Erikson, E. H. *The young man Luther.* New York: Norton, 1958.

Erikson, E. H. Identity and the life cycle. *Psychological Issues,* 1959, **1**, Whole No. 1.

Erikson, E. H. *Gandhi's truth on the origins of militant nonviolence.* New York: Norton, 1969.

Freud, S. *Moses and monotheism.* Translated by K. Jones. New York: Knopf, 1939.

Glick, P. C., Heer, D. M., and Beresford, J. C. Family formation and family composition: Trends and prospects. In M. B. Sussman (Ed.), *Sourcebook in marriage and the family.* New York: Houghton-Mifflin, 1963.

Goslin, D. A. (Ed.) *Handbook of socialization theory and research.* Chicago: Rand McNally, 1969.

Inkeles, A. Social structure and socialization. In D. A. Goslin (Ed.), *Handbook of socialization theory and research.* Chicago: Rand McNally, 1969.

Keniston, K. Youth as a stage of life. *The American Scholar,* 1970, **39**, 631–654.

LeVine, R. A. Culture, personality, and socialization: An evolutionary view. In D. A. Goslin (Ed.), *Handbook of socialization theory and research.* Chicago: Rand McNally, 1969.

Looft, William R. Socialization and personality throughout the lifespan: An examination of contemporary psychological approaches. In P. B. Baltes and K. W. Schaie (Eds.), *Lifespan Developmental Psychology: Personality and Socialization.* New York: Academic Press, 1973.

Maas, H. Long term effects of early childhood separation and group care. *Vita Humana,* 1963, **6,** 34–56.

Mannheim, K. The problem of generations. In K. Mannheim (Ed.), *Essays on the sociology of knowledge.* New York: Oxford University Press, 1952.

Neugarten, B. L. *Middle age and aging: A reader in social psychology.* Chicago: University of Chicago Press, 1968.

Neugarten, B. L., and Moore, J. W. The changing age-status system. In B. L. Neugarten (Ed.), *Middle age and aging: A reader in social psychology.* Chicago: University of Chicago Press, 1968.

Neugarten, B. L., Moore, J. W., and Lowe, J. C. Age norms, age constraints, and adult socialization. *American Journal of Sociology,* 1965, **70,** 710–717.

Neugarten, B. L., and Paterson, W. A. A study of the American age-grade system. In *Proceedings of the Fourth Congress of the International Association of Gerontology,* Vol. 3, 1957.

Parsons, T., and Shils, E. A. The social system. In T. Parsons and E. A. Shils (Eds.), *Toward a general theory of action.* Cambridge: Harvard University Press, 1951.

Riley, M. W. Social gerontology and the age stratification of society. *Gerontologist,* 1971, **11,** 79–87.

Riley, M. W., Johnson, M. E., and Foner, A. (Eds.). *Aging and society: A sociology of age stratification.* Vol. 3. New York: Russell Sage, 1972.

Schaie, K. W. Age changes and age differences. In B. L. Neugarten (Ed.), *Middle age and aging: A reader in social psychology.* Chicago: University of Chicago Press, 1968.

Van Gennep, A. *The rites of passage.* Chicago: University of Chicago Press, 1960.

Warner, W. L. *A black civilization.* New York: Harper and Row, 1958.

Wohlwill, J. F. The age variable in psychological research. *Psychological Review,* 1970, **77,** 49–64.

EIGHT

Time, Age, and the Life Cycle

In considering the relationships between time, age, and the life cycle, it is timely to focus on adulthood and, more particularly, on the second half of life, for our society is now an aging society with increasing proportions of persons over age 50. As the current large numbers of young people, the fruits of the baby boom, move into middle age our society will become, for the first time in history, not a youthful but a mature society.

In the 1940s and 1950s when social and behavioral scientists first turned their attention to the growing numbers of older people, they defined the aged as a problem group, and professionals such as social workers and physicians became preoccupied with the unmet needs of this group. Stereotypes of the aged were based on images of the *needy* aged, that minority of poor, sick, isolated, or desolate persons who require a wide array of supportive services. However, as research findings began to multiply and as more representative samples of older people were studied, both social scientists and professionals began to take a broader view, to acknowledge the enormous diversity of lifestyles among the middle aged and the old, and to see the diversity of patterns of successful aging. They came to recognize that the characteristics of people who will become old in future decades are very different from those of people who are currently old. The stereotypes have therefore crumbled, and we have before us now a more realistic picture of old age.

About 20 years ago gerontologists began to ask about the antecedents of different patterns of old age, to focus on the processes of aging rather than on the aged, and to extend their studies downward is the life cycle. At about the same time child psychologists who had been conducting longitudinal studies of infants and children found themselves following their study populations upward into adulthood. Both groups of investigators joined up in the middle, and there is now a growing interest in the whole life cycle as the unit for study.

Originally presented as an invited lecture at the 131st annual meeting of the American Psychiatric Association, Atlanta, GA, May 8–12, 1978. Reprinted by permission from *American Journal of Psychiatry* 136, no. 7 (July 1979): 887–94.

One of the consequences has been that the views of developmental psychologists are changing. As Clarke and Clarke (1), among many others, have made it clear, it is no longer sufficient to say that the child is father of the man, momentous as that discovery has been. We say, instead, that psychological change is continuous throughout the life cycle and, further, that the psychological realities of adulthood and aging are not to be understood merely by projecting forward the issues that are salient in childhood (2).

Illustrative of the growing interest in adult development are three new scholarly books that have appeared in the last two years. *The Seasons of a Man's Life*, by Levinson and his associates at Yale (3), advances a descriptive framework in which men progress through a series of invariant life eras or stages as they move from early adulthood into middle and late adulthood, with each stage marked off by specific chronological ages. Levinson's group drew on Erikson's stages of ego development, but rather than focusing on the changes that occur within the person, they focused on the concept of life structure and the boundary between self and the interpersonal world.

The second book is *Adaptation to Life*, by Vaillant (4), who studied the longitudinal data accumulated on men followed from the time they were freshmen at Harvard through their mid 40s. This book also fits Erikson's general framework, but it focuses directly on processes of adaptation. Its central thesis is that adaptive styles mature over time, that this maturation is more dependent on development from within than on changes in the interpersonal environment, and that change is continuous rather than stepwise. While not all men show the same rate of development, the change is always unidirectional, with movement forward but not backward.

The third book, edited by Erikson and called *Adulthood* (5), asks whether the earlier historical obsession with childhood and adolescence may now be giving way to "the century of the adult." The book contains a number of papers by authors from different disciplines who approach the topic in very different ways, but most of them ask how various civilizations and religions have defined maturity.

The mass media, having earlier discovered old age, have now also discovered adulthood. Thus *Passages* (6) has just been followed by *Transformations* (7), and other books with similar titles are on the way. Distorting the situation somewhat as perhaps they must do within the constraints of their occupation, journalists have given adulthood the treatment of high drama. They are making news by promoting the midlife crisis or the midlife transition as if it were life's greatest trauma, and there has now appeared the misbegotten term "middlescence." Such exaggeration and distortion notwithstanding, there is a growing public awareness that adulthood is as complex, as dynamic, and, at least in some important ways, as amenable to change as is childhood or youth.

It should be noted that the empirical studies now available are few in number and based on small samples, usually of middle-class men. Levinson's study, important as it is, is based on only 40 men; Vaillant's, on only 95; and we have no comparable study of women. The public should not be too quick to presume that the regularities or, for that matter, the dramatic transitions define what is normal and that the person who has not experienced them is somehow off the track. Many psychologists feel that the mass media's coverage of this subject has come too soon, is based on too few data, and, as will be elaborated below, that we should be wary of the too-quick generalizations regarding the midlife crisis or concepts of adult stages. Furthermore, we are not likely soon to have a Dr. Spock of adulthood, for the course of adult change is too complex and the individual differences are too great for any how-to-do-it book.

TIME AND TIMING

As people think about the life cycle, they use common markers and refer to a succession of life periods. In all societies the differences between children, adults, and the aged have been recognized and rationalized; and unique characteristics and behaviors have been ascribed to each age group. In our own society, life periods have become increasingly differentiated. Historians have pointed out that childhood did not become a discernible period of life until the 17th and 18th centuries (8); adolescence was a social invention of the late 19th century; and only within the last few decades, as the transition from childhood to adulthood has become even more prolonged, a new period of "youth" has emerged (9). Middle age has recently become distinguished from young adulthood, and now the young-old are being distinguished from the old-old. The young-old are a rapidly growing group of retirees and their spouses who are physically and mentally vigorous and whose major characteristic is new leisure time. They are relatively healthy people, relatively comfortable financially, increasingly well-educated, politically active, and they are important consumers of goods and services. This is a new age-group in history, with a sizable proportion who are becoming the first real leisure class of America. They are people who seek interesting ways to use their time, both for self-fulfillment and for contributing to their communities, and they currently represent an underused resource in our society (10).

Whether the life cycle is perceived as consisting of 3, 6, or 10 periods, individuals develop a concept of the "normal, expectable life cycle," a set of anticipations that certain life events will occur at certain times, and a mental clock telling them where they are and whether they are on time or off time. People talk easily about these clocks. They readily tell an interviewer what they regard as the best age to marry, to have a child, to become a grandmother, when a man should be settled in his career, when he should have reached the top, when he should retire, and even what personality characteristics ought to be salient in successive age periods (for instance, it is appropriate to be impulsive in adolescence, but not in middle age). People will also readily report whether they themselves are on time, and if not, why not.

Being on time or off time is a compelling basis for self-assessment. Men and women compare themselves with their friends, siblings, work colleagues, or parents in deciding whether they have made good, but it is always with a time line in mind. It is not the fact that one reaches 40, 50, or 60 which is itself important, but rather, "How am I doing for my age?"

From this perspective it can be argued that the normal and expectable life events are not themselves life crises. Leaving the parents' home, marriage, parenthood, occupational achievement, one's own children leaving home, the climacteric, grandparenthood, retirement—these are the normal turning points, the punctuation marks along the life line. They call forth changes in self-concept and identity, but whether or not they produce crises depends on their timing. For instance, for the majority of middle-aged women the departure of children is not a crisis. It is, instead, when children do *not* leave home on time that a crisis is created for both parent and child. For an increasingly large proportion of men retirement is a normal, expectable event. Even death is a normal and expectable event for the old. Death is tragic only when it occurs at too young an age. Even the death of one's spouse, if it occurs on time, does not create a psychiatric crisis for most men or women.

This observation is not to deny that the expectable life event precipitates crisis reactions in some persons; neither is it meant to deny that some—but by no means all—of the major life events that occur in middle or old age are losses to the individual and that grief is their accompaniment. Yet most such events, when they occur on time, have been anticipated and rehearsed, the grief work completed, and the reconciliation accomplished without shattering the sense of continuity of the life cycle or the individual's coping strategies.

Age norms and age expectations are reflections of socially defined time and timing, and social timing is important in understanding adaptational patterns. In times of rapid social change age norms also change, and the rhythm of the life cycle is altered. In modern America biological timing has been changing: for example, puberty comes earlier than before for both sexes, and although the data are less clear-cut, the climacteric comes later for women; the most dramatic biological change of all is that most people now live into old age. (Because highly educated people live longer than the average, those readers of this paper who have reached 65, especially the women, can look forward to reaching 80 or 85. Younger readers can expect to live even longer.)

It is not only biological timing that has become different; social timing is also changing. Entry into the labor market comes later for men as education lengthens;

but exit from the labor market comes earlier as the age of retirement drops (and is expected to continue to drop for a least the next few decades). The age of marriage has been earlier (until the last 2 or 3 years when it has taken a slight upturn); and while an increasing number of young women, especially the highly educated, are postponing marriage and parenthood, the large majority marry earlier than their grandmothers, have a first child earlier, and have fewer children spaced closer together. In turn, grandparenthood has been coming earlier. But widowhood has been coming later, and there is now a period of nearly 15 years after children leave home when husband and wife are alone in the household, a period we awkwardly refer to as the empty nest. This is a new phenomenon historically—as is true of the increasingly frequent appearance of great-grandparenthood.

There are also changes in the rhythm of the life cycle for the increasing number of men and women who are marrying, divorcing, and then remarrying, and, most striking in young women, for the number who are rearing children first in two-parent, then one-parent, and then in two-parent households. There are increasing numbers of women and men who enter and reenter the labor force, change jobs, undertake new careers, or return to school.

All of this adds up to what Hirschhorn (11) has called the "fluid" life cycle, one marked by an increasing number of role transitions and by the disappearance of traditional timetables, or what may also be described as the proliferation of timetables and the lack of synchrony among age-related roles. Some observers are impressed with other idiosyncrasies in timing: with the "renewal" activities represented, for example, by the middle-aged or old person who becomes a college freshman or the persons who enter May-December marriages and begin new families, with the occasional result that a man may become a father again at the same time he becomes a grandfather.

While there are few studies in which this social change has actually been measured, our society is becoming accustomed to the 28-year-old mayor, the 30-year-old college president, the 35-year-old grandmother, the 50-year-old retiree, the 65-year-old father of a preschooler, and the 70-year-old student, and even the 85-year-old mother caring for a 65-year-old son.

To what extent this new age-irrelevant society is actually affecting the mental health of adults is debatable. Nevertheless, because questions of timing are central to the individual's self-concept, especially to the middle-aged as they take stock of their lives, changing age-norms and changing timetables are significant for the psychiatrist who sees the patient struggling to decide what is age-appropriate or what it means to act one's age.

Whatever the effects on mental health, if the interpretation is accurate that lives are becoming more varied and more fluid, that major life events and major role transitions are becoming more irregular, that age is becoming less relevant and age norms less limiting, then it is of doubtful value to describe adulthood as an invariant sequence of stages, each occurring at a given chronological age.

PSYCHOLOGICAL PREOCCUPATIONS IN ADULTHOOD

Turning to a different level of observation, whatever the changes in timing of discrete life events, is there an imperative of psychological change in the life cycle, a predictable sequence of developmental tasks and preoccupations that become salient as people grow up, grow old, and die?

Young Adulthood

We are accustomed to thinking that in adolescence the major psychological task is identity formation, and that in youth it is to make a comfortable fit between the self and society and to prepare a script for one's life.

In young adulthood the emergent issues are usually described as those related to intimacy, parenthood, and to meeting the expectations of the world of work. The major tasks are to achieve a balance between settling down and moving forward; growing new roots while striving for achievement; meeting new obligations, especially toward spouse and children; and investing oneself in the lives of a few significant others to whom one will be bound for years to come, while at the same time achieving individuation, competency, and job mastery.

The transitions into major family and work roles are coming closer together in time and creating problems for both sexes. The women's movement has brought new role conflicts for women who simultaneously pursue work careers and mothering careers and for men who seek new liberations and new combinations of roles as workers, fathers, and homemakers. It is often said that the task for the young adult is to undertake one's anticipated life script while accepting the reality that the script will be continually altered in ways that cannot be predicted and that can only partially be controlled.

Middle Age

In middle age the psychological issues are described in different terms (12). Some relate to new family roles: the reworking of relationships between husbands and wives, with new expectations of what it means to be male or female; the changing sense of self as children grow up and as one's victories and defeats are reckoned by how well the child is turning out: the need to quickly establish an intimate relationship with a stranger when a son-in-law or daughter-in-law appears; for increasing numbers of middle-aged people, the need to adjust quickly to a child's divorce; the appearance of a grandchild, who brings a new awareness of aging but also a new source of gratification; and the awareness of the self as the bridge between the generations.

There are also the responsibilities and concerns over the welfare of the aging parent, which can be called "parent-caring." One recent study (13) has indicated that it is not marriage, parenthood, grandparenthood, the climacteric, or the empty nest, but parent-caring that is becoming the major problem in the area of family life and a major source of life stress.

Some of the issues of middle age relate not to the creation of biological heirs but to the creation of social heirs. These include the need to nurture and to act as model, guide, or mentor to the young; the care not to overstep the delicate boundaries of authority; and the uncertainties over the use of one's power—in short, the awareness of being the socializer rather than the socialized.

Other themes relate to occupational life and the concerns over moving up, moving down, reaching a plateau, or hanging on. For women there is the often-described sense of new freedom, increased time and energy available when children leave home, freedom from fear of unwanted pregnancy, and, for many, the new pleasure in sexual relations that accompanies the menopause. At the same time, for many of their husbands there is concern over increased job pressure or, equally troublesome, job boredom and the feeling of being stuck in a rut that is to be found among the successful as well as the unsuccessful.

Other issues of middle age relate to the increased stocktaking, the heightened introspection and reflection that become characteristic of the mental life; the sense of being in the prime of life in terms of one's experience and good judgment, and on the other hand, the sense of being newly vulnerable. The personalization of death brings with it, for women, the rehearsal for widowhood, and for men, the rehearsal of the heart attack. For both sexes there is the realization that the body is less predictable than before, and there is new attention to body-monitoring.

Middle age is said to bring with it a changing time perspective. Time becomes restructured in terms of time left to live instead of time since birth. It is not that 50 or 60 years have passed, but the question, how many years lie ahead? What is yet to be accomplished, and what might best be abandoned?

The changing time perspective is not necessarily depressing. One person put it well: "Time is now a two-edged sword. To some of my friends, it acts as a brake; to others, as a prod. It adds a certain anxiety, but I must also say it adds a certain zest in seeing how much pleasure can still be obtained, how many good years one can still plan for, how many new activities can be undertaken. . . ."

Old Age

In old age some old and some new issues arise. Some are related to renunciation: adapting to losses of work, friends, and spouse; the yielding of a position of authority and the questioning of one's former competences; the reconciliations with significant others and with one's achievements and failures; the resolution of grief over the death of others and of the approaching death of self; the maintenance of a sense of integrity in terms of what one has been, rather than what one is; and the concern over legacy and how to leave traces of oneself.

In old age there are also the triumphs of survivorship; the recognition that one has savored a wide range of experiences and therefore "knows about life" in ways no younger person can know; the knowledge that in having lived through physical and psychological pain, one recovers and can deal also with the contingencies that lie ahead; and a sense that one is now the possessor and conservator of the eternal truths.

The preoccupation with time and the time left to live loses some of its poignancy. Dependency and deterioration, not death itself, is the specter of old age. In the innermost parts of the mind the acceptance of one's own death may be, as Freud said, impossible to contemplate (14), yet the old person seems relatively free to talk about death and to express concern not over the fact that death will come, but about the manner in which it will come. And there is, for many if not most, a sense of peace as much as protest, for despite Dylan Thomas' urging, only a few "go raging into that good night . . ." (15, p. 128).

Discussion

These are only some of the themes that enliven the years of adulthood and that call forth a continually changing sense of self and a changing set of adaptations. With the passage of time, life becomes more, not less, complex; it becomes enriched, not impoverished.

The psychological issues mentioned here are the things people talk about to their friends and their spouses, to a sympathetic interviewer, and especially to the psychiatrist. They are the threads that individuals work and rework into the pattern of their lives, like threads of a tapestry. Present in awareness, they are the stuff of which memories are made, the past is reinvented, and the future is planned.

At the same time that the themes of adulthood are usually described in sequential order, as in the preceding paragraphs, they do not in truth emerge at only given moments in life, each to be resolved and then put behind as if they were beads on a chain. Identity is made and remade; issues of intimacy and freedom and commitment to significant others, the pressures of time, the reformulation of life goals, stocktaking and reconciliation and acceptance of one's successes and failures—all of these preoccupy the young as well as the old. It is a truism, even though it sometimes goes unmentioned, that the psychological preoccupations of adults are recurrent. They appear and reappear in new forms over long periods of time. This being so, it is something of a distortion to describe adulthood as a series of discrete and neatly bounded stages, as if adult life were a staircase.

Comment

For many years, as my students and I have tried to learn about the life cycle, I have asked them to locate a three- or four-generation family and to obtain a brief life history of each of its members, then to ask themselves how the trajectory of change in one member of the family has affected the lives of the others. Almost always the student returns after a few weeks with a sense of revelation and with the comment that it is the older persons in the family who have been the most fascinating and from whom the student has learned the most about the subject matter of human development. It is as if the student had never before considered the fact that the longer a life, the more twists and turns it has had and the more challenging a puzzle it is to unravel.

Perhaps the same kind of field experience would be valuable in the training of psychiatrists who might otherwise see only the sick rather than the well and, in particular, only the sick older person rather than the well older person.

What are some of the things that we students of adult development have learned?

1. It does not do justice to middle age or old age, any more than to adolescence or youth, to describe it primarily in terms of its problems and losses rather than its freedoms and gains.

2. As lives grow longer, as the successive choices and commitments accumulate, lives grow more different from each other. Final biological decrements may sometimes reduce the diversities among individuals, but for most persons, their lives end without a final deterioration that erases individuality. Just as no one becomes a child again before death, so most people do not become vegetables.

3. Most persons who have reached age 40, 50, or 60 do not wish to be young again, even though they may wish to feel young. They want instead to grow old with equanimity and with the assurance that they will have had a full measure of life's experience.

DEVELOPMENTAL ISSUES

A third order of observation also warrants attention. In addition to regularity and irregularity in the sequencing of life events and the recurrent nature of psychological issues as they appear in awareness, there are changes in the inner life that do not always appear in awareness or lend themselves to direct expression. It is in this area, in which psychologists and psychiatrists focus on more covert expressions and in which fantasies, dreams, projective techniques, and the clinical interview are the tools of observation, that there are also discernible changes in adulthood. Some of us regard this area as one in which true developmental or age-related changes are to be sought.

A respectable literature is now accumulating on this subject. There is the early but still timely work of Jung (16), who, in describing developmental change in adulthood, commented in particular on the increase in introversion in middle and later life and on the reorganization of value systems. There is the work of Buhler (17, 18), who, in discussing typical shifts in motivations, gave a central place to concepts of intentionality in behavior, to goal seeking and goal restructuring. There is the work of Erikson (19), whose descriptions of eight stages of the life cycle and eight major choice points for the expanding ego are well-known to us all. There is also the work of Lowenthal and her colleagues (20), who are studying adaptational patterns at successive transition points in adulthood. There are others, of course, whose contributions have been important.

A small but growing number of psychologists and clinicians have been focusing on developmental changes in the second half of life. Our group at the University of Chicago began in the 1950s to describe intrapsychic changes in the large samples of middle-aged and older men and women we were studying—for instance, in the perception of the self in relation to the external environment and in coping with "impulse life." Middle-aged people seem to view the environment as one that rewards boldness and risk-taking, while older persons view the self as conforming and accommodating to the demands of the outside world. There seems to be a change from outer-world to inner-world orientation that we described as increased "interiority" (21).

There is also the work of Cumming and Henry (22) and the theory called disengagement, in which it was posited that the individual and the society withdraw from each other in a mutual process, that individuals alter their psychological as well as their social investments, and that this process is inherent and leads to good adaptation in the old (a theory that was later modified in the light of additional data).

Studies of reminiscence by Lieberman and Falk (23), Tobin and Etigson (24), and others[1], which built on Butler's concepts of the life review (25), have indicated that middle-aged persons draw on their memories somewhat differently than do older persons. The middle-aged consciously select from past experience in the solution of current problems; the old put their store of memories in order, as it were, dramatizing some and striving for consistency in others, perhaps as a way of preparing an ending for the life history.

There are also the continuing contributions of Gutmann, who has studied aging in different societies and who has outlined an intrinsic pattern of change in the second half of life that occurs across a range of cultures. The trajectory of change is one in which men move from active to passive mastery modes, but women move in the opposite direction, toward increased instrumentality and assertiveness. Gutmann (26) proposed a tentative explanation—that it is the requirements of parenthood that establish sex-role distinctions in early adulthood, when women need to suppress their aggressive impulses if they are to succeed in caring for children and when men need to suppress their affiliative impulses if they are to succeed as economic providers. After children are grown and the demands of parenthood are over, the earlier suppressed elements of personality can be expressed, so that men and women move in opposite directions but both move toward the "normal unisex of later life" (26).

To cite another example, there are studies by some of my colleagues on survivorship in very aged persons and of the "adaptive paranoia" of old age, when combativeness seems to become a survival asset. Some (27) have suggested that the traditional views of psychological health do not apply to aged persons and that different processes of coping may come to the fore. This is reminiscent of work done by Busse (28) and his associates who some years ago suggested that the psychodynamics of depression are probably quite different in the old than in the young and are based on loss and mourning rather than on aggression turned inward.

There is also the work of the group associated with the Institute for Psychoanalysis in Chicago. Kohut (29) has been explicating the transformation of narcissism in the adult, the capacity for humor, and the achievement of the human attitude we call wisdom. Cohler (30) has described the ways in which memory processes affect the reconstructions that go on in the psychoanalytic setting. The work of Pollock (31) has focused on the mourning process in the older person.

The last-named group is also building on the studies in geriatric psychiatry of Berezin and Cath of the psychoanalytic group in Boston (32) in pursuing the relationship between normal and pathological personality development in the second half of life. Significant questions are being raised about the types of adaptation that may be regarded as pathological in the young but normal in the old. This concern with the relationship between mental health and mental illness, when viewed from the perspective of the life cycle, is the important arena in which developmental psychology and psychiatry come together and in which the development of theory will be of special importance.[2]

DISCUSSION

Whatever the social and social-psychological changes of adulthood, internal personality changes occur slowly. They reflect the accumulations of life events and the continuities and discontinuities in conscious preoccupations, and they are influenced by the perceptions of change in the significant people with whom we interact.

The internal changes, along with the individual's conscious preoccupations, are not necessarily triggered by one life event or another; nor can internal change be paced off by a metric of calendar time, except in the most general sense. The inner life becomes altered over the life span, but it is doubtful that people change internally at, for example, regular 10-year intervals. This is because at both the aware and unaware levels of the mind, the present has always the elements of the past contained within it. One thinks of oneself in the present in terms of where one has been and what one has become. The adult has a built-in dimension of thought that is the present-relative-to-the-past, and it is the blending of past and present that constitutes psychological reality. Time segments are therefore not separable from each other.

This is true also because memory and remembering occupy central positions in the life of the mind. The coexistence of past and present and the dynamic nature of reminiscence have been poetically stated in Proust's *Remembrance of Things Past* (33): "For man is that creature without any fixed age, who has the faculty of becoming, in a few seconds, many years younger, and who, surrounded by the walls of the time through which he has lived, floats within them but as though in a basin, the surface level of which is constantly changing, so as to bring him into the range now of one epoch, now of another" (p. 272).

Given the licenses of metaphor, the inner life of the mind may also be described as a river or a stream, one whose content gradually changes as it accumulates materials from the banks it has touched. The processes of memory bring to the surface different elements that rise and fall and rise again, and it is because of memory that a life has a continuity that encompasses its discontinuities.

What, then, are the implications for psychiatry?

The psychiatrist who uses any of the relational therapies helps the patient to create coherence and to make a meaningful life story from a life history. In doing so, both patient and therapist deal always with time and age and timing, whether it is a young patient who is relating a short past to a long future or an old patient who is relating a long past to a short future. An aging person who comes to the psychiatrist in pain seeks assistance in reintegrating past, present, and future, in determining how to use the time that is left, how to put the mental house in order, and how to find appropriate forms of youthfulness. The old patient may fear that as youth is dying, only the shell of old age will survive.

In working out a balance between the losses and the victories, the mourning and the celebration, the aging patient's grief is real, and periods of depression may be the normal, not the pathological, response. To help an aging patient carry out the grief work is understandably difficult—even threatening—to the therapist who is facing, or denying, the same developmental task.

But an aging patient brings certain strengths to the therapeutic situation: a large repertoire of experience, long practice at working out solutions to problems, and rich resources for recovery. Introspection and stocktaking are well-developed features of the mental life. The past lies close at hand, and the reliving and reworking of the past may come more readily than to a younger person.

The rewards in treating an older patient may therefore be very great. It may even happen that therapists are helped to deal with their own aging when, in using their highly refined empathy, they come in part to identify with their patients. In assisting older patients to come to peace with their lives and to master their narcissism, therapists may come to peace with their own lives and more quickly master their own narcissism. Perhaps aging patients and therapists can together develop a new direction for psychiatry as a whole, a new understanding of the relationship between illness and health in which lifetime is the pivotal dimension. If so, there will be new strength in the field of human healing.

Notes

1. Falk J: The organization of remembered life experience of older people: its relation to anticipated stress, to subsequent adaptation, and to age. University of Chicago, 1970 (unpublished doctoral dissertation)
Revere VL: The remembered past: its reconstruction at different life stages. University of Chicago, 1971 (unpublished doctoral dissertation)
2. Pollock GH: Aging or aged: development or pathology. Chicago, Institute of Psychoanalysis Library, 1978 (unpublished paper)

References

1. Clark AM, Clarke ABD: Early Experience: Myth and Evidence. New York, Free Press, 1976.
2. Neugarten BL: Continuities and discontinuities of psychological issues into adult life. Hum Dev 12:121–130, 1969.
3. Levinson DJ: The Seasons of a Man's Life. New York, Alfred A. Knopf, 1978.
4. Vaillant G: Adaptation to Life. Boston, Little, Brown and Co, 1977.
5. Erikson E (ed): Adulthood. New York, WW Norton and Co, 1978.
6. Sheehy G: Passages. New York, EP Dutton and Co, 1976.
7. Gould R: Transformations. New York, Simon and Schuster, 1978.
8. Aries P: Centuries of Childhood. New York, Vintage Books, 1962.
9. Youth: Transition to Adulthood. Report of a Panel of the President's Social Science Advisory Committee, Washington, DC, US Government Printing Office, 1974.
10. Neugarten BL: Age groups in American society and the rise of the young-old. Annals of the American Academy of Political and Social Sciences 415:187–198, 1974.
11. Hirschhorn L: Social policy and the life cycle: a developmental perspective. Social Service Review 51:434–450, 1977.
12. Neugarten BL: The awareness of middle age, in Middle Age and Aging. Edited by Neugarten BL. Chicago, University of Chicago Press, 1968.
13. Lieberman GL: Children of the elderly as natural helpers: some demographic considerations. Am J Community Psychol 6:489–498, 1978.
14. Freud S: Thoughts for the times on war and death (1915), in Complete Psychological Works, standard ed, vol. 14. Translated and edited by Strachey J. London, Hogarth Press, 1957.

15. Thomas D: Do not go gentle into that good night, in The Collected Poems of Dylan Thomas. New York, New Directions Books, 1957.

16. Jung CG: The stages of life, in The Collected Works of CG Jung, vol. 8: The Structure and Dynamics of the Psyche. New York, Pantheon Books, 1960.

17. Buhler C: Der Menschliche Lebenslauf als Psychologisches Problem. Leipzig, Verlag von S Hirzel, 1933.

18. Buhler C: Genetic aspects of the self. Ann NY Acad Sci 96:730–764, 1962.

19. Erikson EH: Childhood and Society, 2nd revised ed. New York, WW Norton and Co, 1963.

20. Lowenthal MF, Thurner M, Chiriboga D: Four Stages of Life. San Francisco, Jossey-Bass, 1975.

21. Neugarten BL and Associates: Personality in Middle and Late Life. New York, Atherton Press, 1964.

22. Cumming E, Henry WE: Growing Old. New York, Basic Books, 1961.

23. Lieberman MA, Falk J: The remembered past as a source of data for research on the life cycle. Hum Dev 14:132–141, 1971.

24. Tobin SS, Etigson E: Effect of stress on earliest memory. Arch Gen Psychiatry, 19:435–444, 1968.

25. Butler RN: The life review: an interpretation of reminiscence in the aged. Psychiatry 26:65–76, 1963.

26. Gutmann DL: Parenthood: a key to the comparative study of the life cycle, in Life-Span Developmental Psychology. Edited by Datan N, Ginsberg L. New York, Academic Press, 1975.

27. Lieberman MA: Adaptive processes in late life. Ibid.

28. Busse EW: Psychopathology, in Handbook of Aging and the Individual. Edited by Birren JE. Chicago, University of Chicago Press, 1959, pp 389–391.

29. Kohut H: The Restoration of the Self. New York, International Universities Press, 1977.

30. Coher BJ: Adult developmental psychology and reconstruction in psychoanalysis, in The Course of Life. Edited by Greenspan SI, Pollock GH. Washington, DC, National Institute of Mental Health (in press).

31. Pollock GH: On mourning, immortality, and utopia. J Am Psychoanal Assoc 23:334–362, 1975.

32. Berezin MA, Cath SH (eds): Geriatric Psychiatry. New York, International Universities Press, 1965.

33. Proust M: Remembrance of Things Past, vol 11. Translated by Moncrieff CKS. London, Chatto and Windus, 1968.

NINE

The Future Social Roles of the Aged

Without claiming to be a futurologist, in the sense in which that term is becoming current, I am nevertheless happy to have been invited today to comment on the future social roles of the aged. All of us like to predict the future from our interpretations of the present and the past; and gerontologists are no exception to the rule.

The comments to follow will be at two different levels of generality: first, the role or position of older people in the society at large, as compared with other age-groups; second, the particular social role patterns that individual people adopt as they grow old.

THE POSITION OF OLDER PEOPLE IN THE SOCIETY

From a historical perspective, societies—as opposed to individuals—age as the benefits of industrialization, rising standards of living, and modern medical research lead to longer life expectancy, and as the proportions of old people therefore increase in relation to the number of children. This societal aging is common to all industrialized nations. Not only has it appeared earlier in Western countries than in other parts of the world, but, for various historical reasons, it appeared earlier in some European countries than in the United States.

For example, we may use an index of societal aging that reflects the proportions of persons aged 65 and over in relation to the number of children under 15. In the hundred years from 1850 to 1950, this index moved from 20 to 70 in Great Britain; from 24 to 64 in Sweden; and from 10 to 45 in the United States.

As the proportion of older people increases, it is inevitable that their social visibility increases. In some countries the appearance of large numbers of old people has been more "sudden" than in others; and dislocations have occurred because those societies are not yet prepared to meet the needs of large groups of older people. In such countries—and, in some respects, the United States is one of them—a sizable percentage of older people suffer from poverty, illness, and social isolation, and a group

Paper presented at the International Gerontological Symposium, Amsterdam, Netherlands, April 1970.

of *needy* aged appears who create acute problems in the fields of social and medical welfare. In other countries, the historical process has been more gradual, and the needy among the aged are no more numerous than the needy among the young.

In all industrialized societies, however, all members, young or old, must adapt to new phenomena such as multigenerational families, retirement from work, and leisure as a way of life.

The increased visibility of the old has been occurring in a wider context in which other age groups have also become more sharply delineated. With the growing differentiation that characterizes modern societies, there has been increasing awareness of age differences and of the special needs of various age groups. In the United States, for example, there has been a historical process in which it was children, then adolescents, then the aged who were singled out for attention. This fact was evidenced in the legislative programs of political parties, where special legislation on behalf of children appeared well before 1900; but on behalf of the aged, not until the early 1930s.

This sequence is probably not the same in all countries, but it is probably safe to say that in 1970 there is a heightened awareness in all parts of the world of age differences as these are presently reflected in student movements, campus protests, and the appearance of a so-called "youth culture."

To some extent, at least in my own country, the "youth culture," the "revolt of youth," and the "generation gap" are the exaggerated views of the publicists. But because the mass media create as well as reflect genuine social phenomena, it would appear that people are focussing attention upon age differences more than before, and upon the "problems" that presumably occur as the result.

While it is the student movements that are now in the limelight, some social scientists are broadening the perspective and asking if generational conflicts are indeed increasing, and if they will also appear in the other direction—that is, between the old and the society at large. Perhaps a more realistic way of putting the question is whether or not conflicts will appear between the young, on the one hand, and the old, on the other. As age groups become more differentiated, will political and social competition between the groups become more evident? Do the political movements of the young represent a more general age-divisiveness that is appearing in various parts of the world?

Again in my own country, certain antagonisms toward both the young and the old may now be forming that were not present earlier. Anger toward the young has been rising in universities and in legislatures, and is reflected in public opinion polls. At the same time, because industrial societies become gerontocratic societies as they become "aging" societies, and because positions of political and economic leadership are increasingly occupied by older people (a trend which has had, however, some marked reversals in the past decade in the United States), it brings with it resentments on the part of the young and middle-aged. As generational equilibrium becomes an increasing problem in the one direction, it may also appear in the other direction; and the phenomenon that has been called "ageism" (that is, negative or hostile attitudes toward an age-group different from one's own) may be directed toward both young and old.

Another factor which may lead to age-divisiveness is that, at least in the United States, old people are becoming a visible leisure class. As they become accustomed to the politics of confrontation they see around them, they may also become a more vocal and a more demanding group. There are signs that this is so, with, for example, appeals to "Senior Power" (in some ways analogous to the appeal of "black power"), and with occasional newspaper accounts of groups of older people picketing and protesting over such local issues as reduced bus fares or better housing projects. Whether these incidents will remain isolated and insignificant, or whether there is an activist politics of old age developing in the United States is a debatable question.

Ageism is not likely ever to take the virulent forms of racism, but it may emerge as an increasingly important social problem in the short-run future.

SOCIAL ROLE PATTERNS

Let us turn now from the society at large to the lives of individual older people and consider social roles in a narrower sense. What are the social role involvements likely to be for successive groups of older men and women? How are people likely to structure their lives after about age 65? Under what conditions will they achieve life satisfaction?

Here, too, a historical perspective is enlightening. Because gerontology as a whole is a relatively young science, we have operated, understandably enough, with mistaken interpretations that are only now being corrected.

Twenty and thirty years ago, the general view was that as societies become industrialized and urbanized, they would inevitably create situations unfavorable to the old: increased geographical mobility would bring the breakdown of the extended family; rapid rate of technological change would bring obsolescence for older workers; increasing productivity would mean increasing retirement—in short, the result would be what some gerontologists described as a "roleless role" for the aged, and associated with it would be poverty, isolation, loneliness, alienation.

This point of view, it turned out, was in error. For one thing, empirical studies had been few and had been based on atypical samples: the hospitalized, the institutionalized, the recipients of social welfare—in other words, the "problem" aged or the needy aged to whom I referred earlier, rather than the typical aged. When large representative samples of older men and women were studied, the proportions reporting high life satisfaction and who demonstrated socially competent life styles were not markedly different from the proportions at younger ages. The large majority of older people seem to be reasonably competent, reasonably successful—depending, of course, upon health and basic socio-economic conditions, and omitting those at very advanced ages or in the terminal phase of life.

Large-scale surveys showed that older people were not isolated from other family members. To the contrary, while most older people prefer to live in their own households, they live near a child or a relative and see other family members regularly and frequently. This is as true in the United States as in Norway and in Great Britain—indeed the overall patterns of life for older people are remarkably the same in at least these three countries. On the average, men do not decline in health or in morale after retirement; neither do they, after a short period of readjustment, fail to establish meaningful patterns of activity. While attitudes vary according to occupational level, the majority of workers seem increasingly to welcome retirement and to choose leisure over work just as soon as they have sufficient income on which to live. Although there are some signs of increased age-segregation, as in the retirement communities that have multiplied in the United States, this trend involves only a small proportion of older persons, and that proportion is a self-selected group who appear to be exercising a larger rather than smaller degree of freedom in choosing where to live. Furthermore such studies as are available indicate that in such communities where the density of older people is relatively high, social interaction of the older person is increased. On the whole it cannot be said that urban industrial societies preclude the social integration of the old.

A second major conclusion is that there is wide variation of life styles among older people; enormous diversity; and multiple patterns of successful aging. There is no single pattern of disengagement, and no single or modal pattern that produces life satisfaction.

These overall findings apply not only to the younger aged—those in their sixties—but also to persons in their seventies.

Let me illustrate, in this connection, from only two studies of 70-year-olds in which I have participated. In one large-scale study of persons aged 70 to 79 in the United States, whom we followed over a 7-year period, we found a number of patterns: one group whom we called the "re-organizers" were persons who substituted new activities for lost ones—who, when they had retired from work, gave time to their families, to community affairs or to church or other associations. They reorganized their patterns of activity, were competent in a wide variety of activities, and had high levels of satisfaction. One such person was a retired schoolteacher, who, at age

75, was busy with selling life insurance and making more money than ever before. He was an elected officer in an association of retirees, he attended concerts and the theater with his wife, and visited with friends regularly.

Another group who showed high morale had only medium levels of activity. We called them the "focused," because they had become selective in their activities, and now devoted energy to one or two role areas. One such case, for instance, was a retired man who was now preoccupied with the roles of homemaker, parent, and husband. He had withdrawn from work and also from club-memberships, but welcomed the opportunity to live a happy life with his family, seeing his children and grandchildren, gardening, and helping his wife with homemaking which he had never done before.

A third group we called the "disengaged." These were persons who had high life satisfaction, but with low role activity; persons who had voluntarily moved away from role commitments, not in response to social losses or physical deficits, but because of preference. This pattern might be called the "rocking-chair" approach to old age—a calm, withdrawn, but highly contented pattern.

There were other patterns, of course: people who were less content—some of them striving and ambitious, and still eager to hold on to the patterns of their middle age; some who were busily defending themselves against the threats of aging by constricting their social interactions and closing themselves off from new experience; some who had strong dependency needs but who maintained themselves fairly well by having one or two other persons whom they depended on for emotional support.

In another study, this one based on small groups of relatively healthy 70- to 75-year-old men in 6 different countries (the United States, Germany, Austria, Holland, Italy, and Poland) who were either retired schoolteachers or retired steelworkers, we found wide individual differences, differences between the two occupational groups, and differences between countries. Overall, however, we found little social isolation. The most common pattern was one in which there was highest activity in family roles (parent, grandparent, spouse, and kin-member); intermediate activity in the roles that relate to informal social relations (friend, neighbor, acquaintance); and low activity in the roles that reflect formal social relations (club-member, church-member, citizen, and political participant). But other patterns were frequent, also, indicating again that there is no single pattern of social roles that characterizes men in their seventies.

Studies like these are based, of course, on persons who live in their own homes in the community, and who are still relatively healthy. It is true, of course, that there are lonely and isolated old people, sick old people, and old people who live in hospitals and homes for the aged, and for whom the picture is more dismal. There are studies, however, which show that many of the people who are socially isolated in old age are persons who were relatively isolated also when they were younger.

What we certainly cannot do is to generalize about social role patterns even in 75-year-olds, to say nothing of 65-year-olds. What is striking to the investigator is the wide variations, and the different patterns that seem to be associated with contentment or high morale.

From studies such as these we have concluded that people, as they grow old, seem to be neither at the mercy of the social environment nor at the mercy of some set of intrinsic psychological processes that they cannot influence. On the contrary, the individual seems to continue to make his own impression upon the wide range of social and biological changes; to exercise choice, and to select from the environment in accordance with his own long-established needs.

If it is already true that there is no single social role pattern for the aged in 1970, my prediction is that it will become even more true in the future. Differences between older people will probably become greater. With better health, more education, and more financial resources, older men and women will have greater freedom to choose the life-style that suits them. Future generations will also have had more experience with change—changes in jobs, changes in residence and in living arrangements, and changes in the timing of education, work, and leisure—and this experience will probably result in greater adaptability. It is likely that persons who have learned to adapt to change in youth and middle age will be better able to adapt to change in their old age.

All this is not to deny the fact that at the very end of life there will continue to be a shorter or longer period of dependency; and that increased numbers of the very old will need care, either in their own homes or in special institutional settings. For persons who are terminally ill or incapacitated, it will be idle, in the future as in the present, to speak of meaningful social roles. While it must be left to the biologist to predict the future with regard to the prolongation of life and the extent to which men will gain greater controls over death, the problems for the society will continue to be those of providing the maximum social supports, the highest possible levels of care and comfort, the assurance of dignified death, and an increasing element of choice for the individual himself or for members of his family regarding how and when his life shall end.

With the exception of the terminal phase of life, then, and within the biological imperatives that rule men's lives, the social scientist who takes upon himself the role of futurologist sees an encouraging future with regard to the social roles of the aged.

This future will depend, of course, upon conditions of world stability; upon increasing economic productivity, rising standards of living, and equitable distribution of goods and services; and above all, upon population control. Post-industrial societies may fail in achieving these conditions; and predictions at this level of abstraction are perhaps no more than the reflection of optimism or pessimism on the part of the speaker. Still, within the limits of these larger uncertainties, and to the extent that man will continue to create a viable physical and social environment, the trends I have described are not overly fanciful.

Thus, to sum up: From the broad perspective of the relations between age-groups, the near future may witness a rise in the phenomenon I have called "ageism" in at least some industrialized countries: those, perhaps like the United States, in which there is not yet a tradition of valuing older people. This trend will probably not occur at all in other countries where the traditions and the value-systems are different; where the society is more "mature"; or where there is a longer tradition of distributing the goods of the society more equally among age-groups. In any case, in those places where it will appear, it is likely that such a trend toward increased competition among age-groups will be short-lived; and in the longer future, the position of the old will improve as they become successively "younger" in body and mind, and as age differentiations will tend to diminish in importance throughout the whole of adulthood.

From the perspective of social role patterns for individuals, the future would appear to be one of increased social permissiveness, increasing diversity of life styles, increased freedom to develop idiosyncratic patterns that provide for higher levels of life satisfaction. In the long run, as I have suggested, we may come to ignore chronological age as a major distinguishing feature between individuals; and instead of speaking of social roles for *the aged,* come to speak of the social roles of individuals who happen to be young, middle-aged, or old, but more important, who happen to have different tastes, different goals, and different ways of enhancing the quality of their lives.

TEN

The Middle Years

Bernice L. Neugarten and Nancy Datan

Middle life has received relatively little attention from students of the life cycle. The early part of life, paced by a biologically timed sequence of events, continues to attract major attention from behavioral scientists; and in the past few decades a large body of research has grown up about old age. The years of maturity, by contrast, are less understood. Only a few attempts have been made to develop a psychology of the life cycle, and the search for regular developmental sequences of personality change in adulthood is relatively new.[28,32,55,56,69] This neglect of middle life has led by default to the uncritical view on the part of many psychologists that personality is stabilized and the major life commitments completed in the period of youth and that nothing of great significance occurs for the long time until senescence appears. Clinicians, on the other hand, have shown considerable awareness of the potential hazards to mental health that arise in midlife.[9] For women the climacterium is thought to constitute one such crisis;[6,8,23,25] for men the perception of decline in sexual prowess is considered a serious crisis;[73,76] and the phenomenon of depression in middle age has received much attention.[68] All this has led to somewhat unbalanced views of middle age as either plateau or crisis.

The focus of this chapter is upon social psychological perspectives, rather than upon the psychodynamics of personality change. In taking note of salient biological, psychological, and social changes of middle age, we shall draw upon such empirical studies as exist and focus primarily upon investigations of so-called normal or nonclinical populations.

THE CHANGING BOUNDARIES OF MIDDLE AGE

The boundaries of middle age have been defined by various indices. Chronological age definitions are perhaps the most arbitrary. Typically the period being described is 40 to 60 or 65, but it is sometimes as broad as a 30 year span, 30 to 60, or sometimes only a single decade, the forties. There is no consensus that any single biological or

Reprinted by permission of Harper Collins Publishers from *American Handbook of Psychiatry*, edited by S. Arieti, 2d ed., vol. 1, *The Foundations of Psychiatry* (New York: Basic Books, 1974), 592–608. Portions appeared in earlier papers (see references 53 and 54 at the end of this chapter).

social event constitutes the lower boundary of middle age. While it is often said that retirement constitutes the upper boundary for men, there is no agreed upon boundary for women. The major life events that characterize the middle part of the life span—reaching the peak of one's occupational career, the launching of children from the home, the death of parents, climacterium, grandparenthood, illness, retirement, widowhood—while they tend to proceed in a roughly predictable sequence, occur at varying chronological ages and are separated by varying intervals of time. Most behavioral scientists therefore concur that chronological age is not a meaningful index by which to order the social and psychological data of adulthood; and the individual's own awareness of entry and exit from middle age, as will be described in more detail below, seems to emerge from a combination of biological and social cues rather than from a fixed number of birthdays.[53,62,78] Since there are no clear boundaries, it is sometimes said that middle age should be described as a state of mind rather than as a given period of years. If so, it is a state of mind that has an important influence upon the individual's perceptions of himself and his strategies for managing his world.

For both observer and observed, middle age cannot meaningfully be separated from that which precedes and follows it in the life cycle, for the individual always assesses his present in terms of both his past and his future. Accordingly, perceptions of the life cycle are meaningful data in understanding the middle-aged.

PERCEPTIONS OF THE LIFE CYCLE

Perceptions vary from one person to the next regarding the timing and rhythm of major life events and the quality of life at successive periods of adulthood, but important bases of consensus are to be found as well as consistent group differences. In one study of the views of men and women aged 40 to 70 (a community sample drawn from a metropolitan area), adulthood was generally seen as divided into four periods: young adulthood, maturity, middle age, and old age, each period having its unique characteristics. These major periods of life were recognized by all respondents, but there were differences in the views of men and women and differences according to socio-economic level. Men saw a succession of minor dividing points and a relatively gradual progression from one period of life to the next. Women saw one major dividing point that outweighed the others in significance, and they often described adult life in terms of two somewhat disconnected lives, one before and one after 40. Among business executives and professionals, a man did not reach middle age until 50, nor old age until 70. For the blue-collar worker, on the other hand, life was paced more rapidly, and a man was described as middle-aged by 40 and old by 60.

The themes of life associated with middle age varied also with the social status of the respondent. For the upper-middle class, young adulthood (20 to 30) was described as a time of exploration and groping, of "feeling one's way" in job, marriage, and other adult roles, and as a period of experimentation. Maturity (30 to 40) was the time of progressive achievement and increasing autonomy. Middle age was described as the period of greatest productivity and of major rewards, the "prime of life." Women, while mentioning the adjustments required by the departure of children from the home, also described middle age as a period of mellowness and serenity. Old age was viewed as a period of relaxation, leisure, security, partial withdrawal, and resting on one's laurels.

The blue-collar worker had a different view. Both men and women described young adulthood as the period, not when issues are explored, but when they become settled, and when life's responsibilities loom up as inescapable. One becomes increasingly sensible, older, wiser, and quieter. Not only does middle age come early, but it is described in terms of decline—slowing down, physical weakening, becoming a has-been. Old age is the period of withdrawal and progressive physical decline and is described in pessimistic terms, the "old age, it's a pity" theme.[62]

In a related study of over 600 middle-aged men and women, there was a striking consistency in attitudes about growing older. While the largest proportion of responses were neutral, in those persons who expressed negative or contingent attitudes the fear of dependency was paramount. (Contingent attitudes were those in which the respondent said, "Growing old will be fine if my health stays good," or "I don't mind old age as long as I don't become a burden to anyone.") Dependency was always seen as having two sources, loss of income and loss of health. Fear of death was never expressed, nor fear of social isolation. Fear of dependency was the only theme to occur with any frequency, and it occurred approximately as often for men as for women and for people at all social class levels.[57]

THE CHANGING RHYTHMS OF THE LIFE CYCLE

Perceptions of the life cycle are influenced, of course, by social change. From a historical perspective there is documentation to show that not until the seventeenth and eighteenth centuries, with the growth of industrialization, a middle class, and formal educational institutions, did the view appear that childhood was a discernible period of life with special needs and characteristics.[2] The concept of adolescence can be viewed as essentially a twentieth-century invention.[24] Most recently a case has been made for a new stage called youth,[41] a stage that has appeared only in the last few decades when social change has become so rapid that it threatens to make obsolete all institutions and values within the lifetime of each generation and when a growing minority of young persons face the task of reconciling the self with the social order. It has been suggested that, in terms of the developmental polarities suggested by Erikson,[28] in which the central psychological issue of adolescence is identity versus diffusion, the central issue for youth is individuation versus alienation.

A parallel case can be made for the fact that the period of middle age is a recently delineated stage in the life cycle. In this instance the significant dimensions of social and technological change are the enormous increase in longevity that has occurred since the beginning of this century and the growth of leisure in the affluent postindustrial society. At the risk of overdoing these parallelisms, it might be ventured that the central psychological task for middle age relates to the use of time, and the essential polarity is between time mastery and capitulation.

From a somewhat narrower historical perspective, social change creates alterations in the rhythm and timing of life events, alterations that have their inevitable effects upon perceptions of what it means to be middle-aged. This can be illustrated from changes in the family cycle and the work cycle. Dramatic changes have occurred over the past several decades as age at marriage has dropped, as children are born earlier in the marriage and are spaced closer together, as longevity and consequently the duration of marriage has increased.[30]

Census data show, for instance, that in 1890, only 80 years ago, the average American woman left school at about age 14, married at 22, had her first-born child within two to three years and her last-born child when she was 32. Her husband died when she was only 53, her last child married when she was 55, and she herself lived to about 68. The average woman was widowed, then, before her last child left home.

In 1966 this picture was very different. Then the average woman left school at age 18; she married at 20; her first child was born within one year; her last child, by the time she was 26; and all her children were in school full-time when she was only 32. The projections for this group of women were that the last child would marry when she was 48, her husband would die when she was 64, and she herself could expect to live to almost 80. Thus, our average woman can now look forward to some 45 years of life after her last-born child is in school.

These trends are equally reflected, of course, in the lives of men. Historically the family cycle has quickened for both sexes as marriage, parenthood, empty nest, and grandparenthood all occur earlier, and as the interval of time becomes extended (now some 16 years) when husband and wife are the remaining members of the household. (While the family cycle runs its course a few years later for men and women at higher social class levels, the general pattern of historical change is the same for both higher and lower levels.)

Parent-child relationships in middle age have been affected by the fact that parenthood has been coming earlier in life. Changes in parental behavior, with, for example, fathers becoming less authoritarian, may in part reflect this increasing youthfulness. It is the relative youth of both parents and grandparents, furthermore, that may be contributing to the complex patterns of help between generations that are now becoming evident, including the widespread financial help that flows from parents downward to their adult children.[75] In a study of three-generation families in which styles of behavior by grandparents were delineated, it was found that younger grandparents (those under 65 as compared with those over 65) more often followed the fun-seeking pattern.[63] The fun-seeker is the grandparent whose relation to the child is informal and playful and who joins the child for the purpose of having fun, somewhat as if he were the child's playmate. Grandchildren are viewed by these grandparents as a source of leisure activity, as a source of self-indulgence. Authority lines become irrelevant, and the emphasis is upon mutual gratification. Similarly, with grandparenthood coming earlier in life, there is the emergence of an extended family system that encompasses several generations. (In 1962, 40 per cent of all persons in the United States who were 65 or over had *great*-grandchildren.)

Changes in the work cycle are also occurring rapidly, affecting the perceptions of middle age. With longer education and later entry into the labor force, and with earlier retirement, the proportion of the life span spent at work is diminishing for men. For women the trend is the opposite. While fewer women work, and fewer work full-time, the trend is to extend the proportion of the life span spent in the labor force. With more than half of all women aged 50 to 55 now in the labor force, middle-aged women have gained in status relative to men, and relationships are changing not only between the sexes but between the generations within the family. Not only the mother goes to work now, but also the middle-aged grandmother.[52,55]

While direct data are lacking, it is probable that these changes in the family and in the economy are contributing to major differences between the sexes in adaptations to middle age and in patterns of aging. For women, although there is an increased burden of caring for aged parents, lightened family responsibilities, the marriage of the last-born child, and the taking on of new economic and civic roles now tend to coincide with the biological changes of the climacterium, probably producing an increasingly accentuated new period of life and contributing to the new sense of freedom expressed by many middle-aged women.

The rhythms of the work career show great variability at different occupational levels, and there are large differences from one occupation to another in the timing of career stages, in the rewards that come at each stage, and in the relationships between younger and older participants in the work setting. Increased complexity of knowledge is required, not only of the practicing professional, but for a wide variety of occupations. Even more significant is the accompanying problem of obsolescence of skills and technical knowledge, a problem that characterizes most occupational groups. Age lines tend to become blurred and age-deference systems weakened in instances where a younger man's up-to-date knowledge has the advantage over the older man's experience. To take but one example, studies of business leaders show that the average age of the business elite rose steadily from 1870 to 1950.[33,79] The increase in size, complexity, and bureaucratization that characterizes big business today has been accompanied by a lengthening of the early phases of the career line. It has been taking longer than in earlier generations for a man to rise to the top of the administrative ladder, a fact that perhaps underlies some of the efforts now being made by business firms to push young men into leadership roles.

The changing technology, the changing job patterns, as well as the changing family cycle, are all influencing the experience of middle age.

THE SUBJECTIVE EXPERIENCE OF MIDDLE AGE

Middle-aged men and women, while they recognize the rapidity of social change and while they by no means regard themselves as being in command of all they survey, nevertheless recognize that they constitute the powerful age group vis-à-vis other age groups; that they are the norm bearers and the decision makers; and that they live in a society that, while it may be oriented toward youth, is controlled by the middle-aged. There is space here to describe only a few of the psychological issues of middle age as they have been described in one of our studies in which 100 highly placed men and women were interviewed at length concerning the salient characteristics of middle adulthood.[53] These people were selected randomly from various directories of business leaders, professionals, and scientists.

The enthusiasm manifested by these informants as the interviews progressed was only one of many confirmations that middle age is a period of heightened sensitivity to one's position within a complex social environment, and that reassessment of the self is a prevailing theme. As anticipated most of this group were highly introspective and verbal persons who evidenced considerable insight into the changes that had taken place in their careers, their families, their status, and in the ways in which they dealt with both their inner and outer worlds. Generally the higher the individual's career position, the greater was his willingness to explore the various issues and themes of middle age.

The Delineation of Middle Age

There is ample evidence in these reports, as in the studies mentioned earlier, that middle age is perceived as a distinctive period, one that is qualitatively different from other age periods. Middle-aged people look to their positions within different life contexts—the body, the career, the family—rather than to chronological age for their primary cues in clocking themselves. Often there is a differential rhythm in the timing of events within these various contexts, so that the cues utilized for placing oneself in this period of the life cycle are not always synchronous. For example, one business executive regards himself as being on top in his occupation and assumes all the prerogatives that go with seniority in that context, yet, because his children are still young, he feels he has a long way to go before completing his major goals within the family.

Distance from the Young

Generally the middle-aged person sees himself as the bridge between the generations, both within the family and within the wider contexts of work and community. At the same time he has a clear sense of differentiation from both the younger and older generations. In his view young people cannot understand nor relate to the middle-aged because they have not accumulated the prerequisite life experiences. Both the particular historical events and the general accumulation of experience create generational identification and mark the boundaries between generations. One 48 year old said,

> I graduated from college in the middle of the Great Depression. A degree in Sociology didn't prepare you for jobs that didn't exist, so I became a social worker because there were openings in that field. . . . Everybody was having trouble eking out an existence, and it took all your time and energy. . . . Today's young people are different. They've grown up in an age of affluence. When I was my son's age I was supporting my father's family. But my son can never understand all this . . . he's of a different generation altogether.

The middle-ager becomes increasingly aware of the distance—emotionally, socially, and culturally—between himself and the young. Sometimes the awareness comes as a sudden revelation:

> I used to think that all of us in the office were contemporaries, for we all had similar career interests. But one day we were talking about old movies and the younger ones had never seen a Shirley Temple film. . . . Then it struck me with a blow that I was older than they. I had never been so conscious of it before.

Similarly, another man remarked:

> When I see a pretty girl on the stage or in the movies, and when I realize she's about the age of my son, it's a real shock. It makes me realize that I'm middle-aged.

An often expressed preoccupation is how one should relate to both younger and older persons and how to act one's age. Most of our respondents are acutely aware of their responsibility to the younger generation and of what we called "the creation of social heirs." One corporation executive says,

> I worry lest I no longer have the rapport with young people that I had some
> years back. I think I'm becoming uncomfortable with them because they're so
> uncomfortable with me. They treat me like I treated my own employer when I
> was 25. I was frightened of him. . . . But one of my main problems now is to en-
> courage young people to develop so that they'll be able to carry on after us.

And a 50-year-old-woman said,

> You always have younger people looking to you and asking questions. . . . You
> don't want them to think you're a fool. . . . You try to be an adequate model.

The awareness that one's parents' generation is now quite old does not lead to the
same feeling of distance from the parental generation a from the younger generation.

> I sympathize with old people, now, in a way that is new. I watch my parents, for
> instance, and I wonder if I will age in the same way.

The sense of proximity and identification with the old is enhanced by the feeling that
those who are older are in a position to understand and appreciate the responsibilities and commitments to which the middle-aged have fallen heir.

> My parents, even though they are much older, can understand what we are go-
> ing through; just as I now understand what they went through.

Although the idiosyncrasies of the aged may be annoying to the middle-aged, an
effort is usually made to keep such feelings under control. There is greater projection
of the self in one's behavior with older people, sometimes to the extent of blurring the
differences between the two generations. One woman recounted an incident that
betrayed her apparent lack of awareness (or her denial) of her mother's aging:

> I was shopping with mother. She had left something behind on the counter and
> the clerk called out to tell me that the "old lady" had forgotten her package. I was
> amazed. Of course the clerk was a young man and she must have seemed old to
> him. But I myself don't think of her as old.

Marriage and Family

Women, but not men, tend to define their age status in terms of the timing of events
within the family cycle. Even unmarried career women often discuss middle age in
terms of the family they might have had.

> Before I was 35, the future just stretched forth, far away. . . . I think I'm doing
> now what I want. The things that troubled me in my thirties about marriage
> and children don't bother me now because I'm at the age where many women
> have already lost their husbands.

Both men and women, however, recognized a difference in the marriage relationship that follows upon the departure of children, some describing it in positive, others in negative terms, but all recognizing a new marital adjustment to be made.

> It's a totally new thing. Now there isn't the responsibility for the children. There's more privacy and freedom to be yourself. All of a sudden there are times when we can just sit down and have a conversation. And it was a treat to go on a vacation alone!
>
> It's the boredom that has grown up between us but which we didn't face before. With the kids at home, we found something to talk about, but now the buffer between us is gone. There are just the two of us, face to face.

A recent review of the literature on the family of later life points to the theme of progressive disenchantment with marriage from the peak of the honeymoon to the nadir of middle life, and to the fact that a number of studies indicate that middle-age marriages are more likely than not to be unsatisfactory. There are other studies, however, that indicate the opposite.[77] In either case, and whatever the multiplicity of possible interpretations, middle age is not the point at which marriages characteristically break up. On the contrary, nationwide statistics show that divorce rates are highest for teen-age marriages, then drop steadily with age and duration of marriage.

One difference between husbands and wives is marked. Most of the women interviewed feel that the most conspicuous characteristic of middle age is the sense of increased freedom. Not only is there increased time and energy available for the self, but also a satisfying change in self-concept takes place. The typical theme is that middle age marks the beginning of a period in which latent talents and capacities can be put to use in new directions.

Some of these women describe this sense of freedom coming at the same time that their husbands are reporting increased job pressures or—something equally troublesome—job boredom. Contrast this typical statement of a woman,

> I discovered these last few years that I was old enough to admit to myself the things I could do well and to start doing them. I didn't think like this before. . . . It's a great new feeling.

with the statement of one man,

> You're thankful your health is such that you can continue working up to this point. It's a matter of concern to me right now, to hang on. I'm forty-seven, and I have two children in college to support.

or with the statement of another man, this one a history professor,

> I'm afraid I'm a bit envious of my wife. She went to work a few years ago, when our children no longer needed her attention, and a whole new world has opened

to her. But myself? I just look forward to writing another volume, and then another volume.

The Work Career

Men, unlike women, perceive the onset of middle age by cues presented outside the family context, often from the deferential behavior accorded them in the work setting. One man described the first time a younger associate held open a door for him; another, being called by his official title by a newcomer in the company; another, the first time he was ceremoniously asked for advice by a younger man.

Men perceive a close relationship between life line and career line. Middle age is the time to take stock. Any disparity noted between career expectations and career achievements—that is, whether one is "on time" or "late" in reaching career goals—adds to the heightened awareness of age. One lawyer said,

> I moved at age forty-five from a large corporation to a law firm. I got out at the last possible moment, because if you haven't made it by then, you had better make it fast, or you are stuck.

There is good evidence that among men most of the upward occupational mobility that occurs is largely completed by the beginning of the middle years, or by age 35.[18,39] Some of the more highly educated continue to move up the ladder in their forties and occasionally in their fifties. On the other hand, some men, generally the less schooled, start slipping sometime in the years from 35 to 55. The majority tend to hold on, throughout this period, to whatever rung they managed to reach. Family income does not always reflect a man's job status, for by the time of the mid-forties such large numbers of wives have taken jobs that family income often continues to rise. For this and other reasons there is considerable variation in family income in middle age as compared to earlier periods in the family cycle.

The Changing Body

The most dramatic cues for the male are often biological. The increased attention centered upon his health, the decrease in the efficiency of the body, the death of friends of the same age—these are the signs that prompt many men to describe bodily changes as the most salient characteristic of middle age.

> Mentally I still feel young, but suddenly one day my son beat me at tennis.

Or,

> It was the sudden heart attack in a friend that made the difference. I realized that I could no longer count on my body as I used to . . . the body is now unpredictable.

One 44-year-old added,

> Of course I'm not as young as I used to be, and it's true, the refrain your hear so
> often in the provocative jokes about the decrease in sexual power in man. But it
> isn't so much the loss of sexual interest, I think it's more the energy factor.

A decrease in sexual vigor is frequently commented on as a normal slowing down:
"my needs have grown less frequent as I've gotten older," or "sex isn't as important as
it once was." The effect is often described as having little effect on the quality of the
marriage.

> I think as the years go by you have less sexual desire. In fact, when you're younger
> there's a *need*, in addition to the desire, and that need diminishes without the
> personal relationship becoming strained or less close and warm. . . . I still enjoy
> sex, but not with the fervor of youth. . . . Not because I've lost my feelings for
> my wife, but because it happens to you physically.

Although a number of small-scale studies have appeared recently, the data are poor
regarding the sexual behavior of middle-aged and older people. It would appear that
sexual activity remains higher than the earlier stereotypes would indicate and that
sexual activity in middle age tends to be consistent with the individuals' earlier behavior; but at the same time there is gradual decrease with age in most persons, and
the incidence of sexual inadequacy takes a sharp upturn in men after age 50. Masters
and Johnson, making many of the same points made earlier by Kinsey and others,
point to the manifold physiological and psychological factors involved in sexual behavior in both sexes.[19,43,50] Most clinicians seem to agree with their view that in a
high percentage of cases men can be successfully treated for secondarily acquired impotence, and that the diminution of both the male's sexual prowess and the female's
responsiveness is the reflection of psychological rather than biological factors,
mainly the boredom and monotony of repetitious sexual relationship, preoccupations with career or family pressures, mental or physical fatigue, health concerns, and,
particularly for the male, fear of performance associated with any of these factors.

Changes in health and in sexual performance are more of an age marker for men
than for women. Despite the menopause and other manifestations of the climacterium, women refer much less frequently to biological changes or to concern over
health. Body monitoring is the term we used to describe the large variety of protective strategies for maintaining the middle-aged body at given levels of performance
and appearance; but while these issues take the form of a new sense of physical vulnerability in men, they take the form of a rehearsal for widowhood in women.
Women are more concerned over the body monitoring of their husbands than of
themselves.

That widowhood is a critical concern for middle-aged women is borne out by other studies. Not only is there the grief and reorganization of established life patterns to face, but widows experience a drop in status with the death of their husbands.[46] The situation of many resembles that of a minority group who are singled out for unequal treatment and who regard themselves as objects of social discrimination. Many widows feel demeaned by limiting their socializing to other widows and feel that friends avoid them in the attempt to ignore the whole subject of death and grief. The rehearsal for widowhood is obviously reality-based. With 20 to 25 percent of all women aged 55 to 65 living as widows, most married women number among their friends or relatives other women who have been recently widowed.

The Changing Time Perspective

Both sexes, although men more than women, talked of the new difference in the way time is perceived. Life is restructured in terms of time left to live rather than time since birth. Not only the reversal in directionality, but the awareness that time is finite, is a particularly conspicuous feature of middle age. Thus,

> You hear so much about deaths that seem premature. That's one of the changes that comes over you over the years. Young fellows never give it a thought.

Another said,

> Time is now a two-edged sword. To some of my friends, it acts as a prod; to others, a brake. It adds a certain anxiety, but I must also say it adds a certain zest in seeing how much pleasure can still be obtained, how many good years one can still arrange, how many new activities can be undertaken.

The recognition that there is "only so much time left" was a frequent theme in the interviews. In referring to the death of a contemporary, one man said,

> There is now the realization that death is very real. Those things don't quite penetrate when you're in your twenties and you think that life is all ahead of you. Now you know that death will come to you, too.

This last-named phenomenon we called the personalization of death: the awareness that one's own death is inevitable and that one must begin to come to terms with that actuality. Death rates over the life span show a sudden and dramatic rise at middle age. The rate for men aged 45 to 64 is six times as high as it is in the preceding 20-year period, and for women it is three times as high. A second factor that may be equally significant is that from childhood through early adulthood the leading cause of death is accidents, but for the age range 45 to 64, for both men and women, malignant neoplasms and heart disease account for nearly two-thirds of all deaths. To put this another way, in early life death is exceptional and accidental; but in middle age not only does death strike frequently, but it strikes from within.

The Prime of Life

Despite the new realization of the finiteness of time, one of the most prevailing themes expressed by middle-aged respondents is that middle adulthood is the period of maximum capacity and ability to handle a highly complex environment and a highly differentiated self. Very few express a wish to be young again. As one of them said,

> There is a difference between wanting to *feel* young and wanting to *be* young. Of course it would be pleasant to maintain the vigor and appearance of youth; but I would not trade those things for the authority or the autonomy I feel—no, nor the ease of interpersonal relationships nor the self-confidence that comes from experience.

The middle-aged individual, having learned to cope with the many contingencies of childhood, adolescence, and young adulthood, now has available to him a substantial repertoire of strategies for dealing with life. One woman put it,

> I know what will work in most situations, and what will not. I am well beyond the trial and error stage of youth. I now have a set of guidelines. . . . And I am practiced.

Whether or not they are correct in their assessments, most of our respondents perceive striking improvement in their exercise of judgment. For both men and women the perception of greater maturity and a better grasp of realities is one of the most reassuring aspects of being middle-aged.

> You feel you have lived long enough to have learned a few things that nobody can learn earlier. That's the reward . . . and also the excitement. I now see things in books, in people, in music that I couldn't see when I was younger. . . . It's a form of ripening that I attribute largely to my present age.

There are a number of manifestations of this sense of competence. There is, for instance, the 45-year-old's sensitivity to the self as the instrument by which to reach his goals; what we have called a preoccupation with self-utilization (as contrasted to the self-consciousness of the adolescent):

> I know now exactly what I can do best, and how to make the best use of my time. . . . I know how to delegate authority, but also what decisions to make myself. . . . I know how to protect myself from troublesome people . . . one well-placed telephone call will get me what I need. It takes time to learn how to

cut through the red tape and how to get the organization to work for me. . . . All
this is what makes the difference between me and a young man, and it's all this
that gives me the advantage.

Other studies have shown that the perception of middle age as the peak period of life
is shared by young, middle-aged, and older respondents.[3] In one such study there
was consensus that the middle-aged are not only the wealthiest, but the most powerful; not only the most knowledgeable, but the most skillful.[16]

There is also the heightened self-understanding that provides gratification. One
perceptive woman described it in these terms:

It is as if there are two mirrors before me, each held at a partial angle. I see part
of myself in my mother who is growing old, and part of her in me. In the other
mirror, I see part of myself in my daughter. I have had some dramatic insights,
just from looking in those mirrors. . . . It is a set of revelations that I suppose can
only come when you are in the middle of three generations.

In pondering the data on these men and women, we have been impressed with the
central importance of what might be called the executive processes of personality in
middle age: self-awareness, selectivity, manipulation and control of the environment, mastery, competence, the wide array of cognitive strategies. We are impressed,
too, with reflection as a striking characteristic of the mental life of middle-aged persons: the stocktaking, the heightened introspection, and, above all, the structuring
and restructuring of experience—that is, the conscious processing of new information in the light of what one has already learned and the turning of one's proficiency
to the achievement of desired ends. These people feel that they effectively manipu-
late their social environments on the basis of prestige and expertise; and that they create many of their own rules and norms. There is a sense of increased control over
impulse life. The middle-aged person often describes himself as no longer "driven,"
but as the "driver"—in short, "in command."

Although the self-reports quoted here were given by highly educated and successful persons, they express many of the same attitudes expressed less fluently by
persons of less education and less achievement, persons who also feel in middle age
the same increasing distance from the young, the stocktaking, the changing time
perspective, and the higher degrees of expertise and self-understanding.

Furthermore, while these self-reports are taken from a single study, they demonstrate the salient issues identified by researchers who have studied middle age in various biological, social, and psychological contexts, and they are remarkably
consistent with theoretical formulations of development in adulthood as set forth by
psychologists and psychiatrists. They seem to us, for instance, to be congruent with
the views of students of the life cycle such as Erikson,[28] Jung,[40] Buhler,[13,14] and oth-

ers who conceive of midlife as a developmental period in its own right, a period in which the personality has new dilemmas and new possibilities for change; and when the personality is not to be understood as fixated upon the conflicts of childhood.[7,10,12,13,14,15,29] These self-reports are also congruent with the views of Havighurst,[36] Peck,[67] and others who have described the developmental tasks of middle-age, and with the insights of clinicians like Butler,[15] Levinson,[44] Gould,[31] and Soddy,[73] who have turned their attention to gathering data on nonclinical populations.

Is Middle Age a Crisis Period?

As mentioned earlier, middle age is often described in the psychiatric as well as in the popular literature as a period of crisis. The climacterium and the departure of children from the home are usually mentioned as trauma-producing events for women; and for men, health problems, sexual impotence, and career decline. The implication is often that early middle age is second only to adolescence as a period of stress and distress.

The Climacterium

Like puberty and pregnancy the climacterium is generally regarded as a significant turning point in a woman's psychosexual development; one that frequently reflects profound psychological as well as endocrine and somatic changes. Because it signifies that reproductive life has come to an end, it has often been described as a potential threat to a woman's feminine identity, and adaptation to the climacterium as one of the major tasks of a woman's life.[25] Benedek[7] is one of the few psychoanalysts who has taken a more optimistic view; she regards it as a developmental phase in which psychic energy previously used to cope with the fluctuations of the menstrual cycle and reproduction is now released for new forms of psychological and social expansion.

Although there is a large medical and popular literature on the climacterium, there is a conspicuous lack of psychological research with nonclinical samples. While an estimated 75 percent of women experience some discomfort during the climacterium, only a small proportion receive medical treatment, suggesting that conclusions drawn from clinical observations cannot be generalized to the larger population.

For example, in one study of 100 working-class and middle-class women aged 43 to 53, all of them in good health, all with children of high school age, data were obtained on a large number of psychological and social variables, including both overt and covert measures of anxiety, life satisfaction, and self-concept.[61] It was found that these women minimized the significance of the menopause, regarding it as unlikely to produce much anxiety or stress. Among the aspects disliked most about middle age, only one woman of the 100 mentioned menopause, and even after considerable time given to the topic on two different interview occasions, only one-third could think of any way that a woman's physical or emotional health was likely to be adversely affected. Many welcomed menopause as relief from menstruation and fear of unwanted pregnancies. A majority maintained that any changes in health, sexuality, or emotional status during the climacteric period were caused by idiosyncratic factors or individual differences in general capacity to tolerate stress. "It depends on the individual. Personally I think if women look for trouble, they find it."

On a specially devised checklist of attitudes toward menopause, the large majority attributed no discontinuity in a woman's life to the climacterium. Three-fourths took the view that, except for the underlying biological changes, women even have a relative degree of control over their symptoms. Using a checklist of those menopausal symptoms most frequently reported in the medical literature (hot flushes, paresthesia, irritability, and so on), it was found that even those women with high symptom scores discounted the importance of the climacterium as a factor in their current morale. And using several different measures of psychological well-being, some based on standardized tests, others on projective tests, some on direct self-report, very little correlation was found between psychological well-being and measures of climacteric status, symptoms, or attitudes toward menopause. The study produced no evidence, in short, to support a crisis view of the climacterium.

In two related studies the attitudes-toward-menopause and the symptom checklists were administered to several hundred women who ranged in age from 13 to 65.[60,64] It was found that young women (under 40) had more negative and more undifferentiated views of menopause, but the middle-aged and older women saw it as only a temporary inconvenience. Highest frequency of symptoms occurred in the adolescents and in the menopausal women; but at adolescence the symptoms were primarily emotional, at menopause, primarily somatic. In only a few scattered instances were psychological symptoms reported more frequently by menopausal women than by any of the other age groups.

A similar picture among European-born women emerged in a cross-cultural study that included women of three Israeli subcultures: European immigrants, Near Eastern Jewish immigrants, and Israeli-born Muslim Arabs.[22,49] When European-born women were interviewed about their concerns at middle age, they seldom related them to climacteric change. This was not true, however, of the other two cultural groups, both of whom came from traditional settings in which the role of women had altered relatively little since Biblical times. For women in the latter groups climacteric changes were more salient and more closely related to their perceptions of major changes at middle age.

Nor did our data support the common view that the cessation of fertility is perceived as a major loss. Among the 100 American women just described, no regret over lost fertility was expressed: on the contrary, many women stated that they were happy to be done with childrearing.[61] A survey of nearly 1,200 middle-aged women of five Israeli subcultures that varied from traditionalism to modernity produced a parallel finding. Despite great differences in family size (an average of more than eight children among the most traditional women, and an average of two children among the most modern women), women in every cultural group emphatically welcomed the cessation of fertility.[20]

All this is not to gainsay the fact that while perhaps most middle-aged women attach only secondary significance to the climacterium, some experience considerable disturbance and should and do seek out treatment. Some clinicians have proposed that any physiological or psychological distress at climacterium is primarily due to temporary endocrine imbalance and should be treated by correcting the estrogen deficiency;[42] others have come to view the menopause as itself a hormone-deficiency disease, advocating estrogen maintenance from puberty to death;[22,80,81] but still others take a different view and see the distress as primarily due to psychodynamic factors or failure in psychological adaptation.[27] Therapeutic approaches vary accordingly, although it is usual for the therapeutic approach to be geared to both physiological and psychological dimensions.[17,74] In restricting the present chapter to the discussion of social psychological factors, we wish merely to point to the importance of biological and psychodynamic factors as well, but to leave this last topic to be treated at greater length elsewhere.

Climacterium in men is discussed by many writers; it is generally concluded that although there are exceptional occurrences of abrupt involution comparable to ovarian involution, and occasional reports of symptoms such as headaches, dizziness, and hot flushes, if there is any change at all for the majority of men other than the gradual involution of senescence, the change is neither abrupt nor universal.[68,73,76,78] It has been pointed out also that even if there is a decline in spermatogenesis the psychological consequences of such a change are unknown. Redlich and Freedman[68] are among those who suggest that the mild depressive symptoms seen among men in their fifties are perhaps related to a career decline rather than to intrinsic organic change. Soddy,[73] however, compares the climacteric period to adolescence, noting that although there is no definitive physiological marker among adolescent boys comparable to menarche in girls, the psychological changes are probably similar. He suggests that the logical inference is that there are very few differences between the sexes in attitude changes that are due directly to hormonal influences; sex differences are more likely due to cultural and social factors related to the more manifest climacteric changes in women.

The Empty Nest

With regard to another presumed crisis, the empty nest, available studies indicate that it, too, has been given exaggerated importance in terms of its consequences for mental health. One set of evidence comes from the women whose reactions to the menopause have just been described.[61] These women were divided according to family stage: the intact stage, in which none of the children had yet left home; the transitional stage, with one or more gone but one or more remaining; and the empty nest stage. Those women who had children under age 14 at home were also compared with those whose youngest child was 15 or older. Life styles or role orientations were identified, and the sample was separated into those who were primarily home-oriented, community-oriented, work-oriented, or mixed home-community-oriented. These women were studied also for *change* in the pattern of role activities, assessing the extent to which each woman had expanded or constricted her activities in family and in nonfamily roles over the past five to ten years. The women were grouped into "expanders," "shifters," "statics," and "constrictors." The relationships between these social role patterns and measures of psychological well-being were low. Rather than being a stressful period for women, the empty nest or postparental stage was associated with a somewhat *higher* level of life satisfaction than were the other family stages. For at least the women in this sample, coping with children at home was presumably more stressful than seeing their children launched into adult society.

There is other evidence.[26] For example, a study of 54 middle-aged men and women whose youngest child was about to leave home showed that while some persons in the sample had serious problems, the problems were not related to the departure of the children.[47] The authors concluded that the confrontation of the empty nest, when compared with retrospections of the low points in the past and expectations of the future, is not of a nature to justify the use of the term "crisis."

Indices of Mental Health

Somewhat the same case can be made for the effects of other life events. While important alterations in the life space of the middle-aged person take place and may necessitate a certain degree of personal reorganization, it can be argued that the normal life events of middle age do not in themselves constitute emergencies for most people. This argument is supported by national statistics for age of first admission to mental hospitals (1967), which rise from childhood to a peak in the period 25 to 34—that is, during young adulthood—and then drop gradually through middle age, rising sharply after age 65. Similarly, in a study of 2,500 adults 21 and over, reports of past emotional crises were given by about a fifth in all age groups, but by a slightly higher proportion in the group aged 35 to 44, with the proportion then dropping steadily with age.[34] The same study also showed that self-reported symptoms of psychological distress rise somewhat with age, but show no tendency to peak in middle age. Finally, U.S. suicide rates climb steadily with age for males but do not peak in middle age, while for females the rate remains low with a slight drop after age 60 to 69. Thus, neither self-reports nor gross external criteria such as these support the crisis view of the middle years.

We interpret all this as support for our view of the "normal, expectable life cycle." Adults develop a set of anticipations of the normal life events, not only what those events should be, but also when they should occur.[54] They make plans, set goals, and reassess those goals along a time line shaped by those expectations. Adults have a sense of the life cycle: that is, an anticipation and acceptance of the inevitable sequence of events that occur as men grow up, grow old, and die; and they understand that their own lives will be similar to the lives of others and that the turning points are inescapable. This ability to interpret the past and foresee the future, and to create for oneself a sense of the predictable life cycle, presumably differentiates the healthy adult personality from the unhealthy one. From this point of view the normal, expectable life events are seldom trauma-producing. Women in their forties and fifties regard the climacterium as inevitable; they know that all women survive it; and most women therefore take it in stride. Similarly men and women expect their children to grow up and leave home, just as they themselves did in their own youth, and their feelings of relief and pride are important parts of their mixed emotions.

The normal, expectable life event too superficially viewed as a crisis event can be illustrated for events at the upper boundary of middle age as well. To an increasingly large proportion of men, retirement is a normal, expectable event. Yet in much of the literature on the topic, the investigator conceptualizes it as a crisis, with the result that the findings from different studies are at variance, with some investigators unprepared for their discovery of no significant losses in life satisfaction or no increased rates of depression following retirement. The fact is that retirement is becoming a middle-aged phenomenon, with many workers now being offered and accepting the opportunity to withdraw from work at age 55. The latest national survey indicates that a surprisingly large proportion of workers in all industries are choosing to retire earlier and earlier, with the main, if not the single, determining factor being level of income—as soon as a man establishes enough retirement income, he chooses to stop working. A more recent study shows that nearly 70 percent of persons who retired as *planned* were content in their retirement, compared with less than 20 percent of the unexpected retirees, those who retired unexpectedly because of poor health or loss of job.[5] Even death becomes a normal, expectable event to the old, and there are various studies that describe the relative equanimity with which it is anticipated.[51] Judging from our many interviews with old people gathered in the course of large-scale

156   THE LIFE COURSE

16. Cameron, P., "The Generation Gap: Which Generation Is Believed Powerful versus Generational Members' Self-Appraisals of Power," *Develop. Psychol.*, 3:403–404, 1970.

17. Cohen, S., Ditman, K. S., and Gustafson, S. R., *Psychochemotherapy: The Physician's Manual*, rev. ed., Western Medical Publications, Los Angeles, 1967.

18. Coleman, R., and Neugarten, B. L., *Social Status in the City*, Jossey-Bass, San Francisco, 1971.

19. Cristenson, C. V., and Gagnon, J. H., "Sexual Behavior in a Group of Older Women," *J. Gerontol.*, 20:351–357, 1965.

20. Datan, N., "Women's Attitudes towards the Climacterium in Five Israeli Subcultures," Ph.D. diss., University of Chicago, 1971.

21. ——, Maoz, B., Antonovsky, A., and Wijsenbeek, H., "Climacterium in Three Cultural Contexts," *Tropical and Geographical Med.*, 22:77–86, 1970.

22. Davis, M. E., Lantzl, L. H., and Cox, A. B., "Detection, Prevention and Retardation of Menopausal Osteoporosis," *Obstetrics and Gynecol.*, 36:187–198, 1970.

23. de Beauvoir, S., *The Second Sex*, Knopf, New York, 1953.

24. Demos, J., and Demos, V., "Adolescence in Historical Perspective," *J. Marriage and Fam.*, 31:632–638, 1969.

25. Deutsch, H., "The Climacterium," in Deutsch, H., *The Psychology of Women*, Vol. 2, *Motherhood*, Grune and Stratton, New York, 1945.

26. Deutscher, I., "Socialization for Postparental Life," in Cavan, R. S. (Ed.), *Marriage and Family in the Modern World*, 2nd ed., Thomas Y. Crowell, New York, 1965.

27. Dunlop, E., "Emotional Imbalance in the Premenopausal Woman," *Psychosom.*, 9:44–47, 1968.

28. Erikson, E. H., *Childhood and Society*, Norton, New York, 1950.

29. Frenkel-Brunswick, E., "Adjustments and Reorientations in the Course of the Life Span," in Neugarten, B. L. (Ed.), *Middle Age and Aging*, University of Chicago Press, Chicago, 1968.

30. Glick, P. C., Heer, D. M., and Beresford, J., "Family Formation and Family Composition: Trends and Prospects," in Sussman, M. B. (Ed.), *Sourcebook in Marriage and the Family*, 2nd ed., Houghton Mifflin, Boston, 1963.

31. Gould, R. L., "The Phases of Adult Life: A Study in Developmental Psychology," *Am. J. Psychiat.*, 129:521–531, 1972.

32. Goulet, L. R., and Baltes, P. B., *Life Span Developmental Psychology*, Academic Press, New York, 1970.

33. Gregory, F. W., and Neu, I. D., "The American Business Elite in the 1870's," in Miller, W. (Ed.), *Men in Business*, Harvard University Press, Cambridge, 1952.

34. Gurin, G., Veroff, J., and Feld, S., *Americans View Their Mental Health: A Nationwide Interview Study*, Basic Books, New York, 1960.

35. Gutmann, D. L., "An Exploration of Ego Configurations," in Neugarten, B. L., et al., *Personality in Middle and Late Life*, Atherton Press, New York, 1964.

36. Havighurst, R. J., "Changing Roles of Women in the Middle Years," in Gross, I. (Ed.), *Potentialities of Women in the Middle Years*, Michigan State University Press, Lansing, 1956.

37. ———, "The Social Competence of Middle-aged People," *Genet. Psychol. Monog.*, 56:297–375, 1957.

38. Jacques,E., "Death and the Mid-life Crises," *Internat. J. Psychoanal.*, 46:502–514, 1965.

39. Jaffe, A. J., "The Middle Years," *Industrial Gerontology*, September 1971, special issue.

40. Jung, C. G., "The Stages of Life," in C. G. Jung, *The Collected Works of C. G. Jung*, Vol. 8, *The Structure and Dynamics of the Psyche*, pp. 387–403, Pantheon Books, New York, 1960.

41. Keniston, K., "Youth as a Stage of Life," *Am. Scholar*, 39:631–654, 1970.

42. Kerr, M. D., "Psychohormonal Approach to the Menopause," *Modern Treatment*, 5:587–595, 1968.

43. Kinsey, A. C., et al., *Sexual Behavior in the Human Female*, W. B. Saunders, Philadelphia, 1953.

44. Klerman, G. L., and Levinson, D. J., "Becoming the Director: Promotion as a Phase in Personal-Professional Development," *Psychiatry*, 32:411–427, 1969.

45. Lieberman, M. A., and Coplan, A. S., "Distance from Death as a Variable in the Study of Aging," *Develop. Psychol.*, 2:71–84, 1970.

46. Lopata, H., *Widowhood in an American City*, Schenkman Publishing Co., Cambridge, Mass., 1972.

47. Lowenthal, M. F., and Chiriboga, D., "Transition to the Empty Nest," *Arch. Gen. Psychiat.*, 26:8–14, 1972.

48. ———, et al., *Aging and Mental Disorder in San Francisco: A Social Psychiatric Study*, Jossey-Bass, San Francisco, 1967.

49. Maoz, B., Dowty, N., Antonovsky, A., and Wijsenbeek, H., "Female Attitudes to Menopause," *Soc. Psychiat.*, 5:35–40, 1970.

50. Masters, W. H., and Johnson, V. E., *Human Sexual Response*, Little, Brown, Boston, 1966.

51. Munniches, J. M. A., *Old Age and Finitude: A Contribution to Psychogerontology*, Karger, Basel, 1966.

52. Myrdal, A., and Klein, V., *Women's Two Roles: Home and Work*, 2nd ed., Routledge and Kegan Paul, London, 1968.

53. Neugarten, B. L., "The Awareness of Middle Age," in Owen, R. (Ed.), *Middle Age*, British Broadcasting Co., London, 1967.

54. ———, "Dynamics of Transition of Middle Age to Old Age: Adaptation and the Life Cycle," *J. Geriatric Psychiat.*, 4:71–87, 1970.

55. ——— (Ed.), *Middle Age and Aging: A Reader in Social Psychology*, University of Chicago Press, Chicago, 1968.

56. ———, et al., *Personality in Middle and Late Life,* Atherton Press, New York, 1964.

57. ———, and Garron, D. C., "Attitudes of Middle-aged Persons toward Growing Older," *Geriatrics,* 14:21–24, 1959.

58. ———, and Gutmann, D. L., "Age-Sex Roles and Personality in Middle Age: A Thematic Apperception Study," *Psychol. Monog.,* 72, 1958.

59. ———, Havighurst, R. J., and Tobin, S. S., "The Measurement of Life Satisfaction," *J. Gerontol.,* 16:134–143, 1961.

60. ———, and Kraines, R. J., "Menopausal Symptoms in Women of Various Ages," *Psychosom. Med.,* 27:266–273, 1965.

61. ———, Kraines, R. J., and Wood, V., "Women in the Middle Years," unpublished manuscript on file, Committee on Human Development, University of Chicago, 1965.

62. ———, and Peterson, W. A., "A Study of the American Age-grade System," *Proceedings of the Fourth Congress of the International Association of Gerontology,* 3:497–502, 1957.

63. ———, and Weinstein, K., "The Changing American Grandparent," *J. Marriage and Fam.,* 26:199–204, 1964.

64. ———, Wood, V., Kraines, R. J., and Loomis, B., "Women's Attitudes toward the Menopause," *Vita Humana* (now *Human Dev.*), 6:140–151, 1963.

65. Owen, R. (Ed.), *Middle Age,* British Broadcasting Co., London, 1967.

66. Parkes, C. M., "Effects of Bereavement on Physical and Mental Health: A Study of the Medical Records of Widows," *Brit. Med. J.,* 2:274–279, 1964.

67. Peck, R. F., and Berkowitz, H., "Personality and Adjustment in Middle Age," in Neugarten, B. L., et al., *Personality in Middle and Late Life,* Atherton Press, New York, 1964.

68. Redlich, F. C., and Freedman, D. X., *The Theory and Practice of Psychiatry,* Basic Books, New York, 1966.

69. Riegel, K. F., "On the History of Psychological Gerontology," Working Paper No. 8, Center for Research on Conflict Resolution, History of Science Program, University of Michigan, Ann Arbor, 1971.

70. Riley, M. W., Foner, A., et al., *Aging and Society,* Vol. 1, *An Inventory of Research Findings,* Russell Sage Foundation, New York, 1968.

71. ———, Riley, J. W., Johnson, M. E., et al. (Eds.), *Aging and Society,* Vol. 2, *Aging and the Professions,* Russell Sage Foundation, New York, 1969.

72. Rothstein, S. H., "Aging Awareness and Personalization of Death in the Young and Middle Years," Ph.D. diss., University of Chicago, 1967.

73. Soddy, K., *Men in Middle Life,* Tavistock, London, 1967.

74. Sonkin, L. S., and Cohen, E. J., "Treatment of the Menopause," *Modern Treatment,* 5:545–563, 1968.

75. Sussman, M. B., "The Help Pattern in the Middle Class Family," *Am. Sociol. Rev.,* 18:22–28, 1957.

76. Szalita, A. B., "Psychodynamics of Disorders of the Involutional Age," in Arieti, S. (Ed.), *American Handbook of Psychiatry,* Vol. 3, Basic Books, New York, 1966.

77. Troll, L. E., "The Family of Later Life: A Decade Review," *J. Marriage and Fam.,* 263–290, 1971.

78. Vedder, C. B., *Problems of the Middle Aged,* Pp. 45–64, Charles C Thomas, Springfield, Ill., 1965.

79. Warner, W. L., and Abegglen, J. C., *Occupational Mobility in American Business and Industry, 1928–1952,* University of Minnesota Press, Minneapolis, 1955.

80. Wilson, R. A., *Forever Feminine,* M. Evans and Co., New York, 1966.

81. ———, and Wilson, T. A., "The Fate of the Non-treated Post-menopausal Woman," *J. Am. Geriatric Soc.,* 11:347–362, 1963.

ELEVEN

Midlife Women in the 1980's

Bernice L. Neugarten and Lorill Brown-Rezanka

INTRODUCTION

It can be taken for granted that midlife women in the 1980's will be different from midlife women of today. The question is, in what ways? And what will be the implications for public policy? These questions should be approached within a broad context: by looking at the changing rhythms of the life cycle as they are affecting women in the middle years, and by looking at the wider social trends that are transforming the lives of women with regard to educational, family and work patterns.

But first, how is midlife or middle age to be defined? The most arbitrary definition is one based on age, with the period usually signified as 40 to 60 or 40 to 65. In truth, however, age is not a meaningful marker. The major life events that characterize the middle part of the life span—launching children from the home, reaching the peak of one's occupational career, the climacterium, grandparenthood, retirement, the onset of chronic illness, widowhood—while they tend to occur in a roughly predictable sequence, occur at very different ages to different people.

If particular life events themselves are taken as the markers of middle age, it is sometimes said that the last child's departure from the home is the lower boundary, and retirement, the upper boundary; but there is no consensus on this matter.

Without meaningful age markers or life event markers, it is sometimes suggested that middle age should be described as a state of mind. From that perspective, it has been shown that the person's awareness of entry and exit from middle age often emerges from one or another biological or social cue rather than from a fixed number of birthdays, so that the psychological beginning and end of middle age also varies from one person to the next, and there is no broadly applicable definition.[1]

For present purposes, then, we are thrown back upon the use of age to mark off midlife, and we shall focus on the age group 40 to 60. To use age markers is not altogether disadvantageous, for in a bureaucratic society that makes increasing use of age

Reprinted from Select Committee on Aging and Subcommittee on Retirement Income and Employment, U.S. House of Representatives, *Women in Mid-Life—Security and Fulfillment,* pt. 1, Joint Testimony, 95th Congress, 2d sess., 1978 (Comm. Pub., No. 95-170), 24–38.

in sorting people and in creating policies and programs, most of our information about life in the middle years has been gathered in terms of age categories. It should be kept in mind, nevertheless, that age has become an increasingly poor predictor of the way people lead their lives and of attitudes and expectations.

THE CHANGING RHYTHM OF THE LIFE CYCLE

Rapid social change has brought with it changes in the rhythm of the life cycle. Some of the old regularities in timing have disappeared and some of the social clocks that tell people whether they are on time or off time are no longer operating. That is, age norms are less compelling than before, and it is less clear what behaviors are appropriate or inappropriate for one's age.

It is not only that the timing of biological events is different and that, for example, while puberty comes earlier in the life cycle than before, the menopause comes later; or that—the most dramatic biological change of all—with the increase in average life expectancy for women, a majority of midlife women can now look forward to living well into their eighties and a sizable proportion to their nineties.

It is also that the social timing is changing. Historically, entry into the labor market has been coming later for men as education is lengthening, but exit from the labor market has been coming earlier as age of retirement is dropping. The timing of these events affects the life patterns not only of men but also of their wives, mothers and daughters.

Historical changes in the timing of events in the family cycle are particularly clear for women. Age at marriage has fluctuated around 21 ever since the turn of the century, but women married at somewhat older ages during the Depression years of the 1930's and at somewhat younger ages during the affluent years of the 1950's. (Age at marriage has taken a slight upturn again in the last few years.) With the timing of motherhood coming at a younger age, and with children spaced closer together, the period of childbearing and childrearing has become shorter. On the average, mothers are now in their early thirties when they see their last child off to school. They then have more than half their lives ahead of them.

The so-called empty nest has also been coming at a younger age than before. Children customarily left home for the first time when they married, but more children now leave home to go to college or to set up separate households, whether or not they marry. (At present more than half of all young people leave the parental household by age 19.) And because of increasing longevity, the period of the empty nest is lengthening, so that a parental couple now has the prospect of some 13 years together after their last child is gone.

Because present middle aged women married early and had their children early, grandmotherhood is coming earlier. Finally, because the life span for women has lengthened more than that for men, and because wives are usually younger than their husbands, the survivor is likely to be the wife. So while widowhood comes later than before, it lasts longer than before.

Statistical averages like these obscure the great variations that exist, and they produce an oversimplified picture. At any period in history there are not only great individual differences between women with regard to the timing of family and other life events, but there are differences between ethnic and racial groups, religious groups, educational and socioeconomic levels and differences between women who live in rural or urban areas. Nevertheless, the timing of life events has changed for most women; and while the family cycle runs its course a few years later for women at higher-than-average levels of education, the general pattern of change has been similar for the highly educated and the poorly educated.

The Fluid Life Cycle

There are also changes of another kind that are producing a new rhythm of the life cycle, particularly for those who are presently young, who are marrying, divorcing, then remarrying; the large number who are rearing children first in two-parent, then one-parent, then in two-parent households; the women who work outside the home, then stop to rear children, then return to school part-time or full-time, then work again; and the many who follow one kind of work, then another.

All this adds up to what can be called the fluid life cycle, one marked by an increasing number of role transitions, the disappearance of traditional timetables, and the lack of synchrony among age-related roles.[2] To go a step further, ours seems to be a society that is becoming accustomed to the 22-year-old mayor, the 30-year-old college president, the 35-year-old grandmother, the 50-year-old retiree, the 70-year-old student, and even the 85-year-old mother who is caring for a 65-year-old child.

In all these ways, the regularities of adult life and the traditional views of life periods are becoming blurred. Middle age has fewer markers, and it becomes more difficult to distinguish the young, the middle-aged and the young-old in terms that are socially meaningful.

SOCIAL CHANGE AND THE LIVES OF WOMEN

The altered timing of life events is only one of the ways that women's lives are changing. In the last 10 years, Americans have seen a resurgence of feminism unparalleled in scope and fervor since the movement for women's rights that followed the Civil War. Many complex social and economic trends have led to and led from the contemporary women's movement. One has been the increasing levels of education of women; another, the changes in concepts of marriage and parenthood that, for at least large segments of the population, have accompanied modern methods of contraception and the increased control over fertility; another, the growing demand for women in the labor force, particularly as the service occupations have expanded.

Whatever the nature of social change that lies ahead, the feminist movement has thus far had its major effects on the lives of young women. This is to some degree inevitable when seen from the perspective of the life cycle, for many of the major life commitments of middle-aged and older women were made well before the movement began, and it is understandable that many of these women expect the movement to have greater influence on the lives of their daughters than on their own lives. At the same time, the underlying social changes which gave rise to the feminist movement are influencing the lives of all women (and all men): e.g., it is now middle-aged women more than young women who are entering the labor force in newly-increased numbers; it is all women whose lives are being altered by increasing divorce; and it is the attitudes and expectations of middle-aged and older women that are shaping and being shaped by their daughters and granddaughters. In looking toward the future, it is not possible to foresee all the ways in which women's lives will be the same or different from the lives of their predecessors; but as women who are presently young become the midlife women of the 1980's and 1990's, their lives are likely to be increasingly different from those of their mothers and grandmothers.

Education

Higher proportions of women are graduating from college and higher proportions are taking advanced degrees. In the 1977–78 academic year, 49 percent of all college students were women, and college women actually outnumbered college men among 18- and 19-year-olds. If these trends continue, by the end of the 1980's a higher proportion of women than men in the age group 30 to 44 will be college graduates, a situation that would be unprecedented.

College entrance rates for women have accelerated and decelerated in different decades, associated with fluctuations in age of marriage and in birthrates, with economic and technological changes, with the effects of wars upon the supply and demand of manpower, with the overall growth of higher education, and so on. The feminist movement and the accompanying affirmative action programs in education are also significant new factors.

Women college students are moving into occupations that traditionally have been regarded as men's occupations. Although they continue to be overrepresented in the fields of education and the health professions, an increasing percentage of women are now majoring in mathematics, statistics, business, law, public administration, physical sciences, agriculture, and forestry. Today's women, particularly young women, are following more varied career lines than the women of the past, and they are increasing their career options for the future.

An important new trend is that older women are being welcomed back on campuses. There has been a dramatic change in the age of the college population, with well over ten percent of all college students now 35 or older; but the spectacular increase in this age group has occurred among women, rather than men. Most of these women are furthering career-related goals, but as lifelong education becomes a widely accepted way of improving the general quality of life, it will probably be women more than men whose lives will be affected, at least in the near future.

Continuing education programs have mushroomed, and they offer special benefits for those women who interrupted their education to marry and rear children. These programs generally include one or more of the following features: part-time enrollment, flexible course schedules, short-term courses, counseling services, financial aid for part-time study, removal of age restrictions, curriculum geared to adult experiences, credit by examination, refresher courses, child care facilities, and job placement assistance. Other education reforms important to women are variously designated by such terms as "external degrees," "the open university," and "universities without walls."

Returning college students constitute just one part of the larger population of adults involved in education. In 1976 it was estimated that 16 percent of all persons age 17 to 34 were enrolled in some type of adult education, and nearly 13 percent of all those age 35 to 54. These figures do not include the large numbers engaged in educational activities in museums, churches, neighborhood clubs, nor that very large number who pursue self-taught but systematic learning projects which run the gamut from homemaking skills to esoteric types of knowledge.

The numbers of returning college students are expected to rise considerably as colleges seek to maintain enrollments in the face of declining numbers of younger students. In addition, participants in the broader field of adult education are expected to multiply as the level of formal education in the population continues to rise, for the more formal years of schooling a person has had, the more likely that person will be participating in one or another form of adult education.

All these education trends are affecting the life styles of today's women. They will have even greater impact upon tomorrow's women, especially upon those who have experienced the feminist movement when they were young, and who will be building on that experience as they become the middle-aged of the next decades. Because educational levels are directly related to economic and cultural living standards, to political and social attitudes, and to rising levels of expectations (including expectations about the appropriate role of Government), midlife women will become an increasingly articulate group in the 1980's, a group with substantial influence in all areas of political, social and economic life.

Family and Work Patterns

The great majority of American women marry (in 1975 it was 95 percent) and the great majority become mothers (in 1975 it was 90 percent of those who had married). Nevertheless, family life is changing, and it is now only a minority of households in which the wife is the homemaker and the husband is the sole bread winner. Households in which both wife and husband are in the labor force are now almost half of all wife-husband households; and about two-fifths of all children under age 18 are now being reared in families in which both parents have jobs outside the home.

These facts reflect the wider picture: that while 50 years ago one out of five persons in the labor force was a woman, today it is two out of five. These figures are calculated at points in time when counts of the labor force are taken. The more significant figure emerges from looking at successive points over women's life times. It appears that 9 out of 10 of today's women will have been in the labor force at one or more times in their lives. And while it has always been the case that women are most likely to be working when they are young, in recent decades it is also when they are middle aged. (In 1977 over half of all women age 45 to 54 were employed, and the proportion is expected to rise somewhat further in the 1980's.)

This means that increasing millions of American women have chosen to marry, to raise children, and to work, and to work at more than one point in their lives. An increasing proportion, furthermore, enter the labor force and remain there throughout their adult lives without taking out long periods for homemaking or childrearing.

Wife-husband-children is only one form of the family unit, and there is the possibility that significant numbers of women who are now young and who will reach middle age in the 1980's may move away from the traditional pattern. New forms of the family include the couple who live together without marriage, the husband and wife who have had previous marriages, the couple who choose to remain childless, the never-married or divorced parent raising children alone, and the communal family group. The significant trend overall is the increase in households headed by women. Part of this increase is due to divorce. As is well known, divorce rates are rising in all age groups and are soaring among the young. It is estimated that about 40 percent of first marriages of women now 25 to 35 will end in divorce. If this comes true, it will mean that a high proportion of the women who reach midlife by the end of the 1980's will have gone through at least one broken marriage, and given the data on labor force participation, will have had more than one period when they have been self-supporting.

In any case, more than 10 percent of all households are now headed by women, and approximately 15 percent of all those with children. Another significant trend is the increasing number of women who live alone for short or long periods of their lives, reflecting the growing numbers who postpone marrige, the growing numbers of childless divorcees, and the growing numbers of older widowed women who live alone.

With regard to the family life of today's middle-aged women, it appears that it is not relations with children, or with husband, or the empty nest of the menopause that constitutes a major problem (although, of course, some women have problems in those areas), but widowhood and the new concern over parent-caring.

It has already been mentioned that widowhood comes later in the lives of women today than was true for their mothers. Not until women are beyond age 65 do a majority now become widowed, and this picture may change even more in the next decade with the new declines in deaths from heart disease that have been occurring over the last few years. Notwithstanding, a sizable number of women are widowed in their fifties; the mental rehearsal for widowhood is a common theme in the self-reports of middle-aged women, along with the anticipations of grief, loneliness, financial insecurity and loss of social status that are perceived to be its accompaniments.[3] The adjustment to widowhood may be somewhat less difficult in the future as more women become financially self-reliant and more of them have work and community responsibilities that occupy them. Still, it is likely that widowhood, actual or anticipated, will remain a primary stressor for middle-aged women, and that both financial and social support systems for widows will continue to be an important area requiring intervention by both private and public agencies.

The dramatic change in family life which is affecting the lives of women is the appearance of the four- and five-generation family. Increasing longevity in the population brings with it, especially for women who are themselves in midlife, concern over the care of an aging parent or parent-in-law. Parent-caring does not necessarily imply that a woman takes on the daily physical care of a frail old person living in her household. It does mean shouldering or sharing the responsibility for decisionmaking, for planning the living arrangements and the medical supervision and the social support system for an older relative—sometimes for two generations of older relatives, for it is not unusual today for a 40-year-old woman to have both a 65-year young-old mother and an 85-year old-old grandmother to be concerned about.

The significance of parent-caring is confirmed in a recent survey of adults in the metropolitan area of Chicago who were asked what major changes in their lives had occurred in the past 4 years. A perceived change in a parent was the second-most-frequently reported event, a serious health change or increased need for moral support. Of the large proportion of adults who reported such a change in the parent, about 40 percent said the problem was genuinely troublesome to them, the interviewees; of this latter group, the majority had turned for advice or assistance to other family members, to friends, or to other helping persons.[4] About a fourth had turned to formal or professional helpers, such a social workers or psychiatrists.

Parent-caring involves strong components of obligation and commitment, whether or not there is frequent visiting and whether or not the adult child reports a feeling of close emotional bondedness to the aging parent. Indeed, the strong intergenerational family ties among adults may be an aspect of family life that has not been given the recognition it deserves. Many studies have shown that while most older people want to remain independent of their families as long as possible, they expect their children to come to their aid when they can no longer manage for themselves, and that these expectations are usually fulfilled.[5] As has long been true, it is usually the woman rather than the man in the middle generation who fills the role of kin-keeper, maintaining communication across generations and seeing to it that services are provided when needed. It is also the case that the older the individual and the sicker, the more likely he or she is to be living with an adult child. The 1970 census showed that of all persons age 75 and over, one of five women and one of ten men were living in a child's household—or to put it differently, for every older person living in an institution, there were three others living with a child, most frequently with a daughter.

All in all, so far as family patterns are concerned, we cannot yet assess the long-term effects of changes in education, family planning, work patterns, and longevity as they are affecting the family responsibilities of both women and men. It is clear that more women are spending more time in work and community roles that lie outside the traditional roles of mother and homemaker, not only because they work outside the home both before and after marriage and both before and after motherhood, but also because more women have periods of time between marriages and because the periods of the empty nest and widowhood are longer than before. In these ways the family cycle is becoming less dominant in shaping the lives of women. At the same time the family, and especially the multi-generation family, is by no means losing its salience. While most women feel freer of family responsibilities when they reach midlife, there is some increasing number who feel themselves caught between the needs of adolescent children, husbands and aging parents, and who feel no more free to devote themselves to work or community roles in their midlife than they were in their young adulthood.

Whatever the balance of forces will be, it is likely that women who work at increasingly responsible and high-level jobs will be less willing to return to the home to care for an aging relative. Just as younger women have been seeking day-care services to assist them in their child-care role, middle-aged women will be seeking social services and home-health services to assist them in their parent-caring role.

Women as Workers

In thinking ahead to the 1980's, more should be said about women's work roles. The major reason that women work, whether they are young or middle-aged, married or not, mothers or not, is an economic reason, just as is true for men. This is not likely to change in the next few decades. It is significant, however, that the greatest growth of women workers in recent years has taken place among well-educated wives from families whose incomes are moderate but insufficient to maintain the desired pattern of consumption. Before World War II, married women workers came almost exclusively from low-income families, but it is now about as likely for a middle-class wife to be employed as for a working-class wife.

There is a direct relationship between women's levels of education and their levels of employment. The more education a woman has, the more likely she is to be in the labor force. This is true for all women as a group and true also when the data are broken down by different age groups. (Of women who were drop-outs from high school, less than 40 percent were employed in 1976, but of women who had four or more years of college, it was 65 percent.) This latter point makes it clear that there are reasons other than economic that also propel women into the labor force. Especially at higher educational levels, women work for intellectual and social stimulation, for opportunities for service, for self-development, and because they find the work intrinsically satisfying and rewarding.

As educational levels rise, not only the numbers but also the occupational levels of women workers rise. It is this latter fact that has special significance for the 1980's. A higher proportion of young women than of middle-aged women have had college educations and hold jobs at the top of the occupational ladder in professional and technical job categories. As these young women become the midlife women of the 1980's, their length of work experience will have an added effect on their high levels of education, and the two factors together will mean for them higher occupational levels. The total distribution of women workers will become more similar to the distribution of men workers than is true today.

This warrants a closer look. At present, women workers compared to men remain concentrated in a few major occupational categories. (In 1976, well over half of all women workers were in relatively low-paying clerical, operative, or service positions.) But these aggregated data obscure the important age differences. Over the past several decades, there has been a large influx of middle-aged women into the labor force, women who had on the average less education than younger women and who went to work at low-paying, dead-end jobs. This historical trend will come to an end as the proportion of middle-aged women in the labor market tops out (it is predicted, for instance, that of women 45 to 54 the proportion will increase from 55 percent in 1975 only slightly and will reach 60 percent by 1990).

Table 11.1. Social Characteristics of American Women in 1975[1]

	Group A, age 60 to 65	Group B, age 40 to 45	Group C, age 25 to 30
Total number (in thousands)[2]	4,983	5,735	8,909
Average life expectancy at birth	55	63	70
Education:			
Percent completed high school	53	72	84
Percent 1 or more years of college	17	23	38
Percent graduated from college	8	11	20
Labor force participation:			
Percent in labor force at present	33	57	57
Percent in professional and technical jobs	12	17	25
Early family experience:[3]			
Percent whose parents both born in United States	46	85	94
Percent with 1 or no sibling	18	30	20
Percent to age 15 in families with no deaths of parents or siblings	45	71	85
Marriage and family:			
Percent 1st married by age 20	37	50	46
Percent single at age 25 to 29	23	10	15
Percent divorced by age 35 to 39	12	18	([4])
Percent 1st marriage ended (or predicted to end) in divorce	16	26	38
For married women:			
Average number of births by age 27	1.1	2	1.4
Total number of births per woman	2.5	3.2	[5]1.5
Percent 1st birth within 7 mo. of marriage	11	14	23
Percent childless at age 25 to 29	30	13	21

[1] Data are taken from various reports of the U.S. Bureau of the Census and the Bureau of Labor Statistics.

[2] As of July 1, 1977. Parallel numbers of men are 4,380; 5,465; and 8,837.

[3] Data on early family experience are for white native born, both sexes combined; and for group C, for persons born in 1950. See Peter Uhlenberg, "Changing configurations of the life course," a paper prepared for the Conference on the Family Life Course in Historical Perspective, Williams College, July 1975.

[4] 17 percent of this group have already been divorced by age 25 to 29.

[5] This group is still in their childbearing years; their total birthrate will be higher.

The difference in jobs status between younger and older women is illustrated in Table 11.1, where it is shown that as one moves from the older to the younger group, the proportions in professional and technical occupations in 1975 rises from 12 to 25 percent. It is this 25 percent who will be among the midlife women in the 1980's. Together with the additional number who will have raised their educational levels and their job levels by that time, the effect will be an upward shift in the occupational distribution of women as a whole and a generally higher-level work force.

One of the factors that may operate in the opposite direction, however, is that the numbers of presently young people are so large, the outcome of the post-war baby boom. As these numbers of women and men move along, like a bulge in the pipeline of the population, the competition for jobs may become acute and the opportunities for women may diminish more than for men. This is but a reminder that society-wide economic and technological and population trends will continue to have major influences on the employment patterns of women, and that the overall outcomes are not altogether predictable.

Still another set of influences on women's employment patterns relate to changes in public attitudes. It has already been said that sex discrimination undoubtedly plays a role today, even though its extent is difficult to assess. One of the factors that has great potential for improving the status of women workers is the anti-discrimination legislation and the affirmative action programs enacted by Congress and federal agencies: the Equal Pay Act of 1963 and its amendments of 1972; title VII of the Civil Rights Act of 1964 and its extended coverage of 1972; title IX of the Education Amendments of 1972; and the Presidential Executive Order 11246 of 1967 establishing nondiscrimination by sex in Government employment.

Public attitudes are important in yet another way. The fact that today's women are concentrated in low-paying jobs is voluntary in part and reflects the traditional patterns both within family and schools that have led women to set low levels of aspiration for themselves as workers. As more women become educated for and move into higher-level occupations, and as more begin to think in terms of careers rather than jobs, their earnings and their overall status as workers should change for the better.

Minority Women

Unlike the patterns that were true earlier, minority women (black, Mexican-American, Puerto Rican, American Indian, Asiatic, and Eskimo) are no more likely today to be in the labor force than are majority women. This is because the proportions of minority women at work have stayed relatively constant over the past two decades, while the proportions of majority women have climbed.

In the job market, minority women have faced both race discrimination and sex discrimination, and as a group they have been markedly disadvantaged compared to majority women. They not only have lower levels of education; they have usually begun work in lower-status jobs and, with the exception of such occupations as teaching, they remain clustered in less desirable jobs; they have higher unemployment rates; and compared with majority women of equivalent education and experience, their earnings have been less.

While these disadvantages are still severe, the situation for minority women has been somewhat alleviated in the past 20 years, with the proportion rising rapidly in the professional and technical categories (from 7 to 14 percent) and in clerical jobs (from 9 to 26 percent), and with the proportion in private household work dropping sharply (from 35 to 9 percent). The important point is the one made earlier, that changes in the occupational distribution are tied directly to the educational levels of successive age groups, a fact that is even more striking in the case of minority women than it is for majority women. The Civil Rights movement has had its major effects upon young people, and it is successive groups of young minority women who have had improved educational opportunities and improved job opportunities.

As pointed out earlier, it is difficult to disentangle the complex interactions between education, work, and family patterns in the lives of women. This is clearly illustrated when comparing black women to white women. That black women have fared more poorly in the labor market is associated in part with differences in their education, but in part also with differences in family patterns. A higher proportion, for instance, have borne their first child before age 18; a higher proportion have large families of six or more children; a smaller proportion are married and living with their husbands; and a much higher proportion are heads of households (in 1976, 36 percent of all black families were headed by women as compared with 11 percent of white families.)

To the extent that family patterns are changing—and they are changing at a particularly striking rate in middle-class black families—employment patterns for black women can also be expected to change. While the work status of minority women will improve if racial discrimination diminishes, and while the work status of both minority and majority women will improve if sex discrimination diminishes, still work status for both groups will continue, in all probability, to be more directly related to family patterns than to discrimination *per se*.

Successive Groups of American Women

The social trends just described can be understood another way, by comparing the social characteristics of different age groups of American women. This has been attempted in Table 11.1 where, although the data are often only approximate to our purposes, they nevertheless convey some of the major differences in the lives of women born at successive points in history. The first, group A, are women age 60–65 in the year 1975 and represent those who are presently exiting from middle age. The second, group B, age 40–45 in 1975, represent those who are presently entering middle age. The third, group C, age 25–30, represent those who will enter middle age by the end of the 1980's. While the choice of 5-year age groups has been arbitrary, these particular groups serve not only to highlight historical changes but also to demonstrate that major historical events are associated with differences in life outcomes across whole birth cohorts.

The two World Wars and the Great Depression of the 1930's are usually regarded as watershed events in American history. Group A, born 1910 to 1915, were young children during World War I and were reaching adulthood during the depression years. Group B, born 1930 to 1935, were depression babies who were reaching adulthood during the affluent years of the 1950's. Because these two groups are separated by a 20-year interval, group B may be regarded roughly as the daughters of group A. Group C, born 15 years later in 1945 to 1950, were part of the baby boom that followed World War II and were reaching adulthood when the feminist movement was gaining momentum at the turn of the 1970's.

The lives of these three groups of women might well be expected to differ, as indeed they did. Some of the differences can be read from table 11.1, while others can only be inferred. But it is clear that the three groups brought or will bring very different experiential backgrounds with them into middle age.

Of the oldest group, group A, the large majority were born into big families; half had one or both parents who were foreign born; and the majority, by the time they reached 15, had experienced the death of a sibling or of a parent. Of this total group, only half finished high school and only a very few finished college. Entering their childbearing years during the depression, a sizable proportion stayed single to age 30, a sizable proportion delayed having children, and a sizable proportion remained childless. Overall the birthrate in this group was the lowest recorded up to that time.

By contrast, group B women, born in the depression years, were reared in small families; only a minority had a foreign-born mother or father; and only a minority had by adolescence witnessed a death in the immediate family. Of this total group the large majority finished high school, but it was still the unusual young woman who finished college. Entering their childbearing years during a period of economic expansion, this group married early and bore relatively large numbers of children. More of this group have been or will be divorced than is true for their mothers, but fewer will have been widowed by age 60. Because of their high birthrates, furthermore, this group, compared to those who precede and follow them, will have relatively large numbers of children to turn to in their old age, although, unlike their own mothers, they will have relatively few grandchildren.

The youngest women, group C, are markedly different from both earlier groups. Once again it is a group who were reared in large families. Almost half these women have married early, before age 20, but a sizable proportion have delayed childbearing and the majority say they expect to bear only one or two children. If they carry out their plans for small families and if their longevity increases as predicted, these women will have many more child-free years than did any of their predecessors.[6] They are also markedly different from earlier groups in terms of their higher educational and occupational levels, with, as already mentioned, one-fourth who are already employed in professional and technical jobs.

WHAT WILL MIDLIFE WOMEN WANT?

We have been saying, sometimes explicitly and sometimes implicitly, that successive groups of women will be different in midlife because they have had different experiences in childhood and youth. Midlife women in the 1980's will be different also, of course, because the world itself will be different. But to stay with the more circumscribed question before us, what are the implications for the 1980's and 1990's of the changing life patterns we have been describing?

By the year 1990, our group C women will be 40 to 45 and our group B women, 55 to 60. Together with the larger intermediate group, they will constitute a very heterogeneous population, a point that should not be lost sight of despite the fact that we have been describing group averages rather than group variability. We have stressed the differences between age groups, but there are equally striking differences between socioeconomic groups, ethnic groups, and so on. Furthermore, the variability among middle-aged women is greater than among young women. People become more different with the passage of time, as choices and commitments build up into unique life patterns, and as interests and activities become more individualized. That women's lives fan out as they grow older can be seen when women gather, say, for a 25th reunion of their high school or college class; they find how variegated their lives have become as compared to the time they were in school together.

With increasing heterogeneity, midlife women will want a wide range of options—in living arrangements, in the workplace, in education, and in recreation. With long periods of lifetime still ahead, they will want opportunities to try new types of work, new types of service to their communities, and new routes to self-fulfillment. Middle-aged women have already been reporting that they feel and act younger than their mothers did at the same age—that they are not only healthier and more vigorous, but more youthful in outlook and in expectations of life. There is every reason to expect this trend to accelerate.

As it accelerates, women will press for a more egalitarian society; removal of sex, race, and particularly age discrimination; equity for men and women in pension systems; removal of mandatory retirement for themselves and for their husbands; a change toward an age-irrelevant society, one in which arbitrary constraints based on age are removed in both work and nonwork areas of life. They will expect improved programs in health care, with special attention given to the amelioration of chronic illness. They will want new programs of economic assistance for men as well as women during transitions between jobs, school and homemaking. In education they will want financial support as they undertake new or second careers, or as they seek new cultural experiences: scholarships available for part-time as well as full-time study, Federal loan programs, paid sabbaticals from work. They will encourage more entry and exit points into higher education and the expansion of innovative programs geared to their needs for flexibility.

Most midlife women will continue to balance work and family responsibilities. For increasing numbers, this will involve working all through adulthood and moving up the career ladder; others will not wish to work steadily or full-time, and they will seek flexibility without sacrificing the opportunity for interesting and responsible work. This will include job-sharing, especially of career-level jobs, and more jobs specially arranged to match the capabilities of mature and experienced women. Others will choose non-remunerated work in their communities and will seek out a wider range of service opportunities, especially those commensurate with their ability and their life experience. Because the age of retirement is expected to continue to drop, an increasing number of women in their late fifties will seek meaningful leisure pursuits for their husbands and themselves, but also service opportunities planned as husband-wife undertakings.

An increasing proportion of midlife women will be divorced and living alone, or they will be heads of households that include adolescent children and other relatives. Together with the group who are widowed, they will create an increasing demand for varied types of housing. Some who live alone will seek housing that provides not only physical security and recreational facilities, but also facilitates for congregate eating and cooking. Others, married or single, will want architectural arrangements that will allow for the care of an aging relative. Whether married or single, midlife women will want housing and neighborhood facilities that provide greater local flexibility, so that as their households contract or expand they need not keep moving into new neighborhoods or new communities.

We have already mentioned the needs of midlife women for assistance in their parent-caring role. Some women would take an aged parent into their homes if financial reimbursement could be provided to replace lost work income; these women are likely to look to Government for this type of aid. Others want improved home health services or social services or homemaking services to help the older relative live independently. Others want sheltered group housing for older relatives as an alternative to the nursing home; still others, who look to institutional care as the last resort, will press for more acceptable forms of nursing home care.

Counseling services for women will become increasingly important. This includes access to counselors who are themselves middle-aged or older, and who can assist them not only with regard to educational, work, and service opportunities, but also with changing psychological relationships to adult children, husbands, and grandchildren and with psychological transitions related to divorce, widowhood, and retirement. Midlife women will benefit, as will younger women, from counseling that comes to terms with the facts of increasing longevity and that will help them plan for lengthening periods of old age for themselves, their husbands, and their parents.

All in all, as the society moves toward the 21st century and toward a population in which higher proportions will be middle-aged and old—as we move toward the so-called mature society—it will be the middle-aged, and in many ways middle-aged women, who will create a new social and psychological climate. They will create new meanings for the terms midlife and middle age, and new connotations of vigor and activity that will be seen to accompany experience and maturity. In so doing, they will help create a more realistic view of the life cycle, not only for the middle-aged, but also for the old and for the young.

Notes

1. Bernice L. Neugarten, "The awareness of middle age," in Middle Age and Aging, Bernice L. Neugarten (Ed), (Chicago: University of Chicago Press, 1968), pp. 93–98.

2. Larry Hirschhorn, "Social policy and the life cycle: a developmental perspective." Social Service Review 51 (September, 1977), pp. 434–450.

3. Helena Lopata, Widowhood in an American City. (Cambridge: Schenkman Publishing Co., 1973).

4. Grace L. Lieberman, "Children of the elderly as natural helpers: some demographic variables." American Journal of Community Psychology, Special Issue, Autumn, 1978.

5. Ethel Shanas and Marvin B. Sussman (Eds), Family, Bureaucracy, and the Elderly. (Durham, N.C.: Duke University Press, 1977).

6. Roxanne A. Van Dusen and Eleanor B. Sheldon, "The Changing Status of American Women." American Psychologist, 31 (1976), pp. 106–116.

TWELVE

Social and Psychological Characteristics
of Older Persons

THE AGING SOCIETY

Long life is a major achievement of the 20th century in all developed countries of the world. The average life expectancy at birth in the United States has now reached 75 years, and it is expected to keep rising (Table 12.1.). It is not only that people are living longer. Primarily because of lower birth rates, the proportions of older to younger people are increasing, producing a shift in the overall age distribution of the society that is expressed by the term, the aging society.

That the older population itself is growing older is reflected in the fact that during the next 20 years, the fastest growth rates will be, as now, in the group aged 85 years and older. The trend is dramatized even further by the fact that centenarians, while they are rare, are expected to quadruple in number and to reach nearly 110,000 by the year 2000.[1]

The older population is growing older because the newest gains in life expectancy are different from those of earlier decades. In the past, because they were due mainly to the conquest of infectious diseases, the gains were spread relatively evenly across the population, with the result that more people reached old age. But because, for the past two decades, mortality rates have been so low for persons younger than age 50 that they could not be much improved, the new gains have been those that affect older persons: gains that have come from new treatments of chronic diseases and from the amelioration of those conditions internal and external to the individual that are especially lethal to older people. While the effects of new infectious diseases, such as the acquired immunodeficiency syndrome (AIDS), cannot be foreseen, it is nevertheless likely that future gains in longevity will continue to be those that lengthen the period of old age.

HEALTH STATUS

The future health status of older people as a group is not altogether predictable. The evidence is clear that the vigorous and active part of the life span has been lengthen-

Reprinted by permission from *Geriatric Medicine,* 2d ed., edited by C. K. Cassel, D. E. Riesenberg, L. B. Sorenson, and J. R. Walsh (New York: Springer-Verlag, 1990), 28–36.

Table 12.1. Life expectancy at selected ages.*

	Birth	Average remaining years of life at 65 y	75 y†	85 y†
White women				
1960	74.1	15.9	9.3	4.7
1985	78.7	18.7	11.8	6.5
White men				
1960	67.4	12.9	7.9	4.3
1985	71.8	14.6	9.0	5.2
Black women				
1960	65.9	15.1	10.1	5.4
1985	73.7	17.2	11.5	7.4
Black men				
1960	60.7	12.7	8.9	5.1
1985	65.3	13.4	9.0	6.0
Sex ratio, 1986				
(Men/100 Women)	105	83	64	40

* Data from references 5 and 14.
† Entries for the ages of 75 and 85 years are for 1983.

ing, and, in that sense, we have been producing a 20th century version of the Fountain of Youth. But advanced old age may continue to mean, for individuals, failure in one body organ after another.[2] Science and medicine may continue to develop palliative means that delay death, but that prolong rather than shorten the duration of terminal illnesses.[3]

At present, more and more people are surviving into the oldest age group where the need for supportive services is greatest, especially the need for long-term care. For the immediate future, this group will remain a small proportion of persons older than age 65 (Table 12.2.); however, as their numbers multiply, it is the population older than 85 that will dominate health planning for the foreseeable future.[4]

ECONOMIC AND SOCIAL HEALTH OF OLDER PEOPLE

Patterns of aging, and the quality of life once people grow old, are closely related to the economic and social health of the society at large. A strong case can be made that the economic well-being of older persons and the social well-being that is so closely related to it reflect the society's economic level more than its political ideology or its cultural characteristics.

In the decades after World War II, but especially since the late 1960s, the economic condition of older people as a group has dramatically improved. Like other developed countries, the United States has a multitiered system that rests on public

Table 12.2. Selected characteristics of older people by age group.*

	65–74	75–84	85+	All 65+	All 75+
Numbers (millions), (1986)					
Men	7.2	3.3	0.7	11.2	4.0
Women	9.4	5.5	1.8	16.7	7.3
Projected total population (millions)					
2000	17.7	12.3	4.9	34.9	...
2020	29.9	14.5	7.1	51.4	...
Median income, (1985) (thousands)					
Families	20.4	16.4	15.1	...	...
Unrelated individuals	8.2	7.2	6.4	...	...
Percent below poverty level (1986)					
Men	7.0	10.7	13.3	8.5	...
Women	13.0	18.1	19.7	15.2	...
Percent in labor force (1986)					
Men	25.0†	...	...	16.0	10.4‡
Women	14.3†	...	...	7.4	4.1‡
Marital status (percents)$					
Men					
Married with spouse present	79	68	...	75	...
Widowed	9	23	...	14	...
Women					
Married with spouse present	49	23	...	38	...
Widowed	39	67	...	51	...
Living alone					
Men	13	...	...	15	19
Women	35	...	...	41	51
Living in nursing homes (1985)‖					
Men and Women	1	6	22	...	...
Median years of schooling (1986)					
Men	12.1	...	...	11.7	9.6
Women	12.1	...	...	11.9	10.4
Percent who are homeowners (1985)	...	...	...	75	...
(Percent of homes that are mortgage free)¶	...	...	...	80	...

  * Data from references 5 and 15.
  † Data are for those 65–69.
  ‡ Data are for those 70+.
  $ Percent of the never married, married with spouse absent, and divorced are not shown in this Table.
  ‖ Of nursing home residents, over two-thirds are women.
  ¶ In 1980 for the first time a greater number of older persons lived in suburbs (over 10 million) than in central (8 million).

continued

Table 12.2. *Continued*

	65–74	75–84	85+	All 65+	All 75+
Changed residence (from March 1983– March 1984)#					
Same county	...	...	...	3.8	...
Different county	...	...	...	1.0	...

Fewer than 5% of persons 65+ moved in this one-year period, compared to 17% of persons of all ages and 34% of persons aged 20–24. Of the small proportion of older persons who move, most migrate to the sunbelt states. Data from reference 16.

pensions, private pensions, and savings. The system supports people for as long as 30 or more years after retirement, a reflection of the fact that people are retiring earlier but living longer.

Economic Indicators

Most older persons are not poor, although the range of economic differences is very wide.[5] About as many older men have very high incomes as the number who live in poverty. The distribution is different for women, of whom a much larger proportion have incomes near or under the poverty level. This is related to the fact that the majority of women over 65 are widowed; they were in the labor force only intermittently, and as a consequence, they have meager or no Social Security benefits of their own, and few have private pensions. Very old widowed and never-married women are particularly disadvantaged groups.

Minority-group older people, especially blacks, also are very poorly off. In these groups, the social and economic disadvantages that have accumulated throughout their lives are accentuated in old age.

Older persons, on average, have substantially lower cash incomes than younger people. At the same time, they have certain economic advantages because of special income tax benefits provided to persons older than 65, government in-kind transfers that are not available to younger persons (primarily health care costs covered by Medicare), and lifetime accumulations of wealth (primarily the equity in their own homes). Some analysts contend that when these factors are taken into account, the average older person has economic resources roughly equivalent to an average person of working age. Still, there are sizable subgroups of older people who have very limited economic resources, especially very old women and members of minority groups.

Social Indicators

A few additional facts are helpful in rounding out the picture: The vast majority of persons retire before the age of 65 years and begin to draw Social Security benefits at the age of 62 or 63 years. At present, only 16% of men and only 7% of women are in the labor force after the age of 65, and most of them work only part-time.

Most men older than 65 years are married and living with their wives. Not only are most women widowed by the time they reach 65 years of age, but by the time they real 75, more than half live alone.

Most older persons "grow old in place"; that is, they remain in the same communities, often in the same houses that they have occupied for most of their adult lives. Of the small proportion who move, most go to the Sunbelt states of the South and West.

About 75% of older people own their own homes, and about 80% of these homes are mortgage free. For the first time in 1980, more older people lived in suburbs than in the central cities.

The major point to be drawn from the kinds of data shown in Table 12.2. is that old age itself does not define a problem group in today's society. Some older people are economically and socially needy; others are not. On most socioeconomic measures, it is a small minority who are severely disadvantaged. These are mainly very old persons who, compared with persons born later, have been disadvantaged earlier in their lives with regard to education, occupational skills, medical care, and pension systems.

This picture will change rapidly as new cohorts of persons reach old age, a point to be elaborated in a later section of this chapter.

Social Participation and Attitudes

Measures of the social participation and social integration of older people reveal considerable heterogeneity. As Table 12.3. shows, however, the majority report that they have active family ties and close friends whom they see frequently. About the same proportion of younger people attend a church or synagogue, and sizable numbers, up through their 80s, report that they belong to organizations and are engaged in volunteer work.

Moreover, as shown in Table 12.4., a majority report their health to be excellent or good; and most report high levels of life satisfaction. Compared with younger adults, about the same proportion feel that life is better than they expected, and high proportions have positive self-images. Only a small fraction report that insufficient income is a serious problem, or loneliness; a somewhat larger fraction report that fear of crime or poor health poses a serious problem.

Overall, the picture that emerges is that persons over 65, as a group, exhibit relatively high levels of economic and social health.

The data in Tables 12.2. through 12.4. have, at the same time, been broken down to show some of the differences between younger and older subgroups.

Table 12.3. Indicators of social participation (self-reports) by age group.*

	Age, y			
	18–59	60–69	70–79	80+
Of those with children, %				
Saw child in last day or so	65	53	46	51
Give help to child or grandchild, %				
When someone is ill	74	73	75	78
By helping with money	26	21	23	25
Have close friends, %	97	95	94	90
Saw friend in last day or so, %	63	63	59	58
Spend "lot of time" in organizations, %	14	15	17	16

	Age, y		
	18–64	55–64	All 65+
Attend church/synagogue in last week or two, %			
Year 1974	34	...	40
Year 1981	27	...	35
Attended senior center or golden age club in last week or two, %			
Year 1974	...	2	6
Year 1981	...	3	9
In past year 1984†	...	...	15
Used congregate meal services in past year			
Year 1984†	...	...	8
Spend "lot of time" in recreation and hobbies, %			
Year 1974	34	...	26
Year 1981	36	...	26
socializing with friends, %			
Year 1974	55	...	47
Year 1981	45	...	38
caring for younger/older family members, %			
Year 1974	53	...	27
Year 1981	50	...	20

	Age, y			
	65–69	70–79	80+	All 65+
Do volunteer work, %				
Year 1974	28	20	12	22
Year 1981	28	23	12	23

continued

Table 12.3. *Continued*

	Age, y			
	35–54	55–64	65–74	75+
Voted, %				
Year 1980‡	66	71	69	58
Year 1984‡	66	72	72	61

* Data from references 17 and 18.
† Data from reference 19.
‡ Data from reference 5 (pp. 9, 10, 12, 44, 45, 47, 85, 137, 139, 142).

THE LIFE CYCLE PERSPECTIVE

It is important to recognize that aging processes are gradual and continuous, a progression of changes, some orderly and predictable, and others unpredictable. Social, as well as biological, timetables govern the sequence of change.

The life cycle perspective has important implications for health planners and providers. First, except for retirement, old age is not a separable period of life, neither abrupt in its onset nor, for most persons, marked by dramatic changes in interest patterns, personal commitments, or, until a major change in health occurs, in life style. The individual's social and health characteristics in old age are, in large part, the outcomes of earlier life-styles and earlier health histories.

Second, people grow old in very different ways, and they become increasingly different from one another with the passage of time, at least until the very terminal stage of life when biological losses may level out individual differences. Women age differently from men, and there are differences among racial, ethnic, and, particularly, socioeconomic groups. Add to this the idiosyncratic sequence of events that accumulate over a lifetime to create individual variation. The result is that older people are a very diverse group.

Although the incidence of illness and disability increases with age in the second half of life, the association between age and health is far from perfect. In probabilistic terms, age is a good predictor of health status, but for any given individual, it is a poor predictor of physical, mental, or social competence.

Third, some of the major variations in aging are due to cohort differences: each group of people who reach old age has certain unique characteristics. This is because of the changing historical and societal conditions that have influenced their lives. One example is the rising educational level of older persons: by 1990 about half of the population over age 65 will have had some education beyond high school. Another example relates to the increasing number of women in the labor force: now, for the first time, large groups of women are experiencing formal retirement. To plan

Table 12.4. Attitudes of older people by age group.*

	Age, y (1974)					Age, y (1981)
	18–59	60–69	70–79	80+	All 65+	All 65+
Health is excellent or good (self-report, 1981), %	...	64†	52	51	56	...
Life satisfaction, %‡						
Year 1974	...	27†	26	24	26	...
Year 1981	...	26†	24	24	25	...
"My life now compared with what I expected it would be," %						
Better than expected	38	30	33	27	...	...
Worse than expected	11	10	10	13	...	...
Self-image: "very useful member of my community," %	28	38	39	28	...	...
"People over 65 get too little respect," %	73	46	44	45	...	...
"Very serious problem for me," %						
Not enough money to live on	18	19	15	12	15	17
Fear of crime	14	21	26	19	23	25
Poor health	9	23	22	28	21	21
Loneliness	7	12	13	17	12	13
Transportation to stores, physicians, recreation (1981)	10§	...	...	...	...	14

* Data from references 17 and 18.
† For group aged 65 to 69 years.
‡ Median score on the Life Satisfaction Index Z, on scale ranging from 0 to 36.
§ For group aged 18 to 64 years.

health services for the next 20 years, health professionals will thus do well to study the characteristics of people who are presently middle aged.

Finally, social, psychological, and biological changes are not synchronous. Many older people suffer from ill health but consider themselves well; they go about their daily lives without taking on "the sick role." Others, when they retire or become great-grandparents, think of themselves as old even though their health may be excellent.

Expectations and Adaptations

Despite the diversities in patterns of aging, most older people become more preoccupied with their health than when they were young. This produces a greater readiness, not only to seek health services, but to learn about health maintenance. Older people of today are an eminently teachable group for the health educator.

Older men and women, like younger people, make continual adaptations to the changes that occur inside and outside the body. Most older people adapt successfully. As they accumulate life experience, they become practiced in making psychological adaptations. They look ahead with a certain sense of equanimity and with an expectation that, given certain supports, they will succeed in coping with new transitions just as they have coped with earlier ones.

A significant factor in adapting to change is the nature of the individual's expectations. Most people develop a concept of the "normal, expectable life cycle," a set of anticipations that certain life events will occur at certain times, and an internalized social clock telling them whether they are on time or off time.[6]

Being on or off time is a compelling basis for self-assessment. Men and women compare themselves with their friends or siblings or parents in deciding whether they are doing well or poorly, always with a time line in mind. It is not the fact that one reaches 60 or 70 that is important, but rather, "How well am I doing for my age?" This probably poses special changes in self-image for those who reach 90, for they have few peers with whom to compare themselves. In coming years, there will be more people who survive to ages 90 and 100. We may then learn more about the psychology of that age group.

Expectable Life Events

For most people, the normal and expectable life events are not life crises. Marriage, parenthood, occupational achievements, children growing up and leaving home, the climacteric, grandparenthood, retirement, and great-grandparenthood are the normal turning points, the punctuation marks along the lifeline. They call forth changes in self-concept and identity, but whether or not they become critical events usually depends on their timing. For the majority, the departure of children from the home is not a crisis, nor is retirement. Even the death of one's spouse, if it occurs on time, does not usually create a mental health crisis.

The onset of chronic illness is another expectable event. This is one of the reasons why most older people describe their health as being good even when they have one or more chronic diseases (Table 12.4.). They mean that their health is as good or better than they had anticipated.

This is not to deny that illness precipitates crisis reactions in many older persons, nor to deny that some, but by no means all, of the major life events that occur in the second half of life are losses to the individual, accompanied by anxiety or grief. But most such events have been anticipated and rehearsed. Given the appropriate social supports, the psychological adjustment is made without shattering the sense of continuity of the life cycle or the individual's coping strategies.

Young-Old and Old-Old

Across the great range of differences among older people, the most useful distinction for the health planner is between young-old and old-old, a distinction based not on age itself, but on social and health characteristics.[7] The young-old are the large majority of older persons. They are vigorous and competent men and women who have retired or otherwise reduced their time investments in working or homemaking. They are relatively comfortable financially, relatively well-educated, and well-integrated members of their families and their communities.

Old-old persons, by contrast, are those who suffer major physical, mental, or social losses and who require a range of supportive and restorative health and social services. Essentially, these are persons who are in need of special care. While this group probably will remain a minority over the next few decades, their absolute numbers are growing rapidly as medical and social advances help to extend their lives.

It is estimated, based on recent health and social surveys, that, at any one moment, young-old men and women constitute about 80% or 85% of the whole population aged older than 65 years, and old-old persons, about 15% to 20%. These are gross estimates, and the proportions are different in successive age subgroups.

Young-old persons seek meaningful ways to use their time. Some stay at work, some move to part-time jobs, and some undertake second careers. Others seek self-fulfillment through education or various forms of leisure. Some serve as volunteers in health services, social services, or civic affairs. A large number are teaching, counseling, or tutoring in schools, social agencies, churches, or corporations. Young-old men and women are beginning to be recognized as a major resource to the society.[8]

Young-old men and women are also active politically, more so than younger adults, and are becoming more articulate about their political, economic, and social claims on both governmental and private agencies. Old-age advocacy groups are a manifestation of this new political consciousness; the proliferation of government agencies that serve the needs of older people is another. Young-old people are likely to make increasing demands on the health services system and, in doing so, to speak not only for themselves but for old-old persons, whom they see themselves becoming.

Oldest-Old

Recently, a new group has been delineate called the *oldest-old.* It refers to persons over 85, who presently constitute about 1% of the population, a percentage that is expected to grow to more than 2% by the year 2010 and to almost 3% by the year 2030 (by which time it will have reached nearly 9 million in number). This group holds special interest for gerontologists who are interested in studying the biological and social factors associated with survivorship, in the hope that to do so will add important new insights into the processes of aging.

From preliminary studies of this group, it already is clear that it is very heterogeneous: blacks and whites, rich and poor, and extremely high proportions of widowed women and extremely low-income persons. It includes competent, vigorous individuals who report no limitations of everyday activities due to health, and individuals who are in extreme states of disability and deterioration.[9] These preliminary facts seem to support the findings mentioned earlier, that the longer people live, the more different from one another they become, and accordingly, that age becomes an increasingly poor predictor of an individual's level of health or social competency.

PSYCHOLOGICAL ISSUES

Whatever the variations among individuals, and whatever the personality differences, there is a certain directionality of change and a certain ordering of psychological tasks and preoccupations across the long periods of adulthood and old age.[10]

Young Adulthood

We are accustomed to thinking that in adolescence, the major psychological task is identity formation, and in youth, it is finding a niche in society and preparing a script for one's life. In young adulthood, the issues are related to intimacy, to investing oneself in the lives of a few significant others, and to taking on responsibilities for those others, usually a spouse and children. New tasks also arise in meeting expectations in the world of work, developing competency and job mastery, and creating a balance between work and family. A frequent preoccupation of the young adult is how to follow one's planned life script while accepting the reality that the script is being continually altered in ways that could not have been predicted and that can only partially be controlled.

Psychology of Middle Age

In middle age, the psychological issues are new. Some are related to family roles: the reworking of relationships between husbands and wives, with changing expectations of what it means to be male or female; and the realization that one's victories and defeats are reckoned by how well one's children are turning out. The appearance of a son-in-law or daughter-in-law often means establishing a quick but intimate relationship with a stranger, and for increasing numbers of middle-aged persons today, the need to adjust to the divorce of a child. The appearance of a grandchild brings a new awareness of aging, but also, for most men and women, a new source of pleasure.

Some of the psychological readjustments of middle age relate not to the creation of biological heirs, but to the creation of social heirs; the need to nurture and to act as a model or mentor to the young; and the concern not to overstep the delicate boundaries of one's authority either in the family or in the workplace. For women, there is often a sense of new freedom, increased time for oneself when children are gone, freedom from fear of unwanted pregnancy, and for many, a new pleasure in sexual relations that accompanies menopause.

At the same time, there are also the responsibilities that can be called *parent-caring*. Recent studies indicate that, with the increase of multigenerational families, the concern over providing care for aging parents is the major source of stress in the area of family life.[11]

Other issues relate to the occupational life: the concerns about moving up or moving down or reaching a plateau. With large proportions of middle-aged women now in the work force, there is often, for both women and men, increasing investment in work. For some, there are unwelcome job pressures; for others, the restlessness that comes with job boredom, or burnout. But for most middle-aged workers, there is a heightened competence and also a sense of being in the prime of life with regard to the value of one's experience and expertise.

Middle age is also the period of increased stocktaking: introspection and reflection become characteristic of the mental life. The assessment of where one has been and where one is going manifests itself in a number of ways: acceptance of limits and a moderation of ambition; dramatic new questions of identity; for some persons, depression in the face of unrealized hopes or unavoidable life events; and for others, a moving away from conventional patterns that leads to new careers, geographic moves, and new leisure activities.

Concerns Over Health

A psychological change that is probably of special interest to physicians as they interact with middle-aged patients is the heightened concern over health that usually comes as a person moves through the 40s and 50s.

For men, the most dramatic signs that they are entering middle age are often biological. Attention is increasingly centered on the decreasing efficiency of the body. It is not only one's performance on the golf course or one's sexual performance, but it is the heart attack in a friend that prompts many men to describe bodily changes as the most important feature of the transition from young adulthood to middle age.

Health changes are more salient markers for men than for women. The menopause and other manifestations of the climacteric are events to which middle-aged women seldom attach great psychological significance; despite the concerns over cancer, women refer less often than men to health or biological changes. It is, for instance, a false stereotype that the menopause leads to depression in most women.

Body monitoring nevertheless takes on new importance to both men and women as they develop a large variety of protective strategies for maintaining the body at given levels of performance and appearance. While these issues reflect a new sense of physical vulnerability in men, they often take a different form in women, i.e., the mental "rehearsal for widowhood." Women often are more concerned over the body monitoring of their husbands than of themselves.

Changing Time Perspectives

A second set of psychological issues also is likely to be of special interest to physicians: namely, that both men and women are aware of a new way in which they think about their lifetimes. Life is restructured in terms of time-left-to-live rather than time-since-birth. Not only the reversal in direction, but also the awareness that time is finite is a conspicuous feature of middle age, especially for men. Death takes on a new reality; it becomes personalized, i.e., it could now happen to oneself. There is at the same time a new awareness of increased longevity in the population at large and, for most people, the expectation that they will live much longer than their parents.

Many middle-aged persons think of time as a two-edged sword that acts in some ways as a brake on their activities, but in other ways, as a prod, in seeing how many more good years one can plan for and how many new activities one can undertake.

The sense of a long life still ahead has different implications for middle-aged men compared with middle-aged women. In at least some men, it is accompanied by a readiness to marry for a second time and to start a new family. Many women, sensitive to the reality that middle-aged or older women seldom remarry, worry that there may be many years of widowhood ahead and perhaps of living alone. Middle age, then, as is true of other periods of life, has a different set of psychological meanings for the two sexes.

Psychology of Old Age

Many of the concerns of middle age continue to preoccupy older persons, but new themes also arise.

Some of the new psychological issues are related to renunciation: adapting to losses of work, friends, and spouse, and yielding up positions of authority. The resolution of grief over the death of others becomes a repeated psychological task, and grief occurs over one's own approaching death. The sense of integrity is reformulated in terms of what one has been rather than what one is, and the concerns over legacy arise, as how to leave traces of oneself and a proper record of one's life.

There are also the triumphs of survivorship, for instance, the recognition that one has savored a wide range of experiences and therefore "knows about life" in ways no younger person can know. There is, in most old people, the knowledge that, in having lived through physical and psychological pain in the past, one recovers and can cope also with the contingencies that lie ahead. There is also a sense that one is now the possessor and conservator of some of the basic values of one's society and perhaps some of the eternal truths about living and dying.

These are only some of the themes and the preoccupations that give meaning to the long years of adulthood, and that call forth a changing sense of self and a changing set of adaptations. With the passage of time, lives become more, not less, complex, and for most persons, lives become enriched, not impoverished.

Psychology of Illness in Old Age

Older people have been described here as a very diverse group, most of whom, despite their differences, remain young-old for long periods of time and relatively well in terms of social, physical, and mental health. Older persons deal with illness in many different ways, just as is true of young people. This is not to say, however, that older people as a group are the same as younger people in the ways that they think about their health, their illnesses, and their medical care.

The important factor in the psychology of illness in late life is that young-old people become, whether for a very short or a very long period before their deaths, old-old people. Recognizing that this change will come, most men and women become particularly sensitive not only to the quality of the physical care that they are receiving from health professionals, but also the quality of psychological care, and to what kinds of care they can anticipate when they become frail.

The sensitivity to psychological care has many components. One is that older persons have ongoing, not only intermittent, concerns about their health and health care. Given the increased attention to health maintenance and preventive medicine by newspaper columnists, television commentators, and other educators, there is a wider understanding among older people today that many of their illnesses are treatable, and that some are reversible. As a consequence, many old men and women have higher expectations of being benefited by medical treatment than was true only a decade ago.

At the same time, old men and women recognize their biological vulnerability and the fact that the aging body becomes less able to cope with stress, internal or external. As mentioned earlier, illness and disability have different meanings if they occur "on time" or "off time" in the life cycle. To the old person, illness comes "on time," and understandably enough is usually accompanied by premonitions of death.

Most old people talk about death with their spouses or children or friends and are relatively willing to talk about it even with an interviewer who is a stranger. They usually express most concerns not about the fact that death will come, but about how long a period of dependency and deterioration will precede it, and about the manner in which it will come. With the recent advances in high-technology medicine and life-prolonging procedures, there is a new worry that one might die "on the machines." An increasing number of persons are signing a "living will," a directive that, should they be suddenly stricken and unable to make known their wishes, instructs their physicians in advance to forego the use of extreme forms of life-extending treatment.

Another factor is the difficulty for most older persons of acknowledging dependency, especially for women who have been for long periods of their lives the givers of physical and emotional care, rather than the receivers.

Some older persons, after experiencing a catastrophic medical event, such as a major stroke, express the fear of dependency by stating their willingness, even their eagerness, to die. The physician, in attempting to facilitate recovery, may be thwarted by such a patient's desires and may experience a sense of helplessness and frustration.

Other patients react differently to a personal medical catastrophe. They become preoccupied with "buying time"; they may challenge the competence of the physician by continually seeking additional opinions or by insisting on all the newest treatment procedures.

Whatever form the fear of dependency may take, or the fear of pain, or other motivations, older people usually want not the latest possible death that high technology can provide, but what they regard as the "best death," one that provides as much dignity and autonomy as possible.

Some old persons want to discuss this problem with their physicians; others are hesitant about broaching it. Physicians, for their part, have their own sensitivities to issues of death and dying that may, in some instances, create new opportunities for intimate communication with patients who are approaching death, but, in other instances, new difficulties of communication.

In a medical system that has been geared more to cure than to care, it is understandable that the psychological needs of old sick patients sometimes go unmet by otherwise competent physicians whose training has been focused more on scientific and technological than on humanistic aspects of medical practice.[12] The same problems of communication may occur in the interactions between physicians and young patients, but the problems become accentuated in the case of old patients whose remaining lifetimes are short, whose well-being often depends directly on the nature of the patient-physician relationship, and who are therefore especially in need of emotional support and understanding that only the physician can provide. This is especially true because most old-old people suffer from chronic illness, where the relationship with the physician becomes a long-lasting and increasingly complex one.

Although the patient-physician relationship and patient-physician communication are by no means new concerns among physicians or patients, new attention is presently being given to these issues by medical educators, in particular to the cultivation of empathy, caring, and compassion on the part of the physician.[13] It is not clear whether or not the appearance of the aging society plays a major role in bringing these concerns to the forefront. But because more physicians now and in the future will be dealing with increasing numbers of old patients, it is likely that the psychology of illness in old age will command increasing attention, and that communication between physicians and old patients will be a central issue in medical training and in medical practice.

References

1. National Institute on Aging and the US Bureau of the Census. *America's Centenarians*. Washington, DC: US Dept of Health and Human Services, 1987.
2. Avorn JL. Medicine: The life and death of Oliver Shay. In: Pifer A, Bronte L, eds. *Our Aging Society*. New York, NY: WW Norton & Co Inc; 1986:283–297.
3. Brody JA, Brock DB, Williams TF. Trends in the health of the elderly population. *Annu Rev Public Health* 1987;8:211–34.
4. Katz S, Greer DS, Beck JC, et al. Active life expectancy: societal implications. In: Committee on an Aging Society, Institute of Medicine and National Research Council, eds. *America's Aging: Health in an Older Society*. Washington, DC: National Academy Press; 1985:57–72.
5. Special Committee on Aging, (US Congress, Senate) 1987. *Aging America: Trends and Projections*. US Dept of Health and Human Services publication, 1988:38–77.
6. Neugarten BN, Neugarten DA. Changing meanings of age in the aging society. In:

Pifer A, Bronte L, eds. *Our Aging Society.* New York, NY: WW Norton & Co Inc; 1986:33–52.

7. Neugarten BN. Age groups in American society and the rise of the young-old. *Ann Am Acad Political Soc Sci* 1974;415:187–198.

8. Committee on an Aging Society, Institute of Medicine and National Research Council. *America's Aging: Productive Roles in an Older Society.* Washington, DC: National Academy Press; 1986.

9. Rosenwaike I. A demographic portrait of the oldest old. *Milbank Q* 1985; 63:187–205.

10. Neugarten BN. Time, age, and the life cycle. *Am J Psychiatry* 1979;136:887–893.

11. Brody EM. Parent care as a normative family stress. *Gerontologist* 1985;25:19–29.

12. Odegaard CE. *Dear Doctor—A Personal Letter to a Physician.* Menlo Park, Calif: The Henry J. Kaiser Family Foundation; 1986.

13. White KL. *The Task of Medicine.* Menlo Park, Calif: The Henry J. Kaiser Family Foundation; 1988.

THIRTEEN

Women's Attitudes toward the Menopause

Bernice L. Neugarten, Vivian Wood, Ruth J. Kraines,

and Barbara Loomis

The menopause, like puberty or pregnancy, is generally regarded as a significant event in a woman's life; one that is known to reflect profound endocrine and somatic changes; and one that presumably involves psychological and social concomitants as well. Although there is a large medical and biological literature regarding the climacterium,[1] there are few psychological studies available, except those reporting symptomology or those based on observations of women who were receiving medical or psychiatric treatment. Even the theories regarding the psychological effects of the climacterium are based largely upon observations of clinicians—psychoanalytic case studies, psychiatric investigations of climacteric psychoses, and observations of their middle-aged patients made by gynecologists and other physicians (*August*, 1956; *Barnacle*, 1949; *Deutsch*, 1945; *Fessler*, 1950; *Hoskins*, 1944; *Ross*, 1951; *Sicher*, 1949).

Unlike the case with puberty or pregnancy, developmental psychologists have not yet turned their attention to the menopause, and to the possible relationships, whether antecedent or consequent, between biological, psychological, and social variables. [A paper by the psychoanalyst *Therese Benedek* (1952) is a notable exception.] Neither is there a body of anthropological or sociological literature that describes the prevailing cultural or social attitudes to be found in America or other Western societies regarding the menopause.

As preliminary to a larger study of adjustment patterns in middle age, a number of exploratory interviews were gathered in which each woman was asked to assess her own menopausal status (whether she regarded herself as pre-, "in," or postclimacteric). She was then asked the basis of this assessment; what, if any, symptoms she had experienced; what her anticipations of menopause had been, and why; what she re-

This research was facilitated by USPHS Grant no. M-3972, Bernice L. Neugarten, Principal Investigator. Reprinted by permission of the publisher, S. Karger, Basel and New York, from *Vita Humana* 6 (1963): 140–51.

garded as the worst and what the best aspects; and what, if any, changes in her life she attributed to the menopause.

It was soon apparent that women varied greatly in their attitudes and experiences. Some, particularly at upper-middle-class levels, vehemently assured the interviewer that the menopause was without any social or psychological import; that, indeed, the enlightened woman does not fear, nor—even if she suffers considerable physical discomfort—does she complain about the menopause.

"Why make any fuss about it?"

"I just made up my mind I'd walk right through it, and I did . . ."

"I saw women complaining, and I thought I would never be so ridiculous. I would just sit there and perspire, if I had to. At times you do feel terribly warm. I would sit and feel the water on my head, and wonder how red I looked. But I wouldn't worry about it, because it is a natural thing, and why get worried about it? I remember one time, in the kitchen, I had a terrific hot flush. . . . I went to look at myself in the mirror. I didn't even look red, so I thought, 'All right . . . the next time I'll just sit there, and who will notice? And if someone notices, I won't even care . . .'"

Others confessed to considerable fear:

"I would think of my mother and the trouble she went through; and I wondered if I would come through it whole or in pieces . . ."

"I knew two women who had nervous breakdowns, and I worried about losing my mind . . ."

"I thought menopause would be the beginning of the end . . . a gradual senility closing over, like the darkness . . ."

"I was afraid we couldn't have sexual relations after the menopause—and my husband thought so, too . . ."

"When I think of how I used to worry! You wish someone would tell you—but you're too embarrassed to ask anyone . . ."

Other women seemed to be repeating the advice found in women's magazines and in newspaper columns:

"I just think if a woman looks for trouble, she'll find it . . ."

"If you fill your thinking and your day with constructive things—like trying to help other people—then it seems to me nothing can enter a mind already filled . . ."

"If you keep busy, you won't think about it, and you'll be all right . . ."

Underlying this variety of attitudes were two common phenomena: first, whether they made much or made little of its importance, middle-aged women were willing, even eager, to talk about the menopause. Many volunteered the comment that they seldom talked about it with other women; that they wished for more information and more communication. Second, although many professed not to believe what they termed "old wives' tales," most women had nevertheless heard many such tales of the dangers of menopause, and could recite them easily: that menopause often results in mental breakdown; that it marks the end of a woman's sexual attractiveness as well as her sexual desires; and so on. Many women said, in this connection, that while they themselves had had neither fears nor major discomforts, they indeed knew other women who held many such irrational fears or who had suffered greatly. (The investigators interpreted such responses as indicative, at least in part, of the psychological mechanism of projection.)

The Instrument

Following a round of preliminary interviews, a more systematic measurement of attitudes toward the menopause was undertaken. A checklist was drawn up containing statements culled from the exploratory interviews and from the literature on the subject. For example, the statement, "Women generally feel better after the menopause than they have for years," appears in a pamphlet about menopause for sale by the US Government Printing Office (*US Public Health Service,* 1959). "Women who have trouble with the menopause are usually those who have nothing to do with their time," is a statement made by a number of interviewees. "A woman in menopause is likely to do crazy things she herself does not understand" is a statement made by a woman describing her own behavior. Respondents were asked to check, for each statement, 1. agree strongly; 2. agree to some extent; 3. disagree somewhat; or 4. disagree strongly. Because of the projective phenomenon already mentioned, the statements were worded in terms of "other women," or "women in general" rather than "self" (see Table 13.2).

The checklist was then pre-tested on a sample of 50 women aged 40 to 50. Following the analysis of those responses, the instrument was revised and the number of items reduced to 35. Certain statements were eliminated because they drew stereotyped responses; others, because of overlap.

The Samples

The revised Attitudes-Toward-Menopause Checklist, hereafter referred to as the ATM, was administered as part of a lengthy interview to a sample of 100 women aged 45 to 55 on whom a variety of other data were being gathered. These 100 women, referred to here as the C, or Criterion, group, had been drawn from lists of mothers of graduates from two public high schools in the Chicago metropolitan area. None of these women had had surgical or artificial menopause, and all were in relatively good health.

Once the data on the ATM had been analyzed for the Criterion group, the question arose, how do women of different ages view the menopause? Accordingly, the instrument was administered to other groups of women contacted through business

Table 13.1. The Samples: By Age and Level of Education

			Percents		
			High school graduation or less	One or more years of college	No infor- mation
Group	Number	Age			
A	50	21–30	8	90	2
B	52	31–44	33	50	17
C	100	45–55	65	35	0
D	65	56–65	54	46	0

firms and women's clubs. Directions for filling out the ATM were usually given in group situations, and the respondents were asked to mail back the forms to the investigators along with certain identifying information (age, level of education, marital status, number and ages of children, and health status). The proportion responding varied from group to group, with an average of about 75% responses. From this larger pool, Groups A, B, and D were drawn.

The composition of the four samples, by age and level of education, is shown in table 13.1. All the women in all four groups were married, all were mothers of one or more children and, with the exception of a few in Groups B and D, all were living with their husbands. None of these women reported major physical illness or disability.

These groups of women, although by no means constituting representative samples, are biased in only one known direction: compared with the general population of American women, they are higher on level of education, for they include higher proportions of the college-educated. This is especially true of Group A and Group D.

FINDINGS
Level of Education

When responses to the ATM were analyzed for differences between the women in each age group who had and those who had not attended college, only a few scattered differences appeared, a number attributable to chance.

As already indicated, however, the four samples of women represent relatively advantaged groups with regard to educational level. It is likely that in more heterogeneous samples educational level would emerge as a significant variable in women's attitudes toward menopause.

Age Differences

As shown in table 13.2, consistent age differences were found. The statements are grouped in the table according to the pattern that emerged from a factor analysis car-

Table 13.3. Attitudes-Toward-Menopause: By Age

	Percent who agree[a]			
	Age groups			
	A	B	C	D
	21–30	31–44	45–55	56–65
Items subgrouped	(N = 50)	(N = 52)	(N = 100)	(N = 65)
I. *"Negative Affect"*				
28. Menopause is an unpleasant experience for a woman	56	44	58	55
32. It's not surprising that most women get disagreeable during the menopause	58	51	57	43
34. Women should expect some trouble during the menopause	60	46	59	58
30. Menopause is a disturbing thing which most women naturally dread	38*	46	57	53
20. It's no wonder women feel "down in the dumps" at the time of the menopause	54	46	49	49
33. In truth, just about every woman is depressed about the change of life	48	29	40	28
II. *"Post-Menopausal Recovery"*				
24. Women generally feel better after the menopause than they have for years	32*	20*	68	67
26. A woman has a broader outlook on life after the change of life	22*	25*	53	33*
27. A woman gets more confidence in herself after the change of life	12*	21*	52	42
16. Women are generally calmer and happier after the change of life than before	30*	46*	75	80
23. Life is more interesting for a woman after the menopause	2*	13*	45	35
17. After the change of life, a women feels freer to do things for herself	16*	24*	74	65
31. After the change of life, a woman has a better relationship with her husband	20*	33*	62	44*
35. Many women think menopause is the best thing that ever happened to them	14*	31	46	40
21. After the change of life, a woman gets more interested in community affairs than before	24*	31*	53	60

continued

Table 13.3. *Continued*

	Percent who agree[a] Age groups			
	A	B	C	D
	21–30	31–44	45–55	56–65
Items subgrouped	(N = 50)	(N = 52)	(N = 100)	(N = 65)
III. *"Extent of Continuity"*				
14. A woman's body may change in meno-pause, but otherwise she doesn't change much	48*	71*	85	83
15. The only difference between a woman who has not been through the menopause and one who has, is that one menstruates and the other doesn't	34*	52	67	77
12. Going through the menopause really does not change a woman in any important way	58*	55*	74	83
IV. *"Control of Symptoms"*				
4. Women who have trouble with the meno-pause are usually those who have nothing to do with their time	58	50*	71	70
7. Women who have trouble in the meno-pause are those who are expecting it	48*	56*	76	63
8. The thing that causes women all their trouble at menopause is something they can't control—changes inside their bodies	42*	56*	78	65
V. *"Psychological Losses"*				
29. Women often get self-centered at the time of the menopause	78	63	67	48*
25. After the change of life, women often don't consider themselves "real women" anymore	16	13	15	3*
1. Women often use the change of life as an excuse for getting attention	60*	69	80	68
18. Women worry about losing their minds during the menopause	28*	35	51	24*
11. A woman is concerned about how her husband will feel toward her after the menopause	58*	44	41	21*

continued

Table 13.3. *Continued*

Items subgrouped	Percent who agree[a] Age groups			
	A 21–30 (*N* = 50)	B 31–44 (*N* = 52)	C 45–55 (*N* = 100)	D 56–65 (*N* = 65)
VI. *"Unpredictability"*				
6. A woman in menopause is apt to do crazy things she herself does not understand	40	56	53	40
10. Menopause is a mysterious thing which most women don't understand	46	46	59	46
VII. *"Sexuality"*				
3. If the truth were really known, most women would like to have themselves a fling at this time in their lives	8*	33	32	24
19. After the menopause, a woman is more interested in sex than she was before	14*	27	35	21
Ungrouped Items[b]				
2. Unmarried women have a harder time than married women do at the time of the menopause	42	37	30	33
5. A woman should see a doctor during the menopause	100	100	95	94
9. A good thing about the menopause is that a woman can quit worrying about getting pregnant	64	38*	78	63*
13. Menopause is one of the biggest changes that happens in a woman's life	68*	42	50	55
22. Women think of menopause as the beginning of the end	26	13*	26	9*

[a] Those subjects who checked "agree strongly" or "agree to some extent."

[b] These statements did not show large loadings on any of the seven factors represented by the groupings in the table.

* The difference between this percentage and the percentage of Group C is significant at the .05 level or above.

ried out on the responses of Group C.[2] That analysis, although serving a purpose extraneous to the present report, provided groupings of the statements that are meaningful also for studying age differences.

Overall inspection of table 13.2 shows first that, as anticipated, young women's patterns of attitudes toward the menopause are different from those of middle-aged women. When each group is compared with the Criterion group, the largest number of significant differences are found between Groups A and C; then between B and C.

At the same time, it appears that it is not age alone, but age and experience-with-menopause that are probably operating together. There are very few differences between Groups C and D; and relatively few between A and B. The major differences lie between the first two and the last groups—in other words, between women who have and those who have not yet experienced the changes of the climacterium. Although there is not a one-to-one correlation between chronological age and age-at-menopause, approximately 75% of the women in Group C, as well as all those in D, reported that they were presently experiencing or had already completed the "change of life." Only a few of Group B had yet entered "the period of the change."

It can be seen from table 13.2, also, that age differences follow a particular pattern from one cluster of statements to the next. Thus, on the first cluster, "negative affect," there are no significant differences between age groups nor between statements. In each instance, about half the women agree that the menopause is a disagreeable, depressing, troublesome, unpleasant, disturbing event; and about half the women disagree.

On the second cluster of statements, however, there are sharp age differences, and in general, all in the same direction: middle-aged women recognize a "recovery," even some marked gains occurring once the menopause is past. The postmenopausal woman is seen as feeling better, more confident, calmer, freer than before. The majority of younger women, by contrast, are in disagreement with this view.

On the third and fourth clusters age differences, while not so sharp as on the second cluster, are numerous and are again consistent in direction: namely, middle-aged women take what may be interpreted as the more positive view, with higher proportions agreeing that the menopause creates no major discontinuity in life, and agreeing that, except for the underlying biological changes, women have a relative degree of control over their symptoms and need not inevitably have difficulties. This is essentially the view that one woman expressed by saying, "If women look for trouble, of course they find it."

Of the remainder of the statements, those that form the fifth, sixth, and seventh clusters as well as those that fit none of the clusters, age differences are scattered and inconsistent in direction, depending evidently upon the particular content and wording of each statement. It is interesting to note, for instance, that on No. 18, "Women worry about losing their minds," it is the Criterion group, Group C, which shows the highest proportion who agree.

It is also of interest that on Nos. 3 and 19, it is the youngest group who disagree most with the view that menopausal women may experience an upsurge of sexual impulse. In this connection, the interviews with Group C women, many of whom had not completed the change of life, showed a wide range of ideas about a woman's interest in sex relations after the menopause. The comments ranged from, "I would expect her to be less interested in sex, because that is something that belongs more or less to the childbearing period," to, "She might become more interested because the fear of pregnancy is gone." Many women expressed considerable uncertainty about the effects of the menopause on sexuality.

DISCUSSION

That there should be generally different views of menopause in younger and in middle-aged women is hardly a surprise. Any event is likely to have quite different significance for persons who are at different points in the life line.

One reason why fewer middle-aged as compared to younger women in this study viewed menopause as significant event may be that loss of reproductive capacity is not an important concern of middle-aged women at either a conscious or unconscious level. In the psychological and psychiatric literature it is often stated that the end of the reproductive period—the "closing of the gates," as it has been described (*Deutsch*, 1945, p. 457)—evokes in most women a desire for another child. If so, women might be expected to view menopause as most significant at that time in life when the loss of reproductive capacity is imminent. Yet this was not the case in these data.

There is additional evidence on the same point from our interview data. Of the 100 women in the Criterion group, only 4, in responding to a multiple-choice question, chose, "Not being able to have more children" as the worst thing in general about the menopause. (At the same time, 26 said the worst thing was, "Not knowing what to expect"; 19 said, "The discomfort and pain"; 18 said, "It's a sign you are getting old"; 4 said, "Loss of enjoyment in sex relations"; 22 said, "None of these things"; and 7 could not answer the question.) It is true of course, that all these women had borne children; but the same was true of all the younger women in Groups A and B. Many Group C women said, in interview, that they had raised their children and were now happy to have done, not only with menstruation and its attendant annoyances, but also with the mothering of small children.

The fact that middle-aged as frequently as younger women view the menopause as unpleasant and disturbing is not irreconcilable with their view of the menopause as an unimportant event. As one woman put it, "Yes, the change of life is an unpleasant time. No one enjoys the hot flushes, the headaches, or the nervous tension. Sometimes it's even a little frightening. But I've gone through changes before, and I can weather another one. Besides, it's only a temporary condition."

Another woman joked, "It's not the pause that refreshes, it's true; but it's just a pause that depresses."

The middle-aged woman's view of the postmenopausal period as a time when she will be happier and healthier underscores her belief in the temporary nature of the unpleasant period, a belief that is reinforced perhaps by hearing postmenopausal women say, as two said to our interviewer:

"My experience has been that I've been healthier and in much better spirits since the change of life. I've been relieved of a lot of aches and pains."

"Since I have had my menopause, I have felt like a teen-ager again. I can remember my mother saying that after her menopause she really got her vigor, and I can say the same thing about myself. I'm just never tired now."

The fact that most younger women have generally more negative views is perhaps because the menopause is not only relatively far removed, and therefore relatively vague; but because, being vague, it becomes blended into the whole process of growing old, a process that is both dim and unpleasant. Perhaps it is only the middle-aged or older woman who can take a differentiated view of the menopause; and who, on the basis of experience, can, as one woman said, "separate the old wives' tales from that which is true of old wives."

SUMMARY

An instrument for measuring attitudes toward the menopause was developed, consisting of 35 statements on which women were asked if they agreed or disagreed. The instrument was administered to 267 women of four age groups: 21–30; 31–44; 45–55; and 56–65. Differences were most marked between the first two and the last two groups, with the younger women holding the more negative and more undifferentiated attitudes.

Notes

1. *Menopause* and *climacterium* (as well as the more popular term, *the change of life*) are often used interchangeably in the literature. In more accurate terms, *menopause* refers to the cessation of the menses; and *climacterium* to the involution of the ovary and the various processes, including menopause, associated with this involution.

2. Responses were scored from 1 to 4; and on the matrix of intercorrelations, the principal component method of factor extraction by Jacoby and the Varimax program for rotation were used. Seven factors, accounting for 85% of the variance, emerged from that analysis, factors which have been named "negative affect," "post-menopausal recovery," and so on, as indicated in table 13.2. Within each group of statements, the order is that of their loadings on the respective factor. It should be kept in mind that a somewhat different factor pattern might have emerged from the responses of Groups A, B, or D.

References

August, H. E.: Psychological aspects of personal adjustment. In *Irma C. Gross* (Ed.), Potentialities of women in the middle years (Michigan State Univ. Press, East Lansing 1956).

Barnacle, C. H.: Psychiatric implications of the climacteric. Amer. Practit. *4:* 154–157 (1949).

Benedek, Therese: Psychosexual functions in women (Ronald, New York 1952).

Deutsch, Helene: The psychology of women. Vol. II, Motherhood (Grune & Stratton, New York 1945).

Fessler, L.: Psychopathology of climacteric depression. Psychoanal. Quart. *19:* 28–42 (1950).

Hoskins, R. G.: Psychological treatment of the menopause. J. clin. Endocrin. *4:* 605–610 (1944).

Ross, M.: Psychosomatic approach to the climacterium. Calif. Med. *74;* 240–242 (1951).

Sicher, L.: Change of life: a psychosomatic problem. Amer. J. Psychother. *3:* 399–409 (1949).

US Public Health Service: Menopause. Health Information Series Publ. No. 179. (US Govt. Print. Off., Washington, D.C., 1959).

The Changing American Grandparent

Bernice L. Neugarten and Karol K. Weinstein

Despite the proliferation of investigations regarding the relations between generations and the position of the aged within the family, surprisingly little attention has
been paid directly to the role of grandparenthood.[1] There are a few articles written
by psychoanalysts and psychiatrists analyzing the symbolic meaning of the grandparent in the developing psyche of the child or, in a few cases, illustrating the role of
a particular grandparent in the psychopathology of a particular child.[2] Attention has
not correspondingly been given, however, to the psyche of the grandparent, and references are made only obliquely, if at all, to the symbolic meaning of the grandchild
to the grandparent.

There are a number of anthropologists' reports on grandparenthood in one or another simple society as well as studies involving cross-cultural comparisons based on
ethnographic materials. Notable among the latter is a study by Apple[3] which shows
that, among the 51 societies for which data are available, those societies in which
grandparents are removed from family authority are those in which grandparents
have an equalitarian or an indulgent, warm relationship with the grandchildren. In
those societies in which economic power and/or prestige rests with the old, relationships between grandparents and grandchildren are formal and authoritarian.

Sociologists, for the most part, have included only a few questions about grandparenthood when interviewing older persons about family life, or they have analyzed
the grandparent role solely from indirect evidence, without empirical data gathered
specifically for that purpose.[4] There are a few noteworthy exceptions: Albrecht[5]
studied the grandparental responsibilities of a representative sample of persons over
65 in a small midwestern community. She concluded that grandparents neither had
nor coveted responsibility for grandchildren; that they took pleasure from the emotional response and occasionally took reflected glory from the accomplishments of
their grandchildren.

An unpublished study by Apple[6] of a group of urban middle-class grandparents

Paper presented at the Sixth International Gerontological Congress, Copenhagen, August 1963.
Reprinted by permission from *Journal of Marriage and the Family* 26, no. 2 (May 1964): 199–204.

indicated that, as they relinquish the parental role over the adult child, grandparents come to identify with grandchildren in a way that might be called "pleasure without responsibility."

In a study of older persons in a working-class area of London, Townsend[7] found many grandmothers who maintained very large responsibility for the care of the grandchild, but he also found that for the total sample, the relationship of grandparents to grandchildren might be characterized as one of "privileged disrespect." Children were expected to be more respectful of parents than of grandparents.

THE DATA

The data reported in this paper were collected primarily for the purpose of generating rather than testing hypotheses regarding various psychological and social dimensions of the grandparent role. Three dimensions were investigated: first, the degree of comfort with the role as expressed by the grandparent; second, the significance of the role as seen by the actor; and last, the style with which the role is enacted.

The data came from interviews with both grandmother and grandfather in 70 middle-class families in which the interviewer located first a married couple with children and then one set of grandparents. Of the 70 sets of grandparents, 46 were maternal—that is, the wife's parents—and 24 were paternal. All pairs of grandparents lived in separated households from their children, although most lived within relatively short distances of the metropolitan area of Chicago.

As classified by indices of occupation, area of residence, level of income, and level of education, the grandparental couples were all middle class. The group was about evenly divided between upper-middle (professionals and business executives) and lower-middle (owners of small service businesses and white-collar occupations below the managerial level). As is true in other middle-class, urban groups in the United States, the largest proportion of these families had been upwardly mobile, either from working class into lower-middle or from lower-middle into upper-middle. Of the 70 grandparental couples, 19 were foreign born (Polish, Lithuanian, Russian, and a few German and Italian). The sample was skewed with regard to religious affiliation, with 40 percent Jewish, 48 percent Protestant, and 12 percent Catholic. The age range of the grandfathers was, with a few exceptions, the mid-fifties through the late sixties; for the grandmothers it was the early fifties to the mid-sixties.

Each member of the couple was interviewed separately and, in most instances, in two sessions. Respondents were asked a variety of open-ended questions regarding their relations to their grandchildren: how often and on what occasions they saw their grandchildren; what the significance of grandparenthood was in their lives and how it had affected them. While grandparenthood has multiple values for each respondent and may influence his relations with various family members, the focus was upon the primary relationship—that between grandparent and grandchild.

FINDINGS AND DUSCUSSION

Degree of comfort in the role. As shown in Table 14.1, the majority of grandparents expressed only comfort, satisfaction, and pleasure. Among this group, a sizable number seemed to be idealizing the role of grandparenthood and to have high expectations of the grandchild in the future—that the child would either achieve some special goal or success or offer unique affection at some later date.

At the same time, approximately one-third of the sample (36 percent of the grandmothers and 29 percent of the grandfathers) were experiencing sufficient dif-

Table 14.1. Ease of Role Performance, Significance of Role, and Style of Grandparenting in 70 Grandmothers and 70 Grandfathers

	Grandmothers (N = 70)		Grandfathers (N = 70)	
	N	Percent	N	Percent
A. Ease of role performance:				
1) Comfortable/pleasant	41	59	43	61
2) Difficulty/discomfort	25	36	20	29
(Insufficient data)	4	5	7	10
Total	70	100	70	100
B. Significance of the grandparent role:				
1) Biological renewal and/or continuity	29*	42*	16*	23*
2) Emotional self-fulfillment	13	19	19	27
3) Resource person to child	3	4	8	11
4) Vicarious achievement through child	3	4	3	4
5) Remote; little effect on the self	19	27	20	29
(Insufficient data)	3	4	4	6
Total	70	100	70	100
C. Style of grandparenting:				
1) The Formal	22	31	23	33
2) The Fun-Seeking	20	29	17	24
3) The Parent Surrogate	10*	14*	0*	0*
4) The Reservoir of Family Wisdom	1	1	4	6
5) The Distant Figure	13	19	20	29
(Insufficient data)	4	6	6	8
Total	70	100	70	100

*The difference between grandmothers and grandfathers in this category is reliable at or beyond the .05 level (frequencies were tested for differences of proportions, using the Yates correction for continuity).

ficulty in the role that they made open reference to their discomfort, their disappointment, or their lack of positive reward. This discomfort indicated strain in thinking of oneself as a grandparent (the role is in some ways alien to the self-image), conflict with the parents with regard to the rearing of the grandchild, or indifference (and some self-chastisement for the indifference) to caretaking or responsibility in reference to the grandchild.

The significance and meaning of the role. The investigators made judgments based upon the total interview data on each case with regard to the primary significance of grandparenthood for each respondent. Recognizing that the role has multiple meanings for each person and that the categories to be described may overlap to some degree, the investigators nevertheless classified each case as belonging to one of five categories:

1) for some, grandparenthood seemed to constitute primarily a source of *biological renewal* ("It's through my grandchildren that I feel young again") and/or *biological continuity* with the future ("It's through these children that I see my life going on into the future" or, "It's carrying on the family line"). As shown in Table 14.1, this category occurred significantly less frequently for grandfathers than for grandmothers, perhaps because the majority of these respondents were parents, not of the young husband but of the young wife. It is likely that grandfathers perceive family continuity less frequently through their female than through their male offspring and that in a sample more evenly balanced with regard to maternal-paternal lines of ascent, this category would appear more frequently in the responses from grandfathers.

2) For some, grandparenthood affords primarily an opportunity to succeed in a new emotional role, with the implication that the individual feels himself to be a better grandparent than he was a parent. Frequently, grandfatherhood offered a certain vindication of the life history by providing *emotional self-fulfillment* in a way that fatherhood had not done. As one man put it, "I can be, and I can do for my grandchildren things I could never do for my own kids. I was too busy with my business to enjoy my kids, but my grandchildren are different. Now I have the time to be with them."

3) For a small proportion, the grandparent role provides a new role of teacher or *resource person*. Here the emphasis is upon the satisfaction that accrues from contributing to the grandchild's welfare—either by financial aid, or by offering the benefit of the grandparent's unique life experience. For example, "I take my grandson down to the factory and show him how the business operates—and then, too, I set aside money especially for him. That's something his father can't do yet, although he'll do it for *his* grandchildren."

4) For a few, grandparenthood is seen as providing an extension of the self in that the grandchild is one who will *accomplish vicariously* for the grandparent that which

neither he nor his first-generation offspring could achieve. For these persons, the grandchild offers primarily an opportunity for aggrandizing the ego, as in the case of the grandmother who said, "She's a beautiful child, and she'll grow up to be a beautiful woman. Maybe I shouldn't, but I can't help feeling proud of that."

5) As shown in Table 14.1, 27 percent of the grandmothers and 29 percent of the grandfathers in this sample reported feeling relatively *remote* from their grandchildren and acknowledged relatively *little effect* of grandparenthood in their own lives—this despite the fact that they lived geographically near at least one set of grandchildren and felt apologetic about expressing what they regarded as unusual sentiments. Some of the grandfathers mentioned the young age of their grandchildren in connection with their current feelings of psychological distance. For example, one man remarked, "My granddaughter is just a baby, and I don't even feel like a grandfather yet. Wait until she's older—maybe I'll feel different then."

Of the grandmothers who felt remote from their grandchildren, the rationalization was different. Most of the women in this group were working or were active in community affairs and said essentially, "It's great to be a grandmother, of course— but I don't have much time. . . ." The other grandmothers in this group indicated strained relations with the adult child: either they felt that their daughters had married too young, or they disapproved of their sons-in-law.

For both the men and the women who fell into this category of psychological distance, a certain lack of conviction appeared in their statements, as if the men did not really believe that, once the grandchildren were older, they would indeed become closer to them, and as if the women did not really believe that their busy schedules accounted for their lack of emotional involvement with their grandchildren. Rather, these grandparents imply that the role itself is perceived as being empty of meaningful relationships.

Styles of grandparenting. Somewhat independent of the significance of grandparenthood is the question of style in enacting the role of grandmother or grandfather. Treating the data inductively, five major styles were differentiated:

1. The *Formal* are those who follow what they regard as the proper and prescribed role for grandparents. Although they like to provide special treats and indulgences for the grandchild, and although they may occasionally take on a minor service such as baby-sitting, they maintain clearly demarcated lines between parenting and grandparenting, and they leave parenting strictly to the parent. They maintain a constant interest in the grandchild but are careful not to offer advice on childrearing.

2. The *Fun Seeker* is the grandparent whose relation to the grandchild is characterized by informality and playfulness. He joins the child in specific activities for the specific purpose of having fun, somewhat as if he were the child's playmate. Grand-

children are viewed as a source of leisure activity, as an item of "consumption" rather than "production," or as a source of self-indulgence. The relationship is one in which authority lines—either with the grandchild or with the parent—are irrelevant. The emphasis here is on mutuality of satisfaction rather than on providing treats for the grandchild. Mutuality imposes a latent demand that both parties derive fun from the relationship.[8]

3. The *Surrogate Parent* occurs only, as might have been anticipated, for grandmothers in this group. It comes about by initiation on the part of the younger generation, that is, when the young mother works and the grandmother assumes the actual caretaking responsibility for the child.

4. The *Reservoir of Family Wisdom* represents a distinctly authoritarian patricentered relationship in which the grandparent—in the rare occasions on which it occurs in this sample, it is the grandfather—is the dispenser of special skills or resources. Lines of authority are distinct, and the young parents maintain and emphasize their subordinate positions, sometimes with and sometimes without resentment.

5. The *Distant Figure* is the grandparent who emerges from the shadows on holidays and on special ritual occasions such as Christmas and birthdays. Contact with the grandchild is fleeting and infrequent, a fact which distinguishes this style from the *Formal.* This grandparent is benevolent in stance but essentially distant and remote from the child's life, a somewhat intermittent St. Nicholas.

Of major interest is the frequency with which grandparents of both sexes are either Fun Seekers or Distant Figures vis-à-vis their grandchildren. These two styles have been adopted by half of all the cases in this sample. Of interest, also, is the fact that in both styles the issue of authority is peripheral. Although deference may be given to the grandparent in certain ways, authority relationships are not a central issue.

Both of these styles are, then, to be differentiated from what has been regarded as the traditional grandparent role—one in which patriarchal or matriarchal control is exercised over both younger generations and in which authority constitutes the major axis of the relationship.

These two styles of grandparenting differ not only from traditional concepts; they differ also in some respects from more recently described types. Cavan, for example,[9] has suggested that the modern grandparent role is essentially a maternal one for both men and women and that to succeed as a grandfather, the male must learn to be a slightly masculinized grandmother, a role that differs markedly from the instrumental and outer-world orientation that has presumably characterized most males during a great part of their adult lives. It is being suggested here, however, that the newly emerging types are neuter in gender. Neither the Fun Seeker nor the Dis-

Table 14.2. Age Differences in Styles of Grandparenting*

	Under 65 (N = 81)	Over 65 (N = 34)
The Formal:		
Men	12	11
Women	13	9
Total	25 (31%)	20 (59%)
The Fun-Seeking:		
Men	13	4
Women	17	3
Total	30 (37%)	7 (21%)
The Distant Figure:		
Men	15	5
Women	11	2
Total	26 (32%)	7 (21%)

* These age differences are statistically reliable as indicated by 2 × 3 chi-square test applied to the category totals (P = .02).

tant Figure involves much nurturance, and neither "maternal" nor "paternal" seems an appropriate adjective.

Grandparent style in relation to age. A final question is the extent to which these new styles of grandparenting reflect, directly or indirectly, the increasing youthfulness of grandparents as compared to a few decades ago. (This youthfulness is evidenced not only in terms of the actual chronological age at which grandparenthood occurs but also in terms of evaluations of self as youthful. A large majority of middle-aged and older persons describe themselves as "more youthful than my parents were at my age.")

To follow up this point, the sample was divided into two groups: those who were under and over 65. As shown in Table 14.2, the Formal style occurs significantly more frequently in the older group; the Fun Seeking and the Distant Figure styles occur significantly more frequently in the younger group. (Examination of the table shows, furthermore, that the same age differences occur in both grandmothers and grandfathers.)

These age differences may reflect secular trends: that is, differences in values and expectations in persons who grow up and who grow old at different times in history. They may also reflect processes of aging and/or the effects of continuing socialization which produce differences in role behavior over time. It might be pointed out, however, that sociologists, when they have treated the topic of grandparenthood at all, have done so within the context of old age, not middle age. Grandparenthood might best be studied as a middle-age phenomenon if the investigator is interested in the assumption of new roles and the significance of new roles in adult socialization.

In this connection, certain lines of inquiry suggest themselves: as with other roles, a certain amount of anticipatory socialization takes place with regard to the grandparent role. Women in particular often describe a preparatory period in which they visualize themselves as grandmothers, often before their children are married. With the presently quickened pace of the family cycle, in which women experience the emptying of the nest, the marriages of their children, and the appearance of grandchildren at earlier points in their own lives, the expectation that grandmother-hood is a welcome and pleasurable event seems frequently to be accompanied also by doubts that one is "ready" to become a grandmother or by the feelings of being pre-maturely old. The anticipation and first adjustment to the role of grandmother has not been systematically studied, either by sociologists or psychologists, but there is anecdotal data to suggest that, at both conscious and unconscious levels, the middle-aged woman may relive her own first pregnancy and childbirth and that there are ad-ditional social and psychological factors that probably result in a certain transformation in ego-identity. The reactions of males to grandfatherhood have sim-ilarly gone uninvestigated although, as has been suggested earlier, the event may re-quire a certain reversal of traditional sex role and a consequent change in self-concept.

Other questions that merit investigation relate to the variations in role expecta-tions for grandparents in various ethnic and socioeconomic groups and the extent to which the grandparent role is comparable to other roles insofar as "reality shock" oc-curs for some individuals—that is, insofar as a period of disenchantment sets in, ei-ther early in the life of the grandchild or later as the grandchild approaches adolescence when the expected rewards to the grandparents may not be forth-coming.

When grandparenthood comes to be studied from such perspectives as these, it is likely to provide a significant area for research, not only with regard to changing fam-ily structure but also with regard to adult socialization.

Notes

1. Most studies of family relationships of older people have given no specific attention to grandparenthood. Several of the most recent examples are: Ethel Shanas, *Family Relationships of Older People* (Research Series 20), New York: Health Information Foundation, 1961; Arthur J. Robins, "Family Relations of the Aging in Three-Generation Households," in *Social and Psychological Aspects of Aging*, ed., by Clark Tibbitts and Wilma Donahue, New York: Co-lumbia University Press, 1962, pp. 464–474; and Marvin B. Sussman, "Relationships of

Adult Children with Their Parents in the United States," paper given at the Symposium on the Family, Intergenerational Relationships, and Social Structure, Duke University, 1963.

The fact that grandparenthood has not yet come within the central focus of research in social gerontology is evidenced also by examining the three major volumes that have appeared since 1960 in the field of social gerontology: (1) Tibbits and Donahue, *op. cit.,* which comprises one part of the proceedings of the Fifth Congress of the International Associations of Gerontology; (2) Clark Tibbits, ed., *Handbook of Social Gerontology,* Chicago: University of Chicago Press, 1960; and (3) Ernest W. Burgess, ed., *Aging in Western Societies,* Chicago: University of Chicago Press, 1960, the companion volume to the *Handbooks.* In the first of these three volumes, the topic does not occur at all; in the other two, it is treated in only a few pages of text. In none of the three is "grandparenthood" an entry in the index to the volume.

2. Karl Abraham, "Some Remarks on the role of Grandparent in the Psychology of Neurosis" (1913), in *Clinical Papers and Essays on Psychoanalysis,* I, New York: Basic Books, 1955, pp. 47–49; Sandor Ferenczi, "The Grandfather Complex" (1913), reprinted in *Further Contributions to the Theory and Techniques of Psychoanalysis,* New York: Basic Books, 1952, pp. 323–324; Ernest Jones, "The Fantasy of Reversal of Generations" (1913) and "Significance of the Grandfather for the Fate of the Individual" (1913), in *Papers on Psychoanalysis,* New York: William Wood, 1948, pp. 519–524; Maureen Boire LaBarre, Lucie Jessner, and Lon Ussery, "The Significance of Grandmothers in th Psychopathology of Children," *American Journal of Orthopsychiatry,* 30 (January 1960), pp. 175–185; Ernest Rappaport, "The Grandparent syndrome," *Psychoanalytic Quarterly,* 27 (1958), pp. 518–537; and Elsie Thurston, "Grandparents in the Three Generation Home: A Study of Their Influence on Children," *Smith College Studies in Social Work,* 12 (1941), pp. 172–173.

3. Dorrian Apple, "The Social Structure of Grandparenthood," *American Anthropologist,* 58 (August 1956), pp. 656–663. See also S. F. Nadel, *The Foundations of Social Anthropology,* Glencoe, Ill.: Free Press, 1953; A. R. Radcliffe-Brown, *African Systems of Kinship and Marriage,* London: Oxford University Press, 1950.

4. Ruth Shonle Cavan, "Self and Role in Adjustment During Old Age," in *Human Behavior and Social Processes,* ed. by Arnold M. Rose, Boston: Houghton Mifflin, 1962, pp. 526–536; Hans von Hentig, "The Social Function of the Grandmother," *Social Forces,* 24 (1946), pp. 389–392; M. F. Nimkoff, "Changing Family Relationships of Older People in the United States During the Last Fifty Years," *The Gerontologist,* 1 (June 1961), pp. 92–97; William M. Smith, Jr., Joseph H. Britton, and Jean O. Britton, *Relationships within Three Generation Families,* Pennsylvania State University College of Home Economics Research Publication 155, April 1958; Gordon F. Streib, "Family Patterns in Retirement," *Journal of Social Issues,* 14 (No. 2, 1958), pp. 46–60.

5. Ruth Albrecht, "The Parental Responsibilities of Grandparents," *Marriage and Family Living,* 16 (August 1954), pp. 201–204.

6. Dorrian Apple, "Grandparents and Grandchildren: A Sociological and Psychological Study of Their Relationship," unpublished Ph.D. dissertation, Radcliffe College, 1954.

7. Peter Townsend, *The Family Life of Old People,* London: Routledge and Kegan Paul, 1957.

8. Wolfenstein has described fun morality in childrearing practices as it applies to parenthood. Perhaps a parallel development is occurring in connection with grandparenthood. As Wolfenstein has delineated it, fun has become not only permissible but almost required in the new morality. Martha Wolfenstein, "Fun Morality, An Analysis of Recent American Child-Training Literature," in *Childhood in Contemporary Cultures,* ed. by Margaret Mead and Martha Wolfenstein, Chicago: University of Chicago Press, 1955, pp. 168–178.

9. Cavan, *op cit.*

FIFTEEN

The Middle Generations

As adults we are facing a relatively new situation in the family: the increasing number of persons living into advanced old age and posing new problems for adult children, who in turn are trying to define their responsibilities toward aging parents and trying to work out ways of dealing with situations for which they may feel relatively unprepared.

On the other hand, the population at large may feel more prepared than we know. Recently, as I was waiting my turn in the hairdresser's shop, I noticed that the woman in the chair next to me was carrying on a long complaining monologue, while the hairdresser was nodding patiently from time to time. When I moved into the chair to take my turn, I asked, "What was all that about?"

"Oh," said the beautician, "she's a self-pitying type. She's going on and on about the problems she's having with her mother, who is 85 and who's getting feeble and needs more attention. But for heaven's sake, who *doesn't* have an aging mother to worry about these days?"

The anecdote is perhaps an indication that we social scientists may be following along *behind* public attitudes, trying to survey attitudes and to define problems and issues long after they have taken shape and after the social realities have become widely accepted. It may be we social scientists, not the public, who are unprepared for the changes we see in family structure and family relationships.

It is often assumed that there is a three-generation family in America; that there is therefore a middle generation which has responsibilities to both the older and younger generations, and that it may be described not only as the generation in the middle, but as the generation *caught* in the middle.

In truth, however, the family in America is becoming a four-generation—even a five-generation—structure. As long as 15 years ago, some 40 percent of all persons over 65 who had ever had a child were great-grandparents. The proportion has undoubtedly risen over the past 15 years, given increasing longevity and other changes

Reprinted by permission from *Aging Parents,* edited by P. K. Ragan (Los Angeles: University of Southern California Press, 1979), 258–66.

that are producing shortened intervals between generations. We should be talking today about middle generations in the plural and about aging children as well as aging parents, for it is another important demographic fact that a substantial number of families have two generations who are beyond middle age. It is often a young-old 65-year-old child who is concerned over an old-old 85-year-old parent.

Concern over an aging parent or parent-in-law has come to be part of the psychological baggage that most adults carry around in their heads. The widespread problem of "parent-caring" first surfaced in my own research some years ago, when in our first studies of middle-aged women we found that so far as their family life was concerned, it was not the menopause nor the empty nest that was causing problems; but it was the fear of widowhood, and it was parent-caring.

That finding has been confirmed by other investigators, for example in a survey just completed by my colleagues at the University of Chicago. A representative sample of 1,100 adults residing in the metropolitan area of Chicago were asked what changes they had experienced in the past four years—if they had experienced a major life event such as divorce, remarriage, a child starting or finishing school, a health problem in self or in spouse or child; unemployment, widowhood, or retirement; or particular strains in the areas of work, family, or economic well-being. For each event or role strain, the person was asked how bothersome it had been, and if bothersome, whether or not outside advice or assistance had been sought. In another part of the interview, respondents were asked whether their parents or parents-in-law had shown any of four changes: if they had developed serious health problems, were worse off financially, showed increased dependency on the respondent for moral support or advice, or required more of the respondent's time, energy, or money.

The interesting fact is that a perceived change in a parent or parent-in-law was the second most frequently reported change. The only event more frequently reported was the death of a significant other, a relative or close friend. Of all the people in this sample who had living parents, over half perceived that a major change had occurred in a parent: a serious health change or increased need for moral support three times as often as a financial problem (Lieberman, 1978).

Of the large group who reported a change in the parent, about 40 percent reported that the problem was one that was genuinely troublesome to themselves. Of this latter group, the majority had turned for advice or assistance to other family members, to friends, and/or to other helping persons. About one-fourth had turned to formal or professional helpers such as a social work agency or a psychiatrist.

Thus the aging of one's parents is an issue of widespread concern. It is of particular interest also that the problem is reported by adults of all ages and that it does not emerge as a problem particular to the middle-aged. (It is true, of course, that the nature of the parental change is itself age-related; and that a serious health problem in the parent of a 50-year-old is more likely to involve total and long-term care than is true of the parent of a 30-year-old.)

The physical or psychological distance between members of the two generations—that is, whether they lived close to each other or felt emotionally closer than at earlier periods in their lives—were irrelevant factors. Thus parent-caring seems to have strong components of obligation and commitment as the basis for the generational tie, whether or not there is frequent visiting and whether or not the adult child reports a feeling of close emotional bondedness to the aging parent.

It is probably noteworthy also that while women in this study reported a concern over parents somewhat more frequently than did men, the difference was not striking. We are accustomed to thinking of the woman as the kin-keeper in the family network—the one who keeps the family together and keeps the channels of communication open—but it is men as well as women who worry about their parents and who report that a change in the parent has produced a change in their own lives.

This may be a phenomenon of family life that has not been given the recognition it deserves—that cross-generational ties are strong for both men and women when both generations are adults, just as is true when one generation is adult and the other is a child. These ties may be as strong or even stronger than in earlier historical periods. A sense of social obligation may replace financial obligation, as has often been pointed out; and it may persist even when the emotional tie is weak.

There are other types of supporting data: for instance, with regard to living arrangements, there has been a marked trend toward separate households for older persons as levels of income have risen (the generations move apart when they can afford it) and as housing has become more available. At the same time, the telephone and automobile make it possible to maintain family ties without living under the same roof. And with regard to face-to-face contact, the latest national survey carried out only three years ago (Harris, 1975) showed that of all people 65 and over who had one or move living children, more than 80 percent had seen at least one child during the last day or week. Of those who had grandchildren, about 75 percent had seen a grandchild within the last day or week.

There are statistical data, furthermore, that show the older the individual and the sicker, the more likely he or she is to be found living with an adult child. In 1970, of all persons aged 75 and over, one of five women and one of ten men was living in the child's household. It often goes unnoticed that at present for every older person in an institution there are nearly three others living with a child.

There are a number of studies that show also that while most older people want to be independent of their families as long as possible, they expect their children to come to their aid when they, the parents, can no longer manage for themselves. Not only do these expectations exist, but they are usually fulfilled, and there is a complex pattern of exchange of services across generations. There are differences to be found, according to ethnic group, socioeconomic group, and in rural and urban settings, but overall it appears that ties of commitment and obligation remain strong in American multigeneration families and that the family remains a strongly supportive institution for the older person.

Within this context, it is the very aged parent who poses the problem for most families, for, far from becoming indifferent to the needs of an old-old father or mother, the child experiences responsibilities that become more pressing and more strongly felt.

It is easy to find examples of the problem. The one that follows is paraphrased from a new book on parent-caring that happened to reach my desk as I was preparing these comments:

> Marcia wished her 82-year-old father-in-law, Max, the best of health. . . . She knew how difficult it had been for him to get out of his house ever since he broke his hip. But her husband, Ken, could not bring himself to say no to his father's demands for company and attention. . . . After the last of Marcia and Ken's children left for college, she had looked forward to a kind of second honeymoon, where she and Ken would be free to take the vacations they had always postponed, free, most of all, to spend some quiet time together. . . . Instead, she found that her father-in-law's needs were ruining these plans. Three evenings a week Ken had to skip dinner at home to drive across town to visit his father. . . . Every other Saturday evening Marcia found herself in her father-in-law's house, listening to him reminisce about his old job, which bored her, and complain about his infirmities, which seemed endless. . . . Nor did Ken enjoy his new responsibilities. He had certainly not expected this turn of affairs. . . . What was worse, his father was a critical old man who never seemed satisfied with Ken's efforts on his behalf. The two had never been close, but it pained Ken to see his father confronted with so many problems. . . . He wanted to do all he could to make his father's last years (or months) of life as comfortable as possible. . . . But he found himself wishing that the whole responsibility would just go away, even if it meant a quick and painless death for his father. That last thought made Ken feel guilty, naturally enough . . . worse, still, Ken realized the situation was beginning to hurt his marriage, for Marcia was becoming more frustrated and dissatisfied and no longer had the patience to listen to Ken's own complaints about his father. Was it his fault that there wasn't someone else to help care for his father? His brother and sister lived in different parts of the country. Did Marcia really expect him to place his father in a nursing home? Wasn't Ken obligated as a son to do all he could for his father? (Cohen and Gans, 1978)

This example is not only easy to duplicate, but serves also to make the point that the relationship to an aging parent must always be understood in terms of the family as the unit. Here, it was Marcia, as well as Ken, and it was their children who also had to be considered; and it was Ken's feelings toward his brother and sister who were being spared the burden. It is often when a parent takes the turn toward dependency that the whole family constellation comes into focus, when siblings may come together who haven't seen each other for years, and when old feelings and rivalries may surface again—in short, when all the positive and negative aspects of family interrelationships become crystallized.

All this raises an important set of issues about the role of the professional. The particular problem that most often brings the adult child to the professional helper is the care of a parent whose health is failing and who needs physical care and surveillance. The presenting problem most frequently is around the question of living arrangements: "Now that my father has died, my 80-year-old mother cannot take care of herself. What do I do?"

Very often the social worker, in exploring the family relationships and in dealing with the child's feelings and needs, finds himself or herself redefining who the *client* is. It often becomes, unwittingly, the child rather than the aged parent. Indeed, some of the popular books now appearing are aimed directly at assuaging the guilt and making life easier for the child (see, for example, Schwartz, 1977; Cohen and Gans, 1978; Silverstone, 1976).

But whether it is the child or the parent who becomes the primary client, it is clear that the family is not dumping its aged member into a nursing home and making short shrift of their problem. The opposite is true instead. Ties of familial obligation are working *against* the nursing home as the solution. But it is an uphill fight for increasing numbers of families, especially those who live in the centers of the cities and those in which both husband and wife are working.

Some observers are saying that if old age continues to bring physical and mental deterioration, then the costs of health services, home care, institutional care, and social services will become enormous. Questions are already being raised about the preservation of life, the quality of care for the frail elderly, the wisdom of using heroic measures to prolong life for the terminally ill, and euthanasia. These are torturous problems, and they will grow ever more pressing.

Some observers are saying also that we cannot avoid more warehousing of old people in the future—that with the changes in women's roles and value patterns it is harder and harder to come by the feelings of duty and perseverance and willingness to do the "dirty work" of physically caring for an old person; and that we will be unable to provide tender loving care for the sick aged. Such care will not be purchasable outside the family, it is said, and it will be harder and harder to produce within the family.

There are others who, like myself, are more impressed with the numbers of families in which the preference to maintain the aged parent at home (whether in the parent's own home or in the home of the child) is pursued at almost any cost; families who avoid the institution until the last possible effort has been made. It is probably true that most families give up when they think there is no alternative, and only when they have tried everything they know, but not before.

The point is: the family needs help from a wide variety of professionals. The question before us today is how that help can be provided. How can the social worker, the clergyman, the physician help both the aging parent and the responsible child in such a way that the needs of both are given equal attention? How does the community agency provide help for families in which both adults are working and both adults lie awake nights worrying about an aged mother?

How can the educator help? Can he provide education about aging, beginning in the elementary school, and education about home care and self care?

Can the TV producer take his chances with the viewing public? Can he provide realistic accounts of aging, and not only Pollyanna-ish interviews with successful old people who reinforce the paradox in our society—that person who ages well is the person who does *not* age?

And what about the city planner? Can the family be helped—not replaced—by the appropriate planning of physical and social resources in the community?

Is it possible for persons to come together on local levels and seek out solutions? Can we find ways for the working child, the neighbor, the friend, the visiting nurse, the social worker, as well as the Social Security office, to work together?

Most of us think we know what the goals should be: somehow to create or recreate a network of support that will sustain older people and maximize their stability; to avoid relocating old people; and to bring services to where the old persons live, rather than bring the old persons to where the services are. This is, underneath, the problem of creating or recreating the primary community—the face-to-face community where people know each other and share responsibility for each other—the *caring* community.

Can professionals work together across the lines of their private and public agencies to help support the caring family and to build a caring community for the old-old?

References

Cohen, S., and Gans, B. *The other generation gap*. Chicago: Follett, 1978.

Harris, L., and Associates. *The myth and the reality of aging in America*. Washington, D.C.: National Council on the Aging, 1975.

Lieberman, G. L. Children of the elderly as natural helpers: Some demographic variables. In J. C. Glidewell & M. A. Lieberman (Special Issue Eds.), *American Journal of Community Psychology.*

Schwartz, A. *Survival handbook for children of aging parents.* Chicago: Follett, 1977.

Silverstone, B., and Hymen, H. K. *You and your aging parent.* New York: Pantheon, 1976.

SIXTEEN

Retirement in the Life Course

Retirement is an important turning point in the lives of most people. It brings with it a major change in activity pattern, a restructuring of the use of time, a different set of daily associates and, for many, a change of residence.

In contrast to other major events in the second half of life—the menopause, children launched from the home, grandparenthood, death of spouse, illness and death—the timing of retirement is determined primarily not by biological changes in the individual or in family members, but by chronological age. People withdraw from the work force when they reach the ages of entitlement for private and public pensions, ages set in the first instance by the employer and in the second by agreements arrived at among industry, labor unions and government.

A stereotyped and generally outmoded view is that, in part because it is arbitrarily timed, retirement is a negative event, one that represents major losses to the individual, not only in income but also in social status, and is often accompanied by depression and anxiety; in short, that it is a crisis event. This view is to be found not only in the public at large, but sometimes also in those mental health professionals who see relatively few older persons in the course of their own daily work as clinicians and therapists.

A different view is the one that emerges, not just from the glossy magazines that show older persons playing golf or basking in the sun, but from systematic studies of retirement, undertaken by psychologists and sociologists, and confirmed by professionals who are experienced in dealing with older persons as clients or patients. In this second view, retirement is seldom the cause of an older person's visit to the clinician's office, or even the triggering event. Because retirement occurs in the lives of most men and increasing numbers of women, it has become one of the markers of the normal, expectable life cycle, an event that is mentally rehearsed and, in this sense, prepared for. Instead of a crisis-producing event, retirement is a familiar and usual occurrence that most people experience with relative equanimity.

Reprinted by permission from *Triangle,* Sandoz Journal of Medical Science, 29, no. 2/3 (1990): 119–25; © Sandoz Pharma Ltd., Basel, Switzerland.

RETIREMENT AS A SOCIAL INSTITUTION

From a historical perspective, retirement is a social practice created in the twentieth century as one of the accompaniments of industrialization. The modern industrialized nation no longer requires the work of all its members in order to maintain a high level of economic productivity. Accordingly, working life has been shortened at both ends: by extending education and delaying entry into the work force for young people, and by providing private and public pensions that enable early exit from the work force for older people. Retirement has now become an established social institution.[1,9,19] It exists in all the countries of Europe and North America and in Japan[7,16,24] and is beginning to appear also for urban wage earners in developing countries.

RECENT SOCIAL TRENDS

From a shorter time perspective, the most dramatic fact about retirement is the drop in retirement age that has occurred in the past two decades. Despite the fact that 65 is the age of eligibility for drawing full public pensions in most countries, both men and women are exercising the choice to take reduced pensions and to retire early. Large numbers are retiring in their early 60s, many as early as their late 50s. The trend is particularly striking in the 60- to 64-year-old age group. For instance, in the United States fewer than 60% of men in this age group are currently in the work force. In West Germany it is only 40% and, in the two most extreme cases, in France it is only 33% and in Italy fewer than 30%.[13] The trend is similar for women, although women have always been a smaller proportion of the work force and have withdrawn earlier than men. (I shall have more to say about women retirees in a later section of this paper.)

At the same time that the retirement age has been falling, longevity has been rising at a very rapid rate. Average life expectancy in the industrialized nations, although it varies somewhat from one country to another, is now approaching 75 years for men, overall, and 80 years for women. Thus, people are retiring earlier, but living longer. This trend is of growing concern to labor-force economists and policy makers in many countries as they look ahead to higher proportions of old people and lower proportions of young people in future decades, if, as projected, both birth rates and mortality rates stay low.[23]

Another major social trend relates to cultural values. An ethic of leisure has emerged which is as significant as the work ethic in giving meaning to life.[26] Increasing numbers of people find their work less rewarding than their leisure, and they choose to retire as soon as they decide they will have enough money to live on, even though their incomes will be lower than before.[25]

A New Rhythm of the Life Course: The "Third age"

These trends, taken together, are creating a new rhythm of the life course. The period of education has grown longer, the working life shorter, and the period of retirement longer. Not only is there now a real period of "life after work," but for many people that period is nearly as long as their working lives, often as long as 30 years.[11] Some observers now describe the retirement period as a "third age," one that provides more freedom than the first two periods of life, with time to develop new interests and with opportunities to extend not only one's lifetime but also what can be called one's personal biography.[20]

Life in Retirement: Sequences of Change

People often speak of "life in retirement," rather than of retirement as a discrete event. Viewed in this way, many people describe retirement as a period characterized by monotony, boredom and decline, a period of marking time until death. For such people, the third age goes unrecognized.

It is a better representation of reality to think of retirement as a period of life that not only is long, but also encompasses a sequence of attitude changes, events, decisions and adaptations. The events are those that occur after the person withdraws from the labor force, but the sequence has attitudinal precursors earlier in life, beginning when young men and women recognize that one day they will retire.

Most young adults have generally favorable attitudes toward retirement, regarding it as a time of "earned" leisure.[2,3] They hope their health will be good and their incomes sufficient to allow them to enjoy life when that time arrives. How young people view retirement may affect how well they fare later, but their anticipations are not likely to stay the same over the years as they assess and reassess the values of work and leisure, and as they forge commitments to spouses and children whose well-being will be influenced by those assessments.

The Retirement Decision

The actual decision to retire, if it is not compelled by poor health, involves a wide range of personal factors: the importance of work to one's sense of identity, current degree of pleasure in the work itself, the quality of one's relations with fellow workers, how much money one has managed to save, and the attitudes and desires of one's spouse and sometimes of one's children, too.

Institutional factors are equally important: the conditions of the workplace, the physical demands of the job, the employer's pension policies, the norms regarding age of retirement that prevail in the particular company or industry, and what one's public pension will be. At present, employers in some industries are offering various direct and indirect inducements to older workers to leave the labor force. The grounds, as they are often stated, are that places must be freed for young workers, and, in addition, that the firm can save more in labor costs by retiring older workers than by dismissing younger workers. In other industries and occupations, however, labor shortages are appearing and older workers are being encouraged to stay on.

The decision to retire occurs when the worker decides that, on balance, the incentives outweigh the disincentives.

Despite the fact that most men and women have mentally rehearsed how their lives will be after they retire, relatively few have made specific or detailed plans in advance. Even at this point in the sequence of events, when workers have decided to leave their jobs, relatively few choose to take part in the retirement preparation programs that are spreading across Europe and North America. These programs usually offer information and counseling with regard to a range of topics such as maintaining good health, keeping active, and using leisure time in satisfying ways. Despite this range of relevant issues, most retirees who do participate in such programs seem to want information only about what their public and private pensions are likely to provide, and what they might do further to assure their financial security in the future. Perhaps the low rates of participation signify that most men and women do not expect retirement to be an unsettling or wrenching experience because they have witnessed retirement in friends and relatives and have already given considerable thought to what their own preferred lifestyles will be after the event.

Stages of Retirement

Once the decision to retire has been made, life begins to change. One author has described a first "honeymoon" stage, when some people try to undertake all the activities they had too little time for earlier, and when others opt for what they call R and R, or rest and relaxation.[1]

This soon gives way to a stage of settling-in, when a new routine becomes established. For most people this second stage ends within six moths or a year, by which time the retiree has established a pattern of activities that, whether or not it resembles the pre-retirement pattern, is usually described as satisfying, and when retirees describe themselves as keeping busy or too busy at activities they regard as meaningful.[6]

For most people the period of retirement that follows the event itself is not, contrary to the stereotype, a monotonous plateau. It is punctuated by changes in the lives of spouses, children and friends, and by changes in the community. As in other periods of life, some events are positive, for instance the birth of a grandchild or a friend's promotion, and some are negative, for instance a personal accident or injury or the death of a close friend. Obviously enough, these are events that occur whether or not the person is retired. They do not, therefore, relate to this discussion in the same way as other kinds of events and sequences that are made possible by retirement.

In today's world, many retirees move from one part of the country to another, develop new interests, and some begin a second or even a third career.[10] It is no longer unusual to see a retired man or woman "go back to school" and enroll at a college or, in Europe, at a University of the Third Age. Nor is it unusual for a retiree to work at a volunteer job, then at a part-time paid job, then to open a small business of his own; or for a couple to move to a home in a warm climate, then move again to be near a child, then move into a retirement community.

Many retirees remain socially productive for many years. Some assist in the rearing of grandchildren, especially now that so many young women are in the labor market and need help with child care. Others undertake the everyday care of a frail relative, sometimes their own parent who has reached advanced old age.

VOLUNTEERISM AND THE "YOUNG-OLD"

Volunteerism is often described as characteristic of the United States more than of other countries. It has recently been noted that a great many non-profit organizations in the United States, such as schools, hospitals, philanthropic organizations, community service groups, and cultural enterprises such as libraries and museums, succeed only by the efforts of large numbers of people who are better described as "unpaid staff" than as "volunteers."[5] These persons are carefully selected and monitored in their work, and they perform a range of administrative or specialist tasks for which they are well suited by their earlier paid work experience. The numbers of unpaid staff are growing rapidly because of retirees who continue to be socially productive in these ways. Volunteerism is now developing also among older persons in other countries.[10]

By definition, the retirement period comprises those years when retirees remain "young-old," that is, they are people who maintain social and intellectual competence as well as good health and who choose to remain active in their families and communities. This period is shorter for some people than for others but, as stated earlier, on average it has been steadily lengthening.

THE "FOURTH AGE" AND THE "OLD-OLD"

The period of retirement ends when people become "old-old," that is, when declining physical or mental health becomes the focus of their lives and when it creates dependency and the need for special supportive services. If the retirement period is considered the "third age," then this period of dependency is the "fourth age."[17] This period begins earlier for some people than for others, and it lasts a shorter or longer time. Depending on the cause of death, for some it lasts only a few days or a few weeks.

The terms young-old and old-old are intended to signify not chronological age, but the state of physical and mental health and the level of family and community involvement. An 80-year-old may be young-old, and a 60-year-old may be old-old.[22]

The nature and timing of events in the fourth age are seldom related to retirement.

WOMEN RETIREES

The patterns of work and retirement have generally been different for today's older women and men. At present, the proportion of older women who experience formal retirement is relatively small, because these women have had, for the most part, irregular work histories. They have worked at lower-paid and non-unionized jobs, and they have taken time out from work to raise children or to meet other family responsibilities. Because private pension plans are usually those created by large corporations and are tied to consecutive years of full-time work, relatively few older women today have pensions based on their own employment histories. These women depend instead on the pensions of their husbands. Furthermore, because women live longer than men, on average, many have only a widow's pension to live on.

For these and related reasons, many observers have commented that today's older women are generally discriminated against in both public and private pension systems. This picture is expected to change as younger women of today create regular work histories of their own, so that when they reach pensionable age they will have retirement arrangements comparable to those of men.

There have been relatively few studies of women in retirement, compared with the many studies of men. The assumption has been that work outside the home did not constitute a central role in the lives of women and, accordingly, that retirement problems were not to be expected. A related assumption was that those women who experience retirement would have few problems because women are more adaptable than men owing to their earlier experiences with events such as pregnancy, childbirth, departure of children from the home and the menopause. Because the dependency that followed retirement was not a new occurrence, women would take it easily in their stride.

These assumptions reflect traditional rather than contemporary perspectives on age-sex roles. It is quite certain that women who reach old age in the coming decades will have had work experiences different from their mothers' and that, accordingly, their retirement experiences will not be the same. Although differences among cohorts exist also for men, the differences are likely to be greater for women. In other words, with regard to work experience, today's young women will be more different from their mothers than today's young men from their fathers.

Recently, on the basis of studies in both modern and simple societies, the view has been put forward that, because of sex differences that are inherent, the aging of men and women takes different directions.[12] Women in their late middle age become more expressive, self-confident, autonomous and assertive in responding to their social environments. Men, meanwhile, become more passive, nurturant, more focussed on comfort and more accommodating. If these differences are indeed inherent, then retirement may be more stressful for women than for men, for retirement occurs when women are in their surge toward self-enhancement, while men are in their time of social disengagement.

To repeat the point, it may come about, however, that as more women have long work histories of their own and careers more similar to men's, the patterns of retirement and adjustment to retirement will become increasingly similar in the two sexes. This seems to be borne out by a recent study of Israeli men and women from a wide range of white-collar and blue-collar occupations that showed greater differences between occupational groups than between the sexes in attitudes toward retirement.[4]

Adaptations to Retirement

There have been many studies of how well people fare after retirement in terms of their physical and mental health. In most such studies, retirees have been interviewed only once, with the result that the findings can clarify neither the sequences of changes that differentiate older persons over the period of retirement, nor whether well-being is greater at one stage than at another. Other problems arise from the fact that different studies are based on different population samples and different measures of health.

One thing is clear: because such vast numbers of people retire each year, retirement happens to many different kinds of people in very different settings and can therefore be expected to have very different meanings. We should be careful, then, not to view retirement as a uniform social or psychological experience and not to expect consequences that are predictable across subgroups.[18]

One careful review of the literate concludes, however, that although each study by itself may be open to criticism, the consistency of findings across studies cannot be ignored.[15] The reports are consistent in the conclusion that, overall, the transition from work to retirement is not accompanied by adverse impacts on physical health, mental health or well-being. Some studies show that retirement is likely to be the outcome, not the cause, of poor health,[14] and some show that retirement may lead to improved mental and physical health.[24]

This discussion should not lead to the conclusion that retirement does not matter, but instead that it matters in complex ways—in use of time, in friendship patterns, in housing arrangements, often in the development of new interests—and that these changes interact to produce positive outcomes in some people, negative outcomes in others.

This is not to say, furthermore, that retirement is not accompanied by stresses of various kinds. For some people, retirement triggers off a fear of aging and of disabling illness. For some retirees who were previously in positions of responsibility over other workers, retirement may mean a loss of power that diminishes self-esteem. For still others, there is a sense of social uselessness, or distress about idleness, or a sense of loss because of separation from friends at work.

Most investigators report that the most frequent problem of retirees is to adjust to a lower level of income. Others report stress arising from the changed pattern of interaction between husbands and wives, when the presence of husbands at home all day, at least for a temporary period, may interfere with established household routines. Some persons find that their fantasies about life in retirement were unrealistic and therefore feel disenchanted.

These kinds of problem are real enough, but they usually fade after some months, as new patterns of activity become established. Psychiatrists often comment that retirement is seldom accompanied by a serious depression.[27]

PROBLEM GROUPS

Generally speaking, some people are more prone than others to suffer psychological distress at retirement. One such group comprises those who have had low-paid and physically demanding jobs all their lives because of low levels of education. These are likely to be men whose sense of self has been tied to hard work, and whose wage has been the single most important index of their worth. Such people have few personal or social resources for coping with the changes that come with retirement.

Another group are those who have been forced to retire earlier than they wanted, because of poor health or because their jobs were terminated by decisions made by their companies. Such people, to whom retirement comes "off time," are likely to adapt poorly, at least at the beginning.[21]

Others have long-standing psychological problems that are triggered by retirement. As at least one major study has shown, these include persons with conflicts about sex roles, with unfulfilled personal goals and with certain personality characteristics such as the tendency to self-blame.[8]

IMPLICATIONS FOR MENTAL HEALTH PROFESSIONALS

In summary, retirement has become one of the expectable events that occur in the lives of the large majority of men workers and increasing numbers of women. It rarely creates a psychological crisis, as might well be anticipated for any life event that is common to a large proportion of the population. Retirement is regarded favorably both before and after it occurs. Most men and women adapt well to the changes in lifestyle that usually accompany it.

This is not to deny that retirement is an important life event, or that some people experience considerable stress when they withdraw from the work role. Such people may suffer from lowered self-esteem, depression or anxiety. Others suffer from a loss of a creative outlet, a locus for friendship and working relationships or a basis of status and prestige. Clinical depressions rarely accompany retirement.

Mental health professionals may expect to see in their practices some older persons for whom retirement has reactivated a long-standing psychological problem. In other instances, the distress of an older person relates to a recent life change—not often to retirement, but rather to a sudden decline in health, to an "off-time" life event, for example when the death of a spouse comes earlier than expected, or to an event that falls outside the normal expectable life cycle altogether, such as the death of a child.

When seen not as a single event but as a period of life, retirement, like other life periods, is marked by both negative and positive changes. In today's modern societies, life in retirement provides new opportunities for expansion as well as extension of the personal biography. The appropriate role of the mental health professional can often be that of assisting the older person to actualize these opportunities.

References

1. Atchley RC: Social Forces and Aging. Wadsworth Publishing Co., Belmont 1985, pp. 185–204.
2. Atchley RC: Aging: Continuity and Change. 2nd ed. Wadsworth Publishing Co., Belmont 1987, pp. 217–230.
3. Barfield RE: Morgan JN: *Gerontologist* 1978, *18,* 19.
4. Biber A: *In:* Early Retirement: Approaches and Variations: An International Perspective. Eds S Bergman, G Naegele, W Tokarski. Published jointly as Kasseler Gerontologische Schriften 3, Soziale Gerontologie, Fachbereich Sozialwesen, Gesamthochschule Kassell, and in Brookdale Monograph Series, JDC-Brookdale Institute of Gerontology and Adult Human Development, Jerusalem 1988.
5. Drucker PF: The New Realities. Harper & Row, New York 1989, pp. 195–206.
6. Ekerdt DJ: *Gerontologist* 1986, *26,* 239.
7. Ekerdt DJ: The Encyclopedia of Aging. Ed. GL Maddox. Springer Publishing Co., New York 1987, pp. 577–580.
8. Fiske M: *In:* Handbook of Mental Health and Aging. Eds JE Birren, RB Sloane. Prentice-Hall Inc., Englewood Cliffs 1980, pp. 337–373.
9. Friedmann EA, Orbach HL: *In:* American Handbook of Psychiatry (2nd ed.), Vol. 1. Ed. S Arieti. Basic Books Inc., New York 1974, pp. 609–645.

10. Gaullier X: La Deuxième Carrière: Ages, Emplois, Retraites. Editions du Seuil, Paris 1988.
11. Guillemard AM: *Aging Sociology* 1985, *5*, 381.
12. Gutman D: Reclaimed Powers: Toward a New Psychology of Men and Women in Later Life. Basic Books Inc., New York 1987, pp. 185–213.
13. International labor Office. Economically active population estimates and projections 1950–2025. Geneva 1986, Table 2.
14. Johnson ES, Williamson JB: *In:* Retirement in Industrialized Societies. Eds K Markides, CL Cooper. John Wiley & Sons, Chichester 1987, pp. 9–41.
15. Kasl SV: *In:* Current Concerns in Occupational Stress. Eds CL Cooper, R Payne. John Wiley & Sons, Chichester 1980, pp. 137–186.
16. Kii T: *In:* Retirement in Industrialized Societies. Eds K Markides, CL Cooper. John Wiley & Sons, Chichester 1987, pp. 231–269.
17. Lalive d'Epinay CJ, Bolzman CA, Sultan MM: *In:* Retirement in Industrialized Societies. Eds K Markides, CL Cooper. John Wiley & Sons, Chichester 1987, pp. 103–130.
18. Maddox GL: *In:* Middle Age and Aging. Ed. BL Neugarten. University of Chicago Press, Chicago 1968, pp. 357–365.
19. Markides K, Cooper CL (Eds.): Retirement in Industrialized Societies. John Wiley & Sons, Chichester 1987.
20. Munnichs JMA: *In:* Retirement in Industrialized Societies. Eds K Markides, CL Cooper. John Wiley & Sons, Chichester 1987, pp. 209–230.
21. Neugarten BL: *Amer. J. Psychiat.* 1979, *136, 7,* 887.
22. Neugarten BL, Neugarten DA: *In:* Our Aging Society: Paradox and Promise. Eds A Pifer, L Bronte. W. W. Norton, New York 1986, pp. 33–51.
23. Palmer JL, Gould SG: *In:* Our Aging Society: Paradox and Promise. Eds A Pifer, L Bronte. W. W. Norton, New York 1986, pp. 367–390.
24. Parker SR: *In:* Retirement in Industrialized Societies. Eds K Markides, CL Cooper. John Wiley & Sons, Chichester 1987, pp. 77–101.
25. Parnes HS, Nestel G: *In:* Work and Retirement: A Longitudinal Study of Men. Ed. HS Parnes. The MIT Press, Cambridge 1981, pp. 155–197.
26. Robinson PK, Coberly S, Paul CE: *In:* Handbook of Aging and the Social Sciences. Eds RH Binstock, E Shanas. 2nd ed. Van Nostrand, New York 1985, pp. 503–527.
27. Simon A: *In:* Handbook of Mental Health and Aging. Eds JE Birren, RB Sloane. Prentice-Hall Inc., Englewood Cliffs 1980, pp. 653–670.

PART THREE

Personality and Adaptation

The Idiosyncratic Faces of Personality

David L. Gutmann

Bernice Neugarten's papers on personality can be roughly divided into two groups: those covering the dynamic psychology of aging, and those dealing with social-psychological influences on attitudes, self-regard and behavior in later life. In the psychodynamic works, the emphasis is on the intrapsychic aspects: the developmental surges of later life; the liberation (rather than the inevitable decline) of the post-menopausal and post–empty-nest woman; the social impact of varied psychological types in the elderly population; the influence of personality, as a self-maintaining and independent system, on its surroundings and ultimate fate. By contrast, in the social-psychological studies that Neugarten also guided and carried out, the emphasis is put on the social forces that bear on the individual: the effects of age norms on the older person's sense of being "on-time" or "off-time"; the social reality of the "young-old"; and the very special condition of those classified as "old-old."

Jung (1933) and Erikson (1952) were the first theorists to speculate, from their clinical observations, on the possibilities for true psychological development (as opposed to fortuitous adaptations) in later life. But Neugarten and I, mining the projective protocols from the Kansas City studies, were the first investigators to demonstrate the tracings, in empirical data, of what appeared to be a developmental shift in the psychology of older men and women: each sex gained access to gendered qualities that had been, in their earlier years, exclusive to their mates. I went on to test the universal application of the developmental conception across the human cultural range, while Neugarten defended the home turf against disengagement theory. That theory was an ambitious piece of social psychology that claimed—prematurely, and without the necessary cross-cultural evidence—to be *the* sovereign theory of psychological growth in later life.

Cumming and Henry (1961) held that disengagement took place on two fronts: the outer/social and the inner/psychological. On the external side, a necessary, *motivated* withdrawal of the aging individual from social engagement was proposed; and on the inner-psychological side, the individual was presumably "liberated" from

David L. Gutmann is Professor of Psychiatry and Education, Northwestern University.

the internalized norms that govern proper behavior in society. The aging individual who attempts to remain socially engaged, thereby bucking the developmental tide, will pay a psychological price in lowered contentment for such hubris; but the compliant individual who swims with the tide will experience the liberation and heightened morale promised by the theory.

All this is superficially plausible; and so this proto-hippie philosophy of "drop out" and "turn on" captured a following of gerontologists in the early sixties. But though she was a key participant in the Kansas City studies, Bernice Neugarten did not sign on to the research team's doctrine of disengagement. For starters, her highly developed "Nebraskan bull detector" told her that the central method of disengagement theory was irretrievably flawed. After all, the whole grand construction was perched on the shaky "morale scale," an instrument whose items were in actuality more sensitive to passivity and apathy than to self-esteem; not surprisingly then, "morale," so conceived, correlated with major indices of withdrawal and disengagement.

Working with Sheldon Tobin and Robert Havighurst, Neugarten developed the much more sensible, pragmatic "life-satisfaction" scale, and she ran the Kansas City subjects' scores on this instrument against their ratings on disengagement. The rest is history. As key papers in this collection report, while high disengagement scores predicted to elevated "morale," they did not predict to high scores on the more psychologically sophisticated and empirical "life satisfaction index." Thus, while some elders did indeed cut back on their contacts with the environing social world, they were not usually rewarded, as the developmental hypothesis had predicted, with a bonus of heightened life satisfaction. In brief, the claim that disengagement theory described a truly developmental process was decisively squelched.

And so that false but beguiling lead was closed off. Now social scientists were free to think about and study the real nature and manifestations of psychological development in the later years. Unfortunately, though, the majority of established geropsychologists refused that particular jump and turned instead to documenting the weak face of aging: not the elders as bearers of a special developmental promise, but the elders as victims of their bodies, of their burdened caretakers, and of a "youth-oriented society" in the later stages of capitalism. However, those disciplinary shortcomings were not Bernice Neugarten's fault: she did her very best; and in the process she not only blocked the advance of the disengagement monolith, she also helped establish the conceptual basis for an authentic personality theory of later life.

From the social-psychological point of view, disengagement, predominantly a socially driven event, organizes the personality on which it acts as well as the responses of the aging person to the fact of disengagement itself. But the findings of

Neugarten and her colleagues confirmed the more dynamic, inner-directed view of personality: that initiative resides within the person and that the psyche seeks out and even creates the social circumstances to which it will respond. Thus, it turned out that the effects of disengagement on life satisfaction were not predicted by the degree of disengagement but by the personality make-up of the disengaging person. As the folk wisdom has it, one man's meat is another man's poison, and while an essentially passive-dependent person will probably thrive on the disengagement process, an essentially active, autonomous person will fight it and lose morale if it gains ground. Likewise, a person in conflict between active and passive modes might alternately succumb to and then fight the disengagement process. In such passages, the personality acts as an independent rather than dependent variable. For perhaps the first time in the history of geropsychology, the case for personality as a mediator, an organizer of internal-psychological and external-social events, had been powerfully established by Bernice Neugarten and her collaborators.

Neugarten also worked to legitimize the use of the instruments best fitted to the study of personality, as dynamically conceived. These were the projective tests: for example, the Thematic Apperception Test (TAT), the Sentence Completion Test, and the Rorschach. Reviewing the literature of the sixties and seventies on constancy and change in personality, Neugarten found that studies based on self-report instruments reported constancy of the aging personality over time, while those employing the projective instruments almost invariably reported orderly, perhaps developmentally mandated, change. Studies employing both types of instruments rarely reported agreement: the findings of personality change obtained by the projective tests did not predict to the questionnaire findings of stability.

Nowadays, such lack of inter-instrument agreement has led to automatic discreditation of the projective methods as research instruments: since they disagree with the "scientific" self-reports, they must be wrong.

But Neugarten, noting intriguing discrepancy, did not use it as an occasion to bash the projective methods. After all, her closest colleague in the Committee on Human Development was William Henry, and while she disagreed with him about disengagement theory, he was an authentic magician with the TAT; and he had made a believer of her. Thus, Neugarten credited the findings from projectives-based studies, even when these were seemingly at odds with the establishment favorites, the "reliable and valid" self-report instruments. In her view, while the self-report instruments picked up the public relations of the respondent, the projectives were the seismographs of personality, picking up signals from the restless tectonic strata of the unconscious.

By assuming that each set of instruments was tapping into distinct and necessary personality functions, Neugarten was prompted to ask the crucial questions that, until then, had not been raised. These questions, which still agitate geropsychology, concern the dialectical and paradoxical relationship between constancy and change in the workings of personality. For example, do the seeming constancies of the psyche actually deconstruct into a blur of constantly changing functions? Do these same constancies liberate the individual to shake things up, to provoke disorder in the service of growth and new and stable structures?

The questions that Neugarten posed have recently generated clarifying answers. For example, Jordan Jacobowitz (1984) of the Hebrew University demonstrated that the correlations between fantasy and self-report instruments do indeed take place, but not concurrently: they are only revealed over time. Thus, while Time 1 TAT patterns will not correlate with Time 1 questionnaire profiles from the same respondents, they will correlated with their Time 2 profiles from these same instruments. After all, a major purpose of fantasy is to keep conflictual material out of consciousness, out of behavior, and out of the self-report, until—after five years or so—it is detoxified, and accepted into self-awareness. Thus, passive tendencies that are at first only expressed through TAT responses—and denied in the questionnaire items—will finally be openly acknowledged, somewhere down the line, in the Time 2 self-report.

But while ground-breaking, psychologically sophisticated studies of this sort have justified Neugarten's faith in the tools of depth personality research, they have not caught on in the field at large. Though Neugarten's contributions to psychodynamics were as important as those on the social-psychological side, it is by and large the latter that have been remembered, and that dominate contemporary geropsychology. Thus, her clarifying distinctions between those who are "on time" or "off time" or between the "young-old" and the "old-old," have become—along with her liberating doctrine of age-irrelevancy—the received wisdom of our field. By the same token, the life-satisfaction scales, originally developed to test propositions in depth-psychology, are now mainly applied to studies in social gerontology.

Meanwhile, the free-standing, internally complex personality that Neugarten, her students, and her associates once studied has since been deconstructed, dispersed into its social surroundings and antecedents. Conflict is no longer studied or portrayed as intrapsychic, but has been converted into the language of context—an idiom which slides easily into the language of victimology: the aging individual at odds with and oppressed by the aging body, the burdened caretakers, and the gerophobic environment. In the process, the powerful tectonic features of personality per se have been largely forgotten.[1]

All the more reason, then, to recall the forgotten side of Bernice Neugarten's contributions, and to remind our gerontological readers of the potent but hidden variables of the dynamic personality. After all, when the "Doctor Science" types learn about Bernice Neugarten's historic and seminal links to an authentic theory of personality, the fashions in geropsychology could change again.

Note

1. Forgotten, but not completely lost: the hidden variables of geropsychology are still studied, in a few obscure and hidden places, by bold (but, alas, unfunded) graduate students.

References

Cumming, E. and Henry, W. 1961. *Growing Old.* New York: Basic Books.
Erikson, E. 1952. *Childhood and Society.* New York: Norton.
Jacobowitz, J. 1984. "Stability and Change of Coping Patterns During the Middle Years as a Function of Personality Type." Unpublished Doctoral Dissertation. Jerusalem, Israel: Department of Psychology, Hebrew University at Jerusalem.
Jung, C. G. 1933. *Modern Man in Search of Soul.* New York: Harcourt Brace.

SEVENTEEN

Age-Sex Roles and Personality in Middle Age: A Thematic Apperception Study

Bernice L. Neugarten and David L. Gutmann

The original purpose of this investigation was to explore the use of projective techniques in studying adult age-sex roles in the family. At least two considerations prompted the choice of the Thematic Apperception Test technique. The first was that the responses would be relatively uncensored, more closely related to the respondent's personal values and experiences than those he might feel constrained to give in answer to more direct questions. Second, fantasy material, although presenting certain difficulties of analysis as compared with questionnaire data, would have a decided advantage for exploratory research. The richness and unstructured nature of projective data enable the investigator to follow an inductive process; he can follow up clues as they appear in the data rather than check dimensions and hypotheses defined in advance.

The primary concern of the study was with the collective role images of husbands, wives, sons, and daughters, as those images emerged from the projections of different respondents. After the role images had been delineated, the investigators turned to implications in the data regarding the personalities of the respondents. Thus, this investigation broadened in scope as the research progressed, and, as will become clearer in following sections, this report deals not only with familial roles but also with the relations between role image and personality in middle age.

THE SAMPLE

The study population consisted of 131 men and women, distributed by age, sex, and social class, as shown in Table 17.1. The middle-class men were well-to-do business executives and professionals, none of whom were retired. The working-class men were stable blue-collar workers, of whom three had retired. Of both groups of women, the large majority were married housewives, only a few of whom held part-time or full-time jobs outside the home. With only a few exceptions, all the people in the study population were native-born of north European ethnic backgrounds. The

Reprinted in an abridged form, from *Psychological Monographs* 72, no. 17 (1958; whole no. 470): 1–33; © 1958 by the American Psychological Association.

Table 17.1 The Sample

	40–54		55–70	
	Men	Women	Men	Women
Middle class	18	22	14	13
Working class	21	12	15	16
Total = 131				

large majority grew up in Kansas, Missouri, or neighboring Midwest states. Almost all were Protestant. With regard to family status, of the total 131 cases, only four women had never married; only eight of the men and six of the women were childless. One-half of the women and one-third of the men were grandparents.

The Data and Methods of Analysis

A specially drawn picture was used, one designed specifically to evoke the sentiments and preoccupations of middle-aged respondents in relation to family roles (Fig. 17.1).

Three levels of inquiry were employed in using the picture. The person was asked, first, to tell a story about the picture—a story with a beginning, a middle, and an end. Then the interviewer, moving clockwise around the picture and beginning with the figure of the young man, asked the respondent to assign an age and to give a general description of each of the four figures. Again moving clockwise, the respondent was finally asked to describe what he thought each figure in the picture was feeling about the others.

Stimulus Value of the Picture

Almost without exception, all respondents saw the picture as representing a two-generation family. One of the younger figures, most often the young man, was frequently seen as being outside the primary group, usually in the role of suitor or fiancée, son-in-law or daughter-in-law. Although always structured as a family situation, the stories varied widely. It might be a story of a young man coming to ask for the daughter's hand in marriage and being opposed by the older woman; it might be a mother, father, daughter, and son-in-law having a casual conversation before dinner; it might be a young couple asking for financial help from parents; or it might be an older couple coming to visit the younger.

It is within the setting of the two-generation family, then, that the role images of the young man, young woman, old man, and old woman emerged.

General Approach to Role Analysis

Having used the three levels of inquiry, the data for each figure can be regarded as a set of expectations as to how that category of person (YM, YW, OM, OW) relates to

FIG. 17.1

the social environment and to other categories of persons in the family in terms of action and affect. It is this set of expectations which were regarded operationally as the role description. The following assumption was made: granted that the different attributes ascribed by the respondent to the four figures in the picture have their roots in intrapsychic determinants, the respondent's expectations, based on his experiences with real people, will still have a highly determining effect on which aspects of the self he chooses to ascribe to each figure in the picture. In other words, the investigators took the respondent's perceptions as projections, mindful of the fact that what was given was intrapsychically determined, but trusting that the interactional social reality had called out and directed the projection.

Illustration of the Method

The first step in the analysis was to see what was the preoccupation around which the respondent had built his story, for the role descriptions took on greater meaning once the basic theme, or preoccupation, was understood.

For example, a woman tells the following story:

> I think the boy is going away to the service. He's telling the mother and father. That's his wife with him. The father is pretty downhearted about it. He has a downcast look on his face. His wife doesn't feel too good about it, but she's trying to pacify the older couple. They've just been married. I can't tell how it'll end up. If he has to go overseas to fight, there's always the possibility he won't come back.
>
> (General description of the YM) Sort of a boy who had always been close to his parents. Looks like a nice kind of boy.
>
> (General description of the YW) Looks very sympathetic. She's a real nice girl. She's trying to sympathize with the old people.
>
> (General description of the OM) Looks like a nice homebody. Nice fellow.
>
> (General description of the OW) I can't see enough of her face. I couldn't say any more, because there's no face to go by. Sort of refined, from her stature.
>
> (YM's feelings) He thinks they're all right, or he wouldn't have sat down. . . . Well, some boys wouldn't care how their folks felt, but he seems to realize that they're hurt.
>
> (YW's feelings) She thinks her husband is a pretty fine fellow, or she wouldn't be trying to sympathize with his folks.
>
> (OM's feelings) He's pleased with the young folks. He's interested in what his son's going to do.
>
> (OW's feelings) She's in a bad place—can't see enough of her. I really couldn't say.

The theme which underlies this story is the theme of family dispersion, the "empty nest." The respondent tells us, in effect, that the children are leaving home and that they "won't come back."

Looking first at the description of the young man, in the story proper we are told what his action is: to leave home, presumably for some dangerous and rigorous extra-familial environment. His action has emotional consequences for the parents, consequences which he does not seek to mitigate. His face is set beyond the boundaries of the primary group, and his only action in the group is the rather formal one of making this position clear to his parents. "He's telling the mother and father."

We are next told about the young man that he has always been close to his parents. The implication is that an earlier relationship of the son to the parents is now ending. It is of interest that the respondent speaks of the YM's affiliation to the parents only when she discusses him in the general, nonsituational context. When she is asked to consider him in relation to the immediate situation and to the actors in it, the theme of remoteness infuses the portrayal. This point is made clear when the respondent is again asked to put the young man back into the interactive context and to discuss his feelings there. Now he emerges as one who, although essentially detached, still adheres to minimal social forms. The respondent has difficulty in ascribing any but the most qualified feeling to him: "thinks they're all right," and "seems to realize that they're hurt." The YM's reaction to the parents' feelings is a relatively intellectualized one: he "realizes" or recognizes their existence, while it is his wife who "sympathizes" with them. Even this modest affective gesture on the part of the YM is doubted, for the respondent goes out of her way to assure us that the YM is not like other boys who "wouldn't care how their parents felt." In the respondent's whole recital, then, she attributes to the YM only minimal and grudging affiliation to the parents.

We can now make this general statement about the perception of the young man's familial role—his basic orientation is to rigorous and compelling nonaffective extrafamilial concerns, and intimacy for him is to be found with peers of the opposite sex. Although not too long ago (in terms of subjective time) the primary, parental group was a major focus of his interest, his present role there is governed by moral directives (superego demands) rather than by spontaneous warmth. These directives, coming into conflict with his more compelling extrafamilial interests, result in a posture of grudging punctiliousness, of bare attention to formal, socially defined demands. Himself barely participant in the family—although at the same time, a source of concern to the parents—he leaves to his wife the mediation of the emotional issues between himself and his parents. He is generally governed by outside demands, as though those demands were more congenial to his energies and motivations than are the demands made by the parental group.

Turning to the YW, we are given a different image. In the story proper she, too, appears as one whose actions are directed toward the parents, but, whereas the YM's action toward the parents—telling them that he is leaving—begins and ends his contact with them, her action—"trying to pacify them"—implies a continuing and multifaceted relationship with the older group. The young man only tells them about himself and at the most can only "recognize" the effects of his announcement on the parents. The young woman, although she "doesn't feel too good about it," does not deal with her own reaction but attempts to alleviate the parents' grief. The word "pacify" implies maternal behavior, as does the pattern of dealing with the woes of others rather than with her own.

Our interpretation of the young woman's strong, maternal concern with intimate human relations is strengthened when we look at the general description given of her. Here, the respondent persists in seeing the YW in relation to the current crisis. Again she is seen as a person whose actions are nurturant and consoling, but at this point an element of emotional distance enters into the description. The young woman is "trying" to sympathize with the older group. Here is an implication of some barrier against emotional rapport between the old group and the YW, a barrier which she feels impelled to overcome. The description of the YW's feelings give us a clue as to why she attempts to overcome the barrier. It is because of her regard for her husband that she feels a responsibility to his parents. We are told that her primary affiliation is to her husband and that responsibility to the parents is secondary, stemming from her marital tie. She takes form now as a person who must deal nurturantly with various aspects of the interpersonal universe, although institutional and generational barriers may exist between her and certain others. If formal ties exist between her and other people, she seeks to enrich the formal ties with empathic bonds.

Taking the role description as a whole and seeing it against the theme of "empty nest," we see the young woman's role as one of emotional liaison, operating in the widening breach between the parental and filial generations. Her husband moves off into what are viewed as distant and threatening events while she, though drawn after him, bridges the gap and maintains some version of the lost emotional ties between parents and children. Against the background of traumatic family dispersion, her role has a maternal quality: although her primary tie is to her husband, her immediate concern is for those who have been injured by the course of events, and she attempts in maternal fashion to compensate the injured through her nurturance. In sum, her role is complementary to her husband's in that, while he moves off to "do battle," she tarries behind to handle the human consequences of his actions and decisions.

Turning to the figure of the old man, we first see him as feeling sad at the news of his son's leaving. No actions are ascribed to him. He reacts to traumatic situations with feeling, but he is not seen as acting out his feeling or doing anything to alter the situation which made him sad.

At the level of general description, we are told that he is "a nice homebody," positively regarded. His major cathexis or emotional investment is to the family, and it is there that he is gratified. Values relevant to his role are those of comfort and ease in an affiliative setting.

Moving to the feelings ascribed to the old man, we notice a shift away from the initial description given of him. Where he was initially saddened, he is now "pleased" with young people, and he will maintain a meaningful, although somewhat intellectualized interest in his son's future activity. There is still no intimation that he will act to change the course of his son's affairs—the son will "do," and the father will be interested—but a note of equanimity has entered the description. If we examine this shift in light of the theme of family dissolution, we conclude that it represents a concept of defensive adjustment, adjustment to the inescapable reality of the young man's maturity through defensive denial of strong personal feeling. After some initial depression, the old man resigns himself to the fact of the breach and returns to the emotional *status quo*. Although the young group, especially the YM, is no longer reciprocally affiliative, the old man's outward feelings toward them remain basically unchanged.

The old man's role, then, somewhat like the young woman's, is an adjustive one. He buffers the shocks of transition. Accepting the reality of change, he acts to minimize the consequent feelings and to find new bases for intimacy in the new situation. It is of particular interest that the old man attempts to maintain the *status quo* by changing himself and hiding his own feelings. At no point in the protocol does he act to change anything outside himself.

This interpretation of the old man's role gains support when we turn to the old woman. In the story proper we are told nothing about her; her presence is merely noted. At the general level of description, perception of her is again denied. In effect, we are told that she has no emotionally expressive surface ("there's no face to go by"). She is associated only with "refinement," a description which implies that she has no contact with a freely affective, spontaneous environment. (By contrast, the old man is the "homebody.") The word "refined" suggests the values of restraint, pride, and possibly a defensive rigidity.

As to the old woman's feelings, the respondent tells us, in effect, that she cannot imagine any feeling states which might pertain, because the OW is "in a bad place." Although there is a relative paucity of data about the OW, we nevertheless obtain the strong impression of rigidity and withdrawal in the figure. Viewed against the thematic background, this rigidity and withdrawal takes on meaning as a possible mode of coping with crisis, but a mode which is quite different from the one defined for the old man. Faced with the trauma of family breakdown, the old man's role is to adjust to the inevitable by minimizing his own reactions. The adjustive mode ascribed to the old woman seems to stress denial of the trauma and its emotional consequences, strict control, and magical defenses against her vulnerability. The old man's adjustment, although a defensive one, still is oriented toward a social universe and untroubled contact with others in future situations. The old woman's role has a more primitive, egocentric quality, as if the vulnerability of the self were the only concern and as if this concern justifies the use of archaic defenses—such as complete denial of a painful situation.

Granted that both the old man's and old woman's roles may represent possible solutions of the respondent's own problem—her defenses against the problem she has proposed—the investigators' primary interest is with the content of the roles as they emerge from the respondent's fantasy and to which figure in the picture each role is ascribed.

TREATMENT OF THE DATA

Using the method illustrated above, each protocol was analyzed for role descriptions of each of the four stimulus figures. Interpretations were recorded separately for each figure. The protocols were divided according to the sex of the respondent but were analyzed without knowledge of the respondent's age or social class.

Reliability of Interpretations

The question of reliability of interpretations was dealt with at an early stage in the research. Using nine protocols selected at random, two judges rated each of the four figures on a five-point scale for each of twelve personality characteristics, and the ratings were then correlated. The average coefficients of correlation were .81 for the YM, .88 for the YW, .83 for the OM, and .88 for the OW.

This procedure proved to be a somewhat oblique test of reliability, since it was later decided not to deal with the role descriptions on the basis of such ratings, but rather to continue to draw summary descriptions of the figure and then to categorize the descriptions according to similarity. At the same time, this test of reliability was a relatively stringent one for this type of data.

Quantifying the Data

Once all the protocols had been analyzed and decoded, the data for each figure were treated separately. The procedures with reference to the data on the old man will be described here since these were the first to be dealt with and since findings regarding the OM influenced in some ways the organization of the other sets of data.

All the descriptions were grouped on the basis of similarity into mutually exclusive categories, attempting always to judge similarity in terms of the most salient features ascribed to the OM by the respondent. This was a lengthy process since the attempt was to establish categories that would produce the least distortion of the original data. At the same time, having become aware that there were age differences in the perceptions of the OM, the investigators attempted to structure the categories in such fashion as to highlight the age differences.

Six major categories were finally delineated and arranged along a continuum termed "dominance-submission." At one end were those categories in which, whatever other characteristics were ascribed to the OM, he was always a dominant figure within the family. At the other end were those categories in which he was seen as a passive or submissive figure. Dominance or submission was judged in terms of the OM's impact on the situation; the extent to which others deferred to him; the extent to which resolutions of family issues depended upon his wishes, his judgments, or his decisions.

Dealing next with one after another subsample of respondents (middle-class men, middle-class women, working-class men, working-class women), frequency distributions were made in which the role descriptions were plotted by category and by age of respondent. The distributions were then tested for statistical significance by applying the chi-square method.

For each subsample of respondents there was a shift with age in the perceptions of the OM. The role descriptions given by younger respondents (aged forty to fifty-four) more often fell in those categories in which the OM is described as dominant; the descriptions given by older respondents (aged fifty-five to seventy) most often fell in those categories in which the OM is passive. The number of cases in each subsample was too small to establish reliable chi-square values, but the trend was present in every group. Cases were then combined into larger groupings—all male, all female, all middle class, all working class. The age trends were now even more pronounced (P values were between .05 and .01). Finally, when all respondents were grouped together, the age shift was unquestionably reliable (P was .001).

At this point, whereas age of respondent consistently produced variation in the data, it was not clear which of the original variables—age, sex, or social status—was the most important in producing the over-all variation. A further step was therefore taken. Ratings on dominance-submission were assigned to each category of role description; these ratings were then submitted to an analysis of variance. It was found that of all the variables—age, sex, social status, and the interactions thereof—only age was significant (P was beyond 0.001). The data on the OW were also subjected to analysis of variance, with the same result emerging.[1]

THE OLD MAN

The figure of the OM seems to symbolize for respondents the ego qualities of the personality: the rational rather than the impulsive approach to problems, concern over the needs of others, reconciliation between opposing interests, cerebral competence.

The descriptions of the OM fall into six major categories that can be ordered along a continuum from dominance to submission.

　　　1. "Altruistic authority." In this category the OM is seen in a position of authority in the family, and he uses his authority to benefit the young people or the

family as a whole. He is the benevolent monarch, the nurturant wise man, whose actions are altruistically motivated and lead only to benevolent outcomes. He operates effortlessly and easily in this role.

2. "Assertive, but guilty." These descriptions are those in which the OM attempts to further his own ends, but is restrained by inner reluctances, doubts, or guilt. He occupies a position of strength and asserts himself in the family, and, although he is not opposed by others, he nevertheless cannot easily and single-mindedly press for his announced goals. There is always some quality of inner doubt about the justice of his claims. He is conflicted, unsure, the insecure autocrat. "He thinks it's about time those kids left home and earned their own living—he hates to tell them, though."

3. "Formal authority." Here the father is the authority, but by default. His authority is challenged as the story progresses, or other individuals take action to decide outcomes while he acts only to approve those outcomes. He is described here not so much in terms of service to others (as in Category 1), but in terms of pliability to the wishes of others. He merely approves decisions which have already been thrashed out among more active figures.

4. "Surrendered authority." It is indicated here that the OM could be the authority if he desired—he possesses the requisite qualities—but he refuses and/or abandons the role. In some instances, he is initially described as dominant, but, as the story unfolds, he is relegated to a more submissive position. In other instances, he is ascribed the qualities associated with leadership, but these qualities are split away from action—they have no impact on the events of the story, they do not impinge on outcomes, they find no overt behavioral expression. He is inwardly "tough" but overtly passive, or he has "executive qualities" but leaves the decision up to his wife. In no instance is there an intrusion of the OM as a dominant force on the family scene.

5. "Passive, affiliative." Here the OM is described in terms of what might be called maternal qualities. He is unflaggingly and uncritically affiliative toward the others. He "loves everybody." He accepts, resignedly, outcomes which he may not approve. He is dominated by his wife, but seems to feel no discomfort or resentment in the situation. In stories where the OW is opposing some action proposed by the young people, such as marriage, the OM's attitude is one of affiliating with both sides—of saying affectionately to the OW, "Why fight the inevitable?"

6. "Passive, cerebral." Grouped here are those descriptions which present the OM as passive and withdrawn. He lacks any announced affiliative attachments to others. The issue of authority does not even arise. His wife rules the family, and he remains remote, both in terms of action and affect, from the family drama. As this drama swirls about him, he "thinks." (The content of his thought or its relevance to the situation is rarely specified.) The OM controls events from behind the forehead, as it were, and takes a certain satisfaction in the freedom this provides him. As one male respondent put it, "He's made up

his mind about the thing. He's waiting for the old woman to tell them what
to do."

Age Differences

As shown in Table 17.2, there is a consistent shift, with increasing age of respondent,
from seeing the OM in situations of power in the family toward seeing him as passive
and submissive. (This age shift is statistically significant beyond the .005 level.)

The stimulus figure of the OM confronts the majority of younger respondents
with the issue of familial authority. (If Category 4 is included, then approximately 75

Table 17.2. Role Descriptions of the Old Man

	40–54		55–70	
Category	Men	Women	Men	Women
1. Altruistic authority:				
Middle class	5	9	2	1
Working class	3	3	1	3
Total	20*		7	
2. Assertive, but guilty:				
Middle class	2	0	2	2
Working class	6	1	1	1
Total	9		6	
3. Formal authority:				
Middle class	5	5	0	0
Working class	2	3	1	0
Total	15		1	
4. Surrendered authority:				
Middle class	2	3	4	3
Working class	6	1	3	2
Total	12		12	
5. Passive, affiliative:				
Middle class	0	4	2	6
Working class	3	4	3	8
Total	11		19	
6. Passive, cerebral:				
Middle class	4	1	4	1
Working class	1	0	6	2
Total	6		13	

*The chi-square test applied to these category totals. The probability that the distribution occurred
by chance is less than .001.

percent of all younger respondents see the OM either as an authority figure or as one who possesses the potential for authority.)

Each of the first four categories in Table 17.2 represents a different resolution of the issue of male dominance. The first two represent active resolutions. If the issue is met head on—if, that is, the OM defines self-gratifying goals and uses his position of authority to achieve them (Category 2)—then ambivalence and guilt are the necessary results. If, on the other hand, the OM uses his authority nurturantly for the benefit of others, he can act easily and comfortably in his position (Category 1). The more passive solutions involve either the OM's sanctioning of the wishes of others and attempting no intervention in the family scene (Category 3) or the more outright abandonment of the authoritative status altogether (Category 4).

For our forty–fifty-four group, the issue being dealt with around the role of the OM is not only that of male dominance, however, but also that of male aggression in the family. The problem seems to be how the OM can be an authority without being arbitrarily, and perhaps harmfully, self-assertive. How can the cultural demand—that the father is head of the family—be met without exposing the family to male aggression? The solution seems to involve the stressing of the moral function of authority: the OM must be either an active force for good, or, by "letting things happen," he passively cooperates with the others in arriving at positive outcomes.

For older respondents, the OM no longer presents the issue of masculine authority. The stories are now those in which the OM has no impact upon family events, and he presents only one or another image of passivity. (Of all respondents aged fifty-five–seventy, 55 percent are found in the last two categories. If Category 4 is included—the OM abandoning or surrendering authority—then 80 percent of all older respondents see the OM among the categories of submission and denial of authority.)

The age shift in the image of the OM from dominance to submission is elaborated in several ways. The forty-year-old respondent sees the OM as being in doubt about his own assertive tendencies; the sixty-year-old sees him as being the passive object of others' assertion. In the forties, the OM is seen as attempting to control events. In the sixties, he attempts only to control and order the cognitive environment, the symbolic traces of objects and events. In the forties, it is proposed that the OM is aware of the pressures from an impulsive and willful woman, but that he can allow the OW full expression and still wisely control the course of events. In the sixties, it is proposed that impulse, in the form of the OW, is left in charge of the field, that the OM's wisdom can control events only behind the forehead. The OM has moved from a stance of intrafamilial autonomy to "intracranial" autonomy.

In regard to the implications for personality differences in respondents, it has been said that the figure of the OM symbolizes ego qualities of the personality. With

domineering OW tries to extend her control over a resistant environment. While she now dominates her husband, she is successfully opposed and limited by the YW and/or the YM. The OM cannot provide a buffer between the intrusive OW and the young, but the young take up the cudgels for themselves and win out against the OW.

4. "The good mother." Here the issue of dominance-submission is not specifically introduced, though the OW is implicitly given the decisive role in the disposition of affairs. The OW is the good, nurturant mother who guides and supports her gratified husband and children. She is mild, benign, maternal. Though she has the most effective role in the family, there is no tension between her and the others. The view is rather of harmonious interaction, where it is only right and "natural" that the mother holds the most important place in the family.

5. "The matriarch." In this category the OW is seen as a forceful and aggressive authority. While, however, she has complete sway over the others, this leads only to benign results. The family, rather than opposing her, bask contentedly in their dependent and submissive positions. Everyone benefits from her rule.

6. "Hostile self-assertion." Here the OW is a stereotyped figure, one who exercises a harsh, arbitrary, and unopposed control. Her dominance is not tempered by any redeeming strain or affiliation or nurturance, nor does she have any concern for others. The OW is either pictured as the embodiment of amoral id—all impulse and wrath—or the punitive superego who harshly judges others and rigidly defines the moral code—a superego armed, as it were, with the energies of the id.

Age Differences

As shown in Table 17.3, role definitions of the old woman, like those of the other three figures, vary consistently with age of respondent. Whereas the age shift in the perception of the old man's role is in the direction of increasing submissiveness, the OW moves from a subordinate to an authoritative family role. (The age shift is statistically stable at the .001 level.)[2]

Younger respondents view the OW as sensitive to, or checked by, outer demands and pressures. Older respondents propose that the OW has come to be the embodiment of controls, strictures, limits. She has taken over the moral and directive qualities which, for younger respondents, were seen as operating outside herself.

In general, with increasing age of respondent, the OW emerges more and more as the most feeling, demanding, and aggressive figure, as the other figures tend toward greater passivity, colorlessness, and conformity. In stories told by older respondents, the point at which the OW is described tends frequently to signal the breakthrough of impulsivity, as if the OW represents unchecked impulse in a scene otherwise populated by more constricted, conforming, or affiliative figures.[8]

As regards respondents themselves, the old woman symbolizes the impulsive, self-centered qualities of the personality (in contrast to the OM, who symbolizes ego qualities of the personality). The age shift in perception of the OW implies, therefore, increasing pressures from the impulse life in the face of decreasing ego controls.

FANTASY DATA IN RELATION TO SEX-ROLE BEHAVIOR

Since these findings have been derived from projective data, what are their implications for role behavior?

The individual, in filling real-life roles, resolves tensions between personal needs and social expectations. The task of the ego is to organize the various affective components of the personality into a personally expressive, though socially acceptable, pattern of behavior. When presented with the picture, however, a different demand is made of the respondent. He is asked not to act in the real family setting, but to breathe vitality into a representation of family life. The task of the ego is not one of integrating various aspects of the self into a coherent pattern of behavior, but the opposite—in effect, to distribute various components of the self among the various figures in the picture.

This fractionating of the components of personality makes the thematic apperception technique a valuable clinical instrument, but it also imposes qualifications on its use in the study of social roles. In the latter case, the respondent describes a living complexity (the role of OM or OW) in terms of only one or a few facets of the self. The projected aspect of the self, temporarily winnowed out of the total personality, tends to be expressed in exaggerated form. The result is a certain stereotypy and a certain overemphasis in the role descriptions. The task of the role analyst is thus made correspondingly difficult. The role patterns he wishes to describe may have been distorted into nonviable extremes as they have become the focuses for conflicting elements in the respondents' personalities. Rather than objective role descriptions, his data are the affective connotations of role behavior, those which people limit and modify in real life.

The findings presented here must be interpreted with caution, then, in applying them to actual role behavior. It should be kept in mind that, if the respondent speaks of the old man as weak and passive and the old woman as dominant and manipulative, he is describing not only two polar forms of behavior but also two aspects of himself and that both aspects will find some (though not equal) expression in his own behavior. If the respondent is an older man, he cannot be described merely on the basis of his description of the old man as passive and weak, for the respondent is a person who also has needs for strength and dominance. It is the nature of the task—responding to the picture—which allows him to describe the old man in more unitary ways than are actually true of himself.

These considerations apply equally with regard to collective role images that emerge from groups of respondents. For example, many older respondents seem to agree that older men are passive, affectless, and isolated from the stream of family events. They are described as "smoking their pipes" and "thinking." It cannot be assumed, however, that the only role of older men in the family is to stand in the corner, thinking and smoking. People who live in the family setting, young or old, do interact with others and do impinge on the environments of other family members. What can be justifiably assumed from this image is not that older men never interact or relate, but that the very activities through which they express the outward forms of intimacy also tend to highlight their desire for passivity and isolated contemplation. The image does not report the daily reality of the older man's role; rather, it is a sharply drawn, condensed expression of the affective mode which underlies his activities. The sharpness of the image is derived from the condensed expression of what is seen as being central to the figure of the old man and from the affective components of the respondents' personalities identified with this central tendency.

What we have in these data, then, is centrality rather than experienced complexity of role behavior.

To take another example, in many stories, especially in those told by men, the description of the old woman provides a point at which unchecked impulse breaks into a scene otherwise peopled by more restrained or affiliative figures. She is a figure of primal omnipotence and wrath—"a devil. Very strict. Must run everything and everybody." In one sense the description functions to bring the aggressive impulse life of the respondent into the story.[4] What emerges is not an unbiased account of the old woman, but picture of the old woman as it is filled out by aggressive energy that has its locus in the respondent himself. (It is the respondent's own denied rage, projected on to the figure of the old woman, that he calls a "devil.") Women who live in a social environment cannot act purely from unmediated primitive impulse. They would soon be hospitalized, institutionalized, or dead. What we are being told in such accounts is that older women's behavior in the family expresses, for those respondents preoccupied with such issues, a central quality of free aggression.

Bearing such considerations in mind, these findings can nevertheless be related to actual role behavior. This relationship is posited on the grounds that the affective complexes energizing the perception of the stimulus figures are indeed cued by the respondent's expectations of such figures in real life. Granted that various components of the respondent's own personality migrate toward one or another stimulus figure, the impressive fact is the consistency with which the same personality components migrate to the same figure in the picture. For instance, for both men and women respondents, it is almost always the old woman, not the old man, to whom impulsivity, aggressivity, and hostile dominance are ascribed. This consistency cannot be explained by chance. The assumption seems warranted that there is something common to the actual role behaviors of older women that elicits this consistency in respondents' fantasies.

To sum up, projective data do not yield descriptions of the total and complex role of the older woman in the family as that role is expressed in everyday, overt behavior (similarly for other figures). What is obtained instead is a central aspect of the role, an aspect that, in one translated form of behavior or another, is being recognized by both men and women.

The role images of all four figures varied consistently with age and sex of respondent, but not with social class. Most striking was the fact that, with increasing age of respondents, the old man and old woman reversed roles in regard to authority in the family. For younger men and women (aged forty–fifty-four) the old man was seen as the authority figure. For older men and women (aged fifty-five–seventy) the old woman was in the dominant role, and the old man, no matter what other qualities were ascribed to him, was seen as submissive.

The different images of all four figures presented by men and women at the two age levels imply personality changes in the years from forty to seventy. For example, women, as they age, seem to become more tolerant of their own aggressive, egocentric impulses; whereas men, as they age, of their own nurturant and affiliative impulses. To take another example, with increasing age in both men and women, ego qualities in the personality seem to become more constricted—more detached from the mastery of affairs and less in control of impulse life.

Notes

1. Findings *re* the YM and YW are omitted from the present version of this paper.—ED.

2. In a subsequent study of forty-seven older men in which the same TAT card was used, Margaret Thaler Singer found essentially the same perceptions of the OM and OW (Singer, 1963, pp. 230–31).

3. Perhaps the projection of impulsive elements of personality on the figure of the OW is partially stimulated by her facelessness in the picture. If impulsivity is regarded by respondents as ego-alien, it might well be ascribed to that figure in the picture which provides fewest cues regarding social interaction.

4. In real life the respondent's wife may function so as to express elements of the respondent's impulse life that are denied expression in his own behavior. Our findings hint as the possibility that males often handle their aggression in the family by proposing that they are the passive object of attack from a woman, rather than by proposing that aggression stems from themselves.

EIGHTEEN

Personality Changes in the Aged

When I was first invited to participate in this symposium, I was asked to address myself to the topic, "Personality Problems in the Aged." I demurred, saying that because I regard myself as a developmental psychologist rather than a clinician, I was not equipped to speak on that topic.

The conversation reminded me that for the most part psychologists who have been concerned with the aged have, indeed, more often been concerned with problem aspects of behavior—with functional versus organic disorders, with problems of diagnosis in clinical settings, or with problems involved in treatment—than with developmental problems. I was reminded, also, that there are other psychologists who would think the appropriate title for any such paper should be, "The Problem *of* Personality . . . ," since theories of personality, as well as methods of assessment, remain a relatively undeveloped area when the focus is upon the older adult. We have, in other words, few theories, few tried and tested methods, even few agreed-upon definitions of the phenomena to be encompassed.

As you see, I have taken for my topic today neither the problems of the aged, nor the problems of doing research on the personality of the aged, but instead the problem of changes in personality that accompany aging. I shall be describing the point of view of a group of us in the Committee on Human Development at the University of Chicago who have carried out over the past ten years a series of empirical studies in this area (Neugarten and Associates, 1964).

Before proceeding further, I should like to take cognizance of the fact that all of us in our personal as well as our professional lives are aware that changes in personality occur with the passage of time, not only as the child becomes the adolescent; and the adolescent, the adult; but also as the adult moves from middle age to old age. Even though we distrust the method of introspection, we are aware of changes in ourselves, and we witness changes in the other adults about us: spouses, parents, work colleagues. The problem is not to obtain agreement among psychologists that

Paper presented at a symposium sponsored jointly by the American Psychological Association and the American Catholic Psychological Association, Los Angeles, September 8, 1964. Reprinted by permission from *Catholic Psychological Record* 3, no. 1 (spring 1965): 9–17.

this is so; but it is how to delineate those personality processes which are the most salient at successive periods in adulthood, to describe those processes in terms which are appropriate to the phenomena, and to isolate the changes which relate to age from those which relate, say, to illness on the one hand, or to social and cultural change on the other hand (Neugarten, 1964).

It might be added that in the effort to transform common sense observation into scientific data, the student of adult behavior is even farther behind than the student of child behavior. Granted that the term "adult psychologist" does not have parallel connotations with the term "child psychologist" and that we would regard such a term as a pun, there is as yet—more properly speaking—no developmental psychology of adulthood in the sense that we have a psychology of childhood or a psychology of adolescence.

Operating under certain handicaps, then, my colleagues and I have had, as the central problem under investigation in the studies to which I referred, the delineation of changes in personality that are associated with chronological age in the second half of the life span.

These studies share one important characteristic: they are all based on relatively large populations drawn from the same pool of over 700 cases on whom psychological data had been gathered in connection with the Kansas City Studies of Adult Life. This pool was built up from probability samples of adults aged 40 to 90, all of whom were living in their own homes and participating in the usual round of activities characteristic of functioning members of a large urban community. None of these persons were volunteers; they were men and women who, following various degrees of persuasion by members of our field staff, had agreed to be interviewed one or more times in their homes or in their places of work.

We have used various techniques in gathering data: for some samples, a single lengthy interview specially designed to illuminate selected personality variables; for others, projective responses to the Thematic Apperception, the Rorschach, or the Draw-a-Person tests; and for a panel of 275 men and women, repeated interview over a six-year period.

We have been particularly concerned with operationalizing constructs from ego psychology, and in exploring methods of applying such constructs to the analysis of empirical data. In doing so, a variety of conceptual approaches has been used, as well as a variety of research strategies. In some of these studies the approach has been inductive and in others, deductive; some represent relatively more, others relatively less rigorous research designs. In one study, Erikson's stages of ego development were explored (Erikson, 1959); in another, adjustive properties of personality; in another, conceptions of age and sex roles; and in still another, the personality types to be found in an aged sample.

In the time allotted today, I shall not attempt to deal with each of the studies separately, but with the implications of the findings as a whole. Although our focus has been, throughout, upon those personality differences which are related to age, in all but a few instances the data have been cross-sectional rather than longitudinal. Accordingly, because inferences regarding changes with age are based on observed differences among age groups, they should be interpreted cautiously with regard to processes of change over time.

The first substantive point with regard to our findings is that, as might well have been anticipated, in some of our studies age proved to be a consistent and statistically significant source of variation; in others of our studies, age was not an important variable.[1]

To some extent, the findings seem to reflect differences in the degree to which the expressions of personality under observation had been relatively overt or relatively covert. In general, significant and consistent age differences emerged where projective data were used and where the investigator's attention was upon such issues as the perception of the self in relation to the external environment, or with ways of coping with impulse life. For example, in TAT data, 40-year-olds seemed to see the environment as one that rewards boldness and risk-taking, and to see themselves as possessing energy congruent with the opportunities presented in the outer world; while sixty-year-olds seemed to see the environment as complex and dangerous, and to see the self as conforming and accommodating to outer world demands. This change was described in one of our studies as a movement from active to passive mastery.

Different modes of dealing with impulse life became salient with increasing age. Preoccupation with the inner life seemed to become greater; emotional cathexes toward persons and objects in the outer world decreased; the readiness to attribute activity and affect to persons in the environment was reduced; there was a movement from outer-world to inner-world orientations. A constriction seemed to occur in the ability to integrate wide ranges of stimuli and in the willingness to deal with complicated and challenging situations.

Differences with age appeared not only in TAT responses, but also in interview data when the investigator's attention was focused upon relatively latent rather than manifest content. Thus older men and women verbalized their opinions in more dogmatic terms than younger persons, failed often to clarify past-present or cause-effect relationships, used idiosyncratic methods of communication, and in these ways showed a lessened sense of relatedness to others. Although there are important differences between men and women as they age, in both sexes the older individuals seem to move toward more eccentric, self-preoccupied positions.

On the other hand, age did not emerge as a significant source of variation when the investigator's attention was primarily upon socio-adaptational patterns more than upon intrapsychic processes *per se,* and upon certain broadly defined adaptive qualities of personality. Thus, where the focus was upon such generalized variables such as Erikson's "generativity" or "integrity," or upon personal-social "adjustment," or upon "differentiated social perceptions," or "super-ego control," no age differences were found. Also in a typology based on factorial structures of personality, both middle-aged and older persons were to be found in each of the major types that emerged.

When all our studies were considered together, those in which chronological age provided order in the data were those where the focus had been upon processes of personality that were not readily available to awareness or to conscious control, and which did not have direct expression in overt patterns of social behavior. Those studies in which individual differences were relatively independent of age, were those where the focus had been upon more purposive and goal-directed processes in the personality, processes in which attempted control of the self and of the life situation were conspicuous elements. Recognizing that the terms are to some extent arbitrary, I shall refer to the first of these two orders of personality phenomena as the intrapsychic; the second as the socio-adaptational. The second takes into account both the intrapsychic attitudes and reaction modes as well as the overt and regulated responses to environmental pressures.

In demonstrating significant age differences with regard to the intrapsychic aspects of personality, our findings are congruent with those of other investigators who have reported increased introversion in old age, reduction in social interactions, and decline in intellectual functioning. They are consistent also with other reports of increased eccentricity in the aged, of stereotyped attitudes, flattened affect, conservation of energy, avoidance of stimuli—in general, of a shrinkage in the psychological life space.

Similarly, the fact that socio-adaptive qualities of personality were not age-related agrees with the findings of others who have focused more directly upon personal-social adjustment or psychological well-being. No age relatedness was found, for example, in a study of these same Kansas City men and women carried out by a different team of investigators who used a measure called Life Satisfaction (Neugarten, Havighurst, and Tobin, 1961). The same is true also of other populations of older persons in which various measures of adjustment were either unrelated to age (Birren, Butler, Greenhouse, Sokoloff, and Yarrow, 1963), or show positive correlations with age (Reichard, Livson, and Petersen, 1962; Kutner, Fanshel, Toga, and Langner, 1956), wherein seventy-year-old males had higher morale than sixty-year olds. The implication is that other factors such as work status, health, financial resources, and marital status are more cogent than chronological age in influencing degrees of adjustment in persons aged 50 and over.

To return to the intrapsychic, at least two different phenomena seem to be involved in the aging process: first, the increased saliency of the inner life, or what might be called the increased "interiority" of personality; second, the decreased efficiency of certain cognitive processes. The increased interiority seems to reflect certain intrinsic as well as responsive processes of change.

While I view personality processes as transactional throughout life, and the personality as developing only through interactions between the individual and his environment, the increase in interiority has the characteristics of a developmental change in much the same sense as changes in earlier periods of the life span are regarded as developmental: that as the result of accumulative adaptations to both biological and social events, there is a continuously changing basis within the individual for perceiving and responding to new events in the outer world. In this sense the age-related differences that have emerged in those studies are based within the personality rather than in the social environment.

This increased inward orientation was measurable by the mid-forties in this sample of well-functioning adults, well before the social losses of aging occurred and well before there was a measurable decrease in the extent of social interaction (Cumming and Henry, 1961) or in competency of performance in adult social roles (Havighurst, 1957). While there is undoubtedly a circular process between psychological and social elements of personality, the implication is that the psychological changes described here as increased inward orientation and decreased cathexes for outer-world events, seem to precede rather than to follow changes in social behavior.

With regard to the second set of intrapsychic processes, our data indicated that some changes associated with age are deteriorative. There are losses of efficiency in cognitive processes, breakdowns of control over impulses observable in TAT protocols, perceptual impairments, and inabilities to deal with wide ranges of stimuli.

The differences between the intrapsychic and the adaptational qualities of personality shown in our studies pose an interesting question, one which relates to my opening comments regarding the differences between clinical and developmental approaches to personality. In one of the studies in this series, an intriguing set of findings emerged. We had analyzed a large sample of TAT protocols using a set of personality variables that we ourselves had developed; and we had demonstrated, by a three-way analysis of variance design, that age (but not sex or social class) was a significant factor, and that the age differences between subgroups were all in the predicted direction. Wishing to elaborate upon these findings, we took the same set of protocols and applied what appeared to be a similar set of operations and a similar set of variables. This second set had been formulated by a clinical psychologist (Dana, 1959) who had found his system successful in differentiating normals, neurotics, and psychotics among adults aged 20 to 40.

Using the new scheme of analysis, our data not only showed no age differences between subgroups, but that, as a total group, this sample of middle-aged and elderly persons fell outside the "normal" range altogether, with scores similar in some instances to the young neurotics; in other instances, to the young psychotics. Since our study population, as a group, could hardly be regarded as mentally ill, the question arose: To what extent are diagnostic signs of pathology different for different age groups? The question should, obviously, be pursued in future research, but it would appear that many older men and women continue to function effectively in everyday life despite ego defects which, if they appeared in a younger person, would be accompanied by observable mental illness.

Not only did this implication arise in regard to group averages, but it was not uncommon to find in our data a TAT protocol which gave evidence of grossly ineffective thought processes in an individual in whom there was no discernible pathology in everyday behavior. Nor does this point relate merely to unreliability or error in our data. The fact that pathologies of thought and affect are to be found in aged persons who are getting along well in their communities, and who rate high on adaptation, is a finding that has been reported also by other investigators. In one recently reported study of healthy aged men, for instance, performance on tests, including projective tests, did not correlate with other evaluations of adaptational behavior (Singer, 1963). Even more interesting was the fact that in the same study there was little relation between pathology in cognitive and affective processes, and in success in meeting the expectations of everyday life, when these two sets of judgments were made by the same psychiatrists (Perlin and Butler, 1963). Thus it is not only on tests as such, but also on psychiatric assessments, that signs of pathology are discernible in socially well-functioning older persons.

Diagnostic signs, the relations between projective test performance and other aspects of behavior, and definitions of mental health and mental illness are all problems which arise, of course, in studying other age groups as well as in studying older persons. The point, however, is that the relationship between various orders of psychological data may not be the same for young adults and old adults.

If the distinction between intrapsychic and adaptational personality processes is valid, the former may lie closer to biological than to social determinants of behavior. This is a complex problem beyond the scope of our own investigations, but the point made earlier is also relevant here: that measurable changes in intrapsychic processes appeared in men and women in the forties and fifties, at a time when biological changes are occurring, but before measurable changes are noted in the competence of role performance or in the range of social interaction.

The postulated relationship between intrapsychic personality processes and biological processes is not to imply necessarily that change along either of the two dimensions reflects an inherent aging process. Other investigators have suggested that changes observable in a large number of biological functions may be more related to health and disease than to increasing age (Kleemeier, 1961; Birren *et al.*, 1963). This is merely a reminder that chronological age has no meaning in itself, but is used only as a convenient index for representing the events that occur with the passage of time.

Returning once more to our findings,—how is it that individuals, as they grow older, continue to function effectively in their social environments despite the increased interiority and despite the defects in cognitive and affective processes? How do those men and women who give evidence of ineffective thought processes continue to appear integrated? While we have not yet pursued these questions directly, the implication is that there are coping and synthesizing processes which mediate between the two orders of personality we were studying, and which presumably provide continuity. Analysis of individual case materials showed no sharp discontinuity with age in regard to adaptational qualities or in personality organization in the typical man or woman in the Kansas City sample, a conclusion reached also by other investigators for other samples (Reichard, Livson, and Petersen, 1962). Coping patterns seem to remain relatively stable over time and the individual continues to deal with his environment in well-established and habitual ways. Perhaps the most striking phenomena to be seen in these Kansas City cases were the abilities of aged men and women to synthesize, to rationalize, and to reorganize experience. Much in the way that individuals substitute for biological losses as they move from middle into old age, as they learn to conserve physical energy and to compensate for lessened acuity of the senses, so also do they seem to make adjustments for losses of cognitive processes—for the slippage of memory, for example.

In a sense the aging individual becomes a socio-emotional "institution" with the passage of time. Not only do certain personality processes provide continuity, but the individual has built up around him a network of social relationships which supports and maintains him. The "institutional" quality involves an individuated pattern of strategies for dealing with the changing world within and without, strategies which transcend many of the intrapsychic changes and losses that appear.

Along with the increased interiority there seems to go also a certain reduction in complexity. With the shrinkage of psychological life space and with decreased ego energy, the aged individual seems to become increasingly dedicated to a central core of values and to a set of habit patterns, and he casts off many earlier emotional investments. It has been frequently said that behavior in a normal old person is more consistent and more predictable than in a younger person—that as individuals age they become increasingly like themselves—and that the personality structure stands more clearly revealed in an old than in a younger person. These observations may reflect the processes I have been describing.

This description of personality change is based in part upon quantitative findings, and in part upon case analyses. In summary, the direction of personality change from middle to old age seems to be towards increased inner orientation; increased separateness from the environment; a certain centripetal movement which leads to increased consistency and decreased complexity; changes in which the synthesizing and executive qualities, in maintaining their centrality, maintain also the continuity of the personality.

Note

1. The discussion in this paper of the research findings is an adaptation of Chapter 9 of *Personality in middle and late life*, by Bernice L. Neugarten and Associates (New York: Atherton Press, 1964).

References

Birren, J. E., Butler, R. N., Greenhouse, S. W., Sokoloff, L., & Yarrow, Marian R. (Eds.) *Human aging.* (Public Health Service Publication No. 986.) Washington, D.C.: U.S. Gov't. Print. Office, 1963.

Cumming, Elaine, & Henry, W. E. *Growing old.* New York: Basic Books, 1961.

Dana, R. H. Proposal for objective scoring of the TAT. *Percept. Mot. Skills,* 1959, 9, 27–43.

Erikson, E. H. Identity and the life cycle: selected papers. *Psychol. Issues,* 1959, 1, No. 1.

Havighurst, R. J. The social competence of middle-aged people. *Genet. Psychol. Monogr.,* 1957, 56, 297–375.

Kleemeier, R. W. Intellectual changes in the senium, or death and the IQ. Paper read at the annual meeting of the American Psychological Association, St. Louis, September, 1961.

Kutner, B., Fanshel, D., Togo, Alice M., & Langner, T. S. *Five hundred over sixty.* New York: Russell Sage Foundation, 1956.

Neugarten, Bernice L. A developmental view of adult personality. In J. E. Birren (Ed.) *Relations of development and aging.* Springfield, Ill.: Charles C Thomas, 1964.

Neugarten, Bernice L. and Associates. *Personality in middle and late life.* New York: Atherton Press, 1964.

Neugarten, Bernice L., Havighurst, R. J., & Tobin, S. S. The measurement of life satisfaction. *J. Geront.,* 1961, 16, 134–143.

Perlin, S., & Butler, R. N. Psychiatric aspects of adaptation to the aging experience. In J. E. Birren, R. N. Butler, S. W. Greenhouse, L. Sokoloff, & Marian R. Yarrow (Eds.) *Human aging.* (Public Health Service Publication No. 986.) Washington, D.C.: U.S. Gov't Print. Office, 1963. Pp. 159–191.

Reichard, Suzanne, Livson, Florine, & Petersen, P. G. *Aging and personality.* New York: Wiley, 1962.

Singer, Margaret T. Personality measurements in the aged. In J. E. Birren, R. N. Butler, S. W. Greenhouse, L. Sokoloff, & Marian R. Yarrow (Eds.) *Human aging.* (Public Health Service Publication No. 986.) Washington, D.C.: U.S. Gov't Print. Office, 1963. Pp. 259–279.

NINETEEN

Personality and Patterns of Aging

Bernice L. Neugarten, Robert J. Havighurst, and Sheldon S. Tobin

In a report prepared for the International Congress of Gerontology in 1963, my colleagues and I presented a summary of the data obtained in a large-scale study of aging that has been in progress over the past several years in the United States, a study known as the Kansas City Study of Adult Life. We said that, in the light of our findings, neither the "activity" nor the "disengagement" theory seemed adequate. Having followed several hundred persons aged 50 to 80 over a six-year interval, we found a positive correlation between the extent of social interaction and psychological well-being, a correlation that is even higher in persons aged 70 and over than persons aged 50 to 70. In other words, those older persons who are highly engaged in various social roles generally have greater life satisfaction than those who have lower levels of engagement. At the same time the relationship is not a consistent one. There are some older persons who are low in social role activity and who have high life satisfaction; and vice-versa, there are others who are high in activity, but low in satisfaction.

On the basis of these findings, we have moved on to studying differences in personality. Presumably there are certain personality types who, as they age, disengage with relative comfort and who remain highly contented with life. Others disengage with great discomfort and show a drop in life satisfaction. Still others will long have shown low levels of role activity accompanied by high satisfaction and these latter persons will show relatively little change as they age. In this view, then, personality becomes the important variable—the fulcrum around which the other variables are organized.

We have attempted to order our data in such a way as to describe the *patterns of aging* that characterize the men and women in our study. To do so, we have used three sets of data: (1) personality type; (2) extent of social role activity; and (3) degree of life-satisfaction.

1. Our personality types are based on an ego-psychology model, in which individuals were rated on 45 different personality variables personality reflecting both

Reprinted by permission from *Gawein,* Journal of Psychology of the University of Nijmegan, 13 (May 1965): 249–55.

cognitive and affective personality attributes. The types were established empirically, by methods of factor analysis (Neugarten and Associates, 1964).

2. Role-activity measures are made up of ratings of the extent and intensity of activity in eleven different social roles: parent, spouse, grandparent, kin-group member, worker, homemaker, citizen, friend, neighbor, club-and-association member, and church member. For example, with regard to the role of spouse, a man who lives with his wife, but who shares with her few activities other than perfunctory routines such as eating his meals in her company, is rated low in the role of spouse; while a man who plans and carries out most of his day's activities in the company of his wife is rated high in this role. The role-activity score is a sum of ratings in the 11 different-roles.

3. The life-satisfaction measure is a sum of ratings on five different components. An individual is regarded as high in psychological well-being to the extent that he (a) takes pleasure from whatever activities constitute his everyday life; (b) regards his life as meaningful and accepts resolutely that which life has been; (c) feels he has succeeded in achieving his major goals; (d) holds a positive image of self; and (e) maintains happy and optimistic attitudes and moods (Neugarten et al., 1961).

These three sets of measures and the assessments of our subjects were carried out by independent teams of investigators.

In describing the patterns based on these three variables, personality type, role activity, and life-satisfaction, we shall report here only those patterns found in our 70- to 79-year-old men and women. In this age-group almost all the men had retired, and this is the group in which the transition from middle age to old age has presumably been accomplished.

A few words about this sample: Of the larger group who formed the original population in the Kansas City Study of Adult Life, about 60 percent remained after six years. The loss of cases is an important factor; and the overall effect has been to produce a relatively select group over time. Thus the patterns described here do not, by any means, encompass all types of older persons to be found in a community, but only those relatively advantaged 70-year-olds who have better-than-average health, cooperativeness, and general well-being. There are 59 persons in this age group, 50 of whom fell into one or another of eight patterns of aging.

To help keep the patterns in mind, we shall describe them primarily in terms of the four major personality in terms of the four major personality types. As shown in Table 19.1, these are the "integrated," the "defended," the "passive-dependent," and the "disintegrated" personalities. These four groups are then further divided according to role activity score and according to life-satisfaction ratings, to yield eight patterns.

First, there are 17 in this group of 70-year-olds who are "integrated" personalities: well-functioning persons who have a complex inner life and at the same time, intact cognitive abilities and competent egos. These persons are acceptant of impulse life, over which they maintain a comfortable degree of control; they are flexible, open to new stimuli; mellow, mature. All these individuals, it happens, were high in life satisfaction. At the same time, they were divided with regard to amount of role activity:

There is one pattern we called the *reorganizers,* who are the competent people engaged in a wide variety of activities. (Theses are marked A in Table 19.1.) They are the optimum agers in some respects—at least in the American culture, where there is high value placed on "staying young, staying active, and refusing to grow old." These are persons who substitute new activities for lost ones; who, when they retire from work, give time to community affairs or to church or to other associations. They reorganize their patterns of activity.

There is a second pattern which we called the *focused* (Group B in Table 19.1).

Table 19.1. Personality Type in Relation to Activity and Life Satisfaction (Age 70–79) ($N = 59$)

Personality Type	Role Activity	Life Satisfaction			
		High		Medium	Low
Integrated	High	⑨	A	2	
	Medium	⑤	B		
	Low	③	C		
Armored-Defended	High	5	D		
	Medium	6		1	
					E
	Low	2		1	1
Passive-Dependent	High			1	
					F
	Medium	1		4	
	Low	2		3	2) G
Unintegrated	High			2	1
	Medium	1			
	Low			2	5) H
	Total	34		16	9

Name of Pattern
A—Re-organizer   E—Constricted
B—Focused   F—Succorance-Seeker
C—Disengaged   G—Apathetic
D—Holding On   H—Disorganized

These are integrated personalities, with high life satisfaction, but who show medium levels of activity. They have become selective in their activities, with time, and they now devote energy to and gain their major satisfaction from one or two role areas. One such case, for instance, was a retired man who was now preoccupied with the roles of homemaker, parent, and husband. He had withdrawn from work and from club-memberships and welcomed the opportunity to live a happy and full life with his family, seeing his children and grandchildren, gardening, and helping his wife with homemaking which he had never done before.

The next pattern we called the *disengaged* (Group C in Table 19.1). These are also integrated personalities with high life satisfaction, but with low activity; persons who have voluntarily moved away from role commitments, not in response to external losses or physical deficits, but because of preference. These are self-directed persons, not shallow, with an interest in the world, but an interest that is not imbedded in a network of social interactions. They have high feelings of self-regard, just as do the first two groups mentioned, but they have chosen what might be called a "rocking-chair" approach to old age—a calm, withdrawn, but contented pattern.

Next we come to the men and women whose personality type was the "armored" or the "defended." These are the striving, ambitious, achievement-oriented personalities, with high defenses against anxiety and with the need to maintain tight controls over impulse life. This personality group provided two patterns of aging:

One we called the *holding-on* pattern (Group D in Table 19.1). This is the group to whom aging constitutes a threat, and who respond by holding on, as long as possible, to the patterns of their middle age. They are quite successful in their attempts, and thus maintain high life satisfaction with medium-or-high activity levels. These are persons who say, "I'll work until I drop," or "So long as you keep busy, you will get along all right."

The other group of "defended" personalities we called the *constricted* pattern of aging (Group E in Table 19.1). These are persons busily defending themselves against aging; preoccupied with losses and deficits; dealing with these threats by constricting their social interactions and their energies and by closing themselves off from experience. They seem to structure their worlds to keep off what they regard as imminent collapse; and while this constriction results in low role activity, it works fairly well, given their personality pattern, to keep them high or medium in life satisfaction.

The third group of personalities are the passive-dependent types, among whom there are two patterns of aging:

The *succorance-seeking* (Group F) are those who have strong dependency needs and who seek responsiveness from others. These persons maintain medium levels of activity and medium levels of life satisfaction, and seem to maintain themselves fairly well so long as they have at least one or two other persons whom they can lean on and who meet their emotional needs.

The *apathetic* pattern (Group G) represents those persons in whom passivity is a striking feature of personality and where there is low role activity and medium or low life satisfaction. These are also "rocking-chair" people, but with very different personality structures from those we have called the disengaged. This apathetic pattern seems to occur in persons in whom aging has probably reinforced long-standing patterns of passivity and apathy. Here, for instance, was a man who, in the interviews, was content to let his wife do his talking for him; and there was a woman whose activities were limited entirely to those of maintaining her physical needs.

Finally there was a group of unintegrated personalities (Group H) who showed a *disorganized* pattern of aging. These were persons who had gross defects in psychological functions, loss of control over emotions and deterioration in thought processes. They were maintaining themselves in the community, but they were low both in role activity and in life satisfaction.

These eight patterns, in accounting for 50 of the 59 cases, provide considerable coherence in our data on 70- to 79-year-olds. If our original sample had been more representative of the universe of 70-year-olds, perhaps we might have a greater number of discrete patterns, some of them, for example, centered around low physical vitality and poor health. (A larger number of patterns would not necessarily be the case, however, since it may be that persons who survive into their seventies are already a select group, in whom only certain patterns of aging are to be found.)

In any case, it is clear, from this brief description of patterns, that neither the "activity" nor the "disengagement" theory of successful aging accounts for the empirical findings. A "personality-continuity" or "developmental" theory of aging needs to be more formally set forth.

People, as they grow old, seem to be neither at the mercy of the social environment nor at the mercy of some set of intrinsic processes—in either instance, inexorable changes that they cannot influence. On the contrary, the individual seems to continue to make his own "impress" upon the wide range of social and biological changes. He continues to exercise choice and to select from the environment in accordance with his own long-established needs. He ages according to a pattern that has a long history and that maintains itself, with adaptation, to the end of life.

In summary, then, we regard personality as the pivotal dimension in describing patterns of aging and in predicting relationships between level of social role activity and life satisfaction. There is considerable evidence that, in normal men and women, there is no sharp discontinuity of personality with age, but instead an increasing consistency. Those characteristics that have been central to the personality seem to become even more clearly delineated, and those values the individual has been cherishing become even more salient. In the personality that remains integrated—and in an environment that permits—patterns of overt behavior are likely to become increasingly consonant with the individual's underlying personality needs and his desires.

References

Neugarten, B. L., Robert J. Havighurst and Sheldon S. Tobin. "The Measurement of Life Satisfaction." *Journal of Gerontology.* Vol. 16, 1961 (pp. 134–143).

Neugarten, Bernice L. and Associates. *Personality in Middle and Late Life.* New York: Atherton Press, 1964.

TWENTY

Personality and the Aging Process

I am greatly honored by being named the recipient of the Kleemeier award: not only because Robert Kleemeier's own research and teaching interests were close to my own and I valued him both as a friend and mentor, but because the award is given by the Gerontological Society, an organization whose aims and welfare have preoccupied me for much of my professional career. I am deeply grateful to those of you who shared in the decision that puts me on this platform today.

In choosing what to talk about on this occasion and in looking back at the addresses made by earlier winners of the Searle and Kleemeier awards, I find it has become traditional for the speaker to describe where he has been as a researcher in the field of aging. I can comply with that tradition only partially, for having pursued more than one line of investigation over the past 15 years, I will need to be selective if I am to be coherent.

It is traditional also on these occasions to acknowledge the support of one's colleagues. In this respect I can go far beyond the traditional: for who else could stand before you today and name as colleagues the people I am privileged to name? When I was just beginning in this field, and when the Chicago group was just undertaking the studies that later became known as the Kansas City Studies of Adult Life, I began to work with Robert Havighurst and William Henry. The group included, for varying intervals of time, Ernest Burgess, Everett Hughes, Martin Loeb, Robert Peck, Warren Peterson, David Riesman, Ethel Shanas, Sheldon Tobin, and W. Lloyd Warner. We were later joined by Elaine Cumming, Richard Williams, David Gutmann, and others. Some of us have stayed on at the University of Chicago over the years and have outlived the Kansas City Studies—notably, Havighurst, Henry, Tobin, and myself—and we have been joined by Robert Kahn, Ruth Kraines, and Morton Lieberman. Could anyone name a more stimulating group of colleagues?

I have had a further advantage, for we have attracted gifted students in adult de-

The 1971 Robert W. Kleemeier Award Lecture, delivered at the 24th annual meeting of the Gerontological Society, Houston, Texas, October 28, 1971. Reprinted by permission from *The Gerontologist* 12, no. 1 (spring 1972, pt. 1): 9–15; © The Gerontological Society of America.

velopment and aging. A recent study of graduate education in gerontology shows that the University of Chicago, compared with other universities, has graduated by far the largest number of Ph.D.s in this field over the past 35 years (Moore and Birren, 1971). By our own tally, and saying nothing of all those who preceded, we have graduated some 50 Ph.D.s in adult development and aging in the past 14 years since the beginning of a specially-supported training program under our Committee on Human Development. Many of our graduates have gone on to become major contributors to the field, a fact in which we take great pride, just as, on the other hand, we recognize the enormous stimulation we ourselves have had from such a large and able group of junior colleagues. In taking stock of where I have been, it is not surprising that I should find it difficult to separate the teaching function from the research function since they have gone hand in hand; but surely Chicago's contributions to the field of research in aging rests in large part upon our graduates.

We have also been fortunate in having had special support for our program, first through the National Institute of Mental Health, and since 1963 through the Institute for Child Health and Human Development. To many of us the transfer from NIMH to NICHD signalled that the field of aging had been removed from the "special problem" category in the eyes of the federal establishment and was being recognized instead as a basic research area that crosscuts the biological and behavioral sciences. That is, unlike alcoholism or drug addiction or delinquency, with which aging was first associated in the funding of training programs, aging is not a special medical or social problem for which we can one day find a "cure" or a solution. Aging is here to stay. We will always need to study aging processes as part of the life cycle, to study the position of the aged in relation to other age groups, and accordingly to build a multi-disciplinary science of aging.

With this latter view always paramount, our program has thrived at Chicago because of the varied research of our faculty and students, and the scope and significance of some of the social and psychological research issues we have been pursuing. We have been studying the question of successful aging and of personality changes and adaptational patterns over time. Some of us have studied the meaning of work and retirement in various occupational groups, and career lines in lawyers, actors, and mental-health professionals. Others of us have studied two- and three-generation families, the personality consistencies between mothers and their own mothers, between middle-aged parents and their college-age children, and attitudes and values across social-class and generational lines. Some of us have studied middle-age, how women adapt to the biological change of the climacterium and to the so-called empty nest, how both men and women perceive and experience middle age. We have been concerned with changing sex roles in middle and late life. We have struggled over concepts of engagement and disengagement, the measurement of morale and life satisfaction, the delineation of personality types. Some of us have studied the adaptations old people make to institutionalization, and some of us have begun to study the uses of the remembered past as means of adapting to the present. Others of us have studied the age-status system, age-norms and expectations of age-appropriate behavior in adults.

The lines of inquiry I have chosen to describe today concern changes in personality and behavior with the passage of time, and with the attempt to measure some of the effects of life experience.

PERSONALITY CHANGES

In one set of studies we asked, What are the changes in personality associated with chronological age in the second half of life? We worked with cross-sectional data gathered in Kansas City on more than 700 relatively healthy men and women aged 40 to 70 from all social-status levels who were living normal lives in the community and data from another group of nearly 300 people aged 50 to 90 whom we interviewed at regular intervals over a 6-year period. We picked successive samples from this large pool of cases, used different conceptual approaches and different variables (this series of studies is reported in Neugarten, 1964).

We found consistent age differences in the covert or intrapsychic areas of personality, in the ways persons see themselves in relation to the environment. For instance, 40-year-olds saw the environment as rewarding boldness and risk-taking, and themselves as possessing energy to take advantage of the opportunities presented in the outer world. By contrast 60-year-olds saw the environment as complex and dangerous, to be dealt with in conforming and accommodating ways. This age difference was described by David Gutmann as a movement from active to passive mastery.

People of different ages deal differently with impulse life. At successive ages, people become more preoccupied with the inner life than with events in the external environment. We described this as increased interiority. There is also less willingness to deal with wide ranges of stimuli or with complicated and challenging situations. Older people seem to move toward more eccentric, self-preoccupied positions and to attend increasingly to the control and satisfaction of personal needs.

Contrary to these findings regarding intrapsychic processes, age was not significant when we looked at socio-adaptational variables—for example, when we tried to operationalize Erikson's concepts of ego development, or when we tried to measure a whole range of variables related to adaptive, goal-directed, and purposive behavior, processes more readily available to conscious control. Nor were measures of psychological well-being related to age. It would appear that older people, like younger, have different capacities to cope with life stresses and to come to terms with their life situations; and that age itself is not the decisive factor.

A third level of functioning is represented by the nature and extent of the individual's interactions with other persons. Here our studies have shown a long-term decrease with age on several different measures: on social role performance in various life roles, on the amount of each day a person spends in interaction with others, and in the degree of ego investment in present social roles. The general picture regarding social interaction did not show dramatic discontinuities, however, at least through the 60s. For our samples as a whole, a marked drop in role performances did not appear until the late 60s or 70s. While some individuals maintained high levels of activity over the 6-year period in which we followed them, the evidence was nevertheless clear that, over a longer time span, there was shrinkage in social life space, whether it came relatively early or late after middle age.

To sum up these findings, then: in studying the same individuals we found asynchronous trends: in the covert or "inner" life—the eye of the mind—increased interiority and other changes which we interpreted as developmental, occurring as early as the 50s; on the adaptational side, no age-related changes; and in social interaction, decrease occurring not until the late 60s and 70s.

These inconsistent findings—that intrapsychic changes in middle and late life proceed in ways that are not necessarily synchronous with changes in social interaction or in psychological well-being—are compatible with other things we know as students of personality. There are differences between the inner and the outer life; and the inner life is not always translated directly into action. Presumably in older persons, like in younger, there are coping and controlling processes, ego processes, which mediate between different orders of personality; which relate particularly to the ability to organize, to interpret, and to evaluate experience, and to carry out patterns of action in line with one's goals.

SUCCESSFUL AGING

Simultaneous to this line of research was another, focused on the question of *successful* aging. Without going into a long recounting of a story that is familiar to many students of gerontology, the disengagement theory, and then a major modification of the theory, emerged from our Chicago group. When first stated in the early 1960s, it set off a controversy in the field that lasted 10 years; a controversy that has now abated, largely, as I like to think, because of some of our own work regarding personality.

The first statement of the theory was based on a recognition of the significance of our findings regarding intrapsychic psychological changes, especially the fact that these changes seemed to precede changes in social behavior. It was observed, as already mentioned, that as people grow old, their social interaction decreases; but looking at the psychological changes, it was postulated that the decrease in social interaction is characterized by mutuality between society and the aging person—the person has decreasing emotional involvement in the activities that characterized him earlier and thus withdraws from those activities. As a second part of the theory, it was proposed that in old age the individual who has disengaged is the person who has a sense of psychological well-being and will be high in life satisfaction (Cumming and Henry, 1961).

Some of us were uncomfortable with this second part of the theory. As we gathered more data and as we studied the lives of the people in our sample, we did not find the consistent patterns that were predicted from the disengagement theory. Something seemed wrong. Therefore, once all the Kansas City data were in, we devised new and better measures of social interaction and of psychological well-being than the ones originally formulated. Now we found that high life satisfaction was more often present in persons who were socially active and involved than in persons who were inactive and uninvolved. This finding has since been confirmed in our pilot study of men aged 70–75 in six industrialized countries (see Neugarten and Havighurst, 1969).

More important, we found diversity. Some people were high-high on the two sets of variables; some, high-low; some, low-low; and some, low-high (Havighurst, Neugarten, and Tobin, 1968). Noting that the disengagement theory could not account for this diversity, we asked, how could it be accounted for?

By that time we had worked out, with the aid of sophisticated statistical techniques, a set of empirically derived personality types. Now, in assessing all three kinds of data on each person—extent of his social interaction, degree of life satisfaction, and personality type—we found a high degree of order in the data. Certain personality types, as they age, slough off various role responsibilities with relative comfort and remain highly content with life. Other personalities show a drop in role and in social interaction and show a drop in life satisfaction. Still others have long shown low levels of activity accompanied by high satisfaction and show relatively little change as they age. For instance, in one group of 70- to 79-year-olds, persons who were living in the community and carrying out their usual daily rounds of activities, we empirically derived eight different patterns of aging. We attached the names, Reorganizers, Focused, Disengaged, Holding-on, Constricted, Succorance-seeking, Apathetic, and Disorganized, each name conveying something of the style of aging common to each of the subgroups (Neugarten, Havighurst, and Tobin, 1968).

We have concluded from this line of studies that personality organization or personality type is the pivotal factor in predicting which individuals will age successfully and that adaptation is the key concept.

Furthermore, although we lack systematic longitudinal data to confirm this view, it has appeared from the life-history information available on the people we studied that the patterns reflect long-standing life styles and that consistencies rather than inconsistencies in coping styles predominate as an individual moves from middle age through old age. Within broad limits—given no major biological accidents or major social upheavals—patterns of aging are predictable from knowing the individuals in middle age. (This conviction has led us at Chicago, naturally enough, to expand our perspective on the field of aging to include middle age and then young adulthood: in short, to conceive of a broader time-span, adulthood, as the relevant one for studying aging.)

In demonstrating that there is no single pattern by which people grow old, and in suggesting that persons age in ways that are consistent with their earlier life-histories, it is our view that given a relatively supportive social environment, older persons like younger ones will choose the combinations of activities that offer them the most ego-involvement and that are most consonant with their long-established value patterns and self-concepts. Aging is not a leveler of individual differences except, perhaps, at the very end of life. In adapting to both biological and social changes, the aging person continues to draw upon that which he has been, as well as that which he is.

In giving central importance to personality factors and to the continuities in personality, and in seeing people as active rather than passive, this is not to underestimate the importance of various social, economic, and biological conditions. We know, of course, that if minimum levels of life satisfaction are to be achieved, people need enough money to live on, and decent housing, and health services, and an environment that provides opportunities for social interaction. From this perspective, a major research problem for social scientists interested in successful aging will continue to be that of elucidating the economic, political, and social conditions that are associated with psychological well-being for older people.

At the same time, variations in socio-cultural contexts will not solve the problem of individual variation—that is, why some individuals are more content than others who live in the same social setting. Despite the likelihood that some settings will be found to provide greater freedom and permissiveness for a broad range of life style, that some will be found to provide greater pressures for social participation, some, greater economic benefits, and so on, we shall still need to look at the ways individual older people adapt to the settings in which they find themselves.

It is the manner in which the individual deals with a variety of contingencies in his life; some of them social, some of them biological, which will continue to be the second important research issue. What does an old person make of his world, and how is the adaptational process influenced by his past life-history and his expectations? In attempting to understand why one individual copes successfully with retirement while another does not, or with illness, we shall have to pursue in much greater depth the ways in which aging individuals relate their pasts with their presents, how they reconcile expectations with reality, and how they interpret and integrate their lives into meaningful wholes.

EXPECTATIONS

In the course of our own studies, it has become increasingly evident that each person interprets his present situation in terms of what his expectations have been. Man is a thinking and planning animal, he looks around, compares himself with others, anticipates; then compares reality with his anticipations, and assesses his situation in terms of the congruence between the two. Expectations are therefore an important factor in understanding levels of psychological well-being.

What impressed us, however, was that people's expectations seem always to include a time line or an age referent. For example, our respondents say, "I'm in better health than most people my age," or "things are better (or worse) than I expected them to be." One person who recently suffered a heart attack said, "Well, at my age you have to expect these things."

As psychologists, we have not given enough attention to this area: what are the expectational sets about growing old that people carry with them through adulthood? How are these expectations changing? In our own work we began to see that individuals, whether or not they can easily verbalize it, develop a view of the "normal, expectable life cycle" (a phrase suggested by Dr. Robert Butler). They form expectations based upon consensually-validated sequences of life events: what these events should be, when they should occur, and under what conditions they should occur. They make plans, set goals, and reassess those goals along a time-line shaped by those expectations.

Thus far we have explored only one facet of this question: namely, expectations regarding age-appropriate behavior and the timing of major life events. We began by asking, What is the psychological significance of a given chronological age? How does the person mark off and evaluate the passage of time? It is clear that people do not evaluate lifetime merely by reckoning the number of years since their birth. The statement, "I am 50 years old" has little significance; but, rather, "I am 50 years old and farther ahead than I expected to be," or "farther behind than other men in the same line of work." In such everyday phrases, the individual gives content and meaning to the passage of time, and he refers to an implicit normative system in comparing himself to others.

To understand this normative system we undertook some exploratory studies of age status, age norms, and age expectations, perceiving them as forming a cultural context against which to view the person's evaluation of lifetime. First we studied the extent to which there was consensus regarding age norms. We recognized that in a complex modern society, there are multiple systems of age status that characterize different institutions and that changes in age roles are not synchronous. (For example, in the political institutions of this society, a man is adult at 18 when he can vote; but in the family he is adult when he marries and becomes a parent, usually several years later than 18.) We asked if, nevertheless, there was an age-status system common to the society as a whole.

We interviewed a representative sample of 600 middle-aged and older people and found widespread agreement in response to questions like these:

> What would you call the periods of life that people go through after they are grown up? At what age does each period begin for most people? What are the important changes from one period to the next?

We found that middle-aged people perceived adulthood as composed of four different life periods, each with its characteristic pattern of personal and social behavior: young adulthood, maturity, middle age, and old age. Progression from one period to the next was described along one of five dimensions: events in the occupational career; events of the family cycle; changes in health; changes in psychological attributes (e.g., "middle age is when you become mellow"); and/or changes in social responsibilities (e.g., "old age is when you let the other fellow do the worrying").

From these data it was possible to delineate the first gross outline of a system of age expectations that encompasses various areas of adult life. There appeared to be a set of social age definitions that provided a frame of reference by which the experiences of adult life were perceived as orderly and rhythmical. Although perceptions varied by sex and by social class (e.g., old age begins earlier in the perceptions of working-class than in middle-class people) there was nevertheless a striking degree of consensus (Neugarten and Peterson, 1957).

We next asked questions regarding age-appropriate and age-linked behaviors:

> What do you think the best age for a man to marry? to hold his top job? for a woman to become a grandmother? What age comes to your mind when you think of a young man? an old man? When a man has the most responsibilities?

There was widespread consensus, also, in responses to items such as these that pertained to work, to family, and to other areas of life. To illustrate, most middle-class men and women agreed that the best age for a man to marry was from 20 to 25; most men should be settled in a career by 24 to 26; they should hold their top jobs by 40; be ready to retire by 60 to 65; and so on. There appears, then, to be a prescriptive time-table for the ordering of major events in the individual's lifeline. Age expectations seemed more clearly focused—that is, consensus was greatest—for the period of young adulthood, as if the normative system bears more heavily upon individuals as they move into adulthood than when they move into middle or old age. There was greater consensus with regard to age-appropriate behavior for women than for men, and again, consistent variation by social class. The higher the social class, the later the ages associated with all major life events.

We moved next to asking, How does this system of age-norms function? How is it demonstrated in the lives of people? We therefore asked respondents about actual occurrences: how old were they when they left their parents' home? married? had their first full-time job? their first child? grandchild? top job? retired? We found that the similarities between occurrences and norms were striking. In short, the actual timing of major life events, especially in young adulthood, tends to adhere to the prescriptive timetable. The normative system seems to function as a system of social control—as prods and brakes upon behavior. In other words, most people do things when they think they "should" do them; and they seem to follow a social clock that becomes internalized so that they can tell an interviewer readily enough if they are late, early, or on time with regard to major life events and with regard to various types of achievement.

We repeated these studies with other groups of respondents: with a group of young married men and women, all around age 25 who lived in a small midwestern city; with a group aged 70 to 80 who lived in a small New England community; with a sample of middle-class blacks who lived in a medium-sized midwestern city. Although some variations appeared, the same general patterns emerged in each set of data, indicating considerable consensus about these types of age norms and age expectations.

We also explored related questions. How do people learn the norms? What are the sanctions in the system, the types of social approval and disapproval that operate to keep people on time? How, in short, does this normative system operate as social control? We have various data showing that age deviancy is always of psychological significance to the individual, but we have not yet obtained good data on how the social mechanisms operate.

Given our conviction that age norms and age expectations constitute a system of social control, we worked out a method for pursuing the question, Do people vary in the degree of constraint they perceive with regard to those norms? We asked such questions as:

> Would you approve of a woman who wears a two-piece bathing suit to the beach when she is 18? when she's 35? 55?

> What about a woman who decides to have another child at 40? at 35? at 30?

> What about a couple who move across country to live near their married children when they are 40? 55? 75?

We found that middle-aged and old people see greater constraints in the age-norm system than do the young. They seem to have learned that age and age-appropriateness are reasonable criteria by which to evaluate behavior; that to be off-time with regard to major life events brings with it negative consequences. In the young there is a certain denial that age is a valid dimension by which to judge behavior (Neugarten, Moore, and Lowe, 1965).

We have begun to explore the psychological correlates of age-deviancy. For instance, in two studies of Army officers (the US Army is a clearly age-graded set of occupations, where the investigator can create an objective measure of who is on-time and who is off-time) it could be demonstrated that being off-time with regard to career has psychological and social accompaniments. On-time and off-time men differed not only with regard to evaluations of their careers, but also with regard to self-esteem, mobility aspirations, anticipated adjustment to retirement, perception of status in the civilian community, and degree of social integration in the community.

These investigations have been exploratory; some has been carried out as doctoral dissertations (in particular, those by Kenneth Olsen, John Lowe, Margaret Huyck, Helen Warren); not all have been completed; and the studies have not yet been integrated and prepared for publication, a task which lies ahead of us. The studies have been rewarding because we think we have begun to uncover one of the social frameworks that has gone unexplored by social scientists; to point to some of the dimensions by which social-psychological meanings are attributed to age and to time; and to provide a richer context for understanding the changes in behavior and in self-assessments that occur as the individual moves through adulthood. It has not been my purpose here to give a full account of these studies, but rather to use them to illustrate one aspect of expectations that warrants investigation and one way in which expectational frameworks can be studied.

To summarize: I have been interested in change over time in the lives of adults and in the role of personality in predicting patterns of aging. Within broad limits of social and biological conditions, an individual will grow old along a path that is predictable from earlier points in his life, and predictable from knowing something about his personality structure, his coping style, his success in adapting to earlier life events, and his expectations of life. The individual is his own translator and interpreter of experience; he creates his future and recreates his past; he measures his present against the past and against the expectations he has carried forward with him through time. Within that expectational framework he evaluates his situation not only against the present realities—of income, health, social interactions, freedoms and constraints—but also against an internalized social clock, a clock that reflects socially-created age norms and tells him if he is on time. Other aspects of expectational systems need investigation if we are to understand how the personality copes and adapts, and to better understand the enormous complexity of that task we call "successful aging."

References

Cumming, E., and Henry, W. E. *Growing old.* New York: Basic Books, 1961.

Havighurst, R. J., Neugarten, B. L., and Tobin, S. S. Disengagement and patterns of aging. In B. L. Neugarten (Ed.), *Middle age and aging: A reader in social psychology.* Chicago: University of Chicago Press, 1968.

Moore, J. W., and Birren, J. E. Doctoral training in gerontology: An analysis of dissertations on problems of aging in institutions of higher learning in the United States, 1934–1969. *Journal of Gerontology,* 1971, *26,* 249–257.

Neugarten, B. L. and Associates. *Personality in middle and late life.* New York: Atherton Press, 1964.

Neugarten, B. L., Havighurst, R. J., and Tobin, S.S. Personality and patterns of aging. In B. L. Neugarten (Ed.), *Middle age and aging: A reader in social psychology.* Chicago: University of Chicago Press, 1968.

Neugarten, B. L., and Havighurst, R. J. Disengagement reconsidered in a crossnational context. In R. J. Havighurst, J. M. A. Munnichs, B. L. Neugarten, and H. Thomae (Eds.), *Adjustment to retirement.* Assen, Netherlands: Van Gorcum and Co., 1969.

Neugarten, B. L., and Peterson, W. A. A study of the American age-grade system. *In 4th Congress of the International Association of Gerontology,* Vol. III. Florence: Tito Mattioli, 1957.

Neugarten, B. L., Moore, J. W., and Lowe, J. C. Age norms, age constraints, and adult socialization. *American Journal of Sociology,* 1965, *70,* 710–717. (See also, Neugarten, B. L., and Moore, J. W. The changing age-status system. In B. L. Neugarten [Ed.], *Middle age and aging: A reader in social psychology.* Chicago: University of Chicago Press, 1968.)

TWENTY-ONE

Disengagement, Personality, and Life Satisfaction in the Later Years

Robert J. Havighurst, Bernice L. Neugarten, and Sheldon S. Tobin

There are, in the social-psychological literature of gerontology, two general points of view with regard to optimum patterns of aging. Both are based on the observed facts that as people grow older their behavior changes, the activities that characterized them in middle age become curtailed, and the extent of their social interaction decreases. The two theories then diverge.

The first, one that might be called the "activity" theory, implies that, except for the inevitable changes in biology and in health, older people are the same as middle-aged people, with essentially the same psychological and social needs. In this view, the decreased social interaction that characterizes old age results from the withdrawal by society from the aging person; and the decrease in interaction proceeds against the desires of most aging men and women. The older person who ages optimally is the person who stays active and who manages to resist the shrinkage of his social world. He maintains the activities of middle age as long as possible, and then finds substitutes for those activities he is forced to relinquish—substitutes for work when he is forced to retire; substitutes for friends and loved ones whom he loses by death.

In the disengagement theory, on the other hand (Cumming and Henry 1961), the decreased social interaction is interpreted as a process characterized by mutuality; one in which both society and the aging person withdraw, with the aging individual acceptant, perhaps even desirous of the decreased interaction. It is suggested that the individual's withdrawal has intrinsic, or developmental qualities as well as responsive ones; that social withdrawal is accompanied by, or preceded by, increased preoccupation with the self and decreased emotional investment in persons and objects in the environment; and that, in this sense, disengagement is a natural rather than an imposed process. In this view, the older person who has a sense of psychological well-being will usually be the person who has reached a new equilibrium

Reprinted from *Age with a Future: Proceedings of the Sixth International Congress of Gerontology,* edited by P. E. Hansen (Copenhagen, Denmark, 1964), 419–25. For a more detailed exposition of disengagement theory, see Neugarten, *Middle Age and Aging* (Chicago: University of Chicago Press, 1968), Introduction to pt. 3, and (with R. J. Havighurst and S. S. Tobin) "Disengagement and Patterns of Aging."

characterized by a greater psychological distance, altered types of relationships, and decreased social interaction with persons around him.

In order to test these two theories empirically, the data of the Kansas City Study of Adult Life were used, consisting of repeated interviews with 159 men and women aged 50–90, taken over the period from 1956 through 1962. The sample at the end of the study consisted of 55 percent of the people who were originally included in the study. Of the attrition in the sample, 27 percent has been due to deaths; 12 percent, to geographical moves; and the rest to refusal to be interviewed at some time during the series of interviews, usually because of reported poor health. There is evidence also that persons who were relatively socially isolated constituted a disproportionate number of the dropouts.

The original sample excluded people living in institutions and those who were so ill that they could not be interviewed. The original sample also excluded people at the very bottom of the socio-economic scale. However, the original sample contained a few people who would have been diagnosed as neurotic by a psychiatrist, as well as people who were chronically ill if the illness was not one that confined a person to bed. Some of the sample became quite ill, physically or mentally, during the period of the Study; and they were continued in the Study if they could be interviewed.

THE MEASURES OF ENGAGEMENT

The procedure in the Study was to measure the extent of engagement of the members of the sample, and to compare these measures with data concerning the life satisfaction and personality of the subjects.

Two aspects of engagement were measured: social engagement and psychological engagement.

Social engagement refers to interactions with other people in the course of everyday living. This was measured in two ways. The first, called the Interaction Index, is a judgment made by the investigator of the amount of each day R spends in the kind of social interaction with other persons in which the hints, cues, and sanctions which govern and control behavior can be exchanged. Scoring was based on verbatim reports of R's daily round of activities. The score does not relate directly to the variety of roles or the number of people interacted with. An aged man who spends all day at home with his wife may receive as high a score as a person who works at a job with others, who has an active social and recreational life, but who lives alone.

The second approach to social engagement involved a set of three measures, all three related to performance in eleven life-roles: worker, spouse, parent, grandparent, kin-group member, home-maker, friend, neighbor, citizen, club-member, and church-member. The first of these is Present Role Activity, a summation of subscores based on ratings of extent and intensity of activity in each of the eleven roles. For example, a man who lives with his wife, but who shares with her few activities other than perfunctory routines such as eating his meals in her company, is rated low in the role of spouse. A widowed man is scored zero on spouse, thus diminishing his total score on Present Role Activity.

A related measure is that of Ego-Investment in Present Roles—the extent to which the individual is ego-involved in his various life-roles. For example, the man who prides himself on being a good husband and who gives evidence of this as he talks about his wife, is rated high on investment in the role of spouse. Although ego-investment stands somewhere between social and psychological engagement, as we have defined the two, the measure used here correlated .87 with role-activity for this sample. It seemed better, accordingly, to treat it as a measure of social engagement rather than as a measure of psychological engagement.

The third measure of social engagement is Change in Role Activity Since Age 60 (or, for those under 70, change in the past 10 years). For example, a man who had fully retired from a fulltime job would be rated as having had the maximum negative change in that role. Another man who had become a grandfather but who spent only a few days a year with his grandchildren would be rated as having a small positive change in that role.

Each S was rated on all three of these measures with regard to each of the eleven roles. Two independent judges rated each case, and the ratings were eventually averaged. Reliability of ratings was high. For instance, for all ratings on the first 30 cases, and using consecutive pairs from among 10 judges, there was 50 percent exact agreements, and 95 percent agreements within one step on a five-step scale.

There is a decrease of social engagement with increasing age in the sample (Table 21.1). The decrease is greater after the age of 70 than between 54 and 70.

Psychological engagement is the extent to which the person is preoccupied with and/or emotionally invested in persons and events in the external world. It is measured on the basis of a Thematic Apperception Test, in two ways, through ratings on Ego Energy and on Ego Style (Rosen and Neugarten 1960, Gutmann 1962). On the basis of both methods there was a decrease of psychological engagement with increasing age. (These data are not shown here.)

MEASURES OF AFFECT AND LIFE SATISFACTION

With this evidence for disengagement as a *process* of aging, we turn next to the relations between measures of engagement on the one hand, and measures of affect and life-satisfaction on the other hand. The scale of "life satisfaction" as a measure of psychological well-being consists of rating scales for five components of life satisfaction: Zest (vs. apathy); Resolution and fortitude; Congruence between desired and

Table 21.1. Age Differences on Measures of Social Engagement.

Age in 1962	Number		Interaction Index		Present Role Activity	
	M	F	M	F	M	F
54–59	14	11	2.6	2.8	43.7	49.1
60–64	15	14	2.5	2.8	45.9	42.7
65–69	12	11	2.6	2.7	44.1	47.9**
70–74	9	16	2.4	2.5	44.6	38.4
75–79	13	21	2.2	2.4	42.0	37.3
80–94	9	14	2.0	2.1	28.9	31.5
54–69	41	36	2.6	2.8	44.6	46.5
70–94	31	51	2.2	2.4*	38.9*	36.1*

* The difference on the measures between the below-70 and over-70-year-olds is significant at or beyond the .05 level.

** The upward turn in Role Activity for the 65–69 women is due in part to the fact that this group included unusually few widows and never-married women, and therefore had an unusually high proportion with positive scores in the "spouse" role.

achieved goals; Positive self-concept, and Positive mood tone. Ratings were made by judges after reading all the interviews with a given person.

Another measure of psychological well-being was a rating on positive affect regarding present level of activity in the life-roles. A separate rating was made for each life-role, and the ratings were added to give the total "Affect" score. A third measure was a rating on affect regarding change in role activity since age 60, or in the past ten years for people under 70.

Although these ratings and the intercorrelations are not shown here, it was found that affect and life satisfaction are positively related to activity or to engagement. Most respondents regret their losses in activity, and those respondents with higher amounts of activity generally have greater psychological well-being than those who have lower levels of activity. At the same time, this relationship is far from consistent, and all four combinations of activity and satisfaction exist—that is, high activity-high satisfaction and low-low are most frequent; but there also are high-low and low-high patterns.

PERSONALITY TYPES, ENGAGEMENT, AND LIFE SATISFACTION

It appears that engagement, affect and life-satisfaction are not interrelated in any simple way. At least one other variable must be involved in the system of interrelations. That variable is probably personality. That is, it may be presumed that certain personality types will disengage with relative comfort and thus remain high in life satisfaction; others will disengage with great discomfort and will show a drop in life satisfaction. Still others will long have had low levels of activity accompanied by high life satisfaction ratings and will show relatively little change in either dimension.

To follow up this line of inquiry, a clinical psychologist carried out a lengthy interview with each of 88 respondents; then used all the data gathered on each case to make ratings of 45 personality variables. An obverse factor analysis was carried out on these data. This analysis revealed 6 personality types for men and 6 for women. While the types are distinguishable in many other ways as well, they represent varying degrees of effectiveness or competence of ego functioning. An extremely well-functioning group, called here the Integrated, appeared in both sexes. These persons have a complex inner life, and at the same time, intact cognitive abilities. They are acceptant of impulse life, over which they maintain a comfortable degree of control; they are flexible, open to new stimuli; and in general, show a high level of integration between cognitive and affective components, or between rational and emotional elements of personality.

At the other extreme, the Unintegrated are individuals who show defect in perceptual and intellectual functioning, and who have difficulty in maintaining a balance between impulse and control. Some of these persons are rigid and over-controlled; others are impulsive and lacking in ego controls; but all are persons who are ineffective in integrating emotional and rational elements within the personality.

The Integrated numbered 27 of the 88 cases; the Unintegrated, 14. The remaining cases formed four other personality types for men; and four somewhat different types for women. These eight are not described in the present report; they are intermediate in most characteristics between the Integrated and the Unintegrated.

The Integrated are highest on life satisfaction, as shown in Table 21.2; the Unintegrated are lowest. There are clearcut differences, also, in level of role activity, with the Integrated, high; and the Unintegrated, low. The best-integrated personalities—men and women in their 70's and 80's as well as those in their 50's and 60's—are those who maintain a high sense of satisfaction from life, and are those who, on the average, maintain a relatively high level of activity. The poorest-integrated personalities are those who have low levels of life satisfaction; and who, on the average, maintain low levels of activity.

It would be an oversimplification, however, to conclude that the effective or well-integrated personalities are always highly active people, those who do not disengage. The range of scores on role activity for the Integrated, as shown in Table 21.2, is wide, indicating that some Integrated persons keep highly active, while others do not. Perhaps the Integrated person, to a greater extent than is true of other aging persons, is able to "choose" and then to maintain the pattern of activity that suits him best—some of the Integrated, that is, can psychologically support a pattern of high role activity well into their 80's; others move toward the "rocking chair" pattern in their 60's or 70's.

At the other extreme of personality, the Unintegrated personalities seem unable

Table 21.2. Personality Type, Satisfaction, and Engagement.

	Integrated (12M, 15F)	Personality Type Intermediate Ego-integrated (18M, 21F)	Unintegrated (8M, 6F)
Age range	58–92	56–85	60–80
Life Satisfaction			
Mean	19.7*	18.6	14.2***
Range	16.5–24	12.5–25	8.5–19.5
Role activity:			
Mean	45.5*	43.2	38.0
Range	28–64	19–63	10–48
Change in activity:			
Mean	−4.3	−3.2	−7.1
Range	(−16)–(+12)	(−15)–(+12)	(−20)–(+3)
Interaction index:			
Mean	2.9*	2.6**	2.1***
Range	1–4	1–4	1–4

* Difference in means between the Integrated and Unintegrated is significant at the .01 level.
** Difference in means between the Integrated and Intermediate is significant at the .05 level.
*** Difference in means between the Intermediate and Unintegrated is significant at the .01 level.

to sustain more than intermediate levels of activity; and whether low or moderate in role-activity, all these persons are low in life satisfaction.

Conclusions

Our data provide convincing evidence of decline in both social and psychological engagement with increasing age. Disengagement seems to us to be a useful term by which to describe these processes of change.

In some ways our data support the activity theory of optimal aging: as level of activity decreases, so also do the individual's feelings of contentment regarding his present activity. The usual relationships found in this sample are high activity with positive affect; and low activity with negative affect. This relationship does not decrease after age 70.

At the same time, the data in some ways support the disengagement theory of optimal aging: there are persons who are relatively high in role activity who would prefer to become more disengaged from their obligations; there are also persons who enjoy relatively inactive lives.

We conclude that neither the activity theory nor the disengagement theory of optimal aging is itself sufficient to account for what we regard as the more inclusive description of these findings: that as men and women move beyond age 70 in a modern, industrialized community like Kansas City, they regret the drop in role activity that occurs in their lives. At the same time, most older persons accept this drop as an inevitable accompaniment of growing old; and they succeed in maintaining a sense of self-worth and a sense of satisfaction with past and present life as a whole. Other older persons are less successful in resolving these conflicting elements—not only do they have strong negative affect regarding losses in activity; but the present losses weigh heavily, and are accompanied by a dissatisfaction with past and present life.

The relations between levels of activity and life satisfaction are strongly influenced by personality type, particularly by the extent to which the individual remains able to integrate emotional and rational elements of the personality. Of the three dimensions on which we have data—activity, satisfaction, and personality type—we regard personality as the pivotal dimension in describing patterns of aging and in predicting relationships between level of activity and life satisfaction. It is for this reason, also, that neither the activity nor the disengagement theory is satisfactory, since neither deals, except peripherally, with the issue of personality differences.

References

Cumming, E. and Henry, W. E. (1961). *Growing Old.* Basic Books, New York.

Gutmann, D. L. (1962). Personality in Middle and Later Years: A Thematic Apperception Test Study. Committee on Human Development, University of Chicago, Chicago (unpublished).

Rosen, J. L. and Neugarten, B. L. (1960). Ego functioning in the middle and later years: a thematic apperception study of normal adults. *Journal of Gerontology* 15, 62–67.

TWENTY-TWO

Disengagement Reconsidered in a Cross-national Context

Bernice L. Neugarten and Robert J. Havighurst

The purposes of our earlier pilot study have been two-fold, first, to generate hypotheses to be tested in a more systematic and large-scale crosscultural investigation; second, to explore a method and a research design that might be useful in undertaking such a large-scale study.

It happens, however, that these pilot data are themselves worthy of examination for the light they shed upon social-psychological processes that characterize aging, and upon theories of optimum aging—two related, though distinct, questions.

To help assess these data, this crossnational study itself might well be seen within the longer perspective of the line of inquiry that has been underway for the past 15 years by the group of investigators at the University of Chicago, in particular the work that relates to the disengagement theory, and recent revisions of that theory.

At present—and due in large part to findings from the Kansas City Studies carried on by the Chicago group—there are two somewhat different views of successful aging. One is the disengagement theory, which consists of two parts. It is postulated in the first part of the theory that as people grow older the extent of their social interaction decreases; that the decrease is a process characterized by mutuality of withdrawal between society and the aging person; and that the individual's withdrawal is accompanied by decreased emotional involvement in the activities and the social relationships that characterized him in middle age. The second part of the theory postulates that, in old age, the individual who has disengaged (and who has accordingly reached a new equilibrium characterized by greater psychological distance, altered types of social relationships, and decreased social interaction with the persons around him) is the person who has a sense of psychological well-being and will be high in satisfaction. This is essentially the theory as set forth in the book, *Growing Old,* by Cumming and Henry (1961), with whom the present authors were associated in the first years of the Kansas City Studies. It is a theory which has aroused considerable controversy among investigators both in the United States and in Europe.

Reprinted by permission from *Adjustment to Retirement: A Cross-National Study,* edited by R. J. Havighurst, J. M. A. Munnichs, B. L. Neugarten, and H. Thomae (Assen, Netherlands: Van Gorcum, 1969), 138–46.

The second portion of the theory, and that which many investigators regard as the essential portion, is not supported by our more recent work (Havighurst, Neugarten, and Tobin, 1963, 1964; Neugarten, 1965). The latest analysis of the Kansas City data indicated that life satisfaction is *positively* related to social interaction or activity in older persons, rather than to disengagement.

Thus we have, on the one hand, the patterns of activity, involvement, and satisfaction which have been described for aging persons residing in a midwestern city in United States, and the problem of verifying and elaborating one or another of the two interpretations that have emerged from two teams of American investigators.

There is, on the other hand, the body of sociological and anthropological theory which implies that, in societies characterized by increasing industrialization, increasing affluence, and greater longevity, there comes an increase of free time for older persons along with changing values regarding work and leisure (the decreased saliency of the Protestant Ethic); increased geographical mobility; and wider, though perhaps more superficial, patterns of social interaction. These factors should lead to increased rates of voluntary as well as involuntary retirement, as well as to a gain in choice and variety of role patterns that accompanies loss of the work role.

From this second perspective, it would follow that given a permissive social environment, older persons, like younger ones, will choose the roles and role combinations which offer them the most ego-involvement. Some older persons, that is, will continue to work as long as they can; others will retire and enter into family or community roles with increased vigor; and still others will retire and simultaneously disengage from other roles.

This latter set of concepts implies that patterns of aging should vary in direct relation to the social setting—in particular, the extent to which the setting is one that provides a wide range of choices; and that patterns of activity, involvement, and satisfaction should reflect, not a relatively "universal" set of relationships, as implied in the disengagement theory, but systematic variation from one society to the next.

We have drawn a distinction between *processes of aging*, and theories of *optimum aging*. The present crossnational data pertain to both. That is, we have data here which relate to changing levels of social interaction, on the one hand; and, on the other hand, to the relation between social interaction and psychological well-being.

First, to clarify a few terms. The term "disengagement," even when used to refer only to the social-psychological processes of age—and without reference to optimum patterns—was used with ambivalent meanings in the book, *Growing Old*. At times it referred to the level of activity, as when the authors spoke of "the disengaged state"; at other times, to the process of change. When referring to process, sometimes it referred to the relinquishing of the major task, or major role, in life—that is, the work role for men, and the roles of wife and mother for women. (Thus, much of

Cumming and Henry's discussion of the individual's readiness or non-readiness to "disengage" was with reference to retirement from work.) At other times it referred to the wider arena of social interaction in which the work role is only one segment or one type of activity.

In the present discussion we use the term "social interaction" to refer to the level and pattern of overall role activity at any given point in time. We have specifically delineated 12 different social roles (worker, parent, grandparent, spouse, kin-group member, homemaker, friend, neighbor, acquaintance, club-member, civic-and-political activity, church-member); and we have summed across all 12 to obtain a measure of social interaction. It happens also that we have as our subjects in these crossnational samples men who have been retired from their regular jobs for at least 4 years. Thus we deal here with social interaction in the presence of retirement (or in the absence of the work role).

We use the term "disengagement" here to refer to the process of change over time—a term that the present authors regard as accurate in describing the social and psychological changes we observed in the Kansas City data.

With regard, then, to the first part of the disengagement theory—that both social and psychological disengagement occur as persons move from middle age to old age: we have the evidence from the Kansas City data that, despite individual differences, the statement is generally true. In Kansas City, 70-year-olds showed lower levels of social interaction than 50-year-olds. In this crossnational study, we did not gather systematic data on younger persons, but data show that the levels of social interaction in 70–75-year-old men vary from city to city and from occupation to occupation, as do the patterns of role activity. Thus, while a general process of disengagement is probably associated with advancing age, the rate of disengagement and the patterns it takes is by no means the same from group to group.

In this sense these crossnational data support the view of diversity in patterns of aging, a view that we have described on earlier occasions in reference to the diversity within the Kansas City cases (Havighurst, Neugarten, and Tobin, 1963, 1964; Neugarten, 1965). What these crossnational data indicate, then, is the importance of the sociocultural setting in producing variations in patterns of social interaction in old people. We have varied the social settings in terms of country and city of residence, and in terms of differences in socioeconomic level as reflected in former occupation; and we have emerged with different levels and patterns of role activity, or social interaction.

Two examples will serve to illustrate this point further. Among the Chicago retired teachers, 60 percent were working in one or another position—substitute teaching, selling insurance, giving lessons, etc. A few men were earning more money now than ever before. The Chicago sample was different in this respect from the other groups of retired teachers in other cities; and they were even more different from all the groups of retired steelworkers. There are ecological factors operating, then—a combination of factors that relate to life in the Chicago area, and to having been a former teacher, that produces a high probability of continued activity in the role of worker. These factors are probably properties of the social system, the reference groups to which these men are related, their values, and their life-styles.

The second example is the retired steelworkers in Milan. These men had all worked in a particularly large industrial plant; and the owners had provided housing and a social center for their workers. The retired workers continued to live in the apartment blocks maintained by the company, and they used the social center as a club-house. Their ratings on friendship activities, and in the roles of acquaintance and colleague, were higher than for other groups of steelworkers in the other cities, and were higher, also, than that of retired *teachers* in Milan. Here the social provisions are clearly affecting the forms of adaptation to aging, by making it easy for the Milanese steelworkers, but not the Milanese teachers, to interact everyday with friends and former work colleagues.

One need not go, of course, to crossnational data for examples of this type. The value of these crossnational data, however, are the relatively systematic manner in which sociocultural contexts are shown to relate to different patterns of role activity, over and above individual differences; and to demonstrate that even in large urban centers in modern Western societies, differences in cultural traditions, value-systems, and probably in attitudes toward the old produce systematic variations in the patterns of social interaction.

The second part of the disengagement theory, as stated earlier, relates to *optimal patterns* of aging and implies that the person who has been disengaging and who, by his mid-70's, has reached a new equilibrium characterized by greater psychological distance, altered types of relationships, and decreased social interaction with the persons around him will be the person who has a high level of psychological well-being.

The re-analysis of the Kansas City data did *not* support that portion of the theory, for, as reported on earlier occasions, we found that life satisfaction is positively related to the level of social interaction in older persons, with the relationship being even higher in persons over 70 than in those under 70 (Tobin and Neugarten, 1961; Havighurst, Neugarten, Tobin, 1963).[1]

Here, also, the crossnational data do not support that portion of the disengagement theory, for in these samples of men drawn from different occupational backgrounds and different cities in the United States and Europe, we find, in group after group, that psychological well-being is positively related to the level of social interaction.

In this instance, the conclusion rests upon use of the Global Life Outlook (GLO) as the measure of well-being.[2] The correlation between GLO and total role activity for all 300 cases pooled turned out to be .45, almost exactly the same correlation as found in Kansas City data. (There, for a population of 159 men and women aged 54 to 94, the correlation between Life-Satisfaction and total role activity was .46.) The correlation here is particularly significant because the average level of role activity and the average level of life satisfaction varied from subgroup to subgroup. To put this in different words, a group of retired steelworkers living, say, in Warsaw may, as a group, be more socially active and may show a high level of psychological well-being as compared with a group of retired steelworkers living in Milan or Chicago or Bonn. But for the individuals within the group, those who are high in activity tend to be those who are also high on Life-Satisfaction. Given the necessity for caution because of the small size of the present samples, nevertheless this last finding is provocative. Does it mean that in persons who are not seriously impaired biologically the modal pattern—despite the city and country of residence, and despite the former occupation—is high life satisfaction in the presence of medium to high social interaction? Would this relationship hold in societies that are more different one from another than those studied here? In non-Western societies? And if so, would we have evidence in support of a view of the aging process in which aging is not different from other periods of the life cycle—a view, that is, that focuses upon the nature of man as a social animal in old age as well as in youth; and that emphasizes the continued importance of social participation in maintaining a sense of well-being?

Perhaps we might also anticipate, in studies based on larger and more representative samples, the same variations as have been found in Kansas City and now again in the present data, and that are reflected in a correlation around .5—namely, that while the *modal* patterns are high activity–high satisfaction and low activity–low satisfaction, the other combinations also exist with some frequency: namely, that some persons who are relatively inactive will be content; and some who are highly active will be discontent.

If so, in considering the question of individual variation, we shall be thrown back again to the complexity of interactions between biological, social, and psychological factors that operate in any given case—and to the saliency of personality factors and coping styles in establishing our predictions.

To restate this point in different words: there are two research questions involved: (1) What social conditions tend to be associated, on the average, with high psychological well-being in the old? (2) What is the order of the variables in predicting psychological well-being for individuals (or, in more statistical terms, "In what order are the variables to be entered in our regression analyses, when the problem is to predict life-satisfaction?"). The two questions are variants of the problem posed at the outset with regard to maximizing the life-satisfaction of older people. Because the two questions are different, our research approaches must be different.

We may be justified in anticipating that crossnational data such as these described here will go far toward answering the first question; in elucidating the ecological factors that produce variations in the ways people grow old; and in pointing to the social conditions that tend in general to be related to psychological well-being. This is a highly important avenue to pursue in the field of gerontology.

At the same time, variations in sociocultural contexts will not solve the question of individual variation, i.e., why some individuals are more content than others who live in the same general setting. Despite the likelihood that some settings will be found to provide greater freedom or greater permissiveness for a broad range of life styles; others will be found to provide greater "pressures" for social participation; others, greater economic benefits; and so on, we shall still need to look at the ways individual older people adapt to the settings in which they find themselves.

It is the manner in which the individual deals with a variety of contingencies in his life, some of them social contingencies, some of them biological, which will continue to be an important issue—what an old person makes of his world, and how the adaptational process is constantly influenced by his past life-history. In attempting to understand why one individual copes successfully with illness while another does not, or why one individual copes successfully with retirement and another does not, we shall have to pursue in much greater depth the ways in which aged individuals relate their pasts with their presents, and how they interpret and integrate their lives into meaningful wholes.

Notes

1. Part of the difference between the two teams in interpreting the Kansas City data is due to the fact that the Cumming-Henry analysis was based on interviews with the subjects gathered over a 4-year period; the Havighurst-Neugarten-Tobin analysis, on interviews gathered over a 6-year period. More important is the fact that different measures were used. As a measure of social interaction, the second team used ratings of performance in 12 social roles rather than the measures used by Cumming-Henry: Role Count, Interaction Index, and Social Life Space. As the measure of psychological well-being, Havighurst, Neugarten and Tobin used a carefully-validated set of ratings on Life Satisfaction, rather than the Cumming-Henry Morale Index.

For the population of 159 men and women aged 54 to 94, those who remained in the Kansas City study at the end of 6 years of study, the correlation between total role activity and Life Satisfaction was .46. The size of that correlation coefficient, while it provided clear evidence that engagement, not disengagement, is related to psychological well-being, also was evidence that not all persons follow the same general rule. While the most frequent patterns were high engagement-high life satisfaction and low-low, there were persons with high-low, and low-high combinations. While a full exposition of the issues lies outside the scope of the present discussion, Havighurst, Neugarten, and Tobin have attributed this diversity primarily to differences in personality, and have gone on to demonstrate the relationships that hold between personality type, social interaction, and life-satisfaction in the Kansas City cases. (Neugarten, 1965; Havighurst, 1968).

Presumably personality differences would emerge as salient factors, also, in patterns of aging to be found in other countries. Given the differences between countries and the differences between occupations that emerged from the present crossnational study—differences, to repeat, that are over and above the individual differences from person to person—it remains to future studies to establish whether personality differences or socio-cultural differences are the most significant. For the time being, we have no evidence on this point.

2. GLO ratings were made on all 300 cases in the present study, but there was insufficient time for the research team to establish crossnational reliability of the ratings or to refine the scales in the light of preliminary findings. The American team, however, undertook further analysis of the GLO data. First, for the 300 cases, the intercorrelations of the 8 dimensions of GLO were all positive and generally at the level of .3 or .4. Factor analysis of these data showed high loadings on three components which accounted for 70 percent of the variance. The communality over all 8 components was 43 percent. The intercorrelation matrix suggested that it was appropriate to sum over the eight components to obtain a total GLO score. (It also suggested, however, that psychological well-being, as measured by the GLO, is a multi-dimensional phenomenon; that is, there appears to be more than just a single factor involved. The latter is much the same conclusion that the American team had reached earlier in their analysis of the Life Satisfaction ratings when used on Kansas City cases.)

Second, of the 50 American cases, interjudge reliability on the GLO ratings was high.

Next, Life-Satisfaction ratings were made on the 50 American cases, and GLO and LSR were found to be highly correlated (r was .87). Given the fact that the LSR had previously been carefully validated on the Kansas City data; and given this high correlation between GLO and LSR, we proceeded further and computed the correlations between GLO and total role activity for each of the 12 subsamples in this study. The correlations were sizable, with 10 of the 12 coefficients falling between .29 and .76. When all 300 cases were pooled, the correlation between GLO and total role activity was .45.

Given the size of this last coefficient, and the foregoing analyses, the American team is confident that these data support the general relationship between role activity and psychological well-being; and bear out the parallel finding that emerged from the Kansas City data.

To the reader who has special interest in measures of psychological well-being, the differences between the dimensions of GLO, 'morale' as used by Cumming and Henry (1961), and 'Life-Satisfaction' as used by Neugarten, Havighurst and Tobin (1961) should be noted. The Morale Index was based on a tally of responses to four sets of questions asking if the respondent would like to change his place of residence; change the frequency of his contacts with relatives, friends, or neighbors; if he would prefer to be a different age from his present age; and if he was involved in weekday or week-end activities that he disliked. 'Life-Satisfaction' was based upon the total interview data, and was the sum of ratings on five different components. An individual was rated high to the extent that he (a) takes pleasure from whatever the round of activities that constitutes his everyday life; (b) regards his life as meaningful and accepts resolutely that which life has been; (c) feels he has succeeded in achieving his major goals; (d) holds a positive image of himself; and (e) maintains happy and optimistic attitudes and moods.

References

Cumming, Elaine, and Henry, W. E.: Growing old. New York: Basic Books, 1961.

Havighurst, R. J., Neugarten, Bernice L., and Tobin, S. S.: Disengagement and patterns of aging. Presented at International Gerontological Research Seminar. Markaryd, Sweden, August, 1963.

Havighurst, R. J., Neugarten, Bernice L., and Tobin, S. S.: Disengagement, personality, and life satisfaction in the later years. In P. F. Hansen (Ed.) Age with a future. Denmark: Munksgaard, 1964, 419–425.

Havighurst, R. J.: Personality and patterns of aging. The Gerontologist, Spring, 1968, Pt. 2, 20–23.

Neugarten, Bernice L., Havighurst, R. J., and Tobin, S. S.: The measurement of life satisfaction. J. Gerontol., 1961, 16, 134–143.

Neugarten, Bernice, L.: Personality and patterns of aging.: Journal of Psychology of the University of Nijmegen (Gawein), 1965, 13, 249–256.

Tobin, S. S. and Neugarten, Bernice L.: Life satisfaction and social interaction in the aging. J. Gerontol., 1961, 16, 344–346.

TWENTY-THREE

The Measurement of Life Satisfaction

Bernice L. Neugarten, Robert J. Havighurst, and Sheldon S. Tobin

There have been various attempts to define and to measure the psychological well-being of older people, usually with the goal of using such a measure as an operational definition of "successful" aging. Different terms have been used in approaching this problem (terms such as adjustment, competence, morale, or happiness); and different criteria, as well as different techniques of measurement. A number of cogent criticisms have been made of these attempts, largely because they are inextricably involved with value judgments.

In many research studies on aging, however, it becomes necessary to establish some measure of success or well-being in relation to which other social and psychological variables can be studied. In such undertakings, therefore, rather than forego a measure of psychological well-being, it becomes the goal to construct as refined and as valid a measure as possible. Once the investigator makes his value judgments explicit by the choice of his terms and his criteria, the actual construction and validation of such a measure can go forward in relatively straightforward and value-free manner.

In earlier approaches to this problem there have been two general points of view. One focuses upon the overt behavior of the individual and utilizes social criteria of success or competence. Studies that fall within this category tend to be ones in which level and range of activities and extent of social participation are the variables to be measured; and in which the assumption is made, implicitly or explicitly, that the greater the extent of social participation, and the less the individual varies from the pattern of activity that characterized him in middle age, the greater is his well-being.

The other point of view focuses upon the individual's internal frame of reference, with only secondary attention given to his level of social participation. Here the variables to be measured have been the individual's own evaluations of his present or past

Reprinted with permission from *Journal of Gerontology* 16, no. 2 (April 1961): 134–43. A partial report of this research was included in a paper by R. J. Havighurst, "Successful Aging: Definition and Measurement," presented at the International Research Seminar on the Social and Psychological Aspects of Aging, August 1960.

life, his satisfaction, or his happiness. The assumptions are, whether or not explicitly stated, that the individual himself is the only proper judge of his well-being; that the value judgments of the investigator can thus be minimized; and, perhaps most important, that it is not appropriate to measure well-being in old age by the same standards that apply to middle age, namely, standards based upon activity or social involvement.

As an example of the first point of view, Havighurst and Albrecht (1953), using public opinion as the criterion, developed a scale for measuring the social acceptability of the older person's behavior. Another example is the activity score on the schedule, "Your Activities and Attitudes" (Cavan, Burgess, Havighurst, and Goldhamer, 1949; Havighurst and Albrecht, 1953); a score which sums up a person's participation in a number of different activities.

Most of the measuring instruments used in previous studies do, in fact, combine elements from both general approaches. For instance, in the Chicago Attitude Inventory (Cavan et al., 1949; Havighurst and Albrecht, 1953; Havighurst, 1957) a person is asked about his economic situation, work, family, friends, health, and so on, and about his happiness and feelings of usefulness. While the emphasis is upon feelings of satisfaction, a high score depends indirectly upon a high level of activity.

A second such measure is the Cavan Adjustment Rating Scale (Cavan et al., 1949; Havighurst, 1957). This is a rating based on interview data which takes into account not only the person's associations with family, friends, and formal and informal groups, but also his feelings of importance and satisfaction and his emotional stability.

Another measure that combines elements of both approaches is the social role performance measure used by Havighurst (1957). Here competence in the social roles of worker, parent, spouse, homemaker, citizen, friend, association member and church member is rated from interview data; with the ratings based not only upon extent of reported activity, but also upon the individual's investment in and satisfaction with his performance in each role.

As part of a larger study of psychological and social factors involved in aging, the Kansas City Study of Adult Life,[1] the present investigators sought to develop a measure of the second general type—one that would use the individual's own evaluations as the point of reference; and one that would be relatively independent of level of activity or social participation. There have been other attempts to devise a measure with these general characteristics. For example, a few investigators (Kuhlen, 1948; Lebo, 1953; Rose, 1955; Pollak, 1948) have used direct self-reports of happiness. Although they are extremely vulnerable to conscious and unconscious psychological defenses, such self-reports have not usually been checked for validity against a more objective criterion.

Another example is Kutner's Morale Scale (Kutner, 1956), which is based upon responses to seven items such as, "On the whole, how satisfied would you say you are with your way of life today?" This instrument was not regarded as satisfactory for our purposes for several reasons: 1) It has not been validated against an outside criterion; 2) it is based upon the assumption that psychological well-being is a unidimensional phenomenon, for the scale has been constructed to form a scale of the Guttman type; 3) there have been scaling difficulties when the items have been used with populations other than the one originally studied. Thus, one of the seven items had to be scored differently for a New York City population than for an Elmira population (Kutner, 1956, p. 303); and an even greater effect of this type was seen when the scale was adapted for use with rural residents of South Dakota (Morrison and Kristjanson, 1958). In short, the items which are successful in producing a Guttman scale for one population are not altogether the same for another population.

Recently, a Morale Index was developed by our collaborators on the Kansas City Study of Adult Life (Cumming, Dean, and Newell, 1958) consisting of four questions of which one was, "Do you wish you could see more of your relatives than you do now? Less? Your neighbors? Your friends?" (R is scored positively if he answers "Things are all right as they are.")

At the time the present investigators began work on this problem, that Index seemed unsatisfactory for several reasons. It was based on so few items that scores might prove highly unreliable; the Index has been validated against only a small sample of cases; and, most important, it appeared to be a unidimensional measure reflecting, for the most part, resignation or conformity to the status quo. The Index seemed, therefore, not to reflect our own concepts of psychological well-being.

The research reported here had two purposes, each requiring a somewhat different set of procedures. The first, as already indicated, was to devise a measure of successful aging for use in the Kansas City Studies, a measure that would be derived relatively independently from various other psychological and social variables. The second purpose was to devise a short, easily-administered instrument that could be used in other studies and to validate that instrument against Kansas City data.

After a description of the study population, the report that follows deals with the derivation and validation of the Life Satisfaction Ratings (LSR) and the scales upon which the ratings are based; then with the derivation and validation of two short self-administered instruments, the Life Satisfaction Index A (LSIA) and the Life Satisfaction Index B (LSIB).

THE STUDY POPULATION

Table 23.1 shows the distribution of the study population by age, sex, and social class. In brief, the upper-middle class represents business and professional levels;

Table 23.1. The Study Population: by Age at First Interview, Sex, and Social Class.

Social class	Age group					Total
	50–56	57–63	64–70	71–79	80–89	
Upper-middle:						
Men	6	7	5	2	2	22
Women	7	6	6	6	3	28
Lower-middle:						
Men	4	4	7	7	6	28
Women	6	3	5	7	6	27
Upper-lower:						
Men	8	7	4	17	5	41
Women	5	7	6	10	3	31
Total	36	34	33	49	25	177

NOTE.—Social class placements for panel members (the first three age groups in the table) were based upon an Index of Social Characteristics in which occupation (or former occupation), level of education, and area of residence were the three main factors. For the quasi-panel (the last two age groups in the table) this Index is less useful, since, with advancing age of R, neither educational level nor former occupation can be assumed to have the same social-class values as for the group who are presently middle-aged. (For example, the semi-skilled worker today generally occupies a lower position in the social system than 40 years ago). We are indebted to Dr. Wayne Wheeler, present Field Director of the Kansas City Study, for his assistance in analyzing the social data available on these older persons and in arriving at their class placements. Because this whole problem of social-class placements for aged persons remains a difficult one, however, we may still have placed a disproportionate number into the upper-lower class.

lower-middle, white-collar occupational levels; and the upper-lower represents blue-collar levels.

This population was composed of members of two groups. The first, referred to as the panel group, were persons aged 50 to 70 at the time of the first interview in 1956. The panel represents a stratified probability sample of middle and working class white persons of this age range residing in the metropolitan area of Kansas City. Excluded were the chronically ill and the physically impaired. The method by which the panel was selected resulted in a group that is biased toward middle class—in other words, that is better educated, wealthier, and of higher occupational and residential prestige than the universe of 50-to-70-year-olds.

The second group, referred to as the quasi-panel, were persons aged 70–90 who joined the Kansas City Study two years after field work had begun. This older group was built up on the basis of quota sampling rather than probability sampling. The group consists of middle- and working-class persons, none of them financially deprived and none of them bedridden or senile.

While the panel probably has a greater middle-class bias than the quasi-panel, it is likely that the older members of the study population are less representative of their universe than is true of the panel members. Not only are these older persons better off financially, but they are in better health than most 70- to 90-year-olds, and thus represent an advantaged rather than a typical group.

Of the original panel, 74 percent remained as cooperating respondents by the end of the fourth round of interviews, at which time the Life Satisfaction Ratings described below were made. Of the original quasi-panel, 83 percent remained at the same point in time, after two rounds of interviews. Thus, in addition to the various biases operating in the original selection of the two groups (for instance, 16 percent of those contacted refused to join the panel), there is an unmeasurable effect on the present study due to sample attrition. Of the attrition, 15 percent was due to deaths; 10 percent, to geographical moves; and the rest, to refusals to be interviewed the second, third, or fourth time. There is evidence also that persons who were relatively socially isolated constituted a disproportionate number of the drop-outs.

All these factors should be kept in mind in considering the range of Life Satisfaction Ratings obtained for this study population and in considering the generalizations that emerged regarding age differences.

The data. The data consisted of lengthy and repeated interviews covering many aspects of the respondent's life pattern, his attitudes, and his values. Included was information on the daily round and the usual week-end round of activity; other household members; relatives, friends, and neighbors; income and work; religion; voluntary organizations; estimates of the amount of social interaction as compared with the amount at age 45; attitudes toward old age, illness, death, and immortality; questions about loneliness, boredom, anger; and questions regarding the respondent's role models and his self-image. The first interview for the quasi-panel was a special schedule combining questions from the first three panel interviews. Both groups had the same fourth-round interview.

THE LIFE SATISFACTION RATINGS

The first problem was to analyze our concept of psychological well-being into a sufficient number of components to represent its complexity, and then to find ways of measuring these components from interview data. Working with a group of graduate students in a research seminar, the investigators began by examining the measures of adjustment and morale that had been used in previous studies, and by defining distinguishable components. Definitions were tried out against case material; independent judgments of the cases were compared; the concepts were redefined; and so on.[2] Finally, operational definitions of the following components were obtained: Zest (vs. apathy); Resolution and fortitude; Congruence between desired and achieved goals; Positive self concept; and Mood tone. More detailed definitions appear in the scales reproduced below, but in brief, an individual was regarded as being at the positive end of the continuum of psychological well-being to the extent that he: A) takes pleasure from the round of activities that constitutes his everyday life; B) regards his life as meaningful and accepts resolutely that which life has been; C) feels he has succeeded in achieving his major goals; D) holds a positive image of self; and E) maintains happy and optimistic attitudes and mood.

Each of these five components was rated on a five-point scale (with 5, high); and the ratings were summed to obtain an overall rating.

We then sought a suitable term by which to refer to this overall rating. The term "adjustment" is unsuitable because it carries the implication that conformity is the most desirable pattern of behavior. "Psychological well-being" is, if nothing else, an awkward phrase. "Morale," in many ways, captures best the qualities here being described, but there was the practical problem that there are already in use in gerontological research two different scales entitled Morale. The term Life Satisfaction was finally adopted on grounds that, although it is not altogether adequate, it comes close to representing the five components.

In making the Life Satisfaction Ratings, all the interview data on each respondent were utilized. Thus the ratings are based, not on R's direct self report of satisfaction (although some questions of this type were included in the interviews), but on the inferences drawn by the raters from all the information available on R, including his interpersonal relationships and how others reacted toward him.

The four rounds of interviewing had been spaced over approximately two and one-half years. In those few cases where marked changes had occurred in R's life situation within that interval of time, and where psychological well-being seemed to have changed accordingly, the rating represented the situation at the most recent point in time, at Interview 4.

Life Satisfaction Rating Scales[3]

A. *Zest vs. apathy.* To be rated here are enthusiasm of response and degree of ego-involvement—in any of various activities, persons, or ideas, whether or not these are activities which involve R with other people, are "good" or "socially approved" or "status-giving." Thus, R who "just loves to sit home and knit" rates as high as R who "loves to get out and meet people." Although a low rating is given for listlessness and apathy, physical energy per se is not to be involved in this rating. Low ratings are given for being "bored with most things"; for "I have to force myself to do things"; and also for meaningless (and unenjoyed) hyper-activity.

> 5 . . . .Speaks of several activities and relationships with enthusiasm. Feels that "now" is the best time of life. Loves to do things, even sitting at home. Takes up new activities; makes new friends readily, seeks self-improvement. Shows zest in several areas of life.

4 . . . .Shows zest, but it is limited to one or two special interests, or limited to certain periods of time. May show disappointment or anger when things go wrong, if they keep him from active enjoyment of life. Plans ahead, even though in small time units.

3 . . . .Has a bland approach to life. Does not seem to get much pleasure out of the things he does. Seeks relaxation and a limited degree of involvement. May be quite detached (aloof) from many activities, things, or people.

2 . . . .Thinks life is monotonous for the most part. May complain of fatigue. Feels bored with many things. If active, finds little meaning or enjoyment in the activity.

1 . . . .Lives on the basis of routine. Doesn't think anything worth doing.

B. *Resolution and fortitude.* The extent to which R accepts personal responsibility for his life; the opposite of feeling resigned, or of merely condoning or passively accepting that which life has brought him. The extent to which R accepts his life as meaningful and inevitable, and is relatively unafraid of death. Erikson's "integrity." Not to be confused with "autonomy" or the extent to which R's life has been self-propelled or characterized by initiative. R may not have been a person of high initiative, but yet he may accept resolutely and relatively positively that which life has been for him. R may feel life was a series of hard knocks, but that he has stood up under them (this would be a high rating).

There are two types of low ratings; the highly intropunitive, where R blames himself overly much; and the extra-punitive, where R blames others or the world in general for whatever failures or disappointments he has experienced.

5 . . . .Try and try again attitude. Bloody but unbowed. Fights back; withstanding, not giving up. Active personal responsibility—take the bad and the good and make the most of it. Wouldn't change the past.

4 . . . .Can take life as it comes. "I have no complaint on the way life has treated me." Assumes responsibility readily. "If you look for the good side of life, you'll find it." Does not mind talking about difficulties in life, but does not dwell on them either. "You have to give up some things."

3 . . . .Says, "I've had my ups and downs; sometimes on top, sometimes on the bottom." Shows a trace of extrapunitiveness or intropunitiveness concerning his difficulties in life.

2 . . . .Feels he hasn't done better because he hasn't gotten the breaks. Feels great difference in life now as compared to age 45; the change has been for the worse. "I've worked hard but never got anywhere."

1 . . . .Talks of hard knocks which he has not mastered (extrapunitive). Feels helpless. Blames self a great deal (intropunitive). Overwhelmed by life.

C. *Congruence between desired and achieved goals.* The extent to which R feels he has achieved his goals in life, whatever those goals might be; feels he has succeeded in accomplishing what *he* regards as important. High ratings go, for instance, to *R* who says, "I've managed to keep out of jail" just as to *R* who says, "I managed to send all my kids through college." Low ratings go to *R* who feels he's missed most of his opportunities, or who says, "I've never been suited to my work," or "I always wanted to be a doctor, but never could get there." Also to *R* who wants most to be "loved," but instead feels merely "approved." (Expressions of regret for lack of education are not counted because they are stereotyped responses among all but the group of highest social status.)

> 5 . . . .Feels he has accomplished what he wanted to do. He has achieved or is achieving his own personal goals.
> 4 . . . .Regrets somewhat the chances missed during life. "Maybe I could have made more of certain opportunities." Nevertheless, feels that he has been fairly successful in accomplishing what he wanted to do in life.
> 3 . . . .Has a fifty-fifty record of opportunities taken and opportunities missed. Would have done some things differently, if he had his life to live over. Might have gotten more education.
> 2 . . . .Has regrets about major opportunities missed but feels good about accomplishment in one area (may be his avocation).
> 1 . . . .Feels he has missed most opportunities in life.

D. *Self-concept. R*'s concept of self—physical as well as psychological and social attributes. High ratings go to *R* who is concerned with grooming and appearance; who thinks of himself as wise, mellow (and thus is comfortable in giving advice to others); who feels proud of his accomplishments; who feels he deserves whatever good breaks he has had; who feels he is important to someone else. Low ratings are given to *R* who feels "old," weak, sick, incompetent; who feels himself a burden to others; who speaks disparagingly of self or of old people.

> 5 . . . .Feels at his best. "I do better work now than ever before." "There was never any better time." Thinks of self as wise, mellow; physically able or attractive; feels important to others. Feels he has the right to indulge himself.
> 4 . . . .Feels more fortunate than the average. Is sure that he can meet the exigencies of life. "When I retire, I'll just substitute other activities." Compensates well for any difficulty of health. Feels worthy of being indulged. "Things I want to do, I can do, but I'll not overexert myself." Feels in control of self in relation to the situation.
> 3 . . . .Sees self as competent in at least one area, e.g., work; but has doubts about self in other areas. Acknowledges loss of youthful vigor, but accepts it in a realistic way. Feels relatively unimportant, but doesn't mind. Feels he takes, but also gives. Senses a general, but not extreme, loss of status as he grows older. Reports health better than average.

2 . . . . .Feels that other people look down on him. Tends to speak disparagingly
of older people. Is defensive about what the years are doing to him.

1 . . . .Feels old. Feels in the way, or worthless. Makes self-disparaging remarks.
"I'm endured by others."

E. *Mood tone.* High ratings for *R* who expresses happy, optimistic attitudes and
mood; who uses spontaneous, positively-toned affective terms for people and
things; who takes pleasure from life and expresses it. Low ratings for depression, "feel
blue and lonely"; for feelings of bitterness; for frequent irritability and anger. (Here
we consider not only *R*'s verbalized attitudes in the interview; but make inferences
from all we know of his interpersonal relationships, how others react toward him.)

5 . . . ."This is the best time of my life." Is nearly always cheerful, optimistic.
Cheerfulness may seem unrealistic to an observer, but *R* shows no sign of
"putting up a bold front."

4 . . . .Gets pleasure out of life, knows it and shows it. There is enough restraint
to seem appropriate to a younger person. Usually feels positive affect. Optimistic.

3 . . . .Seems to move along on an even temperamental keel. Any depressions
are neutralized by positive mood swings. Generally neutral-to-positive affect.
May show some irritability.

2 . . . .Wants things quiet and peaceful. General neutral-to-negative affect.
Some depression.

1 . . . .Pessimistic, complaining, bitter. Complaints of being lonely. Feels
"blue" a good deal of the time. May get angry when in contact with people.

Reliability of ratings. Ratings were made on every case by two judges working independently. The judges were members of a student-faculty research seminar. A system was followed by which judges and groups of cases were systematically varied. In
all, 14 judges rated the 177 cases, and all but one judge maintained a high level of
agreement with the others with whom he was paired. The coefficient of correlation
between two LSR ratings for the 177 cases was .78. (Since, in all subsequent steps,
the average of the two ratings was used, the Spearman-Brown coefficient of attenua-
tion can be employed to raise the coefficient to .87.) Of 885 paired judgments, 94
percent showed exact agreement or agreement within one step on the 5-step scale.
(On the same basis, inter judge agreement varied only slightly from one component
to the next. It was 97 percent for Zest; 96 percent for Resolution; 92 percent for Congruence; 96 percent for Self-concept; and 92 percent for Mood tone.)

For the 177 cases, LSR scores ranged from 8 to 25, with the mean, 17.8, and the
standard deviation, 4.6.

Intercorrelations between components. Table 23.2 shows the intercorrelations between the five components of Life Satisfaction. While positively interrelated, they

Table 23.2. Intercorrelations of the Components of Life Satisfaction ($N = 177$).

	Resolution	Congruence	Self-concept	Mood Tone
Zest	.67	.56	.79	.84
Resolution		.70	.83	.48
Congruence			.73	.57
Self-concept				.82

nevertheless show a fair degree of independence, supporting the assumption that more than one dimension is involved in the scales. Without submitting these coefficients to a factor analysis, it appears that Zest, Mood tone, and possibly Self-concept involve one factor, with the probability of one or two other factors operating in the matrix.

Characteristics of the LSR. For this sample of 177 cases there was no correlation between Life Satisfaction and age (*r* was − .07).

Using an Index of Social Characteristics (ISC) based on three factors, level of education, area of residence, and occupation (or former occupation), the correlation between LSR and ISC was .39. Thus, there is a positive, but not marked relationship between Life Satisfaction and socioeconomic status.

There was no significant sex difference on LSR scores. The mean for the women was 17.9 (S. D., 3.58); and for the men, 17.5 (S. D., 4.04).

With regard to marital status, the non-married (the single, divorced, separated, and widowed) had significantly lower LSR scores. This relationship held true for both sexes, and for both younger and older subgroups in the study population.

Validity of the ratings. The LSR depended on scoring by judges who had read all the recorded interview material, but who had not themselves interviewed the respondent. In seeking to establish an outside criterion by which these ratings could be validated, the investigators thought it desirable to have an experienced clinical psychologist interview the respondents and then make his own ratings of Life Satisfaction.

For various practical reasons, it was not until some 18 to 22 months had elapsed after Interview 4 that these clinical interviews were begun.[4] By this time, a fifth and sixth wave of interviewing had intervened, and there had been further attrition of the study population due not only to deaths and geographic moves, but also to refusals. Nevertheless, over a three-month period, 80 respondents were interviewed at length by the clinical psychologist; and it is his ratings (LSR-C1) that constitute a validity check on the LSR. These interviews and ratings were made by the clinician without any prior knowledge of the respondent—that is, without reading any of the earlier interviews and without discussion of the case with other members of the research staff.

The 80 cases were representative of the 177 as regards sex, age, and social class. They had, however, a slightly higher mean score on the LSR. (Mean LSR for the 177 cases was 17.8; for the 80 cases seen by the clinician, it was 18.9. Twenty-five percent of the total 177, but only 15 percent of the 80 cases, were persons with LSR scores of 14.5 or less.) In other words, a disproportionate number of drop-outs in the 18 to 24-month interval were persons who were low on Life Satisfaction.

Using the average of the two judges' ratings for the LSR score, the correlation between LSR and LSR-C1 for the 80 cases was .64. Of 400 paired judgments, 76 percent represented exact agreement or agreement within one step on the 5-step scale. (On the same basis, agreement between LSR and LSR-C1 varied somewhat from one component to the next. It was 86 percent for Zest; 76 percent for Resolution; 73 percent for Congruence; 78 percent for Self-concept; and 69 percent for Mood tone).

Further study was made of several cases for whom there was marked disagreement between the LSR and the LSR-C1. As anticipated, these cases were of two types: 1) There were a few who had been rated higher on LSR, and where it seemed a reasonable explanation that the clinical psychologist had succeeded in probing beneath the respondent's defenses and had obtained a truer picture of his feelings.

> Mrs. B, for instance, was a woman whose façade was successful throughout the first four interviews in convincing the judges reading the interviews that she was a person who had achieved all her major goals; that she was resolute, competent, happy, even in the face of repeated physical illnesses. In the more intensive interview, however, she broke down and wept, and said she felt life had been unjust and that she had been an unlucky person. It was the clinician's interpretation that she had long been depressed, and that the somatic illnesses had been a defense against the depression. She was a woman with a strong moral code and with tremendous pride; who went through life feeling that at no time must she reveal her disappointments.

2) There were a few cases where the respondent's life situation had changed drastically in the interval of time between the LSR and the LSR-C1 ratings. The respondent had suffered severe illness, or had been widowed, and the crisis had brought on a depression. In a few instances, however, the change had been for the better, as reflected in a higher LSR-C1 rating.

> One man, at the time of Interview 4, had just been widowed. A year earlier he had been retired from his job as a salesman, and he was worried about money as well as being depressed over the death of his wife. When seen by the clinical psychologist, however, he freely discussed the fact that two years earlier he had experienced a depression, but that now he was recovered. He had found a new

job selling, door to door, and he enjoyed what he called his "contacts with the public." He was living in a small apartment near his daughter's family, and he described with enthusiasm his grandchildren and the outings he had with them on weekends.

In general, the correlation of .64 between LSR and LSR-C1 was interpreted by the investigators as providing a satisfactory degree of validation for the LSR, given the various factors already mentioned: 1) the lapse of time between the two ratings; 2) the fact that a number of persons low on Life Satisfaction had dropped out of the study, thus narrowing the range of LSR scores for the 80 cases; 3) the fact that the LSR was based only on recorded interview data; the LSR-C1, on face-to-face interaction; 4) the greater depth of the clinical psychologist's interviews.

It is of some interest in this connection that the correlation between LSR and LSR-C1 was higher for the older members of the sample. For 30 cases aged 70 and over, r was .70; for the 50 cases aged 69 and below, r was .53. It may be that the aged individual has less of a tendency to give conforming or "normative" responses in the regular interview situation than does the younger individual. It might be, on the other hand, that in some manner of which the investigators were unaware, they devised interview questions and rating scales for Life Satisfaction that are more appropriate for the very old respondent than for the somewhat younger respondent and that, as a result, different judges were more likely to agree in their evaluations of persons over 70.[5]

THE LIFE SATISFACTION INDEXES

While the LSR is likely to prove useful in other studies where the amount of information about a respondent is less extensive than in the Kansas City Study, the LSR will require at least one long interview with the respondent. It may therefore be too cumbersome to be used on a large scale. Consequently, using the LSR as the validating criterion, the investigators devised a self-report instrument which would take only a few minutes to administer. Two such instruments were devised, to be used separately or together.

The derivation of the indexes. From the larger group on whom LSR scores were available, a sample of 60 cases were selected that represented the full range of age, sex, and social class. Of these 60 cases, the high scorers and the low scorers on LSR were used as criterion groups. A long list of items and open-ended questions from Interviews 1 through 4 were then studied to select those that differentiated these two groups. In addition to this item analysis, certain new items were written which reflected each of the five components of Life Satisfaction.

Two preliminary instruments then emerged. The first, called the Life Satisfaction

Index A (LSIA) consisted of 25 attitude items for which only an "agree" or "disagree" response is required. The second, the Life Satisfaction Index B (LSIB) consisted of 17 open-ended questions and check-list items, to be scored on a three-point scale.

These two instruments were then administered to 92 respondents along with Interview 6. (A number of respondents had already been interviewed in this sixth wave of field work by the time these instruments were ready. Because 92 seemed a large enough N for our purposes, no attempt was made to return and administer these instruments to those who had already been interviewed.)

When 60 of the 92 cases were in, preliminary computations were made. Scores on LSIA correlated .52 with LSR; scores on LSIB correlated .59 with LSR. These results seemed to warrant further efforts at refining and trimming the instruments. When all 92 cases were in, therefore, an item analysis was undertaken whereby each item of the Indexes was studied for the extent to which it differentiated the high and low LSR groups among the 92.

As a result of this analysis, five items of LSIA and seven items of LSIB were discarded. In their final form, these Indexes are given below, together with their scoring keys.

LIFE SATISFACTION INDEX A

Here are some statements about life in general that people feel differently about. Would you read each statement on the list, and if you agree with it, put a check mark in the space under "AGREE." If you do not agree with a statement, put a check mark in the space under "DISAGREE." If you are not sure one way or the other, put a check mark in the space under "?." PLEASE BE SURE TO ANSWER EVERY QUESTION ON THE LIST.

(Key: score 1 point for each response marked X.)

	AGREE	DISAGREE	?
1. As I grow older, things seem better than I thought they would be.	_x_	_____	_____
2. I have gotten more of the breaks in life than most of the people I know.	_x_	_____	_____
3. This is the dreariest time of my life.	_____	_x_	_____
4. I am just as happy as when I was younger.	_x_	_____	_____
5. My life could be happier than it is now.	_____	_x_	_____
6. These are the best years of my life.	_x_	_____	_____
7. Most of the things I do are boring or monotonous.	_____	_x_	_____
8. I expect some interesting and pleasant things to happen to me in the future.	_x_	_____	_____
9. The things I do are as interesting to me as they ever were.	_x_	_____	_____

(Key: score 1 point for each response marked X.)

	AGREE	DISAGREE	?
10. I feel old and somewhat tired.		_x_	
11. I feel my age, but it does not bother me.	_x_		
12. As I look back on my life, I am fairly well satisfied.	_x_		
13. I would not change my past life even if I could.	_x_		
14. Compared to other people my age, I've made a lot of foolish decisions in my life.		_x_	
15. Compared to other people my age, I make a good appearance.	_x_		
16. I have made plans for things I'll be doing a month or a year from now.	_x_		
17. When I think back over my life, I didn't get most of the important things I wanted.		_x_	
18. Compared to other people, I get down in the dumps too often.		_x_	
19. I've gotten pretty much what I expected out of life.	_x_		
20. In spite of what people say, the lot of the average man is getting worse, not better.		_x_	

Life Satisfaction Index B
(with scoring key)

Would you please comment freely in answer to the following questions?

1. What are the best things about being the age you are now?

　1___a positive answer

　0___nothing good about it

2. What do you think you will be doing five years from now? How do you expect things will be different from the way they are now, in your life?

　2___better, or no change

　1___contingent—"It depends"

　0___worse

3. What is the most important thing in your life right now?

　2___anything outside of self, or pleasant interpretation of future

　1___"Hanging on"; keeping health, or job

　0___getting out of present difficulty, or "nothing now," or reference to the past

4. How happy would you say you are right now, compared with the earlier periods in your life?

　2___this is the happiest time; all have been happy; or, hard to make a choice

　1___some decrease in recent years

　0___earlier periods were better, this is a bad time

5. Do you ever worry about your ability to do what people expect of you—to meet demands that people make on you?

  2___no

  1___qualified yes or no

  0___yes

6. If you could do anything you pleased, in what part of————would you most like to live?

  2___present location

  0___any other location

7. How often do you find yourself feeling lonely?

  2___never; hardly ever

  1___sometimes

  0___fairly often; very often

8. How often do you feel there is no point in living?

  2___never; hardly ever

  1___sometimes

  0___fairly often; very often

9. Do you wish you could see more of your close friends than you do, or would you like more time to yourself?

  2___O.K. as is

  0___wish could see more of friends

  0___wish more time to self

10. How much unhappiness would you say you find in your life today?

  2___almost none

  1___some

  0___a great deal

11. As you get older, would you say things seem to be better or worse than you thought they would be?

  2___better

  1___about as expected

  0___worse

12. How satisfied would you say you are with your way of life?

  2___very satisfied

  1___fairly satisfied

  0___not very satisfied

As shown in Table 23.3, the coefficient of correlation between the final form of LSIA and LSR was .55. The mean score on LSIA was 12.4, and the standard deviation, 4.4). The correlation between the final form of LSIB and LSR was .58. (The mean score for LSIB was 15.1, the standard deviation, 4.7). For combined scores on the two Indexes, the correlation with LSR was .61. (The mean for the combined scores was 27.6; the standard deviation, 6.7).

Table 23.3. Coefficients of Correlation for Various Measures of Life Satisfaction.

	1	2	3	4	5	6
1) LSR	—	.64 (80)	.55 (89)	.58 (89)	.39 (177)	−.07 (177)
2) LSR-C1		—	.39 (51)	.47 (52)	.21 (80)	.09 (80)
3) LSIA			—	.73 (91)	.36 (79)	−.10 (86)
4) LSIB				—	.41 (80)	−.07 (86)
5) Socioeconomic status					—	—[a]
6) Age						—

NOTE.—The number of cases on which the correlation is based is shown in parentheses.

[a] This relationship is zero by definition, since the sample was deliberately selected to control for age and socioeconomic status.

Validity of the indexes. As just described, the derivation and validation of the Indexes proceeded as a single set of operations; and the LSR cannot be regarded as an outside criterion. It is noteworthy, despite this fact, that the correlations between Index scores and LSR are only moderate in size.

It is true that the sixth wave of interviewing began about 14 months after the fourth wave, so that the interval of time between LSR and the two Index scores for the same respondent was, in some instances, as much as 18 to 20 months. This lapse of time probably operated to lower somewhat the congruence between the measures.

Nevertheless, the more important point is undoubtedly that direct self-reports, even though carefully measured, can be expected to agree only partially with the evaluations of life satisfaction made by an outside observer.

Certain additional steps were carried out in respect to validation. Scores on the two Indexes, for instance, were compared with LSR-C1 (the ratings made by the clinical psychologist). Of the 80 cases on whom LSR-C1 scores were available, only 51 had LSIA scores; 52, LSIB. For this relatively small number of cases, the correlations with LSR-C1 were .39 and .47 respectively. These correlations were probably lowered by the fact, already mentioned, that the respondents interviewed by the clinical psychologist constituted a superior group with regard to Life Satisfaction, thus providing a narrow range of scores on which to assess these correlations.

The question was also raised regarding the extent to which LSIA and LSIB were more reflective of Mood Tone alone than of the other components of LSR. Scores on each of the two Indexes correlated no higher, however, with ratings on Mood Tone alone than with LSR ratings.

Age differences. We have already commented on the fact that, in rating Life Satisfaction (LSR and LSR-C1), agreement between the clinical psychologist and the other raters was greater for the older respondents than for the younger. A parallel phenomenon was true with regard to scores on the two Indexes. For persons under

65, LSR-C1 correlated .05 with LSIA, and .32 with LSIB. For persons over 65, the correlations were .55 and .59 respectively. While the *N*s on which these correlations are based are small, the finding parallels the earlier one with regard to greater consistency between measures for respondents of advanced age.

The question once more arises as to whether this greater consistency is an artifact of the measures themselves, or whether it reflects an increasing consistency in psychological behavior in aged persons.

Whatever the explanation, a review of all the relationships here reported between LSR, LSR-C1, LSIA and LSIB seems to warrant the conclusion that the Indexes are more successful instruments for persons over 65 than for younger persons.

SUMMARY

This paper reports the derivation of a set of scales for rating Life Satisfaction, using data on 177 men and women aged 50 to 90. The ratings were based on lengthy interview material, and were validated against the judgments of a clinical psychologist who re-interviewed and rated 80 cases. The scales appear to be relatively satisfactory and may prove useful to other investigators interested in a measure of the psychological well-being of older people.

In addition, two short self-report Indexes of Life Satisfaction were devised and validated against the Life Satisfaction Ratings. While considerable effort was expended in refining these instruments, the effort was only moderately successful. If used with caution, the Indexes will perhaps be useful for certain group measurements of persons over 65.

The rating scales and the two Indexes are reproduced here.

Notes

1. The Kansas City Study of Adult Life is financed by Grant 3M9082 from the National Institute of Mental Health to the Committee on Human Development of the University of Chicago. It is under the supervision of William E. Henry (Principal Investigator), Robert J. Havighurst and Bernice L. Neugarten. The Study Director has been Elaine Cumming, and the Field Director, Lois R. Dean. The present Field Director is Wayne Wheeler.

2. The investigators were aided by Dr. Lois Dean, who was then Field Director of the Kansas City Study. Dr. Dean had interviewed certain of the respondents at great length and had made an analysis of morale in the aged. Several of the components later incorporated into the LSR stemmed from her analysis.

3. Other investigators may use the Scales and Indexes reproduced in this article without permission from either the present investigators or *The Journal of Gerontology.*

4. We are indebted to Mr. William Crotty for obtaining these 80 interviews and making the LSR-C1 ratings.

5. In this connection, it is not uncommon for psychiatrists to remark that a half-hour in-

terview is sufficient to evaluate the adjustment or mental health of an old person; but that it takes considerably more time to make a similar evaluation of a younger person.

References

Cavan, Ruth S., Burgess, E. W., Havighurst, R. J., & Goldhamer, H. *Personal adjustment in old age.* Chicago: Science Research Associates, 1949.

Cumming, Elaine, Dean, Lois R., & Newell, D. S. What is "morale"? A case history of a validity problem. *Hum. Organization,* 1958, 17 (2), 3–8.

Cumming, Elaine, & Henry, W. E. *Growing old.* New York: Basic Books, 1961.

Havighurst, R. J. The social competence of middle-aged people. *Genet. Psychol. Monogr.,* 1957, 56, 297–375.

Havighurst, R. J., & Albrecht, Ruth. *Older people.* New York: Longmans, Green, 1953.

Kuhlen, R. G. Age trends in adjustment during the adult years as reflected in happiness ratings. *Amer. J. Psychol.,* 1948, 3, 307. (Abstract)

Kutner, B., Fanshel, D., Togo, Alice M., & Langner, T. S. *Five hundred over sixty.* New York: Russell Sage Found., 1956.

Lebo, D. Some factors said to make for happiness in old age. *J. Clin. Psychol.,* 1953, 9, 385–390.

Morrison, D., & Kristjanson, G. A. *Personal adjustment among older persons.* Agricultural Experiment Station Technical Bulletin No. 21. Brookings: South Dakota State College, 1958.

Pollak, O. *Social adjustment in old age.* New York: Social Science Research Council, 1948.

Rose, A. M. Factors associated with life satisfaction of middle-class, middle-aged persons. *Marriage & Family Living,* 1955, 17, 15–19.

Rosow, I. Adjustment of the normal aged: concept and measurement. Paper given at the International Research Seminar on the Social and Psychological Aspects of Aging, Berkeley, August, 1960; to be published in R. H. Williams, J. E. Birren, Wilma Donahue, & C. Tibbitts (Eds.), *Psychological and social processes of aging: an international seminar.*

TWENTY-FOUR

Patterns of Aging: Past, Present, and Future

The topic of aging and longevity has become an "in" thing in the mind of the American public. The mass media have discovered it, as witnessed by the recent cover story in *Newsweek*, the article "Is Senility Inevitable?" in *Saturday Review*, the article in *National Geographic* about remote villages in Ecuador and the Soviet Union where persons are said to live to the advanced ages of 125 and 130, and by a rash of newspaper headlines such as "Scientists Seek the Key to Longevity."

This "discovery" by the mass media stems from the fact that a few biologists are predicting that we stand on the brink of a scientific breakthrough that will add from twenty-five to thirty years to the average life-span. Understandably enough, these claims have caught the attention of the science editors and reporters.

Aging is neither an "in" nor an "out" topic, but one that has always been here and is here to stay. Interest in aging constitutes the wave of the future as far as social scientists, social workers, and medical practitioners are concerned. The reason is obvious. Since the turn of the century, the total United States population has increased nearly threefold; but the number of persons aged 65 and over has increased almost sevenfold. In 1970, there were about 20 million older people in the United States; by the year 2000, there will be over 28 million. The latter figure is based on persons already alive and on projection of present death rates. Because it takes no account of possible medical advances or breakthroughs in biology, it is a conservative estimate.

The growing number of aged persons is not in itself a social problem if a social problem is defined as a state of affairs which needs correction. Few persons would seriously maintain that it is wrong to have many older people in the population or that remedial steps should be taken to pare down their numbers. On the contrary, nations prize longevity and count it an accomplishment, not a failure, that increasing numbers of men and women live to old age. The problem is the lack of preparation for the "sudden" appearance of large numbers of older people and the lag in adapting social institutions to their needs.

Based on the Sidney A. and Julia P. Teller Lecture presented at the School of Social Service Administration, University of Chicago, May 2, 1973. Reprinted by permission from *Social Service Review* 47, no. 4 (December 1973): 571–80; © 1973 by The University of Chicago; all rights reserved.

To be more exact, the social problems are of two types. First, a certain proportion of older people suffer from poverty, illness, and social isolation. These people, whom we call the needy aged, create acute problems in the field of social welfare. Second, broader problems arise from the need of all individuals in the society to adjust to the new rhythms of life that result from increased longevity. All members of society must adapt to new social phenomena such as multigenerational families, retirement communities, and leisure as a way of life. The second set of social problems, as much as the first, leads to the innumerable questions of social policy that arise as the whole society accommodates itself to the new age distribution.

How should society meet the needs of older people? How does their increasing presence affect other groups in the society? What new relationships are being generated between young and old? More and more people are asking these questions in their professional as well as their private lives. For example, biological and social scientists have evolved a new science, gerontology; the Gerontological Society, created in 1940, now has a membership of some twenty-two hundred scientists and professional workers; and there are now some fifty-five gerontological societies and organizations in different countries belonging to the International Gerontological Association. The medical profession is arguing over the creation of a new specialty, geriatrics. While the move toward developing new specialties is regarded by many physicians as a step backward rather than forward, nevertheless the first professor of geriatrics in an American university was appointed in 1973. Social workers are experimenting with new types of services for older clients; adult educators are seeking ways of serving the older as well as the younger adult; recreational workers are trying new programs for older people; a few law schools are turning attention to the special legal problems that arise. Business corporations are concerned with the nagging questions of arbitrary or flexible retirement, the vesting of pension funds, and ways of preparing middle-aged workers for the adjustments they will make after retirement. Commissions, committees, and public agencies are proliferating at local, state, and national levels to cope with problems of older people.

All this is leading to a different climate of awareness and to changing images of old age as one looks to the recent past, the present, and the future.

THE PAST

Negative stereotypes of old age were strongly entrenched in a society that prided itself on being youth oriented, future oriented, and oriented toward doing rather than being. Old people were usually regarded either as poor, isolated, sick, unhappy, desolate, and destitute—the "old age, it's a pity" perspective—or, on the contrary, as powerful, rigid, and reactionary. The first of these inaccurate images, usually inadvertently repeated through the mass media, probably originated from social workers, physicians, and psychiatrists who served the disadvantaged, the poor, and the physically and mentally ill—the needy aged.

In that climate—and, of course, it has not entirely disappeared—most people saw aging as alien to the self, and they tended to deny or repress the associated feelings of distaste and anxiety. In a society in which the frequency of death among the young had been drastically reduced by the conquest of infectious disease, and in which death had become increasingly associated only with old age, these pervasive attitudes, irrational and unconscious though they may have been, served also to maintain a psychological distance between young and old.

There was also the fact—and it is still true, although rapidly changing—that, in comparison with other age groups, the aged were economically and socially disadvantaged. They included a disproportionate number of foreign-born, unskilled men, who had come to the United States without much formal education, who had worked most of their lives at low-paying jobs, who had accumulated no savings through their lifetimes, and who were living in relative poverty after a life of hard work.

To reiterate, the image of old age was, from many different perspectives, a negative one.

THE PRESENT

Images are now changing in the direction of reality; and reality means diversity. Older people are coming to be recognized for what they are: namely, a very heterogeneous group. With 10 percent of our population now over sixty-five years old, and with nearly half that group now great-grandparents, a very large number of young people are interacting with older members of their own families. With people now becoming grandparents between the ages of forty and fifty, and with more than one-half of all women in that age group in the labor market, young children see their grandmothers going to work every day and their mothers staying at home with them. We are beginning to delineate a "young-old" population and to see it as different from the "old-old."

The image of the old man in the rocking chair is now matched by the white-haired man on the golf course. Even television images are beginning to change. "Maude" is a forceful, liberal, middle-aged woman; "A Touch of Grace" portrays an elderly widow being courted by an elderly man, with both persons portrayed sympathetically; "Sanford and Son" are a black father and his adult son who have a close and mutually supportive relationship in which the old father emerges as the wiser and more astute.

A different example of the changing images of aging appears in a newspaper picture a few months ago. Captioned "Happy Pappy," it showed Strom Thurmond, the sixty-nine-year-old senator from South Carolina, with his young wife, their eighteen-month-old daughter, and their newborn son. Only six years earlier, in contrast, a newspaper report of the marriage of Supreme Court Justice Douglas to a twenty-three-year-old coed had included some very venomous comments. Five members of the House of Representatives had introduced resolutions calling on the House Judiciary Committee to investigate the moral character of Douglas; one said he should be impeached. If the newspaper account of Justice Douglas's marriage appeared today, it would probably take a much less hostile form, judging at least from the story about Senator Thurmond.

There are other social forces at work which change the images and status of the aged. The so-called youth culture seems to be recognizing new affinities with older people. That culture forgoes instrumentality—work, achievement, production, competition—for expressivity. "Being" rather than "doing," it values reflection, relatedness, and freedom to express one's authentic self. Some young people regard these qualities as characteristic of older people, and they find allies in the old. Some young people perceive the old as alienated from the dominant culture and from the "establishment," although, of course, there is no evidence that a higher proportion of the old than of the young or middle-aged are in truth alienated.

It is possible, also, that sizable segments of the young are seeking to strengthen their ethnic identifications and turn to their grandparents for reaffirmation of ethnic cultural values.

FINDINGS OF SOCIAL SCIENTISTS

The findings of social researchers are contributing to the changing images of aging. For example, studies of large and representative samples of older people have shown that they are not isolated from other family members. While most older people prefer to live in their own households, they live near children or relatives and see other family members regularly. Overall, a higher proportion of old people who are sick live with their families than do those who are well. Old persons, contrary to the stereotype, are not dumped into mental hospitals or nursing homes or homes for the aged by cruel and indifferent children. Furthermore, older persons are not necessarily lonely or desolate if they live alone.

Few older persons ever show overt signs of mental deterioration or senility. Only a small proportion ever become mentally ill; for those who do, psychological and psychiatric treatment is by no means futile.

Retirement is neither good nor bad; some men and women want to keep on working, but more and more choose to retire early, as soon as they have enough income to live without working. The newest studies show that there is an increasing alienation from work and that increasing proportions of the population seem to value leisure more than work. Retired persons do not grow sick from idleness or from feelings of worthlessness. Three-fourths of the persons questioned in a recent national sample reported they were satisfied or very satisfied with their lives since retirement, a finding that is in line with earlier surveys. Most persons over sixty-five years old think of themselves as being in good health and act accordingly. On the average, after a short period of readjustment after retirement, men do not fail to establish meaningful patterns of activity.

Although there are some signs of increased age segregation, as in the retirement communities that have multiplied in the United States, this trend involves only a small proportion of older persons, and they constitute a self-selected group who appear to be exercising a larger rather than a smaller degree of freedom in choosing where to live. Furthermore, what studies are available indicate that in such communities, where the density of older people is relatively high, social interaction has increased. On the whole, it cannot be said that urban industrial societies preclude the social integration of the old.

In a series of studies of individuals between the ages of fifty and eighty carried out over a period of years at the University of Chicago, great diversity was found in the social and psychological patterns associated with successful aging. Various kinds of data were gathered on several hundred persons, all living "normal" lives in the community, including information on types of social interaction, role performance, investment in various roles and life-styles, degree of satisfaction with life—past and present—and personality type. It was found that as they grew older some persons sloughed off various role responsibilities with relative comfort and remained highly content with life. Others showed a drop in social role performance (e.g., as worker, friend, neighbor, or community participant), accompanied by a drop in life satisfaction. Still others, who had long shown low levels of activity accompanied by high satisfaction, changed relatively little as they aged.

For instance, in one group of seventy- to eighty-year-olds, eight different patterns of aging were empirically derived. They included the Reorganizers, Focused, Disengaged, Holding-on, Constricted, Succorance-seeking, Apathetic, and Disorganized. It appeared, furthermore, that the patterns reflected long-standing life-styles; within broad limits—given no major biological accidents or major social upheavals—an individual's pattern of aging was predictable from his way of life in middle age. In other words, aging is not a leveler of individual differences—until, perhaps, at the very end of life.

If there is no single social role pattern for the aged in 1970, the diversity is likely to become even greater in the future. With better health, more education, and more financial resources, older men and women will exercise—or at least will wish to exercise—greater freedom to choose the life-styles that suit them.

All this is not to deny the fact that, at the very end of life, there will continue to be a shorter or longer period of dependency, and that increased numbers of the very old will need care, either in their own homes or in special institutional settings. For persons who are terminally ill or incapacitated, it will be idle, in the future as in the present, to speak of meaningful social roles or of increased options in life-styles. For the advanced aged, the problems for the society will continue to be those of providing maximum social supports, the highest possible levels of care and comfort, the assurance of dignified death, and an increasing element of choice for the individual himself or for members of his family regarding how and when his life shall end.

QUESTIONS FOR THE FUTURE

In looking to the future, rather than focus upon the diversities among individual older people, one might well look at the society as an age-differentiated system and at relationships among age groups. In this context, questions about the prolongation of life can be reconsidered.

Generational conflict and relationships among age groups fluctuate according to historical, political, and economic factors. Under fortunate circumstances, an equilibrium is created whereby all age groups receive an appropriate share of the goods of the society and an appropriate place for their different values and world views. Under other circumstances, conflict may increase, as when the old, through some presumed historical failure, become "de-authorized" in the eyes of the young or when the young become overly advantaged in the eyes of the old. Whatever the forces of social change, the quality of life for all members of society and the social cohesion among age groups are influenced by the relative numbers of young, middle-aged, and old present at any given time.

If, indeed, the life-span is to be further extended, resulting in a dramatic increase in the numbers of the old, will industrialized societies be more ready for them than before and better prepared to meet their needs? Will the status of the aged become better or worse?

The answers are by no means clear. For one thing, generational conflicts may be increasing. If so, will they involve, on the one hand, the young and society at large and, on the other hand, the old and society at large? Is a new age divisiveness appearing and are there new antagonisms that can be called "ageism"? Is the world entering a period of social change in which, like earlier struggles for political and economic rights, there is now also a struggle for age rights? If so, will the struggle be joined not only by the young but also by the old who might otherwise become its victims?

Such questions have no easy answers, for the underlying social dynamics are complex. In the United States, for example, resentments against delinquency, student activism, the drug culture, and the counterculture often become uncritically fused into hostility toward the young as an age group. At the same time, there have been new attempts to integrate the young, as witnessed by the recent lowering of the voting age from twenty-one to eighteen. And there are the dramatic instances, such as the election of a youthful mayor or youth-controlled city councils of Berkeley or Madison, in which traditional age values were swept aside by other political considerations.

Anger toward the old may also be on the rise. In some instances, because a growing proportion of power positions in the judiciary, legislative, business, and professional arenas are occupied by older people, and because of seniority privileges among workers, the young and middle-aged become resentful. In other instances, as the number of the retired increases, the economic burden is perceived as falling more and more upon the middle-aged taxpayer.

These issues are not merely academic, as illustrated in recent journalistic accounts:

An editorial, syndicated in many metropolitan newspapers and occasioned by the 20 percent rise in social security benefits, was headlined, "Budget Story: Bonanza for Elderly." It said, "America's public resources are increasingly being mortgaged for the use of a single group within our country, the elderly." It went on to distort the situation by saying, "One-fourth of total federal spending is earmarked for only one-tenth of the population . . . clearly this trend cannot continue for long without causing a bitter political struggle between the generations."

Another example is an article that appeared two years ago in the *New Republic*. The author advocated that all persons lose the vote at retirement or age seventy, whichever was earlier. Reviewing changes that had occurred in his native California, he said: "We face a serious constitutional crisis—California faces civil war—if we continue to allow the old an unlimited franchise. There are simply too many senile voters and their number is growing."[1]

However, older people are becoming more vocal and more active in the political process. As they become accustomed to the politics of confrontation they see around them, they are beginning to voice their demands. For instance, appeals to "senior power" came into prominence in 1971 at the White House Conference on Aging. There are more frequent accounts of groups of older people picketing and protesting over such local issues as reduced bus fares or better housing projects. Whether such incidents remain isolated and insignificant or whether an activist politics of old age is developing in the United States is still a debatable question, but it would be a mistake to assume that what characterized the political position of older people in the past decades will be equally characteristic in the future.

Another factor to be considered is the creation of advocacy groups. The American Association for Retired Persons, which makes its appeal primarily to middle-class older persons, claims a membership of 3.5 million. The National Council of Senior Citizens, oriented primarily toward blue-collar groups, claims a membership of some 3 million. The Grey Panthers, smaller but more militant, is now organizing nationwide.

Given the complexity of such trends, we presently lack good indexes for assessing the degree of social cohesion among age groups. As we develop so-called intangible social indicators (e.g., of levels of life satisfaction or levels of alienation), social scientists might well build indexes relating to expectations and attitudes of various age groups toward each other and monitor those attitudes in assessing the social health of the nation.

Some observers take an optimistic and others a pessimistic view of the progress thus far achieved in equalizing the needs of various age groups. All in all, it is probably fair to say that, in at least the affluent societies of the world, the status of the aged has begun to show marked improvement during the past few decades. The question is whether such gains as have been achieved can be continued in the face of a dramatic extension of the life-span.

Two general strategies for lengthening the life-span are being pursued: the first is the continuing effort to conquer major diseases. It has been variously estimated that, if the problems of cancer and cardiovascular diseases are solved, life expectancy at age 65 will be increased five to ten years, thus redistributing deaths so that they will come more often at the end of the natural life-span, at about age eighty to ninety.

The second strategy involves altering intrinsic biological processes, which are presumed to underlie aging and which seem to proceed independent of disease processes. That is, the genetic and biochemical secrets of aging should be discovered, and then the biological clock that is presumably programmed into the human species could be altered. This second approach is directed at control of the rate of aging rather than control of disease. A few biologists claim that such a breakthrough will occur within the next twenty years and that it will result in an extension of the natural life-span itself, so that men will have not an additional ten, but an additional twenty-five years of life.

If the natural life-span were to be increased in the relatively short period of a few decades, the effects upon society might well be revolutionary. It is an unhappy fact that few social scientists, and even fewer biological scientists, have given serious thought to the social implications, although speculative essays and fictional accounts by journalists have begun to appear alongside more familiar forms of science fiction.

One writer has published a social satire describing a society in which people when they reach the age of fifty are automatically segregated from others, even from their own children, then painlessly put to death when they reach sixty-five. Another has described the solution in opposite terms in a society in which the old are in control, and the few young who are allowed to be born seek ways to accelerate their own aging in order to take their places in the society of elders. These parodies are examples of ageism carried to the extreme: in the first instance ageism is directed against the old; in the second, against the young.

There have been few serious attempts to extrapolate from available data in pondering such questions as these: Can an increased life-span be achieved without keeping marginally functioning individuals alive for extended periods? Would a major increase in the proportion of the aged so aggravate the problem of health, medical care, income, and housing that the old would be worse off than now? What would be the major deleterious and the major beneficial effects of a prolonged life-span upon the rest of society? Given present economic and governmental institutions, can even the affluent societies support greatly enlarged numbers of retired persons? Can income be divorced from work rapidly enough to balance off inequities among age groups? Will free time be truly free—that is, will it be desired by most individuals? Can it be supported by adequate income and by a reasonable level of good health? Will it be socially honored—that is, will the work ethic change rapidly enough into a leisure ethic? Or, if the employable age were to be extended, would the effects be deleterious upon both young and old? Could spectacular unemployment be avoided in either or both groups? Could technological obsolescence be overcome in the old? Could our educational systems be transformed rapidly enough into opportunity systems for self-fulfillment for the middle-aged and old as well as for the young? Will our social and humanistic and ethical values accommodate to a drastically altered age distribution? What will be the effects upon successive groups of young, and what will be the eventual effects upon their old age?

Lest we be overwhelmed by unanswerable questions, it should be said that, in contrast with those biologists whose statements make newspaper headlines, most biologists take a more conservative view of the future and believe that dramatically lengthened life-spans are still far off.

But whether or not a breakthrough is imminent, we are nevertheless already witnessing transformations in the age distribution of the society, in which the number of older people is rapidly increasing. And we can be quite sure that medical advances will continue to prolong life, even if we are far from solving the biochemical or genetic secrets of aging. Many gerontologists believe that if average life expectancy is increased by only five more years—to say nothing of twenty-five years—the effects upon our present economic and welfare institutions will be profound.

Man's desire for longevity can now be whetted by the findings of social scientists, such as those already mentioned. If—as now appears true—the institutional arrangements of industrialized societies do not inevitably lead to the social isolation of the old, if—as also appears true—man does not lose his ability to learn as he grows old, and if there is no universal set of personality changes that lead inevitably to disengagement from society, then the old person stands to benefit as much from social advances as does the young person.

What, then, will be the new social and ethical pressures for prolonging life? What will be the risks of a prolonged life-span, not only to older people themselves, but to the society as a whole? How can these risks be weighed against the benefits? How can social values be weighed against economic values, and how can a new priority of social values be effected?

These are questions that will inevitably preoccupy us more and more over the next decades. In pursuing our research programs and our action programs and in working out broad-scale social solutions, the social scientist will join with the biological scientist, the policy maker, the jurist, the ethicist, and the social worker. We will need, as never before, the insights and the experience and the social philosophy of the profession of social work.

Notes

1. Steward, Douglas J. "The Lesson of California: Disfranchise the Old." *New Republic* (August 29, 1970).

TWENTY-FIVE

Successful Aging in 1970 and 1990

It is the stated goal of this conference to hasten the day when successful aging becomes a commonplace in America, rather than a rarity. From my own perspective, that day has already arrived, even though it has gone largely unnoticed. All too many Americans are still under the misapprehension that aging is an unmitigated process of decline, and that old age can be summed up by the words illness, poverty, isolation, desolation, and depression.

These views of old age, all too often reinforced through the mass media, are one-sided. They are based largely upon the observations of social workers who serve the poor and the lonely, and the observations of physicians who serve the physically and mentally ill. They do not reflect the findings of social scientists who have studied large representative samples of older people, and they do not reflect the attitudes of most older people themselves.

Our task at this conference might therefore be two-fold: to present to the public a more accurate and well-rounded picture of aging, and to ask how we can hasten the present trends and produce a successful old age not only for most people, but for all people.

WHAT IS SUCCESSFUL AGING?

The question is, first, how to define successful aging. What frame of reference shall we use?

Shall we take the psychiatrist's perspective? Shall we look at levels of stress, presuming that stress must be accompanied by anxiety, depression, and ill health? Shall we look at scores on symptom check-lists that purport to measure mental health?

Shall we take the social psychologist's perspective, and ask to what extent the aging individual remains socially engaged, performing the same range of social roles that were characteristic of him in his middle age? Shall we accept the prevailing paradox that the successful ager is he who does not age at all?

Reprinted by permission from *Successful Aging: A Conference Report,* edited by E. Pfeiffer (Durham, NC: Duke University Press, 1974): 12–18.

Should we take the perspective of family members? And call him successful who becomes neither a financial nor emotional burden, but who maintains mutually rewarding relationships with his children and his children's children?

Shall we adopt the philosopher's or the theologian's perspective? That the successful ager is the man who faces death with relative equanimity? He who has come to terms with the finiteness of life, who has accepted or worked out for himself an explanation of the meaning of life and of his relation to his God or to his version of the unknown?

Or shall we take a closely-related perspective that is identified with Erikson—namely, that a successful ager has achieved what can be called integrity? The acceptance that one's life has not only been meaningful, but that the course of one's life could not have been otherwise? The readiness to take responsibility for what one's life has been, and to become reconciled to one's past as well as to one's future?

The point, obviously enough, is that we live in a world of pluralistic values; and successful aging is in the eye of the beholder.

My colleagues and I at the University of Chicago, who have for many years been studying the social and psychological changes in people as they move from middle age through old age, have made our own value decision in attempting to use the perspective of the individual himself.

We constructed a measure of life-satisfaction based upon five components. An individual is rated high to the extent that he (1) takes pleasure from whatever round of activities that constitute his everyday life—the person who enjoys sitting at home watching television can rate as high as the one who enjoys his work as a lawyer; (2) regards his life as meaningful and accepts responsibility for what his life has been; (3) feels he has succeeded in achieving his major life goals; (4) holds a positive self-image and regards himself as a worthwhile person, no matter what his present weaknesses may be; and (5) maintains optimistic attitudes and moods.

We have found that life satisfaction is not age-related; that it does not necessarily drop off as people grow older. By and large, as many 70-year-olds as 50-year-olds rate high on this measure; and the typical 50- or 60- or 70-year-old reports himself relatively content with his life. A sizable proportion say the present is the best time of their lives. It may be argued, of course, that a person's evaluations are colored by his expectations, and that many old persons hold too low expectations and settle for too little. But if we are to take the person's own evaluations, then we have no right to quarrel with his criteria. (Neither is there evidence that older persons go out of their way more than younger people to make a good impression upon the interviewer, or to give the "socially desirable" rather than an honest report of their feelings about life.)

We are impressed also, after our many years of research, with the wide range of social and psychological patterns associated with high levels of life satisfaction. Some persons we call reorganizers, persons who remain engaged in a wide variety of roles and activities or who substitute new activities for lost ones; others are the focussed, who choose to concentrate on one or two activities which give them pleasure and involvement; others are the disengaged, persons who move voluntarily away from earlier work and family and community commitments and choose the rocking-chair approach to old age. Some older people are satisfied with life only as long as they remain in the labor force; others, only when they retire; some, so long as they can maintain a dependent relationship with at least one person; others when they become free from earlier emotional ties they regard as entanglements. And so on. To give a slight twist to the aphorism, what is one old man's meat is another old man's poison.

Given relatively good health and given at least modest levels of income, then it is the variations rather than the uniformities among older people that are impressive; and the wide range of life styles that accompany satisfaction with life. There is no single pattern of social or psychological change that characterizes people as they move from middle to old age; and there is no single formula which spells satisfaction or success.

From this perspective, if successful aging is to occur for ever-increasing proportions of people, our society will need to provide ever-increasing options. In 1970, there remain sizable groups of older persons in America for whom poor health and inadequate income are the major obstacles. There are also sizable groups whose lives represent the accumulation of past discriminations based on race, ethnicity, or sex, persons for whom new freedoms in old age are more difficult to create. In both instances, however, the social policies to be followed are relatively clear, even though it may appear to many of us that we are moving at too slow a pace.

Thinking about where we are going in the 1970s has led some of us at Chicago to think about the future of older people in America. We have begun to gather data about persons who are presently middle-aged; to ask what kinds of old people they will be, what they will want from life by the year 1990, and how the society should prepare to meet those needs.

A PROLONGED LIFE SPAN?

We have been intrigued by some of the forecasts appearing in the press which quote a few eminent biologists who say the world now stands on the verge of a scientific breakthrough that will mean a dramatic prolongation of the human lifespan. If such a breakthrough occurs, the numbers of aged persons might mushroom, with a dramatic change in the age distribution of the society and perhaps a dramatic change in the possibilities for meeting the needs of older people.

How likely is it that such a breakthrough will occur?

To pursue this question, it should be noted that there are two general strategies for lengthening the life-span. The first is the continuing effort to conquer disease. If we could wipe out deaths from cardiovascular disease and malignancies, it has been variously estimated that the gain would be somewhere from 5 to 10 years at age 65. Thus deaths would be redistributed so that by occurring at 80 or 90 they would occur closer to the end of the natural life-span.

All the advances in medical care and in public health measures over the past century have contributed to this method of lengthening life—they have contributed to a decreased vulnerability to disease.

The second strategy is one of altering the intrinsic biological processes which are presumed to underlie aging and which seem to proceed independently from disease processes—that is, to discover the genetic and biochemical secrets of aging, to delineate the factors that underlie the rate of aging, then to alter the biological clock that is presumably programmed into the human species. The second approach is directed at *rate* control, rather than disease control. It is a discovery of this second type that a few biologists are predicting will occur within the next 20 years and that will result in an extension of the life-span by some 20 to 25 years.

It is obvious why these claims have caught the attention of newspaper reporters.

Our group in Chicago has been attempting to verify these claims, and we have therefore begun to make inquiries of leading biological and bio-medical researchers, asking if, in their opinion, the state of biological knowledge and biological technology is so advanced that an extension of the life-span itself is a likely occurrence. Of the dozen researchers who have thus far responded, there is agreement that no major new anti-aging treatment is yet on the horizon, nor is one likely to appear within the next twenty years that can produce a dramatic increase in the numbers of older persons. We expect to pursue these inquiries further, but we are meanwhile impressed with the consistency of these responses.

A number of our respondents have also volunteered the comment, "So much the better!" For IF a rate-retarding treatment were discovered; and IF it were administered over a major portion of the life-span; and IF a decrease in the rate of aging were to be achieved without an accompanying decrease in the vulnerability to disease, the effects on the society would be grossly detrimental. The reason is that a decrease in rate of aging alone would have the effect of stretching out the entire life span. The individual would undergo a prolonged senescence as part of his prolonged life; and the added length of life would probably be more a burden than a blessing.

The negative effects upon the society at large would also include a higher proportion of dependent to independent persons, and a higher proportion of sick and deteriorated.

OLDER PERSONS IN 1990

In giving up the science fiction approach to the prolongation of life, what will be the numbers of older people in 1990, and what will be their likely characteristics? According to the census, persons aged 65 and over will number 28 million as compared with the present 20 million; and they will constitute 10 to 11% of the population as compared with the present 10%. Not a dramatic difference. Beginning in the year 2010, however, there will be a very sharp increase in the numbers of older people because of the large numbers who are presently young. Indeed by the year 2020 the numbers of older persons are expected to be double the present numbers.

Let us consider a few other projections:

An increasing proportion of persons 65+ will be women, with the difference in numbers particularly marked in those aged 75+, where the ratio of men to women is expected to drop to 58 to 100. . . . Over half of all older women will be widows. . . . Labor force participation will continue to go down, with one of 5 men and one of 10 women aged 65+ in the labor force, and with a large proportion of both sexes employed only part-time. . . . Nearly 50% of those aged 65+ will be high school graduates (compared to 28% in 1970). . . . An increasing proportion will be living in the "rings" of metropolitan areas, with only half as many living in central cities. . . . Older people will be increasingly overrepresented in the voting electorate. . . . Assuming a constant rate of disease incidence, 2 of 5 will experience some limitation of activity due to chronic physical or mental conditions. . . .

Such projections are for the total population of persons 65+, and thus obscure the very wide differences that already exist between various age subgroups, various income groups, ethnic groups, and so on, to say nothing of the differences in life styles that exist within any subgroup.

It is important also to consider that persons who will be old in 1990 will have different attitudes from those of the present older population. They have experienced major political and cultural movements; for example, the challenge to government leaders over the Vietnam war, the civil rights movement, the women's liberation movement, the attack upon corporate enterprise represented by the consumer movement, and the challenge to such institutions as the public school system.

Older persons in 1990 will exhibit different behaviors, for they have experienced both the benefits and the problems of the present age. New devices to enhance mobility, new modes of entertainment and self-expression, new agents for reducing pain, all have their effects upon behavioral characteristics, just as do overcrowded cities, increased crime, and higher degrees of air pollution.

Along with various goods and bads has come an important change in ideology regarding the individual's relation to the state. Persons increasingly look to government, whether federal or local, to improve the quality of their lives and to protect them from harm. This attitudinal set, combined with higher educational and occupational levels in the older generations of 1990 to 2000 is likely to exert a potent influence upon government. In the future, more than in the present, older persons will be inclined not only to wield their influence through direct political action, but to make demands of both the public and private sectors to bring benefits in line with their raised expectations.

Older persons in 1990 will exhibit a wider range of life patterns with regard to the three related areas of work, education, and leisure. Some will opt for early retirement; others will want to continue working beyond age 65; others will want to undertake new work careers at one or more times after age 40. The demand for continuing education is likely to be magnified, and for varied types of education. The extent to which options will increase will depend not only upon the state of the economy, but upon other factors: the extent to which the present trend becomes accelerated toward separating income from work; how rapidly the work ethic is replaced by a leisure ethic; and which age groups will be defined in 1990 as the expendable members of the labor force.

As compared to 1970, when attention must still be focussed upon meeting the basic needs of disadvantaged groups of older persons, by 1990 it is likely that attention will shift increasingly to the needs of self-enhancement and for social relatedness. Every person, regardless of age, is concerned with his "self": and he seeks to develop his capabilities and to maximize his personal gratifications. At the same time, he also seeks avenues for social interaction and for making social contributions as ways of adding to a sense of self-worth.

The Young-Old and the Old-Old

In addition to these more general trends, by 1990 it is likely that at least two populations of older persons will become more clearly delineated. Trends toward early retirement for both men and women, on the one hand, and increased life expectancy, on the other, will lengthen the post-retirement period. We are likely to see a "young old" group, the group that is roughly 55 to 74, and an "old old" group, aged 75 and over, each with a somewhat different set of needs.

The majority of the "young old" are likely to be healthy and relatively vigorous. They will probably develop new needs with regard to the meaningful use of time. Some will have retired involuntarily; they will want new work options, or education which will facilitate their re-entry into the labor force. A larger proportion will have retired voluntarily, and will want opportunities for cultural enrichment, for local political involvement, and for other types of community participation.

The needs of the "young old" in housing, location, and transportation will be increasingly affected by the decisions they make with regard to the use of leisure time.

The large majority will be living independently, apart from children and other relatives, and this fact, combined with the desire to find interesting things to do, will lead them to seek environments which will maximize options for meaningful pursuits. The needs for counseling services are likely to become increasingly varied.

It can be anticipated also that with improved economic status and health care, the "young old" will maintain ties to other family members that are primarily affectional in nature. The tradition of turning to family members in times of crisis will probably continue, although it will obviously be affected by the extent to which other supportive systems are established. Some observers predict that as the more instrumental aspects of life (education, income maintenance, health care) are increasingly shifted to other social institutions, the family may become more, rather than less, important within the expressive aspects of life—for instance, in providing lasting emotional ties, a sense of identity, and a sense of self-worth.

With large numbers who will be vigorous, educated, politically active, and who will have the rising expectations mentioned above, the "young old" are likely to become advocates of an "age-irrelevant" society: that is, one in which arbitrary constraints based on chronological age are removed, a society in which every individual has opportunities consonant with his needs, desires, and abilities, whether he is young or old.

For the "old old," meaningful ways of spending time, and needs for special housing and transportation will depend in large measure upon health status. The majority will probably live independently, but many will need supportive social services, new forms of home health services, and special features in the physical environment to enable them to function as fully as possible. Some older persons will wish to move to different quarters without leaving their communities; some will wish to remain in their same homes; some will wish to move to age-segregated housing; and some will wish to form group households with non-family members.

As the probability of illness increases, the "old old" will need a range of restorative health services, as well as a range of social services designed to prevent unnecessary decline in feelings of dignity and worth. Opportunities for social interaction and social contribution will continue to be important.

The family will probably play a larger role in seeing that aged persons receive the increased support they need. More "young old" persons will be involved in caring for an "old old" parent. Families will probably want more choices in the setting and types of care available for a family member whose health is declining. Such institutions as nursing homes will continue to be necessary, but more families may seek ways of maintaining an older person at home, either in his separate household or in the child's household.

It is also likely that more choices will exist for the family of the person who is dying. If re-education of the society can be accomplished regarding the individual's right to die with dignity, more families may become active in seeing to it that their oldest members are provided with the best possible death rather than with the latest possible death.

These comments represent only a few predictions of the future. Whatever the shape of things to come, the goals will probably remain the same; to be the "enabling society" for older people, and to help produce successful aging for everybody. In short, we shall want to help old people, like young people, do their own thing.

PART FOUR

Social Policy Issues

The Prescience and Influence of Bernice Neugarten

Robert H. Binstock

Bernice Neugarten has been especially prescient and influential in the realm of social policy and aging. Through her work on aging and age relations, she has identified and set forth innovative concepts and concerns about policy that have shaped the agendas of leaders in the worlds of ideas and action.

THE YOUNG-OLD AND THE OLD-OLD

The foundation for Neugarten's intellectual leadership in the arena of social policy issues was expressed in "Age Groups in American Society and the Rise of the Young-Old," which appears in part 1 of this volume. In this seminal article she began to question the soundness of public policies that provide benefits and protection to older people primarily on the basis of old-age criteria, without much reference to the considerable diversity in the economic status, health status, and other characteristics of the older population. She did so by presenting data that illustrated substantial aggregate differences between the characteristics of Americans aged 65 to 74, whom she termed the "young-old," and those aged 75 and older, the "old-old."

Ironically, Neugarten's attempt to break down stereotypes of older people became misused by others in the field of aging to engender an age-based stratification of old-age stereotypes, undoubtedly because she had used two age groupings to illustrate her basic point about the diversity of older people. It soon became a widespread practice to label persons aged 65 to 74 as the "young-old," and to perceive all persons in this age group as healthy and/or capable of earning income. If retired, people in this age range have been seen as a rich reservoir of resources to be drawn upon for providing unpaid social and health services and for fulfilling a variety of other community roles. In contrast, persons aged 75 and older became commonly termed the "old-old" and stereotyped as poor and frail.

Through her leadership as a member of the presidentially appointed Federal Council on Aging in the late 1970s, Neugarten helped to rectify this distortion. The

Robert H. Binstock is professor of Aging, Health, and Society at the School of Medicine, Case Western Reserve University.

Council issued a report prior to the White House Conference on Aging of 1981 that
reiterated her basic point, namely that most older Americans are competent, yet
many are frail and vulnerable and need a range of supportive and restorative services.
Neugarten's paper "Family and Community Support Systems," which appears in the
pages that follow, fleshes out this fundamental observation very well. Among other
things she observes that old age itself is not a parameter that defines a problem group
in modern American society because it is increasingly a poor indicator of an older
person's abilities, behaviors, and needs. Neugarten also sets forth an extensive agenda
of broad public policy goals that gives attention both to the competent and to the
frail and vulnerable within the older population.

AGE OR NEED ENTITLEMENT?

Bernice Neugarten's sharpest challenge to public policies that primarily use old age
as a marker for determining a person's need for governmental assistance was expressed in her paper "Policy for the 1980s: Age or Need Entitlement?" Building on
her observations that societal age norms and characteristics were changing, she
argued:

> . . . In a society in which age is becoming increasingly irrelevant as a predictor of
> lifestyle or as a predictor of need, policies and programs formulated on the basis
> of age are falling increasingly wide of the mark. . . . Income and health care and
> housing and other goods and services should be provided, not according to age,
> but according to relative need.

She recognized the political complexities of designing, administering, and politically sustaining massive public transfer programs based on the relative needs of individual citizens. So, in a subsequent book (Neugarten, 1982), she assembled a
number of policy analysts and scholars to address these complexities.

Shortly thereafter, Congress began a process of implementing the types of
changes that Neugarten had been suggesting. Through a new legislative trend,
which has continued into the mid-1990s, policies on aging have been reformed to
reflect the diverse economic and social characteristics of older persons.

The Social Security Reform Act of 1983 started this trend by taxing Social Security benefits for the first time, making 50% of benefits subject to taxation for individuals with incomes exceeding $25,000 and married couples over $32,000. The
Tax Reform Act of 1986, even as it eliminated the extra personal exemption that had
been available to all persons 65 years and older when filing their federal income tax
returns, provided new tax credits to very low-income older persons on a sliding scale.
The Older Americans Act programs of supportive and social services, for which all
persons aged 60 and older are eligible, have been gradually targeted by Congress to
low-income and minority older persons. The Qualified Medicare Beneficiary pro-

gram established in 1988 requires that Medicaid pay deductibles, co-payments, and Part B premiums for Medicare enrollees who have incomes that are below specific poverty guidelines.

Legislation in the 1990s has continued to apply the principle of sensitivity to economic status in setting standards for responsibilities and benefits in old-age programs. The payroll income ceiling on the Medicare portion of the Federal Insurance Contributions Act (FICA) payroll tax has been eliminated. And the Omnibus Budget Reconciliation Act (OBRA) of 1993 continued this tendency by subjecting 85% of Social Security benefits to taxation for individuals with incomes over $34,000 and couples over $44,000. Many proposals for continuing this trend in policies on aging are under active consideration.

AGE DIVISIVENESS IN POLITICS

Neugarten's prescience is further manifested in "New Perspectives on Aging and Social Policy," originally delivered as the Leon and Josephine Winkelman Lecture at the University of Michigan in 1982. In this work she anticipates the emergence of the so-called "intergenerational equity" construct. After beautifully integrating her earlier observations, she observes that, "the issue that underlies all the others and that will determine all the outcomes is how to maintain an age-integrated society and to guard against age divisiveness." She specifically observes that the political activities of aging advocacy groups may be contributing to a politics of age.

Three years later an organization called Americans for Generational Equity was established in Washington. It publicized the large amount of public funds dedicated to programs on aging (at that time, more than one-quarter of the federal budget), and was "dedicated to forging a coalition to protect the future of young Americans" (*Generational Journal,* 1989). Shortly afterwards, the epithet "greedy geezers" was coined (Farlie, 1988) to describe older Americans and their political activities, and it became commonly used in descriptions of budgetary politics. By the end of the decade the themes of age divisiveness and intergenerational equity had been adopted by the media, academics, and elite sectors of American society as routine perspectives for describing many social policy issues. As the president of the prestigious American Association of Universities asserted: "The shape of the domestic federal budget inescapably pits programs for the retired against every other social purpose dependent on federal funds, in the present and the future" (Rosenzweig, 1990, p. 6).

SOCIAL ETHICS IN AN AGING SOCIETY

Another area of social policy inquiry in which Neugarten has been a pioneer is aging and social ethics. In the mid-1970s she obtained funding from the National Science Foundation to explore a broad range of such issues through a working group at the University of Chicago. Based on these efforts she and her colleague Robert J. Havighurst published two important monographs, *Social Policy, Social Ethics, and the Aging Society* (Neugarten and Havighurst, 1976), and *Extending the Human Life Span: Social Policy and Social Ethics* (Neugarten and Havighurst, 1977). This strand of her work is expressed in "Social Implications of Life Extension," a paper she presented in 1978 at the 11th International Congress of Gerontology in Tokyo. In it she distinguishes between (1) life-extension achieved through disease control, and (2) life-extension through the possibility that the biological clock of the human species could be altered. She sets forth an impressive agenda of ethical and societal challenges that are raised by these two modes of life extension, an agenda which is actively pursued today by scores of ethicists.

Neugarten herself followed through on many of these issues in collaboration with a physician colleague, Christine K. Cassel. In "The Goals of Medicine in an Aging Society," she and Cassel developed a framework for considering how complex questions about appropriate medical care for patients of advanced age could be addressed most rationally, most effectively, and most humanely. In the process they reject the notion that old-age–based rationing of medical care would be either necessary or desirable in the context of rapidly escalating health care costs for an ever-growing population of older people. Constructively, they outline a model of medicine for the aging society that combines the best of the heroic and the humanistic traditions of the medical profession.

The selections in this part of the volume necessarily represent only a small portion of the corpus of Neugarten's publications in the area of social policy issues. Nonetheless, they are sufficient to convey the superlative quality and importance of her contributions to the efforts of societies to deal with the changing nature of old age and the implications of aging populations.

References

Farlie, H. (1988). Talkin' 'bout My Generation. *New Republic,* Vol. 198, no. 13, pp. 19–22.

Generational Journal (1989). Untitled statement of organizational purpose and tax status of Americans for Generational Equity, *1*(4), unnumbered page following 103.

Neugarten, B. L. (ed.) (1982). *Age or need? Public policies for older people.* Beverly Hills, CA: Sage Publications.

Neugarten, B. L., and Havighurst, R. J. (1976). *Social policy, social ethics, and the aging society.* Washington, D.C.: U.S. Government Printing Office.

Neugarten, B. L., and Havighurst, R. J. (1977). *Extending the human life span: Social policy and social ethics.* Washington, D.C.: U.S. Government Printing Office.

Rosenzweig, R. M. (1990). Address to the President's Opening Session, 43rd Annual Scientific Meeting, the Gerontological Society of America. Boston: November 16.

TWENTY-SIX

Social Implications of Life Extension

The "aging society" is appearing in all parts of the world. In the decade 1970 to 1980 the rate of increase of persons over 65 will everywhere be greater than the increase in the total population, and greater than the increase in any other age group.

This is related not to one but to two trends: fertility and mortality. While it has been the drop in fertility which has thus far had the greatest influence upon the proportion of old people in given societies, it is also true that mortality rates have dropped and average life expectancy has increased dramatically, especially in the industrialized societies.

While the figures vary by country and by region of the world, a over-simplified way of summing them up is that in the most industrialized countries of North America and Europe, average life expectancy at birth is now over 70; while in the less developed regions, it is now approaching 60. In Africa, it is about 45; in Asia, it varies in the 50s—with the notable exception of Japan, where it is now in the 70s and is second highest in the world, second only to Sweden; in Latin America, it is in the 60s; and in Europe and North America, it is in the 70s.

As stated in the United Nations report of 1975, it is anticipated that life expectancy will increase for the more developed regions of the world by about two years between now and the year 2000, moving from 71 to 73; but for the less developed regions, it will increase some 13 years, moving from 52 to 65. There is the possibility (in the minds of some gerontologists, the probability) that average life expectancy in countries like the United States will rise another five years rather than two years. If these trends become reality, they will force reconsiderations of a wide range of social and economic policies at national levels. Policy decisions will become increasingly difficult as they come to involve the equitable distribution of resources to the old and to the young.

Future gains in life expectancy are likely to produce quite different outcomes in the more industrialized as compared to the less industrialized nations. Gains have thus far been due primarily to the conquest of infectious diseases with the gains

Paper presented at a symposium entitled "Extending the Human Lifespan," 11th International Congress of Gerontology, Tokyo, Japan, August 1978.

spread relatively evenly across the population. More people have been reaching old age. But in the industrialized countries, future gains will be different because mortality rates cannot be much improved for persons under age 50. The new gains must therefore be of the kind that will affect primarily the older part of the population— that is, by the conquest of chronic disease and by the identification and amelioration of those conditions, internal and external to the human organism, that are specially lethal to older people. This means that new gains in life expectancy in industrialized countries will affect people *after* they reach old age. Again, in oversimplified terms, as the less developed countries follow the more developed countries with regard to medical practices, public health and health education, more people there will reach old age, but in the developed counties, where very high proportions already reach old age, the future will mean a greater extension of old age itself.

Increasing longevity is affecting all our social institutions in all regions of the world. Everywhere the young and the old are adapting to the new rhythms of life: to changing perceptions of the life span, to changing age norms, to new social phenomena such as multigenerational families, retirement, increased leisure, changing health status, and to the new opportunities and new problems of adaptation that accompany a long life. And for the society at large innumerable policy questions arise as the whole social fabric accommodates itself to the changing age distribution.

The full social implications of the aging society need not be elaborated here, but in mentioning only a few such implications my purpose is to remind us that the questions are of two types: first, the ways in which underlying social trends are affecting the numbers and the lives of older persons; but second also, the ways in which the growing numbers of older persons are affecting the lives of all members of society.

Among the accompaniments of increased longevity, there is first the unequal life expectancy of men and women, with the difference much more marked in industrialized than in non-industrialized societies. (In the developed regions of the world, it is projected that men will pull somewhat ahead of their present proportions by the year 2000, but the differential in favor of women is very substantial and will remain so. In developed countries, of all people over 60, some 40 percent are men and 60 percent are women. In the less developed countries, the sex difference is much less: it is about 48 percent men, and 52 percent women.)

There is, therefore, the increased prospect of widowhood for women, and in many countries, the economic deprivation that accompanies it.

There is, at the same time, the multigenerational family with its new gratifications but also its new problems, particularly the one I have called "parent-caring." It appears that the planning for care of an aged parent—whether that care is given directly or indirectly—is becoming part of the psychological baggage that adults now carry about with them, at least in my own country, and it is becoming a major source of life stress.

There are changing health needs of the population, with growth in chronic illness and long-term disability, a trend which may not be alleviated with future life extension. (It is not clear that present gains have shortened the terminal period of illness and disability. Medical advances may be lengthening that terminal period.)

There are the issues of retirement, both for the individual and for the society: provision of meaningful roles and economic security for retirees, and at the same time, programs of social security and pension systems that will be in keeping with manpower needs and economic resources.

There are the problems of providing social services and health services and preventive services. . . . and so on. The litany is a long one.

The social status and the economic status of the old vary enormously in different regions of the world. In some societies the old maintain their traditional economic, political and religious positions, and the infirm aged are cared for within the family system. In other societies, with increasing urbanization and industrialization, social status of the old may be declining at the same time that their economic status and health status are improving. In some countries the aging society has brought increasing proportions of needy aged, those who require special services to overcome poverty, illness, and isolation, while in other countries the aging society has brought decreasing proportions of needy aged.

In industrialized and more affluent counties two different sets of issues are arising: The "young-old" are healthy and vigorous retirees in their 60s and 70s who seek meaningful ways to use their time, and who, while they represent an under-utilized resource to the society, are in some ways becoming the new leisure class of the world. The "old-old" are people in their 80s and 90s, a majority of whom need supportive and restorative services. Successive cohorts who reach old age in the 1980s and 1990s in countries like my own will have higher levels of education and higher expectations. The young-old will want a wide range of options and life-styles and they will advocate an age-irrelevant society, one where arbitrary constraints based on age are removed. The old-old will want improved services and special features in the physical and social environment aimed at slowing physical and mental deterioration.

In the developing and less affluent countries some of these same issues will arise, but attention will presumably be focussed more upon problems of economic support and health services for the old, and upon the effects of urbanization and industrialization on changing family patterns and cultural values.

Altogether, the social implications of life extension have been both good and bad, and increased longevity has cut both ways. The period of life in which people remain physically and intellectually vigorous has thus far been lengthening. At the same time it is producing a larger proportion of ill and deteriorated persons of advanced old age.

From another perspective, we should ask what kind of world will it be, generally speaking, in the next few decades? A wide range of predictions have been put forth. Some observers say that man will solve the problems of overpopulation, food and energy shortages, inflation, environmental pollution, and the threat of nuclear destruction, and that he will do so largely by the continued growth of science and technology. Others say that, because of the very growth of science and technology, the problems are now so vast that man's efforts are doomed to failure. In the latter view, economic and political crises will escalate, genuine economic decline will occur, and social disorganization will follow. If man survives at all, a century from now he will move from an industrialized to a deindustrialized society.

A different view is one of an "equilibrium" society in which new sources of energy will replace petroleum, pollution will be partially controlled, and large-scale war will be avoided. While the picture will be different in different parts of the world, especially in the developing nations, overall it will be a world of dynamic equilibrium, not growing, not diminishing. The tasks for the more affluent nations will be to achieve a stable state of population and production, and then to cooperate with poorer nations in helping them achieve similar goals.

The position of the aged would be very different in these various worlds. In one instance, there would be increasing alienation, conflicts between age groups as well as between other groups, and the old-old would be greatly disadvantaged, even expendable. In another instance, older persons would get a fair share of whatever goods would be produced, for on the one hand their labor would be needed, and on the other hand, the presence of many frail elderly would come increasingly to symbolize man's most humane achievements.

Given these considerations, what, then, is to be said about further extension of the human life span? Should we do all we can to extend the life span in both industrialized and non-industrialized societies?

In this connection, a group of us working at the University of Chicago became interested in the ethical questions involved, and recently held a small conference in which social and biological scientists, policymakers, and social ethicists met together for an exchange of views regarding the pros and cons of research aimed at extension of the life span. The participants were asked to leave aside those issues, important as they are, that have to do with prolonging the life of the individual patient in the terminal stage of illness, the issues that have come to be known as "death with dignity." They were asked to focus, instead, upon the more general question of basic biological research that might lead to extending the longevity of the human species.

It should first be said that two general strategies for lengthening the life span are now being pursued by biomedical and biological scientists. The first is the continuing effort to conquer disease. The second is the attempt to identify the intrinsic biological processes that are thought to underlie aging and that proceed independently from disease processes—that is, to discover the genetic and biochemical secrets of aging and to alter the biological clock that is presumably programmed into the human species. The second approach is directed at rate control, rather than disease control.

The first approach is the one that seeks ways of preventing and slowing atherosclerosis. The second is the one that studies pharmacological, dietary and thermal manipulations in attempting to alter cellular processes.

The participants in the Chicago conference were asked, What should be the primary objective of the science of biogerontology—to improve the quality of life for older people, or to extend the life span of the human species? Can the latter be achieved without cost to the former? If the human life span could be extended beyond the present maximum of 110 or 115 years, what would be the major deleterious and the major beneficial effects upon the society? Is it likely that an increased life span can be achieved that will lengthen the period of healthy, active life without lengthening the period of deterioration at the end of life? Can those risks be weighted against the benefits? How are social and ethical values to be weighed against economic values? Can a new priority of social values be effected?

In that conference, one participant compared the two approaches. The thesis was developed that a major new improvement in disease control (or improving the vigor of the body) would save lives from the time treatment began—say, at age 40; it would save many lives up to age 90; then, after 90, it would save few lives. By contrast, a change in the rate of aging—whether it comes from pharmacological, dietary, or thermal manipulation—would not reduce mortality much in the period from age 40 to 65, but after 65, and particularly after age 80, the effect would become more pronounced.

In short, disease control would give us more young-old people; rate control, more old-old people.

The proponents of both methods of lengthening life say it will be possible to stretch out the active part of life without increasing the period of physical disability. But the evidence for that proposition is scanty, whether it is related to one method or the other. There is nothing thus far to indicate that a reduced rate of aging would be accompanied by a reduction in morbidity, or in the average duration of time a person stays alive with a terminal disease. It seems reasonable to believe that the amount of medical care and health service needed by a particular elderly subgroup is bound to increase with the age of that subgroup, no matter what kind of anti-aging treatment or preventive health care it has received. The amount of disability and dependence upon care by others is sure to be higher for the oldest ten percent of the population than for younger age groups—and if the last survivors live more years, they will in all probability require a greater total amount of health care. If the thesis that major new improvements in disease control would save lives is correct, then biogerontologists are facing a significant ethical problem—or, perhaps more realistically, it is policymakers who will face the problem.

The ethicists at the Chicago conference raised a number of additional points: first, that in order to assess the issues of ethics and human values, one would need to know what would be the *actual* consequences for individuals, for particular societies, and for the human species if life extension were to be achieved—knowledge that we do not now have.

Following up that question, what reasons can be given to *justify* the extension of life? Is it because *individuals desire* to extend their active lives as long as possible? Or because *society* would benefit? Or would the human species benefit? Or because individuals have a moral *right* to live as long as possible under conditions that insure activity?

Other questions were raised: Since a distributive principle is always operating as a society allocates its goods and services, how choose, say, between preventing diseases of the young or postponing aging? Or between feeding the hungry of other countries or supporting our desire to give longer life to our own people? Such questions obviously have no easy answers. Does fairness or justice within a society mean that everyone should be given a fairly equal life expectancy before we expand the life expectancy of some? Do not those who would otherwise die young have a moral claim to be helped to live a statistically average life? And should this not be provided before resources are expended to increase general life expectancy? Knowing that the criteria for such decisions can never be clearcut, the issues must nevertheless be discussed and our conflicting values made explicit. Finally, one of our ethicists asked a set of questions about the uses of knowledge. Presuming that basic research will one day lead to an understanding of the working of the biological clock, we shall have to decide how to use that understanding. There will be many possibilities. But to make it possible to live indefinitely? To what end? If the life span is to be extended, we should know what goals we are trying to achieve.

There is no intent to suggest solutions for any of the social, economic, political or ethical issues mentioned here, for it goes without saying that they are all enormously complex. I have wished instead to raise some of the questions that are in the forefront of public attention—how to provide support and care for growing numbers of older persons and at the same time to maximize their potential contributions to the wider society, or, in different words, how to improve the quality of life for older persons and at the same time to improve the quality of life for aging societies.

Social policies will continue to be formulated and reformulated in the light of changing social trends. They are also being formulated in the light of ethical and value questions, although the latter are often implicit rather than explicit, and often they are conflicting.

As gerontologists we have not only the responsibility to carry on our scientific work, but to help influence the public debate by making explicit the relations between social ethics and social policy.

TWENTY-SEVEN

Policy for the 1980s: Age or Need Entitlement?

In considering what should be the policy agenda for the 1980s, we should take a broad view of some of the trends regarding aging and the aged that are occurring in the society at large, and ask if future public policies will be congruent with these trends. In the past century medical and social advances have produced the most dramatic of changes in the human life cycle—its increased duration. The result is an aging society, one in which the large majority of the population reach old age, and in which increasing numbers live to their 80s and 90s.

The social implications of increased longevity have been both good and bad. The long period of the life cycle in which people remain physically and intellectually vigorous has been lengthening, and in this sense we may be said to be slowly creating a 20th century version of the fountain of youth. At the same time life extension is producing larger numbers of ill and deteriorated persons of advanced old age.

The major problem for biological and biomedical gerontologists is how to increase the active and vigorous part of life without increasing the period of disability, a problem whose solution may continue to escape us for the foreseeable future. The major problems for social scientists and policy makers are how to improve the lives of present and future older persons, and how, at the same time, to facilitate the changes occurring in the family and in the educational, economic, political and human services systems because of the presence of increasing numbers of older people in the U.S. population.

People grow old in very different ways, and the range of differences—whether biological, psychological or social—becomes greater, not narrower, with the passage of the lifetime. There are striking differences between the sexes and among ethnic and socio-economic groups, to say nothing of the many other factors that produce diversity, with the result that 60-year-olds or 80-year-olds are very heterogeneous groups.

Reprinted by permission from *Aging: An Agenda for the Eighties,* A National Journal Issues Book (Washington, DC: November 1979), 48–52; ©1979 by National Journal, Inc.

Wide Limits

While it is true that, over-all, the frequency of illness and disability increases with age in the latter part of life, the association between age and physical capacity is far from perfect and it sets very wide limits within which individual variation is the important reality. This being the case, it does not help much in predicting a person's health, or marital status, or economic status, or life satisfaction, to know only that the person is 60 rather than 50, or 70 rather than 60. This is a finding that has emerged over and over as research accumulates; and it is this generalization that gerontologists have in mind when reporting that in the second half of life age is a poor predictor of physical or intellectual or social performance. In this sense, age is becoming a less relevant characteristic than it was in earlier periods of our history.

There are other ways of making the same point. There are, for instance, changes in the traditional rhythm of the life cycle: increasing numbers of men and women who marry, divorce, then remarry; increasing numbers who rear children in two-parent, then one-parent, then two-parent households; some men who, in May-December marriages, create second families when they are middle-aged. There are increasing numbers of women, but also of men, who enter, exit and re-enter our educational institutions, who enter and re-enter the labor force; who change jobs at various points and who undertake second and third careers. All this adds up to what some observers are calling the fluid life cycle, one marked by an increasing number of role transitions, by the proliferation of timetables and by the lack of synchrony among age-related roles.

The society is becoming accustomed to the 70-year-old student, the 30-year-old college president, the 22-year-old mayor, the 35-year-old grandmother, the 50-year-old retiree, the 65-year-old father of a preschooler and even the 85-year-old mother caring for her 65-year-old son. Age norms and age expectations, then, are diminishing in importance as regulators of behavior and in this sense, too, we are creating a society in which age is losing its relevance.

Group Differences

For policy purposes, one gross way of dealing with the irregularities and diversities among older people is to differentiate between those whom I earlier named the young-old and old-old. Because these terms have often been misused, it should be pointed out that the distinction is based, not on age, but on health and social characteristics.

The young-old are those men and women who are healthy and vigorous retirees and those women who have reduced their investment in their careers as homemakers. They are a large group, relatively comfortable financially, integrated members of their families and their communities, relatively well-educated and politically active.

The young-old seek meaningful ways to use their time. Some want to stay at work, some want to retire, some seek new ways of self-fulfillment through education or through various types of leisure, some seek new ways of serving their communities either in remunerated or non-remunerated jobs. They represent a great resource of talent to the society, much of it under-utilized. The young-old want irrational constraints based on age to be removed; they want age to become irrelevant as they pursue a wide variety of life styles.

The old-old, by contrast, are persons who have suffered major physical or mental deterioration or losses in their ordinary social support systems, and who therefore require a range of supportive and restorative health and social services. These are the older persons who are in need of special care.

From this perspective, the historical appearance of the young-old in the modern society is itself a good example of how age has lost some of its earlier significance, and how age stereotypes need to be reexamined.

RETIREMENT

It is not age, but retirement that marks off the young-old from the middle-aged. Because different people retire at different ages, the young-old are not to be identified as those who reach, say, 55 or 65. On the one hand, age of retirement has been dropping dramatically over the past few decades, with a greater number of persons beginning to draw social security benefits at ages 62, 63 or 64 than at age 65; with increasing numbers choosing to retire after a given number of years of service (the "after 30 years" pattern is spreading); and with sizable numbers taking at least a first retirement at 55.

On the other hand, now that Congress has passed the new law forbidding mandatory retirement until workers reach 70 (and forbidding mandatory retirement altogether for federal employees), and now with the eroding influence of inflation on pensions, larger numbers are likely to stay at work beyond age 65. So the age of retirement is becoming more variable. It is also becoming more blurred by the extent to which persons retire from one job, take another, then retire again, or phase out their work lives gradually, moving from full-time to part-time work. Retirement is therefore not the clear-cut transition that it is often made out to be; and the variation demonstrates the diminishing importance of age as the determiner.

It is usually a major deterioration in health that marks off the old-old from the young-old, although it may also be the sudden loss of family support that precipitates dependency.

DIFFERENT NEEDS

For obvious reasons, the young-old and the old-old have very different needs when it comes to both public and private programs, and different claims on policy makers. It is not only that the young-old want a wide range of options with regard to work and leisure. They also want a wide range of educational opportunities, and of housing and living arrangements. Some choose age-segregated communities, but many want flexible housing in their present communities. Because there are large numbers who are widowed, single and divorced, they want opportunities to form group households, with appropriate financing arrangements. And because parent-caring is becoming so widespread a problem, many want housing arrangements and supportive family services that make it possible to maintain the parent in the parent's own home.

The majority of old-old people live in independent households, but by definition most of them need supportive social services as well as health services. Many need special features in the physical environment to enable them to function as fully as possible. The old-old want medical and social supports to slow physical and mental deterioration, and to prevent unnecessary declines in feelings of self-worth and dignity. There is no denying the fact that for increasing numbers of old-old there is a lengthening period of dependency, and there will be increasing demands for special care, to be given either in independent or in institutional settings.

For both young-old and old-old, the major policy questions revolve around the extent of government responsibility for income maintenance and health care, but beyond this, it is fair to say that it is the needs of the old-old that are causing the greatest concern to policy makers. This is because health care expenditures have escalated so rapidly in the past few years, most notably because of inflation, but also because of the increased numbers of old-old and increased costs of new medical technologies. The Congressional Budget Office recently estimated that without increases in authorization levels, public costs for long-term care alone will be tripled by 1985. While some of these expenditures are for services to ill and disabled young people, most of them are for the old-old.

How well our policies and programs are meeting the needs of the young-old or the old-old cannot be easily determined, not only because the assessment of need is so difficult a problem in the welfare fields, but because we so often use age rather than need in creating our categories. So long as we collect and report our data in terms of age levels rather than need levels, it will remain impossible to monitor our progress. To take a well-worn example: it is often reported that the 11 percent of the population who are over 65 used about 30 percent of all health care resources in 1977. Is that too much, or too little?

POLICY IMPLICATIONS

Turning now to some of the implications for future policy decisions, to what extent will we develop policies and programs that are in line with the new realities regarding age and aging?

A case can be made that at the same time that age itself is becoming less relevant in the society, legislators and administrators have been proliferating laws and regulations that are age-based. In the legitimate concern over the welfare of older people, we have seized upon age as the convenient dimension for creating programs of income maintenance, housing, transportation, health services, social services and tax benefits.

Not only is the major part of the social security system pegged to age, but medicare is pegged to age, and we have also created a special nationwide government network through the Administration on Aging for planning and coordinating social services to persons over 60. The Congressional Research Service of the Library of Congress in 1977 listed some 47 major federal programs that benefit older people. Others, using a narrower definition of the term "program" have listed as many as 134. This is to say nothing of the proliferation of programs at state and local levels.

There has been a certain justification for this proliferation, of course. In the 1950s and 1960s a large proportion of older people in the United States were poor and were without health insurance or easy access to health services or social services. To create programs based on age eligibility did, in fact, catch a large proportion of persons who were in need. But today the situation is changing. The number of persons over 65 who fall under the poverty line is not much different from the number of younger persons under the poverty line. In fact, if all government supported income programs for both young and old are counted in—the direct payments, the transfer programs and the in-kind programs, like social security, supplementary security income, medicare, medicaid, aid to families with dependent children, food stamps, rent subsidies, tax benefits—then it turns out that the proportion of the old who are under the poverty line is substantially smaller than the proportion of young. And, as a reminder that there are many ways of looking at economic well-being, if we look at what people report about themselves, then in a national survey in 1975 about 15 percent of people over 65, but 18 percent of people under 65 said they did not have enough money to live on.

This is not to say that we have done enough about the problem of poverty in older people, or poverty in the wider population. But it cannot be said that older people are not getting a fair share of these efforts. Indeed, some observers are saying we have done enough for the old, even that the old are now an advantaged group compared to other groups whose needs may be equally compelling, even that we are developing a discriminatory system favorable to the old at the expense of the young and the middle-aged.

To argue that we have done enough for the old is, of course, the same distortion that arises whenever we talk about "the old" as if it were a homogeneous group. So long as we do not draw distinctions between the young-old and the old-old, or between the needy and the non-needy, then policy makers will be vulnerable to this type of uncritical argument.

Age-based legislation may have the eventual effect of denying services to those older persons who are most in need. By most estimates about 10 to 15 percent of people over 65 require some form of special health or social services. In a period of inflation and shrinking economic resources, when the public clamors for a curb on government spending, the worry is that this 15 percent may not be served adequately because it is being obscured by the other 85 percent in the age category.

Thus we must be wary lest we define our target populations in ways that are not meaningful but only expedient for the legislator and the administrator.

There is still another danger—that if age-based rather than need-based legislation continues, those of us who consider ourselves advocates for older people may inadvertently be creating age discrimination at the very same time we decry it. Policies and programs aimed at "the old," while they may have been intended to compensate for inequity and disadvantage, may have the unintended effect of adding to age segregation, of reinforcing the misperception of "the old" as a problem group, and of stigmatizing rather than liberating older people from the negative effects of the label, "old."

Some observers have pointed out that "oldness" is a social and political invention that serves not those older people who are most in need but the providers of services to older people. Other observers, taking a broader target, argue that the status of older persons as a group must be raised, and that to do so requires major alterations in the economic, political and social structures of the society. While there is much to be said for such views, the thesis being proposed here is a different one: at the risk of repetition, the thesis is that older persons are a heterogeneous, not a homogeneous, group; that in a society in which age is becoming increasingly irrelevant as a predictor of lifestyle or as a predictor of need, policies and programs formulated on the basis of age are falling increasingly wide of the mark; and that income and health care and housing and other goods and services should be provided, not according to age, but according to relative need.

Age Irrelevancy

But the policy issues are complex and do not, in the actual instance, take the form of simple either-or decisions. It is usually some combination of age and need, as well as other economic and political factors, that policy makers are struggling with, and it is not always an easy matter to disentangle the issue of age irrelevancy. A few examples will illustrate the point:

"Greying of the budget." There is a growing concern over the so-called "greying of the budget." In 1978 some 25 percent of total federal expenditures went to older people. This figure may rise over the next several decades to 40 percent. The projection involves the fact that the baby boom will become the senior boom of the early 21st century, and that it will probably be followed by small numbers of young if, as is anticipated, birth rates stay low. The alarm is that there will be fewer workers to support the great numbers of retirees, and that—without attempting to estimate the effects of inflation, costs of energy or levels of productivity—the total economy will be put out of joint and the social security system may be jeopardized. The latter is probably an ill-founded fear, for Congress is not likely to withdraw its attention from the social security system, and whether or not the present system is changed in major or minor ways, the society is not likely to abandon public programs of income maintenance for older people. Among many other reasons, young workers are likely to prefer a public program for supporting their aged family members to one that places the responsibility back on the family.

But what about the factor of age? Some policy analysts suggest raising the age of eligibility for social security benefits, a suggestion that sets off immediate opposition from others who argue that more incentives should instead be created to keep people at work, such as extra benefits for every additional year spent in the labor market after age 65. Improved conditions in the workplace, more part-time jobs, flextime and phased retirements could also be increased—in short, to create not a longer work life for everyone but greater options for everyone.

Shall policy makers deal with the problem, then, by manipulating age as the variable, or by building upon economic and other motivational factors that underlie the diversities among workers? Or, from the still broader perspective of age versus need, should policy makers concentrate first upon providing a guaranteed minimum income for persons of all ages, and only then shape the social security program to fit the wider framework?

Anti-discrimination legislation: A related example is one already mentioned: the recent legislation that abolishes age as the basis for retirement until age 70 in the private sector. In this instance age is not treated as irrelevant but the law is nevertheless a step in that direction. While the legislation may have been intended by some members of Congress to keep more people in the labor force beyond age 65 and to relieve some of the burden on the social security system, it is likely to have a greater effect instead in broadening the options for older persons, and by permitting some to stay at work who would otherwise face mandatory retirement, to extend the civil rights of all workers.

An example of a very different kind is the new Age Discrimination Act passed in 1975 and amended in 1978 that prohibits discrimination on the basis of age in any program receiving federal support. While the regulations created by HEW (now the Department of Health and Human Services) allow for major exceptions that have the effect of watering down its effects, the act is nevertheless a formal step toward making age equality a civil right, and in making the point that age is not a relevant characteristic in distributing goods and services.

The problems are enormous, however, in implementing the act and in deciding what constitutes age discrimination. Is it discriminatory, for instance, to establish special benefit programs for older people? Or to require a 65-year-old, but not a 64-year-old, to pass a test of vision before obtaining a driver's license? Or to allow a 16-year-old, but not a 15-year-old, to drive an automobile? These distinctions are legal under the present exceptions to the act, but they may come to be regarded as unjust or inequitable, as the legislation leads to continuous self-studies by federal agencies. It may prompt studies by state and local agencies as well, and a rising consciousness about age rights on the part of the public at large. What kinds of age discriminations will come to be regarded as justified? Which ones will be based on scientific evidence, and which ones on mere stereotypes?

Age advocacy: Another example is one outside the government itself but one that relates clearly enough to government policy making. The age advocacy groups such as the National Council of Senior Citizens, the National Retired Teachers Association, the American Association of Retired Persons, and the recently formed Ad Hoc Leadership Council of Aging Organizations led by the American Association of Homes for the Aged are not only growing in size but they are becoming more sophisticated as legislative advocates. (There are also advocacy groups for children and for adolescents, but because the underlying age issues are different, they are omitted from the present discussion.) It has been accepted wisdom that there is no real politics of age in the United States; that age has not been a sufficiently potent factor to cause persons of diverse economic and political persuasions to form cohesive political groups; that the age-based organizations may therefore be paper tigers. In short, political behavior has been regarded as an area in which age is not the relevant factor.

This is probably true, but there is also evidence that older voters coalesce around specific issues that affect them directly, such as increased social security benefits or, on the local level, school taxes or property tax relief. There is some reason for uneasiness that the age advocacy groups may become a divisive force in American life, especially if economic and demographic changes lead to a drop in pension levels or in service programs for older people.

From the present perspective, the growth of age advocacy groups may be another instance of how the irrelevant factor—age—may be creating an artificial social grouping—artificial, that is, with regard to policy initiatives. These organizations may become advocates for the problem elderly, those who are living in poverty or near-poverty, those who need long-term health care, and so on. Or they may put their efforts toward improving the quality of life for the population at large. But if, instead, they advocate for older people as a separate age group, they may help create a backlash in which the needs of the needy aged will be left out.

QUESTIONS

There are many other examples that could be raised, if space permitted. Common to them all are the difficult ethical and philosophical as well as political issues involved. There is, for instance, the value position that because people are old, they deserve more support than people who are young. This value position is rejected by those who are concerned about the needy young—who, if neglected, may be condemned to a blighted old age of their own. If government policies are restructured to support the poor or the disabled or the isolated, rather than to support persons who happen to be old, then what new definitions of need are necessary?

There are needs other than economic needs, but in those instances in which economic need were to be substituted for age entitlement, how could the stereotypes best be countered that income tested programs are demeaning, and that people, especially old people, should not be asked to establish poverty status before becoming eligible for benefits? To what extent does this last mentioned value come into conflict with other values of equity and justice for the population at large? And to what extent are attitudes against income tested programs likely to be present in successive generations? All these are troublesome questions, and they require searching examination. Resolutions will not come easily, but surely in considering the agenda for the 1980s, we should begin to rethink our policies based on age.

There are different ways of being an advocate for older people. One way has been to establish special benefit programs. But another is to insist on the integration of older people in the larger population or, for lack of a better term, to use the approach of mainstreaming by ignoring age differences wherever possible and by focusing on more relevant dimensions of human differences. In the society of the 1980s, what will be the best and most equitable way of caring about older people?

TWENTY-EIGHT

Family and Community Support Systems

I. Introduction

This is the age of aging. Long life is a major achievement of the twentieth century, and this White House Conference is an occasion to celebrate that achievement. It is not only that the majority of persons are living into old age, but the proportions of older to younger people are rising, so that ours is an aging society.

These facts need no elaboration here. They serve to remind us, however, that in line with the mandate of this Conference to focus on a national policy that is future-oriented as well a present-oriented, a policy that embraces both the opportunities and challenges, we should keep in mind that a national policy on aging has two equally important goals. The first is to enhance the lives of older women and men and to multiply the benefits of long life. The second goal is to facilitate positive changes in our social institutions as they accommodate to increasing numbers of older people.

We should be reminded also of the values we seek to implement. Very briefly, to reach out two goals means to maintain an age-integrated society, one in which mutual supports between generations are strengthened and in which involuntary age segregations are removed; to produce equity among age groups in sharing the goods and services of the society, its rights and responsibilities; to utilize the knowledge, experience and energies of older persons in improving the quality of life for all the society; to give priority to meeting the special needs of those minorities of older persons who are handicapped by poverty or illness or social isolation; to maintain the economic and social independence of older persons but at the same time to insure humane programs of care and protection if and when they become necessary; to provide a wide range of options to all older persons in the use of time, living arrangements, ways of self-fulfillment and community involvement, options that take into account the heterogeneity of cultural backgrounds, religious traditions and life styles; to increase our knowledge base with regard to the processes of aging and of so-

Paper presented to Committee #7, White House Conference on Aging, Washington, DC, November 1981.

cial and biomedical factors that influence physical and social health; and to help both young and old unlearn outmoded stereotypes, and to engage both formal and informal educational agencies in recognizing the opportunities for change and renewal that accompany long life.

Another set of considerations forms the context for our deliberations:

The long period of adulthood in which people remain physically and intellectually vigorous has been lengthening, and in this sense we are creating a 20th century version of the Fountain of Youth. At the same time, life extension is producing larger numbers of ill and disabled persons of advanced old age.

The implications for the future health status of older people are not clear. Some believe that in the next few decades the large majority will stay well until about age 85, that there will be a very short period of debility, and that relatively few will live much beyond that age. In this view there will be no great new need to develop systems of medical and social services for the debilitated. A contrasting view is that science and medicine will continue to develop palliative means that will prolong rather than shorten the terminal stage. Whether the first or second view is correct, is relatively certain that more and more people will move into the oldest age categories where, at least for the next few decades, the need for supportive services is greatest.

Older women outnumber older men and increasingly so at the oldest ages. The gap between the sexes in longevity has been widening.

There will be rapid increases in the numbers of older persons of the minority groups of Blacks, Hispanics, Asian-Americans and Native Americans. The gaps in longevity between these groups and the majority whites have been narrowing.

People grow old in very different ways. This is the most consistent finding to emerge from the field of gerontology. Biological and social factors interact to produce striking differences in patterns of aging among groups born at successive times in history, between the sexes, between racial and ethnic groups, urban and rural, and particularly between socio-economic groups. The result is that 60-year-olds or 80-year-olds are very heterogeneous groups.

Age is therefore losing its utility as a simple basis for understanding the conditions and capabilities of older adults. It is becoming a poor indicator of an older person's ability, behavior or need. In different words, age itself does not define a problem group in today's society.

This is not to deny that economic and social hardships may accompany old age, but these are the reflections of social and cultural factors. Aging is therefore social destiny as well as biological destiny. Socially-created destinies can be altered and improved.

Across the great range of differences among older people, it is useful to distinguish the two major groups who can be called, for convenience, the competent and the frail or vulnerable. This distinction is based, not on age, but on health and social characteristics. The competent are the large majority. We are vigorous and active and independent women and men, usually retired, who are well-integrated members of our communities, relatively secure economically, and increasingly well educated. We represent a great pool of expertise and talent to the society, much of it under-utilized.

The frail or vulnerable, by contrast, are those who among us suffer major physical or mental or social losses and who require a range of supportive and restorative services. Essentially, the frail are those who need special care. A very rough estimate is that of all persons over 60, the competent constitute 80 or 85 percent; the frail, about 15 to 20 percent. The proportions of the frail rise, of course, in the oldest subgroups, but even among 85-year-olds a sizable proportion have no major disabilities and are therefore among the competent. Most of us older people report high levels of life satisfaction and do not regard ourselves as deprived. Compared with younger adults, about the same proportions of us hold positive self-images and report that life is better than we had anticipated.

The fact that most older people are competent should not blind us to the sizable numbers who are the vulnerable and needy. Those who are severely handicapped in terms of economic or social need are mainly the very old who, compared to persons born at later periods in history, have been disadvantaged with respect to education, occupational skills, pension systems, and earlier medical care. A large proportion of older women are living in poverty. It is the group of very aged widowed or never-married women who constitute the special problem group in terms of both economic and social disadvantage. Minority-group elderly are disproportionately represented, for disadvantage has existed throughout their lives and has become accentuated in old age. Rural older people are often disadvantaged because of relative isolation and because they have less access to services.

The fact that most older people are competent is itself the second major achievement of our aging society, one that has come about only in the past few decades. To acknowledge this progress is not to answer the question of whether it has been sufficient, nor whether it has been consonant with the expansion of the society's total resources. But this is not the point I wish to debate, for the moment. The point is, instead, that what I call the 80/20 distribution holds when we look at all the older population at one point in calendar time. It says nothing about what happens to older persons over time. It is the worry of most of us and most of our families that we will move from the competent to the frail as we advance in years. The specter that haunts us older people is not death itself, but the prospect that social death might precede biological death. To ignore this point is to ignore a major reality of old age.

II. The Underlying Issue

To come now to the topic immediately before us—the social support system for older people and how it can be improved. I suggest that the underlying issue that concerns us is the changing interrelationships between the components of a four-part system. The four components are, first, older persons ourselves; second, the family and other informal supports; third, the formal agencies and organizations in the private sector; fourth, the government or public sector. How do we create an optimum balance of responsibilities among the four? And how do we create a support system that is flexible and resilient in the face of rapid social change?

III. Older Persons as Actors in the System

To comment first on older individuals who stand in the center of the system: Most of us competent older people have the desire to exercise our competence, both for our sense of self-worth and for social recognition of our worth. This desire lasts all through life. It becomes curtailed only by major biological decline or by repeated social frustration. Our mental apparatus and our learning abilities—if not blocked by overwhelming physical or social impediment—stay sharp and alive.

Not every older person is wise nor altruistic. Yet across all our differences, we share a few important characteristics that differentiate us from the young. We have had long experience, which usually gives us a better understanding of people and events. And we have a commitment not only to our personal welfare but to the welfare of our children, and thus to the welfare of the society at large. So we are likely to have a longer-term and a broader social outlook. A third important advantage is that we have a certain freedom to speak out and to take certain social risks that younger people are often unable to take.

Thus we can take responsibility for ourselves. But we can do more. We can be not only the culture-bearers for the society, but the conscience of the society. This is as relevant to the social support system as it is to the other topics of this Conference. We older people have an investment in the other three parts of the support system; and we are responsible, along with the other parts, for the success of the whole system.

What does this mean, specifically? That no plan aimed at our social welfare as individuals or as members of an age group is to be undertaken without our participation in its formulation and in its implementation; that we share in the responsibility for other older people and in the responsibility for younger people; that we make our contributions to our families, our neighbors and our community organizations in all the ways appropriate to our abilities; that we enter the debates at the community, state, and national levels over the distribution of resources and services. In short, we need to demonstrate that we are an influential part of the system and that we give as well as take.

IV. THE FAMILY

I wish to comment at somewhat greater length on the second part of the social support system, the family, for this is the only Committee in this Conference that is instructed to deal with that all-important institution.

This is the age of the multigenerational family, with its many attendant benefits. An increased span of lifetime is being shared by family members; more parents and offspring have overlapping years of vigorous adulthood; a network of intimate ties provides psychological and social support for both younger and older members; it provides the primary arena for maintaining a sense of self-worth and for opportunities to contribute to the well-being of others.

The family is being affected in dramatic ways by changes occurring in other societal institutions: in the economy, with its changing composition of the labor force, new technology, and particularly inflation; geographical mobility; new patterns of social and medical services; changes in housing and residential patterns, in work and education patterns, especially for women; and changes in attitudes such as the movement toward mid-life options. These are only a few.

The family structure is itself undergoing major alterations. Most older men are married, but most older women are widowed. A widow in her sixties can expect to live another 15 or 20 years. As younger people reach their sixtieth birthdays, there will be higher numbers of divorced older people. There are often two sets of grandchildren born to the same child. A high proportion of middle-aged women are in the labor force. A particularly important fact is the dramatic trend toward separate households for older persons. This reflects the rising economic status of older people, for when they can afford it, both parents and their adult children prefer to live separately. At the same time, the major increase in the numbers of older people who live often brings the risk of social isolation.

Despite all these changes, the support system for older people remains anchored in the family. Whatever its changing structures, the family still provides various forms of financial support to those older persons who need it, and it provides the great bulk of health care and social care for all older persons. It is important also in providing the linkage functions to both private and public services.

Supports go in both directions. We older persons are making important contributions to family well-being. We provide economic support to other family members—studies show that financial aid flows downward from older to younger generations about as much as it flows upward. We provide emotional support; we help in child care, nursing, counseling, and homemaking. We conserve and transmit the traditions and values of our cultural group, and we provide historical continuity for our younger members. Both these latter elements are important to the individual's sense of identity.

The large majority of us are well-integrated members of our families. Most of us live close to at least one of our children; we see children and grandchildren frequently; we stay in contact by telephone and automobile and letter with relatives who are geographically remote, creating what has been termed "intimacy at a distance." And we participate in a complex exchange of goods and services with other family members. Intergenerational ties of commitment and obligation are strong.

It is a myth, then, that the family dumps its older members. Concern over an aging parent—it can be called concern over parent-caring—is widespread, as reported by adults of all ages. Parent-caring has strong components of commitment, whether or not there is geographical distance between parent and child, or frequent contact, or even close affectional ties. In different words, not everybody loves his mother, but almost everybody worries that she be properly cared for.

Despite all these positive aspects, there are two major problems with the family as a support system.

The first is that a sizable minority of older people have never married, or are childless or without kin, or are geographically or socially isolated from other family members. This group is composed mainly of persons of advanced old age, mainly widowed women who live in poverty and who live alone—the subgroup who is most at risk with regard to institutionalization. It includes, also, disproportionate numbers of minority-group older people. It is for this group that the bulk of social services must be provided by private or public agencies.

The second major problem is that in many cases where an older person becomes physically or mentally disabled, the burden on the family becomes too great. In these cases, the family needs assistance. Family crises involving the dependency of a previously independent older person are to be expected when people live to advanced old age. Although most families manage fairly well, and manage the stresses produced in both older and younger members, some families cannot cope.

I am aware that another Committee in this Conference is discussing the issues of long-term care. Yet it is precisely the problem of long-term care of the older person that is the major problem for the family.

Long-term care involves a wide array of services: family counseling, nutrition services, friendly visitors, visiting nurses, homemaker services, senior centers, day care centers, hospitals, nursing homes and hospices, and self-help groups of older people. Institutionalization is only one small part of it, yet it is an important part. Although only a small proportion of older people are likely to become institutionalized—about 5 percent of the total number who are 65 and over when counted on any one day, a percentage that, interestingly enough, has not changed over the past 15 years, and about 8 percent of those persons who live into their 80s—still it is the dread of institutionalization that hangs heavy on older persons.

One important need is for education about the intergenerational family, its strengths and its problems—education aimed at the society at large. That requires the active participation of both formal and informal educational agencies—the schools and colleges, the mass media, and other organizations such as churches and synagogues, community centers, museums, business and labor organizations. It is important also that more studies be carried out on the intergenerational family as a unit, and that research findings be disseminated to both the private and public service agencies.

If we want to help the family fulfill its obligations, there are several directions to follow:

1) Consider the family, not the individual older person alone, as the unit for services and supports, as well as the unit for research and education;

2) Develop neighborhood networks which can offer preventive services as well as assistance to families in crisis situations;

3) Involve older persons as volunteers, foster grandparents, tutors and teachers, and as care-givers for other older persons;

4) Give special attention to the problems of women. They must be helped at earlier as well as later ages to achieve equity and adequacy in education, employment and benefits that are tailored to their multiple roles as spouse, mother and worker—help that prepares women for independence and self-sufficiency. The skills of homemakers are critically needed, and educational, voluntary and government service agencies should cooperate to upgrade the occupational role of homemakers;

5) Give special attention to the disadvantaged families, rural families, ethnic and minority-group families, and new immigrant families—above all, to families of low income;

6) Re-examine government and non-government policies and alter them in ways that will strengthen rather than weaken intergenerational ties. These include private and public pension schemes, especially Social Security and Supplemental Social Insurance, housing policies and zoning regulations that fragment the intergenerational family, tax policies, reimbursement mechanisms for health and social services;

7) Recognize the lag between needs and family-oriented programs. Many programs such as in-home services of homemakers, service-supported living arrangements, and respite care financial supports such as family allowances to help defray parent-caring costs have been suggested, and some are already being implemented on the local level. But implementation at the national level has been slow. National efforts have progressed much further in many other countries. Nearly all industrialized nations except the United States and Canada provide financial "constant attendance allowances" on behalf of those who need care at home; in some countries, as in Sweden, home-help and home-health services are widely available; in other coun-

tries like Japan or the United Kingdom or Australia, loans or grants are available to remodel an extra room for an older person; and so on.

This last issue is one I know will be debated here in a particular way: Should the government provide financial assistance directly to families in caring for their frail older members? One or another form of this recommendation has been made by 24 of the 34 state conference reports that I have seen. Still the question is not a simple one. There is the view—one supported by the few small-scale studies thus far available—that financial incentives, direct or indirect, are not the most important part of the problem, and that there are other more compelling factors in determining which families do and which families do not undertake the direct and daily care of their older members. These factors are related to affection and obligation and cultural values, and to questions of women's responsibilities for child-care and their work outside the home.

V. OTHER INFORMAL SUPPORTS

In addition to the family there is the large and indispensable sector of informal supports that come from friends, neighbors, volunteers, self-help groups, religious institutions, fraternal, educational and civic organizations, business organizations and labor unions. Some are formally organized at local and national levels in the so-called "voluntary organizations." Some are organized along age-specific lines and serve only older people; others, along age-neutral lines and serve those with a common need irrespective of age. The more informal supportive arrangements may have greater outreach capacities than the formal.

While the informal support arrangements are often differentiated from the more formal social services, it is difficult to discuss their functions and their contributions separately. Under both headings we have trouble in assessing how many people are being helped, the extent to which these efforts are effective, and how these organizations are changing as, for example, for-profit organizations are now multiplying for those older persons who can afford to pay. We have no statistical data comparable, say, to our data on health services. Nevertheless there is no disagreement that this whole network is of primary importance to the support of older people, a view supported by a number of local studies (e.g., one carried out in Cleveland by the General Accounting Office of the government). By and large this voluntary sector is aimed at promoting in-home services, and at producing a continuum of services that meet physical, social, emotional, financial, and spiritual needs of older people.

One of the endemic problems in this area is that the persons who are often most directly involved with caring for the older person are those who have had the least training. Quality care is a major concern for all four components in the support system, but it is most often articulated by the professionals in both health agencies and social agencies.

Another problem is that the voluntary organizations are plagued by shortages of volunteers, and—just as is true of public agencies—by inflation and shrinking budgets.

The overarching issue is, of course, how to provide better coordination at the local community level among these informal and voluntary organizations, how they relate to the family as the unit of service, and how they relate to the public and governmental agencies.

VI. The Private and Public Sectors

In commenting further about the third and fourth components of the social support system, the private and the public, the major issue is the one just mentioned—that of coordination, or perhaps more accurately, the lack of coordination, in building upon the informal supports, in using private and public resources most effectively, and in relating federal decision-making to local decision-making.

It should go without saying that the responsibility of government is as great as the responsibilities of the other components in the social support system. The role of government is indispensable, and must not be diminished. From a historical perspective, governments in the industrialized countries are in a third phase with regard to national policy for older people. First came the attention to economic supports; next, the attention to health supports; and now, the attention to social supports.

We all know that, overall, the existing system of service delivery is duplicative and fragmented. While there is already a great deal of public and voluntary coordination, there are enormous variations at the local level.

We all know that the social supports are as critical to the care of older people as are health supports; and that, in many instances, if the former were greater, the latter could be smaller.

We all know that at local, state and national levels the problem is one of creating a proper integration of medical and social services, that federal programs are dominated by the medical model, with medical rather than social supports receiving the large share of resources. Within the federal health programs alone, Medicare and Medicaid are tilted toward institutional care rather than family-based or community-based care. And within the federal social services programs, it is not only the lack of funds that plagues us, but problems in relating such funds as exist under Title XX of Social Security to those available under the Older Americans Act.

In closing, I shall select two of the major issues in this area: the relation of federal to local decision-making, and the problem of the most effective use of resources. And

I shall refer to the recent report of the Federal Council on the Aging—a report of the study which the Congress in 1978 directed the Federal Council to undertake—of the programs being conducted under the Older Americans Act. This report is focused only on the Older Americans Act, but it deals therefore with social support systems for older persons, and the recommendations may well be generalizable.

The report sets out a few major principles: that the focus should not be on groups of categorical services, but on the groups of persons in need of services or in need of opportunities for purposeful activity; that attention must be given to both the formal and informal support systems, to both age-specific and age-neutral programs; that federal funds should not be used to create a new, distinct and limited service delivery system solely for older persons, but that federal funds should be used, instead, to assist communities in planning and developing a comprehensive and coordinated community-based support system; that while the planning and implementation rests with the local community, the federal government has a vital responsibility to provide substantial financial support to the local communities for this purpose.

The Federal Council spent many hours on the issue of the best use of resources, an issue often called targeting. It said first that there are two questions involved here: first, should older people as a group receive special attention by creating special governmental structures and by specific allocation of public funds on their behalf? Recognizing that ageism is still a reality in our country, the Council answered yes to this question, and recommended therefore that the Older Americans Act be reauthorized.

Second is the question of identifying the persons in greatest need. Taking cognizance of the strong arguments in favor of the view that it is the federal government that should define those groups, and that it is primarily the low-income and the minority groups who require special attention, still the Council recommended that—in recognition of local differences in ethnic and racial composition, income levels, culture, extent of voluntary services and informal support systems, and in the availability of resources—the delineation of needy groups and the plans for meeting those needs should be left to the local community.

I have described these recommendations of the Federal Council, but not because I think they should settle these matters. On the contrary, those recommendations are likely to provoke strong opinions among all the members of this group. I recommend them as issues to be debated here, in the belief that they refer to important elements in a national policy on aging.

In closing, I realize that I have touched only lightly on many issues that are of importance to members of this group, and that I have done justice to none of them. I hope, nevertheless, that you will have identified the issues that should take priority in your discussions—and, in particular, that you will have identified some of the actions that should follow—and that you will incorporate them into a few major recommendations. I thank you for this opportunity to come before you, and I wish you success in your deliberations.

TWENTY-NINE

New Perspectives on Aging and Social Policy

When I was invited to present this lecture, it was suggested that I describe how it has come about that, as an investigator who began long ago to study age-related changes in adulthood and old age, I regard age as an irrelevant dimension in policy-making for older people. Following that suggestion, my comments will be organized here around four major generalizations and how they are related in my thinking: first, the life-span perspective is the proper framework for studying aging; second, individual and group differences and irregularities in patterns of change are the over-riding realities; third, age is therefore a poor indicator of the individual's condition or behavior and a poor basis for policy-making; fourth, age integration is a major policy goal for the society.

These four points can be stated in idiomatic terms: Everybody grows older *all* the time . . . Everybody is different . . . Everybody knows that age itself isn't important . . . Everybody is in this aging business together.

EVERYBODY GROWS OLDER ALL THE TIME

It has become customary to introduce a lecture on aging by mentioning some of the well-known facts about increases in longevity: for example, that life is growing longer in all the industrialized nations of the world; that the newest gains in life expectancy are affecting people after, rather than before, they reach old age; or that there have been unanticipated new gains in life expectancy in the United States in the very oldest age group, those over 85.

The implications of these demographic facts are not clear with regard to the future health status of older people. Some biomedical investigators believe that in the next few decades the large majority of people will stay healthy until about age 85; they will experience a very short period of debility; and few persons will live much beyond 85 (Fries and Crapo, 1981). This is the model suggested in the poem about the "one-hoss shay," where the shay operated with splendid efficiency for many years, then broke down suddenly and completely. This model implies that there will

The Leon and Josephine Winkelman Lecture, presented at the School of Social Work, University of Michigan, Ann Arbor, January 25, 1982.

be no great need in the future to develop new systems of medical and social services to care for very aged persons.

Other investigators hold contrary views: that advanced old age will continue to mean, for the individual, failure in one body organ after another, and that science and medicine will continue to develop palliative measures that will prolong rather than shorten the period of disability (Brody, 1982). This is a model of a lifeline in which the downward turn is gradual and drawn out, forming, as it were, a long tail to the curve.

Whichever of these views proves to be correct in the long run, there is little doubt that for at least the next few decades more and more people will move into the oldest age categories where the needs for supportive services are greatest; and, although the debilitated will continue to be a minority of older persons, they will be the group of greatest concern to policy-makers.

Although these demographic trends and projections are themselves leading to new perspectives on aging and the life span, it is not the increase in longevity that is intended here by the phrase, "Everybody grows older all the time." Instead, the emphasis is upon the words "everybody" and "all the time." The processes of aging, rather than the group of persons whom we define as old, are becoming the focus for gerontological research. Aging begins from the moment of conception. It characterizes the infant just as it does the 80-year-old. The change is therefore to see aging as a life-long set of processes and to adopt what has come to be called the life-span perspective.

Given this framework, gerontologists are interested in long life and in studying older people, not as a separate and atypical group but as those persons who have lived the longest. Philosophers and poets and biographers, of course, have had the life-span perspective for a very long time in history, and at least a few social scientists were adopting this framework in graduate teaching and research several decades ago. In the late 1940s, for example, the Committee on Human Development at the University of Chicago added a graduate course in adulthood and old age to the existing courses in childhood and adolescence to form the core of an interdisciplinary doctoral program called Human Development.

Growing numbers of behavioral and social scientists, as well as biological scientists, are now adopting the life-span perspective and hold the position that changes, both incremental and decremental, occur in old age just as they do in childhood; that an understanding of later patterns of behavior depends on understanding earlier patterns; and that earlier patterns should themselves be studied in terms of their influence on later ones. The old question of the relation of early to late development, or the question of antecedents and consequences, is coming under new and critical scrutiny in the last few years, particularly among psychologists (e.g., Brim and Kagan, 1980; Gergen, 1980). It is tied to the question, To what extent, and in what areas of thought and behavior, is it true that the child is father to the man?

The life-span perspective is inherently interdisciplinary, a fact that is self evident given that we study persons who are biological, social and psychological creatures moving through time within socially created contexts. But an intellectual perspective cannot always be translated directly into empirical research, and truly interdisciplinary studies are rare. This may change in the coming decade, for the life-span orientation is now appearing, or re-appearing, within each of a broad range of disciplines—not only in biology and psychology but also in sociology, anthropology, history, and economics (Featherman, 1981). It is apparent that investigators of very diverse persuasions are organizing their data and reorganizing their theories to reckon with change, not only over historical time by also over life-time, and to consider the life span or the life course as the unit of study. Still, it remains an open question whether or not some of these strands can come together to form an interdisciplinary rather than a multi-disciplinary area of inquiry.

A number of concepts encompassed in the life-span orientation are of particular importance to gerontologists: Development and aging are similar, perhaps synonymous terms. It would be well if we no longer used the terms as contrasts, as if development were desirable, but aging, undesirable. . . . Change is continuous. . . . Changes are multiple and multidirectional. . . . Human behavior is flexible and malleable throughout life. . . . Persons learn best that which they are motivated to learn. . . . Patterns of aging (or development) reflect the social and historical settings in which they occur. . . . Successive cohorts of persons therefore age differently. . . . Aging (or development) is social as well as biological destiny. . . . Social destinies can be altered more readily than biological. . . . Persons are active, exploring creatures who influence their environments and who, to a significant degree, create their own lives. . . . Persons seek ways of exercising their competencies as long as they live. . . . Accordingly, the individual's decisions and commitments are important components of change. . . . Chance events, lucky or unlucky, are important components of change. . . . The individual is influenced by the changes occurring in other persons who are significant in his life.

Because of all these factors, the differences between individual life histories increase with the passage of life time, at least until major biological decrement occurs that reduces the range of individual differences. It is difficult, therefore, to speak of constancies or continuities or universal laws in human development, except in the very broadest terms (Neugarten, 1969). All people grow up, grow old, and die, but the variations are legion.

Everybody Is Different

To restate the last point, perhaps the most consistent finding to emerge from gerontology is that people grow old in very different ways. Biological and psychological and social factors interact in complex ways to produce striking variations in patterns of aging between successive cohorts, between the sexes, between racial and ethnic, urban and rural, and particularly between socio-economic groups. This is to say nothing of idiosyncratic sequences that widen the divergence between individuals. The result is that 40-year-olds or 80-year-olds are extremely heterogenous groups. Even in matters of health, where on probabilistic grounds the frequency of illness and disability increases in the latter half of life, the association between age and physical condition is far from perfect and it sets very wide limits within which individual variation is the important reality.

It is not surprising, then, that investigators report, for a wide array of measures drawn from different domains, that variance increases in successive age groups. When investigators look, not at single variables or even multi-factorial patterns at given points in time, but at measurements and observations taken sequentially, variance becomes even more dramatic. It is not the regularities but the irregularities of change across individuals, across groups, and across historical periods that compel our attention.

This can be illustrated from research of various types and various levels of observation. For one, the sequence and the rhythm of major life events has been changing historically. Puberty comes earlier than before; death, later. Social timing is also changing. Entry into the labor market comes later; exit, earlier. Marriage, parenthood, and grandparenthood are differently timed. Increasing numbers of men and women marry, divorce, then remarry, care for children in two-parent, then one-parent, then two-parent households, enter and re-enter the labor force, change jobs, undertake new careers or return to school. All this adds up to what has been called the fluid life cycle (Hirschhorn, 1977), one marked by increased numbers of transitions, the disappearance of traditional timetables, and the lack of synchrony among age-related roles (Neugarten and Hagestad, 1976). Age norms and age expectations are diminishing in importance as regulators of adult behavior.

At another level of observation, the psychological themes and preoccupations of adults, although they are often described by psychologists as occurring in succession, do not in truth arise at regular moments in life, each to be resolved and put behind as if it were a bead on a chain. Identity is formed and reformed. Issues of intimacy and autonomy and commitment to significant others, the pressures of time, the reformulation of life goals, stocktaking and reconciliation and acceptance of successes and failures, all these preoccupy the young as well as the old. The themes are recurrent, emerging, and re-emerging in new forms over long periods of time. It is therefore a distortion to describe the psychology of adulthood and old age as a series of discrete stages, as if adult life were a staircase.

A third level of observation relates to other changes in the inner life, those aspects of the mind that do not always appear in awareness or in direct expression, where psychologists analyze fantasies, dreams, responses to projective techniques and to depth interviews. This is an area few developmental psychologists have been eager to pursue, being neither intrepid enough nor patient enough, leaving it usually to the clinician, or the novelist, or the poet. Nevertheless, from such fragmentary studies that have been carried out by developmental psychologists, it appears likely that changes occur in the quantity and quality of introspection, in cognitive styles, in the ability to abstract from experience and to utilize reminiscence, in the ease of coping with crises, and in the subtler qualities of the self image. At the same time it appears that such internal changes come slowly, are not systematically triggered by the same events in all persons, and do not emerge at stated or predictable intervals. Here, too, regularities are difficult to delineate.

The diversities and irregularities and unpredictabilities among people have important implications for all of us interested in aging. The researchers among us shall need to become more comfortable in the presence of complexity and unpredictability, to reach out for a broad range of models, and to look to the interpretive social sciences as well as to the natural sciences. At least some of us shall probably abandon explanation and prediction, and instead, accept understanding as the goal, where we will use the narrative as well as the experiment, hermeneutics as well as statistics. We shall have to keep before us the dictum that reductionism is the biggest error of all.

The professionals among us will need to keep in mind that different persons need different kinds of services and interventions. Social workers and teachers and psychiatrists will require a wide range of theories and methods, and for them, too, the task will be to avoid single-factor approaches and uni-causal explanations of behavior.

For policy-makers the difficulties are of another kind, because policies and programs, especially at the national level, must be directed at very large groups of persons and it is not easy to deal with individual differences and to provide a wide range of options for people, even though the latter is clearly the goal.

Everybody Knows That Age Itself Isn't Important

How shall we relate what we know as gerontologists to some of the social policy issues of the 1980s? From the preceding statements about individual differences that widen with the passage of life time, it follows that age is a poor indicator of physical, or intellectual, or social competence, especially in the second half of life. This has led me to suggest, on several earlier occasions, that age is becoming less relevant than before in determining patterns of adult life, and it is becoming irrelevant as the basis for policy-making for adults (Neugarten, 1974, 1979 [a], 1981). This is not to imply that age is insignificant in the person's view of himself or in his patterns of social interactions, but that age is a poor basis for creating programs of benefits and services.

For instance, if age is not a reliable index of the adult's ability to learn, can we provide educational opportunities that will maximize human potential at all ages? Can we build an educational system geared less to age and more to the person's changing interests and abilities—one with more exit and re-entry points for adolescents as well as for adults? Can we redistribute periods of education, work, and leisure across the life span in ways consonant with the irregular patterns of adult change?

Another important policy issue is the elimination of age discriminations against both younger and older adults. Shall we re-examine some of the age distinctions that have become formalized in our laws and remove those that are dysfunctional to the society and others that operate, overtly or covertly, in the workplace, the community organization, the medical or social service agency?

What other steps can be taken to maximize the social benefits and minimize the social costs that accompany the fluid life cycle? What kinds of new family policies and work policies can be established for women as well as for men? What kinds of counseling services and social support systems are needed?

It is the national policies aimed at older people that are now in the forefront of public attention. Here it would be useful if the policy-maker, faced with the great range of differences among older men and women, were to make at least a gross distinction between the two groups who can be called the competent and the frail. These are the two groups I once named the young-old and the old-old. Those terms have become widely used, but often misused by referring to 60-year-olds as the young-old, and 80-year-olds as the old-old. Because this was not my intended meaning, I am now suggesting the words competent and frail, repeating once again that the distinction is not based on age, but on health and social characteristics.

The competent are the large majority of older persons in this country, usually retired but vigorous and active, integrated members of their families and communities, relatively secure economically, and increasingly well-educated. A rough estimate is that they constitute about 80 to 85 percent of all persons over 60. Competent older people seek meaningful ways to use their time. Some stay at work, some seek fulfillment through education or various forms of leisure, many are serving their communities in non-remunerated jobs. They represent a great pool of expertise and talent to the society, much of it underestimated and underutilized. It is this majority of older persons whom we have in mind when we speak of older people as a national resource, a theme that surfaced repeatedly in the policy recommendations emerging from the 1981 White House Conference on Aging.

The frail are the minority of older persons who are handicapped by poverty, or illness, or social isolation, those who suffer major physical or mental or social losses and who therefore require special services, the group among whom very aged women and members of minority groups are over-represented. The proportion of the frail rises, of course, in the oldest sub-groups, but even among 85-year-olds, a sizable proportion remain among the competent.

For obvious reasons, these two groups of older people have very different needs and different claims on policy-makers. The competent want a wide range of options regarding work and leisure, educational opportunities, housing and living arrangements. They want irrational constraints based on age to be removed, and age to be recognized as irrelevant as they pursue a wide variety of life styles.

Frail older people, by definition, need a wide range of supportive and restorative health and social services that will enable them to function as fully as possible and that will prevent unnecessary declines in feelings of self-worth.

So the policy issues for the two groups are very different.

Despite the differences and despite the fact that age itself is becoming less meaningful, legislators and administrators have been proliferating laws and regulations that are age-based. In the legitimate concern over the welfare of older people, they have seized upon age as the convenient dimension for creating programs of income maintenance, housing, transportation, health services, social services, and tax benefits. Not only is the major part of the social security system pegged to age, but Medicare is also pegged to age, and a special nationwide network has been created through the Administration on Aging for planning and coordinating social services to persons over 60. The Congressional Research Service of the Library of Congress in 1977 listed some 47 major federal programs that benefit older people. This is to say nothing of the proliferation of programs at state and local levels.

This age-based legislation had a certain justification. In the 1950s and 1960s a large proportion of older people were poor and without health insurance or easy access to health services or social services. To create programs based on age eligibility did, in fact, catch a large number of persons who were in need of special attention. But today the situation is changed. For instance, the most recent census data show that the proportion of persons over 65 living in poverty is not much different from the proportions of younger persons living in poverty. This is substantiated in the latest national survey, in which fewer than one in five persons aged 65 and over, but somewhat more than one in five persons aged 18 to 64, reported that "not enough money to live on" is a serious problem for them (National Council on the Aging, 1981).

In other life domains, the situation of older persons is also relatively favorable, as, for example, in self-reported well-being. In the survey just mentioned, and in earlier surveys including those carried out by the Institute for Social Research, older people appear to be more contented in most areas of life than are younger people (Campbell, Converse and Rodgers, 1976).

This does not deny that minorities of older people have special problems and needs, but says once again that age itself does not define a problem group. Accordingly, I have been advocating that wherever possible we should abandon age as the basis for policy-making and focus instead on meeting needs—to focus on special economic programs for the poor, special health services for the disabled, social supports for the isolated, employment opportunities for those who want to work, and educational opportunities for those who want to study.

If we continue to multiply age-based programs and policies, the eventual effect may be to deny services to those older persons who are most in need. In a period of inflation and shrinking economic resources, when the public clamors for a curb on government spending, the concern is that the 15 to 20 percent who require special attention may not be served adequately because they become obscured by the other 80 to 85 percent.

We must be careful, therefore, to define our target populations in ways that are meaningful, not in ways that are only expedient for the legislator or the administrator. There is another danger: that if age-based rather than need-based legislation continues, some of us who consider ourselves advocates for older people may be inadvertently creating age discrimination at the same time we decry it. Policies and programs aimed at "the old," although they are well intended, may have the unanticipated effect of reinforcing the misperception of older people as a problem group and of stigmatizing rather than liberating them from the negative effects of the label, "old."

To mention one concrete example of how age may be an inappropriate basis for policy decisions, some policy analysts are now arguing, in light of improved health and longevity, that the age of eligibility for social security benefits should be raised as one way of lessening the social security burden on the national economy. Others argue that, instead, more incentives should be created to keep older people at work, such as extra social security benefits for each extra year spent in the work force after age 65, improved working conditions, more part-time jobs, more flex-time and more phased retirements—in short, to create, not a longer work life for everyone, but greater options for everyone. Should policy-makers deal with the problem, then, by manipulating age as the variable or by building upon economic and other motivational factors that underlie the diversities among older workers? This is but one of many such policy questions that need the input of gerontologists.

EVERYBODY IS IN THIS AGING BUSINESS TOGETHER

National policies on aging have two overarching goals. The first is to enhance the lives of older people, to enable their full participation in society and to multiply the advantages of long life. The second is to facilitate the changes occurring in all the economic, social, and political institutions of society as they become transformed by the changing age distribution.

Despite the arguments for moving away from age categories, it is likely that policy-makers will continue to focus on older people as an age group for at least the next decade. Income maintenance and health care for all older people will continue to be the top priorities, but more specific issues will revolve around the sub-groups of the needy. The question will be how best to define the groups in greatest need and how to target resources in the most effective way. For the majority who are competent and independent, the problem, as already suggested, will be how to remove age constraints and age discriminations and how to eradicate the stereotype that older people are a burden to society. For the frail, the particular issue will be the provision of long-term care, of creating community-wide systems in which medical and social services are integrated and in which volunteers and professionals will cooperate in providing programs that are cost-effective but also meet standards of quality care. Major attention must also be given to enlarging our knowledge about aging in both the social and biological sciences and to applying that knowledge. Education will become a more major topic—applying education for older people themselves, for the personnel who will be serving older people, and, in particular, education for the society at large about the implications of an aging society and about the opportunities and benefits of long life.

The issue that underlies all the others and that will determine all the outcomes is how to maintain an age-integrated society and to guard against age divisiveness. This is another way of saying that, "Everybody is in this together." In the United States, as is even more evident in some European countries, there is a growing uneasiness lest a politics of age take shape in the next decade that will be detrimental to the society at large. It stems from the "greying of federal budgets," the concern that there will be fewer young people to support the greater number of retirees, that social security systems and private pensions might be curtailed, and that these issues will polarize younger and older voters. Some observers are worried over what they regard as the growing political power of older voters; others, over a possible political backlash that will be harmful to older people.

One factor may be the growing visibility of the "aging-advocacy" groups that focus their efforts on the welfare of older people and that have become increasingly sophisticated in influencing legislatures and administrative agencies at both national and local levels. For instance, "silver-haired legislatures" are now appearing in various states, settings where older people meet to formulate specific legislation and then urge it upon the regularly elected legislators. Another example is the Leadership Council of Aging Organizations organized a few years ago that now speaks for over 20 organizations, some that have millions of older persons as their members. Another example is the 1981 White House Conference on Aging, where a few of the large advocacy groups worked quickly and effectively in influencing the resolutions that came forth. That Conference itself is interpreted by some political observers as evidence of the growing political power of older persons, even though it is an open question whether or not such Conferences have a direct effect on Congressional actions.

This is not to disparage the efforts of such groups or such Conferences, but only to recognize that their activities may be contributing to a politics of age.

Another factor is the extent to which both public and private agencies have been creating programs that are age-specific. An increasingly wide range of age-based programs are sponsored by local, state, and federal government agencies, as already stated, but the same is true of religious, educational, philanthropic, and self-help organizations. There are also the mushrooming senior clubs and senior centers in which older people are learning to take on age-advocacy roles. All these programs and organizations are undoubtedly enhancing the lives of their clients and their members, but they may also be adding to age segregation in the society.

Whether or not a divisive politics of age emerges will depend upon countless decisions that are value-laden and that involve difficult ethical as well as political questions. It is a widely-held view that because people are old they deserve more support than people who are young. This position is refuted by others who are concerned about the needy young who, if neglected, may be condemned to a blighted old age of their own. Another problem arises if policies are to be restructured to support the needy of all ages rather than to support persons who are young or old, for how is need to be satisfactorily determined and how are efficient eligibility standards to be administered? These are all troublesome questions.

The goal of an age-integrated society will require different strategies in different areas of decision-making. In some cases age-categorical programs will increase equity among age groups; in other cases, age-neutral programs. Overall, the fastest route to an age-integrated society is probably to mainstream people by ignoring age differences wherever possible, and by focusing on more relevant dimensions of human ability and human need.

References

Brim, O. G., Jr., and Kagan, J. (Eds). *Constancy and Change in Human Development.* Cambridge: Harvard University Press, 1980.

Brody, J. A. Life expectancy and the health of older people. *National Forum,* forthcoming, Autumn, 1982.

Campbell, A., Converse, P. E., and Rodgers, W. L. *The Quality of American Life.* New York: Russell Sage Foundation, 1976.

Featherman, D. L. The life-span perspective in social science research. In a Report of the National Research Council, Committee on Basic Research in Behavioral and Social Sciences, forthcoming (untitled).

Fries, J. F., and Crapo, L. M. *Vitality and Aging.* San Francisco: W. H. Freeman, 1981.

Gergen, K. J. The emerging crisis in life-span developmental theory. In Baltes, P. M., and Brim, O. G., Jr. (Eds). *Life-Span Development and Behavior, Vol. III.* New York: Academic Press, 1980.

Hirschhorn, L. Social policy and the life cycle. *Social Service Review,* 1977, *51*; 434–450.

Lerner, R. M., and Bush-Rossnagel, N. A. (Eds). *Individuals as Producers of Their Development: A Life-Span Perspective.* New York: Academic Press, 1981.

National Council on the Aging. *Aging in the Eighties: America in Transition.* Washington, D.C.: National Council on the Aging, Inc. 1981.

Neugarten, B. L. Continuities and discontinuities of psychological issues into adult life. *Human Development,* 1969, *12*, 121–130.

———. Age groups in American society and the rise of the young-old. *Annals of the American Academy of Political and Social Sciences,* Sept., 1974, 187–198.

———. Policy for the 1980s: age-entitlement or need-entitlement? In *Aging: Agenda for the Eighties, a National Journal Issues Book.* Washington, D.C. 1979 (a), 48–52.

———. Time, age, and the life cycle. *American Journal of Psychiatry,* 1979 (b), *136* (7), 887–894.

———. Aging: Policy Issues for the Developed Countries. In *Gerontology in the 1980s: Recommendations by IAG to the 1982 World Assembly on the Aging.* Hamburg: International Association of Gerontology, July, 1981.

———, and Hagestad, G. Age and the life course. In B. Binstock and E. Shanas (Eds). *Handbook of Aging and the Social Sciences.* New York: Van Nostrand and Reinhold, 1976, 35–55.

THIRTY

The Goals of Medicine in an Aging Society

Christine K. Cassel and Bernice L. Neugarten

The unprecedented aging of our society has recently set off a vigorous debate about the appropriate use of expensive and extensive medical care for elderly persons. This debate involves very complex issues, which are too often and too easily oversimplified both in the media and in the professional literature. Some argue that because the increases in longevity in the past two decades are largely the result of advances in medical technology, we can and should continue, by means of research and the implementation of new technologies, to push back the age barriers that presently create limits to good health and to length of life (e.g., Schneider, 1989). Others argue that there must be a natural end to the human life span, that old age is a reasonable and acceptable indicator of proximity to death, and that it is both unseemly and wasteful to keep augmenting medical technology in a struggle against the inevitability of death (e.g., Callahan, 1987).

In this chapter we will examine the goals of medicine in light of the dramatic demographic and epidemiologic changes in our society. We do this in the hope of developing a framework within which the complex questions about appropriate medical care for patients of advanced age can be addressed most rationally, most effectively, and most humanely.

THE "STATE" OF MODERN MEDICINE

The decade of the 1970s saw the beginning of a reexamination of modern medicine. Many different and often conflicting voices were heard, as is true to the present day. Critics included John Knowles (1977), who edited an issue of the journal *Daedalus* entitled *Doing Better and Feeling Worse*. The title referred to the apparent difference between objective indicators of health, which showed improvement; and subjective reports from patients, which indicated increases in health-related complaints as well as growing dissatisfaction with physicians and hospitals.

Carlson's book *The End of Medicine* (1975) also was an indication of the introspection going on in the medical profession and the public examination of the prac-

Reprinted by permission from *Too Old for Health Care?* edited by R. H. Binstock and S. G. Post (Baltimore, MD: Johns Hopkins University Press, 1991), 75–91.

tice of medicine and its role in our society. The title of the book suggested both a critique of the end(s), or the goal(s), of medicine, and a prediction that an oversized technocracy that has outgrown its human roots must inevitably decline and come to an end. Similar apocalyptic visions were popularized by Ivan Illich in his book *Medical Nemesis* (1976), which put forward the view of modern medicine as too narrowly focused on reductionist technical approaches to problems that would be better approached through social reforms or preventive practices. Howard Waitzkin, in *The Second Sickness* (1983), argued that perverse financial incentives were responsible for the imbalances described by Illich, Carlson, and others.

This reexamination of the goals of medicine and the proper place of medicine in society continued through the 1980s, but the themes became more focused. In the 1970s attention was concentrated on the role that unbridled technology has played in diminishing the humanism of medicine. In the 1980s, it was focused on the costs of that technology and on the ways to stem the steadily increasing expenditures (see Hiatt, 1987).

Today, increasing costs are often described as being closely linked to the increase in life expectancy, because older people use far greater amounts of medical care than do younger people. The increasing life expectancy of Americans is, at least in part, due to advances in medical care. Moreover, because today people seldom die prematurely, they need more medical care to help cope with the chronic diseases of senescence. The special interplay between advanced medical technologies and increasing life expectancy has led to even greater questioning of the goals of medicine. The issues of cost containment and the risks of dehumanized technology are often invoked to argue for setting limits on the use of medical interventions, especially for aged persons (e.g., Callahan 1987; Callahan, 1990).

The goals of medicine in today's society must be examined in the context of medical technology and the rising costs of health care. Also, however, they must be reconsidered in light of the increasing longevity of the population, and the moral and ethical issues that underlie the practice of medicine.

The Increase in Life Expectancy

Longevity has increased dramatically in this century, with average life expectancy almost doubling in the period from 1900 to 1965. During that period, two basic assumptions were made. The first was that most of the decline in mortality was due to advances in social conditions rather than to advances in medical treatment. Better sanitation, nutrition, education, and working conditions were largely responsible for the drop in premature deaths that occurred, historically, long before the advent of any specific life-saving medical discoveries, such as insulin or antibiotics.

The second assumption was that the genetically determined life span of the human species is probably about 75 years. It was recognized that a gap exists between maximum life span and average length of life. By the mid-1960s, however, as average life expectancy began to approach 70 years, it was assumed that the gap had been narrowed about as much as possible: that, in short, we had come close to maximizing life expectancy in this country.

Within a decade, however, the latter assumption was proved wrong, and the great demographic transition of the 1980s had begun. Life expectancy, after remaining stable for two decades, began to increase again. This transition has been described in extraordinary detail by demographers, epidemiologists, and health policy specialists (e.g., Olshansky and Ault, 1986).

The increase in longevity has not yet reached a plateau, nor has it ended. In fact, it is continuing at an unprecedented and unanticipated rate. Average life expectancy is now nearly 80 years for women and nearly 74 years for men, and mortality rates are declining most rapidly among the persons who are over 85. The latter group presently constitutes about 1 percent of the population, but it is projected to be over 2 percent in the next 20 years (U.S. Senate, Special Committee on Aging, et al., 1987). While still a small percentage, the numbers of people in this age group, now some 5 million, will increase to as many as 20 million in two decades. A sense of how dramatic this phenomenon has been can be seen in the U.S. Bureau of the Census publication *The Centenarians* (1988), which describes the growth in the number of persons over the age of 100, a number that jumped from 15,000 in 1980 to 25,000 only five years later, in 1985. At that rate, it is predicted that the number will reach 110,000 by the year 2000 and will perhaps be tripled 30 years later, in 2030.

The recent sharp increase in life expectancy is probably due much more to advances in medical treatment than was the increase seen before the mid-1960s. It is difficult to explain the latest gains as the reflection of new social advances, and even more difficult to imagine that a genetic or other biological change has occurred in the human species that would account for such a dramatic demographic transition in a period of only two decades. Instead, the single major factor often described is the decline in mortality from cardiovascular disease which has occurred in the past 20 years. There is some evidence to support the idea that preventive health measures, combined with advanced medical treatment, are probably responsible for the fact that the onset of severe or potentially fatal coronary disease now occurs at a much later age than it did 10 to 15 years ago. Clearly enough, more research is needed to identify the factors contributing to the drop in mortality rates.

Added Longevity: Good or Bad?

The gain in longevity among Americans has been a remarkable phenomenon, and it is probably the mark of an advanced industrialized civilization, for it has also appeared in other industrialized countries of the world. But is it a good thing? Are we to be pleased that people are living so much longer than we ever thought they would? How we answer such questions has a great deal to do with our understanding of society's response to the demographic transition, and it related directly to the basic issue of the goals of medicine in an aging society.

One way of looking at the issue is by asking, as people reach such advanced old age, how healthy and happy are they? Today, the majority of persons over 65 report at least one chronic illness. Reported illness and impairment, however, do not necessarily result in disability. It is the number and the severity of functional disabilities that are the preferred measures of health status. Persons consider themselves in ill health primarily when an illness or impairment interferes with their activities of daily living, usually defined as the tasks related to personal care and to maintenance of the home environment. As might be anticipated, such health-related difficulties increase with advancing age, yet it is noteworthy that of persons aged 65 to 74, the most recent data show that more than 80 percent report no limitations in carrying out these daily activities. Of those aged 75 to 84, more than 70 percent report no such limitations, and even of those over age 85, half report no limitations (U.S. Senate, Special Committee on Aging, et al., 1987).

This is not to underestimate the problems of those persons who are significantly burdened by ill health or those who are dependent on others for their day-to-day care. It is instead to point out that only a minority of older persons, even at advanced older ages, are ill or disabled. National surveys have also found repeatedly that older people report high levels of life satisfaction, as high as or sometimes higher than the levels reported by younger people (Campbell et al., 1976; Harris et al., 1975; Harris et al., 1981).

Not only are old people as a group faring well, but of at least equal importance in the present context is the fact that, as individuals, people grow old in very different ways, and they become increasingly different from one another with the passage of years. Women age differently from men, and there are differences among racial, ethnic, and particularly, socioeconomic groups. Added to this are the idiosyncratic sequences of events that accumulate over lifetimes to create increasing individual variation. The result is that older people are a very diverse group.

Although the prevalence of illness and disability increases with age in the second half of life, the association between age and health is far from perfect. Age is a good predictor of health status in statistical terms, but for any given individual, age is a poor predictor of physical, mental, or social competence. This finding has emerged repeatedly in systematic studies of performance in which a wide range of physiologic and psychological variables has been examined (Shock et al., 1984) and has come to be called a "superfact" in gerontological research (Maddox, 1986; see also chapter 2 of this book).

The most optimistic analysts, exemplified by Fries (1980), predict that the overall health status of the elderly population will continue to improve, leading to a "compression of morbidity" in the last period of life. Others, exemplified by Brody and Schneider (1983), argue that an increase in life expectancy will lead to an increase in the average period of morbidity and dependency before death.

Recent studies that examine "active life expectancy" (e.g., Katz et al., 1983) attempt to forecast patterns of morbidity and disability, as well as length of life. In these studies, it appears that with advancing age, an increasing percentage of the remaining years of life is likely to be spent in a dependent or disabled state. For example, for persons who reach age 65, an average of 16.5 years of life remain. The forecast is that this period of 16-plus years will include, on average, 6 years (or 40 percent) spent in a state of disability and dependency. For persons who reach 85, it is projected that 7.5 years of life remain, a period that includes more than 4.5 years (or 60 percent) in a disabled state. These data support the prediction that the added years of life will be characterized by disability and dependency, and contradict the optimistic view that, as Fries predicts, most persons will stay healthy until about age 85, then die quickly.

It is the specter of disability, particularly mental impairment from chronic dementing diseases such as Alzheimer's disease, that is most frightening for older people and their families. Disability also creates the greatest need for long-term care, either in institutional or home settings. Alzheimer's disease, hip fracture, and other disorders that result in major loss of function increase exponentially after approximately age 75 to 80 (see Hing, 1987; Kane and Kane, 1990; Manton, 1990). This would suggest to some observers that it may be inappropriate to provide life-extending medical care to individuals in their late seventies or older if the life that is extended is simply a life of disability and dependency. These averages, however, do not adequately describe the tremendous physiologic, psychological, and social variability among members of any age cohort, as mentioned above.

Health Care Costs and the Appropriateness of Treatment

Many factors are contributing to the rise in health care costs, including general inflation, the rapid escalation of physicians' fees, and the mushrooming costs of hospital care, as well as the increase in the number of old people, with their needs for health care (see chapter 2, above). In this connection, it is important to note that a small proportion of older people, about 17 percent, account for over 60 percent of

Medicare payments. This statistic confirms the fact that it is only a small fraction of older persons in any one year who are responsible for the high usage of medical services. It also is consistent with the observation that most old people are not very sick until the last year of their lives. One study showed that the 6 percent of Medicare beneficiaries who died during the year 1978 accounted for 28 percent of Medicare reimbursements in that year (Lubitz and Prihoda, 1984). Other studies of high-cost Medicare patients have shown that a considerable fraction of hospital costs are attributable to patients who die during their hospitalization or shortly after discharge (Scitovsky, 1984).

Such data have led to overly simplistic exhortations that old people, instead of irresponsibly consuming all these medical resources, should accept death and thus allow more resources to be used for the young (Callahan, 1987; Callahan, 1990; Lamm, 1987). Some commentators argue that investment in acute health care yields more potential years of life in the young than in the old, and thus it is a more prudential investment plan for society's health care dollars (Daniels, 1988).

Such statements raise fundamental moral questions about the value of human life. They also make misleading generalizations about the goals of most medical treatment, describing it as "life extension" rather than as providing comfort to the patient or enhancing the patient's functional status and quality of life. Just as it is difficult to generalize about the health status of "the elderly," it is equally difficult to generalize about the appropriate use of "medical technology." When the specific uses of the resources spent on patients in their last year of life are examined, it becomes clear that most such patients were functioning at a high level prior to their last illness. Furthermore, the large expenditures in the last year of life are much more likely to be for persons aged 65 to 80 than for persons aged 80 and over (Scitovsky, 1984).

In addition, physicians cannot predict at the onset of hospitalization which patients are likely to survive. As studies have suggested, half of the high-cost patients survive at reasonable levels of functional status for a year or more (Scitovsky, 1984). In other words, the high-cost Medicare patient has a 50:50 chance of meaningful survival. It would be difficult, on grounds of morality, to argue that for reasons of economy, not for medical reasons, all such patients should be allowed to die.

A basic question about the goals of medicine arises here. Persons in danger of dying are, by definition, persons who are extremely ill and are therefore likely to need extensive and expensive hospital care. It is not enough to look simply at the expenditures incurred for them; it may be quite appropriate to provide extensive hospital care for a person with a serious illness, especially if there is a reasonable likelihood of a successful outcome and if such care is consistent with the patient's values or expressed preferences.

The number of dollars spent does not necessarily reflect the appropriateness of any given medical intervention selected by the patient's physician. There is no doubt that life-extending technologies are sometimes used in treating elderly patients, as well as in treating some younger patients, where the prognosis does not warrant aggressive medical intervention and where the patients, if able to express their wishes, would probably refuse such treatment.

Physicians have learned a great deal from the new and emerging field of medical ethics about becoming aware of patients' preferences, which they elicit by encouraging the use of verbal or written "advance directives," or by holding discussions with family members who can report attitudes and values of the patient that might be relevant to making a decision to allow death to occur. Advance directives include legal instruments such as "living wills" and "durable powers of attorney for health care" (Kapp, 1989). They can also include conversations between the physician and the patient regarding the use or nonuse of life-sustaining treatments in the event of critical illness; in this case the patient's preferences are written down and become part of the medical record.

More and more physicians and hospitals are accepting the patient's right to die with dignity. More and more hospitals have explicit policies for do-not-resuscitate orders (Miles and Cranford, 1982). More and more physicians and hospitals are accepting the concept of hospice care for patients who are not likely to regain any meaningful level of existence. More and more state supreme courts, in cases of hopeless illness, have decided in favor of the patient's or the family's petition for the withdrawal of life-sustaining medical treatment (Wanzer et al., 1989).

There is still room for progress in this area, however, for many physicians and other personnel in hospitals and nursing homes are still unduly worried about their legal liability in such situations. They may continue to use medically unwarranted and morally unacceptable medical treatment because of their fear of legal repercussions if treatment is discontinued. Such fear is largely unwarranted, for there are few instances of successful lawsuits brought against physicians for withholding or withdrawing life-sustaining measures when the patient and the family have been involved in the decision, and when the treatment adheres to stated institutional protocols (Miles and Gomez, 1989).

Nonetheless, in the litigious environment of the United States the physician or the medical institution can never be entirely immune from lawsuits. Physicians need to reassert their moral courage to advocate the course of treatment most consistent with caring medical practice and respect for the patient's wishes. Malpractice reform and increasing attention to statutes that encourage the use of advance directives would enhance the physician's likelihood of making sensible decisions regarding the care of hopelessly ill patients. It is most important that such decisions should continue to be based on the individual case, not on some sweeping policy or regulation, especially not on a policy that uses age as the decisive criterion for withholding intensive medical treatment.

For example, some families would want the physician to administer antibiotics to treat pneumonia in a parent with advanced Alzheimer's disease, even though the quality of that parent's life may be very low when assessed by others. The family may find simple physical caregiving to be meaningful to both the aged parent and the caretakers, and may not regard it as too burdensome, even in the home setting. At the same time, treatments such as cardiopulmonary resuscitation or mechanical ventilation, which are ordinarily used only in comparatively severe life-threatening episodes, may not be indicated for the same patient because the burdens of treatment for that patient would not be justified by the chances of success. In most such instances, the situation is seen by everyone concerned as offering no chance of the patient's recovery, and no disagreement arises. In other instances, families and physicians together come to such decisions. The decision reached depends on the patient's condition, the views of the patient and the family, and their relationship with the physician.

Decisions to withhold medical treatment are never easy, nor should they be. Struggling through the management of such cases should help physicians to become more sensitive to the needs of hopelessly ill patients, to the subtleties of clinical treatment decisions for the most frail elderly patients, and to the skills needed for communication with families who are under the stress of caring for a severely impaired relative.

What Are the Basic Values of Medicine?

Concerns about health care expenditures have raised some fundamental questions about the goals of medicine. What is medical care for? Is it for prolonging the lives of the disabled, or is it only for prolonging the lives of those who can be functioning members of society? Is a person's functioning to be measured in terms of economic productivity, and is economic productivity the predominant value by which to judge human life? Should the criteria for medical treatment be different for patients who are financially covered by publicly funded programs such as Medicare and Medicaid than for patients who are privately insured and those who can pay out-of-pocket?

These issues arise not only in regard to elderly persons but also in regard to expenditures for the long-term care of disabled children and young adults. Such questions are now being raised increasingly often, especially with regard to intensive care for infants with severe birth defects. New developments in the care of AIDS patients, treatments that promise longer life expectancy but not complete recovery, will probably raise similar concerns.

In spite of these conflicting values—cost containment and patients' right to medical care—the basic values of medicine remain the same as before: the preservation of life, the relief of suffering, and respect for patients. Advances in medical technology have made the implementation of these values more complex, for in addition to problems of cost containment, the striving to save life often creates great emotional burdens for patients and families, and sometimes seems to conflict with a humanistic approach to patient care. The latter problem needs clarification if we are to understand the goals of modern medicine in an aging society.

It is useful to realize that policy controversies about the costs of medical care and about setting limits to medical interventions for old people center around two different models of medicine. Although these models are not necessarily mutually exclusive, and although, for some patients, the models may lead to identical modes of care, their primary goals are nevertheless clearly distinguishable.

The "Heroic" Model of Medicine

The overriding goal of the heroic model of medicine is the extension of life. In this model, life itself is of irreducible value; and the goal for the medical researcher, as well as for the practicing physician, is to postpone death, regardless of the patient's quality of life and regardless of the cost of treatment. In its most simplistic form, the heroic model of medicine does not ask whether a death is premature, appropriate, or acceptable, but asks only how death, the enemy, can be held at bay. The physician experiences the death of a patient as a personal failure, and perhaps also as an unwelcome reminder of his or her own mortality.

The intoxicating successes of medical technology—such as routine cardiac monitoring and defibrillation, mechanical ventilation, and kidney dialysis—that appeared during the 1960s probably created a receptive environment for the growth and acceptance of this heroic model. Certainly this model did not exist in earlier periods of history, when the physician's role was as much to "abide with" families during the illness of a patient as to dramatically rescue the patient from death.

Perceptions of the inhumanity of highly technical medical care, especially in cases of terminal disease, have led to public expressions of frustration with the heroic model of medicine, especially by those who demand a right to "die with dignity." Researchers in thanatology (the study of death and dying) have examined why some physicians are unable to accept their own mortality and why other physicians can deal patiently and compassionately with their patients' deaths. Accordingly, thanatologists have suggested a range of educational and institutional changes to enable society to deal better with death and dying. One result has been the development of hospice care for patients with terminal illness. Another is the increased discussion of death and dying in the medical curriculum.

The heroic model of medicine has brought with it, of course, an emphasis on medical research, as symbolized by the growth of the U.S. National Institutes of Health, by the "wars" on cancer and on heart disease, and by the enthusiastic search for "cures." In medical training, however, this model has resulted in much less emphasis being placed on the management of chronic disease and on the treatment of the more common but not life-threatening problems that patients present, and more emphasis being placed on the diagnosis and treatment of less common but potentially curable disorders.

The heroic model has indeed won many heroic victories, and it is a glamorous and exciting model both for health care professionals and for the public at large. It is undeniable that the goal of a longer life and the fantasy of being rescued from death are attractive to most people. However, the heroic model cannot deal with uncertainty, with decline, or with death. It cannot encompass the wide range of clinical experience or the humility and compassion that are necessary for medical care in a society characterized by increasing longevity and increasing chronic illness.

The Humanistic Model of Medicine

In the second model of medicine, the one called the "humanistic" model, the primary goal is the improvement of the quality of life. In this model, the physician is much more likely to accept the patient on the patient's own terms and to establish goals of treatment which improve or maintain that person's level of functioning and quality of life. The prolongation of the patient's life is not necessarily what the physician strives for if that is not the patient's goal.

One example of this humanistic model is seen in the palliative approach of hospice care, in which the aim is to control the patient's symptoms and to make the patient comfortable. The application of this model is fairly straightforward in the care of a patient who is suffering from a clearly terminal illness and whose life expectancy is measured in days or weeks. However, in the great majority of elderly patients, multiple chronic diseases are the rule. The distinction between treatment aimed at improving the quality of life for these persons and treatment aimed at life prolongation is not so clear. This is particularly true in patients of advanced old age.

The humanistic approach must extend to psychological, social, and other issues, and it often requires a multidisciplinary team approach. This is especially true in treating older people, because the health problems that cause them distress often cannot be dealt with simply by prescriptions or surgery. The old patient may require economic, psychological, and social support, possibly including improved transportation, suitable housing, education about nutrition, and more.

In the humanistic model, the physician seeks medical interventions that place a low burden on the patient and have a high likelihood of benefit. The physician is unlikely to subject a patient to a procedure or treatment that involves a great deal of pain, as, for example, in resuscitating a frail elderly patient where there is only a small likelihood of improvement in that patient's life after the treatment ends.

In many of the interventions that improve the quality of life, particularly in a very old person, the prolongation of life may be an inevitable side effect. A good example is when a physician recently prescribed a pacemaker for a 99-year-old woman who was experiencing attacks of fainting caused by cardiac arrhythmia. While it may be agreed that extraordinary efforts to prolong the patient's life would be unseemly, "contraindicated," or perhaps even rejected by the patient herself, nonetheless the implantation of a pacemaker will prevent her from continually fainting, and thus falling and risking a broken hip, with its likelihood of protracted disability. The goal of such treatment is palliative—to prevent falling and potential fracture—but the salutary effect that the pacemaker will have on her heart rhythm will undoubtably extend her life.

The observation that treatments that improve life and those that extend life are often indistinguishable applies to almost any palliative measure, ranging from the administration of insulin to persons with diabetes and the administration of oxygen to persons who suffer from shortness of breath, to modern, technology-intensive treatments for heart failure or symptomatic malignancies.

A MODEL OF MEDICINE FOR THE AGING SOCIETY

Why is it that we are seeking a principle by which to limit medical treatment? Is it not obvious to the clinician when a certain treatment is or is not indicated? Clearly, physicians themselves often feel at sea, particularly in the care of very old patients. Old people are a new population to be served, and how best to serve them is a question that has only recently been receiving attention in medical research and training (Cassel, 1987). The guidelines are not clear, and they become especially problematic in a society in which physicians are pressured to be the gatekeepers of society's wealth and to prevent the wasteful use of dollars on people who will not "benefit."

Who is to decide what it means for the patient to benefit? Must the patient's life also be of present benefit to society? One assumption often made in this discourse is that if we could identify the best-functioning elderly person, or perhaps the best-functioning person of any age, we could then produce proper guidelines and would then know to whom medical care should best be offered.

Optimal Care Only for Those Who Function Well?

Various indexes of functioning have been explored by investigators who believe that when the patient's quality of life is very low, it is appropriate to limit medical care, particularly life-extending medical care. Those who are arguing for the rationing of medical care for old people advocate such decisions in treating all older patients, even those who are not extremely ill or terminally ill, and the establishment of a general policy of this kind.

This would mean that over time medical care would be provided more often to old persons whose quality of life is relatively high—those who are often described as "aging successfully"—than to persons whose quality of life is low.

One problem is that, for many observers, the quality of life is defined in reductionist terms, as the level of functioning. In one notable instance, it has been defined in even more reductionist terms, as the level of physiologic functioning; in that instance, old persons who score high on tests of half a dozen physiologic functions are termed the "successful agers" (Rowe and Kahn, 1987).

If the level of functioning were to become, for policy makers, the criterion for determining the type of medical care to be provided, the outcome would be to give more medical care to those who are physically and mentally able, and less to those who are disabled. Not only would such a policy increase inequities in the allocation of health care, but it also raises other underlying ethical questions. Except for the most extremely ill patients, about whom disagreements are rare, how and by whom shall the patient's quality of life be determined? At what point is any given type of medical care no longer warranted? Is it acceptable, on ethical grounds, to make such distinctions and then to act on them, in the interest of cost containment?

If such a policy mandating old-age-based rationing of medical care were to be implemented, it would represent a major departure from the prevailing goal of medicine in our society. Perhaps more importantly, however, for most persons in the society it would represent, on ethical grounds, too high a price for the society to pay.

Optimal Care for All Persons?

The goal of medicine our society has been pursuing to date is to provide medical care that enhances not only the level of functioning but also the quality of life for all persons. Today that goal focuses more sharply than before on the expectation that over time a larger and larger proportion of the population will age "successfully." However, to produce a population most of whose members are at high levels of functioning may not necessarily be the optimum, or even the preferred, goal for a society like our own.

We have been experiencing a tidal wave of improvement in health, which is most clearly shown by the dramatic rise in average life expectancy. Although not all subgroups in the population are experiencing the same rapid gains, still there is no disagreement that the population as a whole has benefited enormously. There is a price to be paid for this, however: the one implied by the metaphor "The rising tide lifts all boats equally." That is, the frail as well as the sturdy are being lifted. Although most people who survive to an advanced old age remain quite vigorous and independent, we shall never be without a certain number who, while they too are now surviving, do so with significant disability and with great need for both medical and social support.

In light of all the advantages of an increase in life expectancy, is the task of caring for those who are aging less than successfully too great a price for our society to pay? A related question is the one already suggested above: namely, whether our measures of success are too narrow. We have learned the sobering lessons of eugenics from a recent society in which only those persons who were regarded as the most highly functioning were allowed to survive. Equally sobering, in the present context, is the fact that the genocide practiced by the Nazis began with physician-supported "mercy killing" of persons who were retarded, mentally ill, or aged and infirm.

Whether or not our own society would move along the same downward path is debatable, but our medical successes have led some of us to view chronic disability and dependence, no matter what the cause, as simply undesirable, as a drain on our resources, or as our failure. These attitudes could lead to a harsh and unforgiving society, one that values only the healthy or only those who can pay their own way. It would be a regressive society, rather than one that reflects the successes of modern civilization. The civilized society allocates resources, both financial and emotional, for including in the life of the community those of its members who are less fortunate, and for providing care to them.

EMBRACING THE AGING SOCIETY

Some observers believe that caring for disabled elderly persons will be an unbearable burden on society and will enervate and destroy us. Perhaps, to the contrary, society will benefit if it is challenged by the need to care for the vulnerable and the frail. Society's vitality and productivity may be improved if it learns how to sustain the lessons of compassion and how best to care for those who need care—in so doing, developing attributes such as loyalty and trust—as well as how to increase community cohesion.

Caring for the disabled may lead, also, to the creation of institutions of medicine and health care which reflect the needs of the modern society—to provide more home care and long-term care, and to be more prudent in the use of expensive medical commodities of unproven value (Brook and Lohr, 1986). We might learn to cut costs by using governmental power to limit the profits generated by entrepreneurial pharmaceutical and medical equipment companies, and to discourage their marketing practices that lead to wasteful overutilization of high-priced therapeutic and diagnostic procedures. We might learn instead how to create policies and methods for the strict assessment of technological procedures. Modern technology is not an evil in itself, but its indiscriminate use is medically inappropriate and wasteful, for it often diverts resources that could be used for long-term or preventive care (see Hiatt, 1987, especially pp. 13–33).

The appropriateness of any technology or treatment must be decided separately for each individual patient. The physician's role is to understand the potential efficacy or lack of efficacy of a given treatment, and to recommend treatment consistent with the patient's condition and the patient's values, regardless of the patient's age, sex, skin color, or income level.

Medicine in today's world needs to embrace the changing society in which people are living so much longer, and to create a humane model of medical care that fits the new social realities. It should focus not on setting age limits for medical care but, rather, on adding opportunities for a continuing sense of the value of life, especially for the very old. In this approach one is neither nihilistic nor fatalistic about the chances of helping old as well as young people.

The complexity of modern medicine requires an integration of the heroic and the humanistic, the technologic and the psychosocial approaches to health. The welfare of the individual patient is the measure by which any medical intervention must be assessed. The aging of our society, and the critique of modern medicine it has engendered, can lead to a medical practice that is better for all patients, and therefore for the society at large. At the same time, it requires a careful examination of the complexities involved. Otherwise it could lead to discrimination against sick and disabled persons and to the dehumanization of our society.

References

Brody, J. A., and Schneider, E. I. (1983). Aging, natural death, and the compression of morbidity: another view. *New England Journal of Medicine, 309*, 854–856.

Brook, R. H., and Lohr, K. N. (1986). Will we need to ration effective health care? *Issues in Science and Technology, 3*(1), 68–77.

Callahan, D. (1987). *Setting limits: medical goals in an aging society.* New York: Simon & Schuster.

Callahan, D. (1990). *What kind of life: the limits of medical progress.* New York: Simon & Schuster.

Campbell, A., Converse, P., and Rodgers, W. (1976). *The quality of American life.* New York: Russell Sage Foundation.

Carlson, R. J. (1975). *The end of medicine.* New York: John Wiley & Sons.

Cassel, C. K. (1987). Certification: another step for geriatric medicine. *Journal of the American Medical Association, 258*, 1518–1519.

Daniels, N. (1988). *Am I my parents' keeper? an essay on justice between the young and the old.* New York: Oxford University Press.

Fries, J. F. (1980). Aging, natural death, and the compression of morbidity. *New England Journal of Medicine, 303*, 130–135.

Harris, L., and Associates (1975). *The myth and reality of aging in America.* Washington,

D.C.: National Council on the Aging.

Harris, L., and Associates (1981). *Aging in the eighties.* Washington, D.C.: National Council on the Aging.

Hiatt, H. H. (1987). *America's health in the balance.* New York: Harper & Row.

Hing, E. (1987). *Use of nursing homes by the elderly: preliminary data from the 1985 National Nursing Home Survey, Advance Data No. 135.* Hyattsville, Md: National Center for Health Statistics, May 14.

Illich, I. (1976). *Medical nemesis: the expropriation of health.* New York: Pantheon Books.

Kane, R. L., and Kane, R. A. (1990). Health care for older people: organizational and policy issues. In R. H. Binstock and L. K. George, eds, *Handbook of aging and the social sciences* (3rd ed.), pp. 415–437. San Diego: Academic Press.

Kapp, M. (1989). Medical treatments and the physician's legal duties. In C. K. Cassel and D. Reisenberg, eds., *Geriatric medicine* (2nd ed.), pp. 623–639. New York: Springer-Verlag.

Katz, S., Branch, L. G., Branson, M. H., Papsidero, J. A., Beck, J. C., and Greer, D. S. (1983). Active life expectancy. *New England Journal of Medicine, 309*, 1218–1224.

Knowles, J. H., ed. (1977). Doing better and feeling worse: health in the United States. *Daedalus: Journal of the American Academy of Arts and Sciences, 106*(1).

Lamm, R. D. (1987). Ethical health care for the elderly: are we cheating our children? In T. M. Smeeding, ed., *Should medical care be rationed by age?*, pp. xi–xv. Totowa, N.J.: Rowman & Littlefield.

Lubitz, J., and Prihoda, R. (1984). The uses and costs of Medicare services in the last two years of life. *Health Care Financing Review, 5*(3), 117–131.

Maddox, G. (1986). Dynamics of population aging: a changing, changeable profile. In *America's aging workforce: a Traveler's symposium,* pp. 30–37. Hartford, Conn.: Traveler's Insurance Co.

Manton, K. G. (1990). Mortality and morbidity. In R. H. Binstock and L. K. George, eds., *Handbook of aging and the social sciences* (3rd ed.), pp. 64–90. San Diego: Academic Press.

Miles, S. H., and Cranford, R. (1982). The do-not-resuscitate order in a teaching hospital. *Annals of Internal Medicine, 96*, 660–664.

Miles, S. H., and Gomez, C. F. (1989). *Protocols for elective use of life-sustaining treatments.* New York: Springer Publishing Co.

Olshansky, S. J., and Ault, B. A. (1986). The fourth stage of the epidemiologic transition: the age of delayed degenerative diseases. *Milbank Memorial Fund Quarterly/Health and Society, 64*, 355–391.

Rowe, J. W., and Kahn, R. L. (1987). Human aging: usual and successful. *Science, 237*, 143–149.

Schneider, E. L. (1989). Options to control the rising health care costs of older Americans. *Journal of the American Medical Association, 261*, 907.

Scitovsky, A. A. (1984). The high cost of dying: what do the data show? *Milbank Memorial Fund Quarterly/Health and Society, 62*, 591–608.

Shock, N. W., Greulich, R., Andres, R., Arenberg, D., Costa, P., Jr., Lakatta, E., and

Tobin, J. (1984). *Normal human aging: the Baltimore longitudinal study of aging.* Washington, D.C.: U.S. Government Printing Office.

U.S. Bureau of the Census, Office of the Actuary (1988). *The centenarians.* Washington, D.C.: U.S. Government Printing Office.

U.S. Senate, Special Committee on Aging, in conjunction with the American Association of Retired Persons, the Federal Council on the Aging, and the U.S. Administration on Aging (1987). *Aging America: trends and projections.* Washington, D.C.: U.S. Government Printing Office.

Waitzkin, H. (1983). *The second sickness: contradictions of capitalist health care.* New York: Free Press.

Wanzer, S., Federman, D., Adelstein, S. J., Cassel, C., Cassem, E., Cranford, R., Hook, E., Lo, B., Mortel, C., Safar, P., Stone, A., and van Eys, J. (1989). The physician's responsibility toward hopelessly ill patients: a second look. *New England Journal of Medicine, 320,* 844–849.

PART FIVE
Postscript

Speculations about the Meanings of Age

Dail A. Neugarten

The last two papers in this volume summarize and speculate. The first traces the development of the field of aging and outlines the issues facing an aging society. It provides a synopsis of Bernice Neugarten's best reflections on the history and prospects of the field. Neugarten concludes that the academic discipline of gerontology has matured and needs now to formulate new questions about lives, life spans and the life course. She also suggests that we know relatively little about the aging of societies—about the impacts of an aging population on families, institutions, communities and on the society at large. Thus she poses a challenge to those researchers and practitioners interested in furthering knowledge about the psychology, sociology and politics of human lives.

In the last paper of this volume, Neugarten prophesies that the field of aging will be replaced by one called "the study of lives"—one which will include a comprehensive and developmental portrayal of life periods, life patterns and life events. Neugarten also conjectures about (and advocates for) social policies and programs based on a more ethical balance of "age" with "need" with "entitlement." She thus raises, as she has many times before, the ultimate question of age-irrelevance.

Shall we see a totally age-integrated society in the twenty-first or twenty-second century? It is doubtful. In her speculating, however, Neugarten has done much to help us understand what we know and what we have yet to learn. Her chief accomplishment has been to frame, then to study, and finally to write about the important issues in the study of lives.

Dail A. Neugarten is Associate Professor of Public Affairs, University of Colorado at Denver.

THIRTY-ONE

Gerontology and the Aging Society

It is a special privilege to stand before this audience today and to speak on behalf of myself and my fellow honorees. I want first to express for all of us our thanks and appreciation for having been singled out to be given that which we prize most highly of all possible rewards, an honorary degree from an outstanding university. This is a highly significant event in our lives.

I wish also to express our congratulations to Catholic University for having reached an important milestone of its own, its 13th lustrum and the 65th year of its illustrious history.

Formerly, age 65 represented entry into old age, that period of life presumably marked by declines in mind and spirit. But, as I shall elaborate later in this talk, age 65 has today become associated, instead, with that period of maturity when a person has all the advantages of accumulated experience and expertise and has, at the same time, a long intellectually productive period still ahead. An academic institution can be likened to a person in this regard; and I congratulate this University, therefore, for now being in that happy position of entering into this new period of maturity.

I will speak today on the topic of how people grow old; a topic that, if it is not of professional interest to us all, is likely to be of personal interest to us all. I shall comment briefly on three aspects: first, on the growth of the academic field of gerontology; second, on a few major findings that have emerged from that field of study; and third, on the aging society: That is, a society in which increasing proportions of the population are old.

THE ACADEMIC FIELD OF GERONTOLOGY

The academic field of gerontology is itself young. It embraces, not one, but a large group of sciences; for the study of aging has become an important line of inquiry in a wide range of biological and social sciences, from genetics to political science. Although human aging has for centuries intrigued philosophers and poets and other observers of the human condition, gerontology, as now defined, is only fifty years

Reprinted by permission from *Dies Natalis,* Katholieke Universiteit Nijmegan, October 28, 1988: 21–28.

old. It had its beginnings in the 1940s, when a few biologists began to pursue the question, "How and why do human cells and bodily organs age?" And when a few psychologists and sociologists began to ask, "How do persons as they grow old change in their psychological capacities, in personality, and in attitudes and activities of everyday life?"

But the development of gerontology was driven, in larger part, by the fact that demographers were pointing to the increasing longevity and the increasing numbers of older people in industrialized societies and were projecting that the numbers would multiply dramatically in the decades ahead. Researchers and policymakers began to ask what this demographic revolution might signify for the welfare of persons as they grow old and for the welfare of the society at large.

Before the 1940s it had been largely professionals who were concerned about older persons. Physicians were caring for the ill and disabled; social workers for the poor and isolated; and mental health professionals were seeing almost no older people at all because the problems of old age were regarded as untreatable—a view that has now been replaced by a more enlightened one.

Research, sparse as it was, had been based primarily on the hospitalized or the institutionalized. The prevailing stereotypes were that old people, as a group, were not only sick, but needy and desolate. Aging was perceived almost entirely as a set of inevitable processes of physical and mental decline. Age 65, because it had been designated as the age of retirement, marked the beginning of those declines.

In the 1940s a few social scientists began to study health status, psychological and social functioning, family interactions, and patterns of work and retirement, and in doing so, to study, from all walks of life, the presence of a wide range of older men and women leading normal everyday lives in their communities. Investigators in a few universities and in a few biomedical research institutes in the United States, and a few in Denmark, England, France, Germany, The Netherlands and the Soviet Union became the pioneers in the field—among them, a small group at my own University of Chicago, and not too long thereafter, a small group at this university in Nijmegen.

By 1940, there were large-scale investigations of older persons underway in Chicago; and by the late 1940s, the first graduate course in aging was created there for doctoral students. So far as I can determine, this was the first such course offered in any university. The course was named, at first, Maturity and Old Age; but it was soon renamed Adult Development and Aging. The new title reflected some of the changes in perspective already appearing: namely, that development occurs in adults as well as in children.

The number of investigators and the number of universities that support research and teaching in aging have now multiplied dramatically, especially in my own country where there are now more than 1,000 colleges and universities offering courses or special programs in aging at both undergraduate and graduate levels. The trend has also been international, as shown by the fact that there are now more than 50 national societies of gerontology and geriatrics across the world, all of them with the express purpose of furthering research and education. And there are some 70 journals in the field, research oriented or practice oriented.

It has been recognized from the outset that biological, psychological, and social processes of aging are interactive, most of them interdependent. If we are to understand how individuals grow old, and how the lengthening of lives interacts with other forms of social change, multidisciplinary approaches are of central importance. This understanding is reflected in today's academic institutions, where research in aging is proceeding within the traditional disciplines, but where Centers of Gerontology are also appearing, where scientists from different backgrounds carry out interdisciplinary studies and interact to educate each other as well as to educate students. Aging has become a major growth industry in academia, one that is likely to continue to expand.

MAJOR FINDINGS

What have we gerontologists learned thus far? There is time here to mention only a few of the major generalizations, drawn largely from the social sciences. Because biomedical advances—such as new treatments for heart disease, or the discovery that Alzheimer's disease has a genetic component; or new evidence that diet, exercise, smoking and other life-style factors play primary roles in health status, and therefore in biological and psychological aging—are widely reported in the news media, they need not be described here.

Social science research has shown, on the basis of systematic and repeated studies, that:

1. The myths and negative stereotypes about middle age and old age do not fit the realities. Major life events such as the biological climacterium in women, children growing up and leaving the family home, the psychological transitions of mid-life, retirement, grandparenthood, and great-grandparenthood, are not crises. They are normal, expectable punctuation marks in the life cycle. Even chronic illness and widowhood, while they represent major losses, do not often provoke psychological crises.

2. The large majority of persons over 65 are retired, and the trend is toward earlier and earlier retirement in all postindustrial countries.

3. Most older people have high levels of life satisfaction, and the majority report that life is better than they had anticipated. The level of life satisfaction is not related to whether one is 60 or 70 or 80.

4. There is no single pattern of optimal aging or what is sometimes called "successful" aging. It is not the common pattern for persons to disengage from their communities or to withdraw psychologically as they grow old. Some are happy when they stay at work; some when they undertake a new hobby or volunteer role; some when they opt for a rocking chair pattern.

5. Not only do people grow old in very different ways, but the differences between persons become greater with the passage of life time. Older persons are more diverse than any younger group, and they become more diverse the longer they live.

6. Across the great range of differences among older people, it is useful, especially for the policymaker, to distinguish the two groups who can be called, for convenience, the independent and the dependent. These terms are not altogether felicitous, but they serve to indicate that the distinction is based, not on age, but on health and social characteristics. The independent are the large majority of older persons in the developed countries. They are vigorous and active and competent men and women, usually retired, who are well-integrated members of their families and their communities, relatively secure economically, and increasingly well-educated, and increasingly active politically.

7. The dependent, by contrast, are those who suffer major physical or mental or social losses and who require a wide range of special health services and social services.

The majority group changes in membership, of course, as new generations reach 65 and as persons move from independence to a shorter or longer period of dependence before they die, but the large proportion who remain competent and independent until very advanced old age may serve to indicate how far we have come in the past 50 years in our developed societies—where not only do the large majority reach old age but the large majority of those who do so, fare so well.

8. For the population of older people considered as a whole, age is related to physical and social health (the increase in chronic illness among older people is of course well known). But for individuals, age is not closely related to physical or social or intellectual competencies, interests or needs. In this sense, age has lost much of its significance in distinguishing among middle-aged and older people.

9. Older persons can continue to learn, as is demonstrable from systematic experimental studies; and more important, they do continue to learn, as demonstrated in the ways in which they make new adaptations to their changing physical and social worlds.

10. A final generalization emerges from those just mentioned. Aging is not an immutable process, either in the social or biological patterning of lives, as the increases in longevity in developed countries has itself made so clear. We do not yet know the limits of change, but the prevailing view among gerontologists now is that a vast

range of positive interventions can be made; that the changes that accompany old age are in many ways treatable, some are reversible. To have changed the climate of opinion among researchers, professionals and the public at large has been the major contribution of both social and biological scientists over the past 50 years.

THE AGING SOCIETY

When we turn to the aging of societies rather than the aging of individuals, the findings are less clear. We have had relatively little research on the effects of the presence of so many older people, effects on younger age groups and on the structures of society. Health planners and epidemiologists are focusing on the implications for health care systems as the numbers and proportions of older people grow larger. And labor economists are focusing on the composition of the work force, on tax and wage adjustments that are needed to provide public and private pensions for the increasing numbers who retire earlier and earlier but live longer and longer. But many questions are yet unexplored. For instance, the family has become a multi-generational structure, but we know little about patterns of social interaction or economic transfers in the four- or five-generation unit. What is the influence of the changing age distribution on our educational institutions? On political structures and legal institutions? How are persons planning or managing their lengthening lives and how are our views of living and dying changing? With women living longer than men, and with greater numbers of older women than older men, what changes in gender roles are occurring in middle and old age?

As we look ahead, some of the issues will be more troublesome than others. An aging society will need a broader definition of productivity, one that goes beyond paid work to include non-paid work, and to include both economic and social productivity. The society will need to nurture the potential for social productivity wherever it is to be found—not only among the old, but also among the young. Can we create a 21st century version of "the elder"—the role in which older people maximize their long experience and expertise for the good of the whole society?

Can we change the ways in which education, paid work and leisure are distributed in a fixed order across the life cycle, and instead create a new pattern in which education and re-education are interspersed with periods of work and periods of leisure, in line with the individual's preferences and changing abilities?

Given that age is not closely linked to the adult's abilities and desires and needs, perhaps we will learn to focus, not on age at all, but on more relevant dimensions of human needs, human competencies, and human diversity.

The aging society provides new opportunities and new challenges: for individuals, opportunities for more varied and enriched experiences and relationships and sensibilities—in short, the possibilities of a longer and richer human development.

And for the society at large, new opportunities, in learning to care for our old, to learn also how better to care for our young. In learning how to nurture the human qualities of each person without regard to the person's age, the possibilities are that the aging society may become a more humane society.

THIRTY-TWO

The End of Gerontology?

When I am asked about the future of gerontology, I am greatly tempted to predict that the field of gerontology is going to disappear over the next couple of decades. I think this is increasingly evident on at least three fronts.

People on the intellectual or academic front, who teach and do research in gerontology, know that the phenomenon called aging doesn't begin when people are in their 60s. It begins at birth, and is a lifelong process. The persuasion is becoming ever more compelling that lives are indivisible. If you study aging, you know that the age that you define as "old" is totally arbitrary. Many think that in order to understand aging, you must begin to study people long before they become what society calls "old." So the realization is now pretty well-established that chronological age is not a useful concept for either research or education.

On the policy front, entitlements keyed to age are also coming into question. This is what I referred to in my book *Age or Need?* in discussing the dilemma of policy makers and how they ought to reconcile the competing needs of populations. Policy makers in this country can tell you that creating policy and services for particular age groups turns out to be ineffective and unsupportable. There was nothing magical, of course, about establishing age 65 as the age of entitlement when policies such as Social Security and Medicare were created. It emerged from a tradition which began when 65 really meant old, and in the United States the decision was part of a political compromise which failed to support universal income security and health insurance at the time those laws were passed. But in today's environment of need, we can see with greater clarity that need without age must override age without need.

And on the front lines, where services are delivered, service providers are today finding it ever more difficult to provide services solely on the basis of age. Service providers recognize and are often intensely sensitive to the needs of their clients. It is therefore stressful and demoralizing for them to be unable to provide benefits when need is obvious, and at the same time to provide benefits in the absence of need.

Reprinted by permission from *Center on Aging,* a publication of the Buehler Center on Aging, McGaw Medical Center of Northwestern University, 10, no. 1 (Spring 1994).

More and more of them are trying to do something about it, to make the allocation of services age-neutral.

There is more and more evidence of the irrelevance of age in related initiatives as well. National health care reform is surely being debated today in terms of universal coverage for persons of all ages. Community agencies are reorganizing to include children's advocacy groups as well as aging advocacy groups. The recent Americans with Disabilities Act is age-neutral.

A caveat is in order. Turning to need as the single criterion for entitlement will require us to be much more explicit and to achieve a higher level of consensus about the nature and relative importance of our needs. Just as age-based entitlements can result in maldistribution of resources, so can need-based entitlements, if the latter are not objective and well understood.

If I am right, then you will forgive a word to the wise when I say that gerontology is not going to last. The trend is undeniable. In the last analysis, chopping up the life cycle was not a very good idea to begin with. In its place, there will be a proliferation of need-driven, age-neutral policies and programs.

The study of aging as it is presently defined will become less and less viable as age becomes less and less a criterion of anything. For the word "gerontology," we will substitute something we now call "the study of lives," based on the concept of the life cycle as a whole and the processes of change from infancy through old age. As that concept emerges, it will improve our understanding of child development, as well as old age, and will be useful to those who use the life-course perspective in teaching, in policy making, and in delivering services.

BIBLIOGRAPHY

OF BERNICE L. NEUGARTEN

1937

An Experiment in Remedial Reading at the College Level. M.A. thesis, Department of Education, University of Chicago.

1943

Family Social Position and the Social Development of the Child. Ph.D. dissertation, Committee on Human Development, University of Chicago.

1946

Social Class and Friendship among School Children. *American Journal of Sociology,* 51: 305–13.

1946–50

Growing up; Being Teen Agers; High School Life; Discovering Myself; Planning My Future; Toward Adult Living. Chicago: National Forum, Inc. (Senior author of a series of six textbooks on personality and guidance for school grades 7 through 12.)

1949

The Democracy of Childhood. Chapter 5 in W. L. Warner and Associates, *Democracy in Jonesville,* pp. 77–88. New York: Harper.

1950

Body Processes Help to Determine Behavior and Development; Encouraging the Child's Spontaneous Interests (with N. Wright). Chapters 4 and 8 in *Fostering Mental Health in Our Schools.* 1950 Yearbook, Association for Supervision and Curriculum Development. Washington, D.C.: National Education Association.

1951–54

Your Heredity; Your Children's Heredity; How You Grow; Getting along in School (with P. J. Misner); *How to Get along with Others; Becoming Real Men and Women.* Chicago: Science Research Associates. (Six guidance booklets for adolescents and parents.)

1953

Review of Florence Greenhoe Robbins, "A Study in Child, Youth, School and Community." *Educational Sociology;* December.

1955

American Indian and White Children: A Sociopsychological Investigation (with R. J. Havighurst). Chicago: University of Chicago Press. Reprinted (1969).

1956

Women's Implicit Views of Women. Chapter 4 in *Potentialities of Women in the Middle Years*, pp. 35–45. I. W. Gross (Ed.), East Lansing: Michigan State University Press.

1957

Society and Education (with R. J. Havighurst). Boston: Allyn and Bacon. 2nd Edition (1962). 3d Edition (1967). 4th Edition (1975).

Social Change and Our Aging Population. *Journal of the American Association of University Women* 50: 2.

A Study of the American Age-Grade System (with W. A. Peterson). In *Proceedings*, 4th Congress, International Association of Gerontology. Merano, Italy, 3: 1–6.

A Study of Male-Female Roles in Middle Age (with D. L. Gutmann). *Human Development Bulletin*, 30–35. Eighth Annual Symposium.

1958

Age-Sex Roles and Personality in Middle Age: A Thematic Apperception Study (with D. L. Gutmann). *Psychological Monographs*, Vol. 72, No. 17 (Whole No. 470): 1–33. Abridged as Chapter 3 in Bernice L. Neugarten and Associates, *Personality in Middle and Late Life*. New York: Atherton Press (1964): 44–89. Abridged as Chapter 6 in Bernice L. Neugarten (Ed.), *Middle Age and Aging*. Chicago: University of Chicago Press (1968): 58–60.

1959

A syllabus and annotated bibliography for an interdisciplinary course in social gerontology (with R. J. Havighurst and C. F. Ryder). Ann Arbor, Michigan: Institute for Social Gerontology, University of Michigan. 31 pp.

Attitudes of Middle-Aged Persons toward Growing Older (with D. C. Garron). *Geriatrics* 14: 21–24.

Social Class and Age-Graded Behavior in Adulthood: An Empirical Study (with Kenneth M. Olsen). Committee on Human Development. University of Chicago, September 3; 7 pp., unpublished.

1960

Ego Functions in the Middle and Later Years: A Thematic Apperception Study of Normal Adults (with J. L. Rosen). *Journal of Gerontology* 15: 62–67.

1961

The Measurement of Life Satisfaction (with R. J. Havighurst and S. S. Tobin). *Journal of Gerontology* 16: 134–43.

Life Satisfaction and Social Interaction in the Aging (with S. S. Tobin). *Journal of Gerontology* 16: 344–46.

Women's Changing Roles through the Life Cycle. *Journal of the Association of Women's Deans and Counselors* 24: 163–70.

1962

Social Role Change and Mental Health in the Climacteric Years (with Vivian Wood).

Paper presented at the American Sociological Association meeting, Washington D.C.:
September 1; unpublished.

Personality Changes in Adulthood and Old Age. *Proceedings of Seminars, 1951–1961*, pp.
22–34. Duke University Council on Gerontology, Durham: Duke University Press.

La satisfaction de vivre: Une measure de la santé mentale dans la viellesse. *L'Hygiène
mentale* 51, 2: 65–69.

Factors Related to the Mental Health of Women in the Climacteric Years (with Ruth J.
Kraines). Paper presented at the American Psychological Association meeting, August
31; unpublished.

1963

Personality and the Aging Process. Chapter 17 in R. H. Williams, C. Tibbitts, and
W. Donahue (Eds.), *Processes of Aging*, pp. 312–34. New York: Atherton Press.

Women's Attitudes toward the Menopause (with V. Wood, R. J. Kraines, and B. Loomis).
Human Development (formerly *Vita Humana*) 6: 140–151. Abridged as Chapter 21 in
Middle Age and Aging, pp. 195–200.

Personality Changes during the Adult Years. Chapter 3 in R. G. Kuhlen (Ed.),
Psychological Backgrounds of Adult Education: 43–76. Center for the Study of Liberal
Education for Adults.

Biological and Psychological Aspects of Aging, Washington, D.C.: U.S. Department of
Health, Education, and Welfare. Welfare Administration, Office of Aging. March;
unpublished.

Review of S. Reichard, F. Livson, and P. G. Peterson, *Aging and Personality,* in
Contemporary Psychology 8: 276–77.

1964

A Developmental View of Adult Personality. Chapter 12 in J. E. Birren (Ed.), *Relations of
Development and Aging*. Springfield, IL: Charles C. Thomas.

The Changing American Grandparent (with K. K. Weinstein). *Journal of Marriage and
the Family* 26: 199–204. Reprinted as Chapter 31 in *Middle Age and Aging*, 280–85.

Review of J. E. Birren, R. N. Butler, S. W. Greenhouse, L. Sokoloff, and M. R. Yarrow,
Human Aging, in *Journal of Gerontology* 19: 234–35.

Personality in Middle and Late Life: Empirical Studies (with Associates). New York:
Atherton Press. Reprinted in the series *Classics in Gerontology*, Arno Press, Salem, NH,
1984. Of the nine chapters in the book, six were authored or coauthored by Bernice
L. Neugarten:

Introduction, xv–xxi.

Ego Functions in the Middle and Later Years: A Thematic Apperception Study (with
Jacqueline Rosen). Chapter 4, 90–101.

Ego Functions in the Middle and Later Years: A Further Exploration (with David L.
Miller). Chapter 5, 105–13.

Personality and Social Interaction (with Alexey Shukin). Chapter 7, 149–57.

Personality Types in an Aged Population (with William J. Crotty and Sheldon S.
Tobin). Chapter 8, 158–87.

Summary and Implications. Chapter 9, 188–200.

Review of F. I. Nye and L. W. Hoffman, *The Employed Mother in America*, in *American Journal of Sociology* 19: 386–87.

Disengagement, Personality and Life Satisfaction in the Later Years (with R. J. Havighurst and S. S. Tobin). In P. F. Hansen (Ed)., *Age with a Future: Proceedings of the Sixth International Congress of Gerontology*, pp. 419–25. Denmark: Munksgaard.

1965

Age Norms, Age Constraints, and Adult Socialization (with J. W. Moore and J. C. Lowe). *American Journal of Sociology* 70: 710–17.

Menopausal Symptoms in Women of Various Ages (with R. J. Kraines). *Psychosomatic Medicine* 27: 266–73.

Personality Changes in the Aged. *Catholic Psychological Record* 3: 9–17.

Personality and Patterns of Aging (with R. J. Havighurst and Sheldon S. Tobin). *Gawein* (Journal of Psychology of the University of Nijmegen) 13: 249–56. Reprinted as Chapter 17 in B. L. Neugarten (Ed.), *Middle Age and Aging* Chicago: University of Chicago Press (1968): 173–77.

Human Development in Adulthood and Old Age: The Role of Longitudinal Studies. Prepared for the National Institute of Child Health and Human Development Colloquium on Longitudinal Methods. February; unpublished.

1966

Adult Personality: A Developmental View. *Human Development: An International Research Journal* (formerly *Vita Humana*) 9: 61–63.

The Aged in American Society. Chapter 4 in H. Becker (Ed.), *Social Problems*, pp. 167–96. New York: John Wiley.

Cross-national Studies of Adulthood and Aging (with V. L. Bengtson). *Interdisciplinary Topics in Gerontology*, 2: 18–36. Basel/New York: Karger.

Some problems of Method in the Cross-national Study of Adjustment to Aging (with V. Bengston). *Proceedings*, 7th Congress, International Association of Gerontology, 6: 103–05.

Psychological Issues of Middle Age (with J. E. Birren and R. J. Kraines). In *Proceedings*, 7th Congress, International Association of Gerontology 6: 299–300.

A Crossnational Study of Adjustment to Retirement. (R. J. Havighurst and V. L. Bengtson). *The Gerontologist* 6: 137–38.

1967

Society and Education (with R. J. Havighurst). Boston: Allyn and Bacon, 3d Edition; 4th Edition (1975).

Society and Education: A Book of Readings (with R. J. Havighurst and J. M. Falk). Boston: Allyn and Bacon.

A New Look at Menopause. *Psychology Today* (December): 43–45 and 67–69.

Social Mobility in a Midwestern City (with R. J. Coleman). In R. J. Havighurst, B. L. Neugarten, and J. M. Falk (Eds.), *Society and Education: A Book of Readings*, 3d Edition, pp. 38–49. Boston: Allyn and Bacon.

The Awareness of Middle Age. In Roger Owen (Ed.), *Middle Age*, pp. 54–65. London:

British Broadcasting Corporation. Reprinted as Chapter 10 in B. L. Neugarten (Ed.), *Middle Age and Aging,* pp. 93–98. Chicago: University of Chicago Press (1968).

1968

Developmental Perspectives. Chapter 4 in A. Simon and L. J. Epstein (Eds.), *Aging in Modern Society,* pp. 42–48. Washington, D.C.: American Psychiatric Association.

Middle Age and Aging: A Reader in Social Psychology. (Ed.) Chicago: University of Chicago Press.

The Changing Age Status System (with Joan W. Moore). Chapter 1 in Bernice L. Neugarten (Ed.), *Middle Age and Aging: A Reader in Social Psychology,* pp. 5–21. Chicago: University of Chicago Press.

Adult Personality: Toward a Psychology of the Life Cycle. Chapter 14 in Bernice L. Neugarten (Ed.), *Middle Age and Aging: A Reader in Social Psychology,* pp. 137–47. Chicago: University of Chicago Press.

Disengagement and Patterns of Aging (with R. J. Havighurst and S. S. Tobin). Chapter 16 in Bernice L. Neugarten (Ed.), *Middle Age and Aging: A Reader in Social Psychology,* pp. 161–72. Chicago: University of Chicago Press.

1969

Continuities and Discontinuities of Psychological Issues into Adult Life. *Human Development* 12: 121–30.

Adjustment to Retirement. R. J. Havighurst, J. M. A. Munnichs, Bernice Neugarten and H. Thomae (Eds.), Assen, The Netherlands: Van Gorcum. Distributed also by Humanities Press, New York.

The Aims and Methods of the Crossnational Research on Aging (with R. J. Havighurst). Chapter 1 in Havighurst et al. (Eds.), *Adjustment to Retirement.* Assen, The Netherlands: Van Gorcum. Distributed also by Humanities Press, New York.

Disengagement Reconsidered in a Crossnational Context (with R. J. Havighurst). Chapter 9 in Havighurst et al. (Eds.), *Adjustment to Retirement.* Assen, The Netherlands: Van Gorcum. Distributed also by Humanities Press, New York.

Review of T. Lidz, *The Person,* in *Contemporary Psychology* 14: 409–11.

Review of M. W. Riley, A. Foner, and Associates, *Aging and Society, Journal of Gerontology* 24: 375–76.

Similarities in Values and Other Personality Characteristics in College Students and Their Parents (with L. E. Troll and R. J. Kraines). *Merrill-Palmer Quarterly* 14: 323–36.

The Old and the Young in Modern Societies. *American Behavioral Scientist* 14 (September/October): 448–50.

1970

A New Look at the Crises of Middle Age. *Geriatric Focus* 9: 1, 6–7.

Adaptation and the Life Cycle. *Journal of Geriatric Psychiatry* 4: 71–87.

Women in the University of Chicago. Report prepared in collaboration with the other members of the Committee on University Women (B. L. Neugarten, chairman). May; 122 pp.

The Future Social Roles of the Aged. Paper presented at the International Gerontological Symposium. Amsterdam, The Netherlands.

1971

Social Status in the City (with R. P. Coleman). San Francisco: Jossey-Bass.

Grow Old along with Me. Psychology Today (December): 45–48, 79–81.

Introduction to the Symposium: Models and Methods for the Study of the Life Cycle. Human Development 14: 81–86.

1972

Education and the Life Cycle. School Review 80 (February): 209–16.

Social Implications of a Prolonged Lifespan. The Gerontologist 12: 437–40.

Personality and the Aging Process. The Gerontologist 12: 9–15.

Review of S. de Beauvoir, The Coming of Age. In Psychology Today (December): 20–22.

1973

Personality Change in Late Life: A Developmental Perspective. In C. Eisdorfer and P. Lawton (Eds.), The Psychology of Adult Development and Aging, pp. 311–35. Washington, D.C.: American Psychological Association.

Patterns of Aging: Past, Present and Future. Social Service Review 47: 571–80.

Sociological Perspectives on the Life Cycle (with N. Datan). Chapter 3 in P. B. Baltes and K. W. Schaie (Eds.), Life-Span Developmental Psychology: Personality and Socialization, pp. 53–69. New York: Academic Press.

Women in Administrative Roles. Proceedings of the Conference. "The Challenge: Rational Administration in Nursing and Health Care Services," Arizona State University.

Older People in 1990: Social Policy Issues. University of Chicago Task Force Report, prepared for the Sloan Foundation. June.

1974

Age Groups in American Society and the Rise of the Young-Old. The Annals of the American Academy of Political and Social Sciences 415 (September): 187–98.

Aging and Society (with M. Riley and B. Foner) American Journal of Sociology 80: 807–9.

The Middle Years (with N. Datan). Chapter 29 in Silvano Arieti (Ed.), American Handbook of Psychiatry, 2d Edition, Vol. 1: The Foundations of Psychiatry. pp. 592–608. New York: Basic Books.

The Socialization of Parents by Young-Adult Children: A New Perspective on Social Change (with G. Hagestad). Paper read at 15th Inter-American Congress of Psychology, December. Bogota, Colombia.

Successful Aging in 1970 and 1990. In E. Pfeiffer (Ed.), Successful Aging: A Conference Report, pp. 12–18. Durham, NC: Duke University Press.

The Older Person in the Family. Paper presented at the American Psychological Association Symposium, "The Role of Psychology in Studying and Helping Families with Problems," University of Chicago. 5 pp.; unpublished.

1975

Society and Education (with R. J. Havighurst). 4th Edition. Boston: Allyn and Bacon.

Women in Education. Chapter 18 in R. J. Havighurst and B. L. Neugarten, *Society and Education,* pp. 382–398 4th Edition. Boston: Allyn and Bacon.

Aging in the Year 2000: A Look at the Future. (Ed.) *The Gerontologist* 15: 3–40.

The Future and the Young-Old. *The Gerontologist* 15: 4–9.

A Pioneer of Social Gerontology, R. J. Havighurst. Sonderdruck aus *Zeitschrift für Gerontologie* 8 (March/April): 82–86.

Persönlichkeitsveränderungen bei alteren Menschen: Die Chicagoer Untersuchungen (with W. J. McDonald). In U. M. Lehr and F. E. Weinert (Eds.), *Entwicklung und Persönlichkeit,* pp. 67–76. Stuttgart: Kohlhammer.

The Aged in the year 2025. In *Aging in America's Future,* pp. 10–21. Proceedings of a symposium sponsored by Hoechst-Roussel Pharmaceuticals. Sommerville, NJ, November.

A Follow-up Study of Adaptation in Middle-Aged Women (with M. Noberini). Paper presented at the meetings of the Gerontological Society, October. 6 pp.; unpublished.

1976

Age and the Life Course (with G. Hagestad). Chapter 2 in J. E. Birren (Ed.), *Handbook of Aging and the Social Sciences,* pp. 35–55. New York: Van Nostrand Reinhold.

Social Policy, Social Ethics, and the Aging Society (with R. J. Havighurst) (Eds.) Washington, D.C.: National Science Foundation, RANN-Research Application Directorate. Government Printing Office: NSF/RA 76-000247.

1977

Our Future Selves: A Research Plan toward Understanding Aging (with G. Maddox). Report of a panel on Behavioral and Social Sciences Research, National Advisory Council on Aging. DHEW Publication (NIH) 78–144.

Extending the Human Life Span: Social Policy and Social Ethics (with R. J. Havighurst). (Eds.) National Science Foundation, Washington, D.C.: Government Printing Office: NSF/RA 770123.

Personality and Aging. Chapter 26 in J. E. Birren (Ed.), *Handbook of the Psychology of Aging,* pp. 626–49. New York: Van Nostrand Reinhold.

Aging in the Future. Collection I: Selected Papers. Proceedings of Sixth Annual Canadian Association on Gerontology.

Commentary. In A. N. Exton-Smith and J. G. Evans (Eds.), *Care of the Elderly,* pp. 99–105. New York: Gruen and Stratton Inc.

1978

Aging: Social Implication. In W. T. Reich (Ed.), *Encyclopedia of Bioethics* pp. 54–58. New York: Free Press.

Midlife Women in the 1980s. Joint testimony, *Women in Midlife—Security and Fulfillment,* pt. 1. Select Committee on Aging and Subcommittee on Retirement

Income and Employment, U. S. House of Representatives, 95th Congress, 2d Session: Committee Publ. No. 95-170, 24–38.

Social Implications of Life Extension. In H. Orimo et al (Eds.), *Recent Advances in Gerontology,* pp. 669–74. Proceedings of the 11th International Congress of Gerontology. Tokyo, August 20–24.

Personality Changes in Adulthood. Master Lecture on the Psychology of Aging. American Psychological Association, Tape Series 14, Tape 14/16. Comments. In "Forum on Aging and the Family," *Family Coordinator* (October): 436–45.

1979

The Young-Old and the Age-Irrelevant Society. In "The Young-Old: A New North American Phenomenon." Sponsored by the Couchiching Institute on Public Affairs. Toronto, Canada. February; pp. 1–12.

The Psychology of Aging: An Overview. Master lecture in developmental psychology, American Psychological Association (on tape). Also in reader, *The Adult Life Cycle.* University of Kansas Adult Life Resource Center.

Women in Education. Revised version is Chapter 18 in R. J. Havighurst and D. Levine (Eds.), *Society and Education,* 5th Edition, pp. 480–508. Boston: Allyn and Bacon.

The Middle Generations. In P. K. Ragan (Ed.). *Aging Parents,* pp. 258–67. Los Angeles: Ethel Percy Andrus Gerontology Center, University of Southern California Press.

Time, Age, and the Life Cycle. *American Journal of Psychiatry* 136 (July): 887–94.

Age and the Changing Life Course. Paper presented at the annual meeting of the American Sociological Association, Boston. August; unpublished.

Teaching in Adult Development and Aging: The Road to Maturity. Invited address Divisions 7, 20. American Psychological Association annual meeting, New York. September.

Policy for the 1980s: Age-Entitlement or Need-Entitlement? In *Aging: Agenda for the Eighties,* pp. 48–52. A National Journal Issues Book, November. Reprinted in B. L. Neugarten (Ed.), *Age or Need? Public Policies for Older People.* New York: Sage Publications (1982).

1980

Must Everything Be Midlife Crisis? *Prime Time* (February): 45–48. Adapted from Time, Age, and the Life Cycle, *American Journal of Psychiatry* 136 (July 1979): 887–94.

1981

Social-Psychological Factors in Women's Changing Self-Concepts. In Proceedings of the 6th International Congress on Obstetrics and Gynecology, Berlin. Pp. 11–15.

Foreword. In Elizabeth Kutza, *The Benefits of Old Age: Social Welfare Policies for the Aged,* pp. ix–xxii. Chicago: University of Chicago Press.

Education for Long Life. *The Northwestern Educator* (January): 1–2.

Growing Old in 2020: How Will It Be Different? *National Forum* (Summer): 28–30.

Education for an Aging Society. In Schooling and Society: The Perry Dunlap Smith Memorial Lectures. Roosevelt University, Chicago. Unpublished.

Age Distinctions and Their Social Functions. In *Chicago Kent Law Review* 57 (Fall): 809–25.

United States Policies and Policy-Making for Older People. Presented at a meeting of the Research Committee on Aging, International Sociological Association, Paris. July; unpublished.

Family and Community Support Systems. Paper presented to Committee #7, White House Conference on Aging, Washington D. C. November 30. 11 pp.; unpublished.

Age Integration Statement. Prepared for White House Conference on Aging, Washington D. C. November 30.

A National Policy on Aging. Prepared for White House Conference on Aging, Washington, D. C. November 30.

1982

Older Americans: A Profile of Social and Health Characteristics. In *The Hospital's Role in Caring for the Elderly: Leadership Issues,* The Hospital Research and Educational Trust, Chicago (June): 3–16. Excerpted as Chapter 2 in Bernice L. Neugarten (Ed.), *Age or Need?* pp. 33–54. Beverly Hills: Sage Publications.

Aging: Policy Issues for the Developed Countries of the World. In H. Thomae and G. L. Maddox (Eds.), *New Perspectives on Old Age: A Message to Decision Makers,* pp. 115–26. New York: Springer Publishing.

Age, Society and the Law: An Annotated Bibliography (with Nancy Zweibel et al.). School of Education and Social Policy, Northwestern University, Evanston. Unpublished.

Redefining Education. *Northwestern Educator* (Spring): 1–11.

New Perspectives on Aging and Social Policy. The Leon and Josephine Winkelman Lecture. University of Michigan, Ann Arbor, January 25; 10 pp.

Human Behavior Is Malleable throughout Life. *Psychology Today.* Fifteenth Anniversary Issue (May): 54.

Middle-Aged Parents and Their Children. Paper given at a conference honoring Professor Ethel Shanas, University of Illinois at Chicago, Circle. May 7; unpublished.

Older People: A Profile. University of Illinois College of Medicine Centennial Celebration, "Medicine for Mankind in Transition." June 3–4; unpublished.

Reflection on Metaphors in the Study of Aging. Proceedings of the Conference on Metaphor in the Study of Aging. University of British Columbia, Vancouver. June; unpublished.

Successful Aging. Public lecture, American Psychological Association, Washington, D.C., August 26. 20 pp.; unpublished.

The Dilemma in Developmental Psychology. Invited lecture, American Psychological Association, August. Unpublished.

The Aging Society. Guest editor, *National Forum* Fall: special issue.

Age or Need? Public Policies for Older People. (Ed). Beverly Hills: Sage Publications. Of the eleven chapters in this book, three were authored by Bernice L. Neugarten: Introduction, 11–18.

Policy for the 1980s: Age or Need Entitlement? Chapter 1, 19–32.

Older People: A Profile. Chapter 2, 33–54.

1983

Health Care, Medicare, and Health Policy for Older People: A Conversation with Arthur Flemming. *American Psychologist* (March): 311–15.

Comments. In J. E. Birren, J. M. A. Munnichs, H. Thomae, and Maurice Marois. (Eds.), *A Challenge to Science and Social Policy*. Oxford University 3: 459–62.

The Study of Aging and Human Development. Paper presented in honor of Allison Davis at the symposium Race, Class, Socialization and the Life Cycle. University of Chicago, October. Unpublished.

1984

Psychological Aspects of Aging and Illness. *Psychosomatics* 25 (February): 123–25.

1985

The Process of Disengagement: The Origin and Development of an Idea. Invited paper, annual meeting, Gerontological Society of America. November. Unpublished.

Interpretive Social Science and Research on Aging. In A. Rossi (Ed.), *Gender and the Life Course*, pp. 291–300. New York: Aldine Publishing.

Age and the Life Course (with G. Hagestad). Revised version in E. Shanas and R. Binstock (Eds.), *Handbook of Aging and the Social Sciences*, 2d Edition, pp. 35–61. New York: Van Nostrand Reinhold.

Aging in the 1980s: Agenda for Psychologists and Policy-Makers. In R. A. Kasschau, L. P. Rehn, and L. P. Ullmann (Eds.), *Psychology research, public policy and practice: Toward a productive partnership*, pp. 95–123. Houston Symposium 5. New York: Praeger.

1986

Age in the Aging Society (with D. A. Neugarten). *Daedalus* (Winter): 31–49. Appears also as Changing Meanings of Age in the Aging Society. In A Pifer and L. Bronte (Eds.), *Our Aging Society: Paradox and Promise*, pp. 33–51. New York: W. W. Norton. Adapted as "The Changing Meaning of Age." *Psychology Today* (1987): 29–33 and 72.

Thirteenth Congress of the International Association of Gerontology: A Postscript. In George L. Maddox and E. W. Busse (Eds.), *Aging: The Universal Human Experience*. New York: Springer.

The Kansas City Studies of Adult Life. In G. L. Maddox (Ed.), *The Encyclopedia of Aging*, pp. 372–73. New York: Springer.

1988

Personality and Psychosocial Patterns of Aging. In M. Bergener, M. Ermini, and H. B. Stahelin (Eds.), *Crossroads in Aging: The 1988 Sandoz Lectures in Gerontology*, pp. 205–16. Newbury Park, CA: London: Academic Press.

The Aging Society and My Academic Life. In Matilda White Riley (Ed.), *Sociological Lives: Social Change and the Life Course*, 2: 91–106. Newbury Park, CA: Sage Publications.

The Aging Society: A Look Toward the Year 2020. The Center for Applied Gerontology, *Issues in Aging.* 5: pp. 34–39.

Gerontology and the Aging Society. In *Dies Natalis,* pp. 21–28. Katholieke University of Nijmegen, The Netherlands.

Studies in the Social Psychology of Aging. *Sandorama,* pp. 11–13.

A Forecast of Women's Health and Longevity: Implications for an Aging America (with C. K. Cassel). *Western Journal of Medicine* (December): 149, 712–17.

1989

Policy Issues in an Aging Society (with D. A. Neugarten). In M. Storandt and G. R. VandenBos (Eds.), *The Adult Years: Continuity and Change,* pp. 147–67. Washington D.C.: American Psychological Association.

1990

Retirement in the Life Course. *Triangle.* Sandoz Medical Journal of Medical Science 29: 119–25.

Growing as Long as We Live. Interview, *Second Opinion* 15 (November): 42–51.

The Changing Meanings of Age. In M. Bergener and S. I. Finkel (Eds.), *Clinical and Scientific Psychogeriatrics: The Holistic Approaches,* pp. 1–6. New York: Springer.

Social and Psychological Characteristics of Older Persons. Chapter 3 in C. K. Cassel and D. Riesenberg (Eds.), *Geriatric Medicine,* 2d Edition, pp. 28–36. New York: Springer-Verlag. Revised as Chapter 4 in B. L. Neugarten and S. C. Reed (Eds.), *Geriatric Medicine,* 3d Edition. New York: Springer-Verlag (1995).

1991

The Goals of Medicine in an Aging Society (with C. K. Cassel). In R. H. Binstock and S. G. Post (Eds.), *Too Old for Health Care?* pp. 75–90. Baltimore, MD: Johns Hopkins University Press.

1992

Building Age-Neutral Community Services: The Case of Home Care (with S. Reed and H. Richman). Report prepared for the Chapin Hall Center for Children, University of Chicago.

1993

Foreword. In Vern L. Bengtson and W. Andrew Achenbaum (Eds.), *The Changing Contract across Generations,* pp. xvii–xviii. New York: Aldine de Gruyter.

Enhancing the Caring Community: The Case of Home Care (with H. Richman and S. Reed). Report prepared for the Chicago Community Trust. 35 pp.

1994

The End of Gerontology? *Center on Aging Newsletter,* Vol. 10, No. 1. Evanston, IL: Buehler Center on Aging, Northwestern University.

Oral History of Bernice L. Neugarten. By Jerrold Neugarten. Available in the Oral History Research Office, Butler Library, Columbia University.

1995

Nothing as Rich as Human Life: A Conversation with Bernice Neugarten, Ph.D.
    Evanston, IL: Buehler Center on Aging, Northwestern University. Videotape.
The Costs of Survivorship (with Celia Berdes). Center on Aging Newsletter, Vol. 11, No.
    4. Evanston, IL: Buehler Center on Aging, Northwestern University.

Index

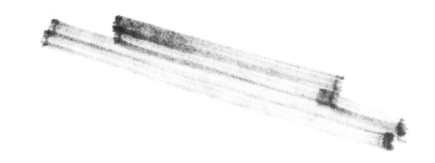